Teaching Culture and Psychology

The fourth edition of *Teaching Culture and Psychology* (previously *Cross-Cultural Explorations*) provides an array of carefully designed instructor resources and student activities that support the construction and implementation of courses on culture and psychology.

Revised and expanded from previous editions, the book enables instructors to use selected activities appropriate for their course structure. Part One explores a variety of pedagogical challenges involved in teaching about culture and psychology and details specific strategies for addressing these challenges. Part Two (instructor resources) and Part Three (student handouts) center around 90 activities designed to encourage students to think critically about the role of culture in a wide range of psychology content areas. These activities are based on current and classic cross-cultural research and take the form of case studies, self-administered scales, mini-experiments, database search assignments, and the collection of content-analytic, observational, and interview data. For each activity, instructors are provided with a lecture/discussion module as well as suggestions for variations and expanded writing assignments. Student handouts are available in this text as well as on the Routledge website as fillable forms.

Contributing to the inclusion of cultural perspectives in the psychology curriculum, this wide-ranging book enables instructors to provide students with hands-on experiences that facilitate the understanding and application of major concepts and principles in the study of culture and psychology, making it ideal for cultural psychology, anthropology, sociology, and related courses.

Susan B. Goldstein received her Ph.D. in Psychology from the University of Hawaii while a grantee of the East West Center. She is a Professor of Psychology at the University of Redlands, U.S.A., where she teaches Cross-Cultural Psychology, and Study Abroad Pre-Departure and Re-entry Courses. Her research and publications have focused on study abroad, intercultural attitudes, social justice allies, stigma, and strategies for diversifying the psychology curriculum.

Teaching Culture and Psychology

Pedagogical Strategies, Instructor Resources, and Student Activities

Fourth Edition

Susan B. Goldstein

Routledge
Taylor & Francis Group

NEW YORK AND LONDON

Cover image: GettyImages\Jackyenjoyphotography

Fourth edition published 2024
by Routledge
605 Third Avenue, New York, NY 10158

and by Routledge
4 Park Square, Milton Park, Abingdon, Oxon, OX14 4RN

Routledge is an imprint of the Taylor & Francis Group, an informa business

First edition published by Pearson 2000
Second edition published by Pearson 2008
Third edition published by Routledge 2019

Library of Congress Cataloging-in-Publication Data
Names: Goldstein, Susan B., author.
Title: Teaching culture and psychology : pedagogical strategies, instructor resources, and student activities / Susan Goldstein.
Other titles: Cross-cultural explorations
Description: Fourth edition. | Abingdon, Oxon ; New York, NY : Routledge, 2024. | Includes bibliographical references.
Identifiers: LCCN 2023052354 (print) | LCCN 2023052355 (ebook) | ISBN 9781032412108 (hardback) | ISBN 9781032394336 (paperback) | ISBN 9781003356820 (ebook)
Subjects: LCSH: Cross-cultural studies--Textbooks. | Intercultural communication--Problems, exercises, etc. | Social psychology--Textbooks.
Classification: LCC GN345.7 .G65 2024 (print) | LCC GN345.7 (ebook) | DDC 155.8--dc23/eng/20231129
LC record available at https://lccn.loc.gov/2023052354
LC ebook record available at https://lccn.loc.gov/2023052355

ISBN: 978-1-032-41210-8 (hbk)
ISBN: 978-1-032-39433-6 (pbk)
ISBN: 978-1-003-35682-0 (ebk)

DOI: 10.4324/9781003356820

Typeset in Times New Roman
by MPS Limited, Dehradun

Access the Support Material: www.routledge.com/9781032412108

CONTENTS

Acknowledgments

The first edition of this book was published in 2000 as a student workbook with tear-out pages. In the years since there have been countless publishing professionals, reviewers, colleagues, students, and family members who formally or informally contributed to this effort. On this fourth edition, I am particularly grateful for the guidance and creativity of Routledge editors Eleanor Taylor and Emilie Coin, and editorial assistant Yashika Tanwar, and for the wisdom, perspective, and limitless encouragement provided by my husband, Paul, my sister, Cynthia, and my daughters, Lauren and Rachel.

There are handouts available to students as fillable forms on the Routledge website at www.routledge.com/9781032394336

Introduction

When I finished graduate school and began interviewing for college teaching positions in the early 1990s, I found I often had to explain to potential employers what it meant to be trained in cross-cultural psychology (in fact, one department chair asked if my academic background prepared me to teach parapsychology – the study of psychic phenomena!). In the four decades since, there has been a virtual explosion of psychology publications with a cultural perspective (Lonner, 2018). For example, the number of articles under the subject "cross-cultural psychology" in the PsycInfo database more than tripled between 2000 and 2020. Psychology as an academic discipline has come to recognize the importance of culture in understanding human behavior and, as a result, increasingly questions the universality of research findings, and grapples with the essentially monocultural perspective that has shaped its goals, content, and methods.

Along with far greater attention to culture in psychological research, there have been corresponding changes in the teaching of psychology, with cross-cultural perspectives playing a more prominent role in course content across the psychology curriculum and rapid growth in the number of courses focused exclusively on culture and psychology. Once found only at the graduate level, these courses have increasingly made their way into the undergraduate curriculum (Norcross et al., 2016). Yet, despite the growing demand for and interest in courses addressing culture and psychology, few psychology instructors have received formal training in this area (Summers & Poelker, 2017). This book was designed to address this gap between training and demand, and support instructors seeking to contribute to the cultural inclusivity of the psychology curriculum.

Earlier editions of this book were designed as a student workbook with an accompanying instructor's manual. However, in recent years, users of this text have expressed greater concern about the pedagogical challenges of teaching about culture and psychology. Instructors are faced with such dilemmas as how to discuss cultural differences without reinforcing stereotypes, how to acknowledge the social justice issues embedded in the conduct of cross-cultural research, and whether and how to address their own positionality relative to the course material. These are some of the issues addressed in this new edition. As in previous editions, my goal is to provide students with hands-on activities

DOI: 10.4324/9781003356820-1

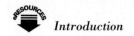

that facilitate the understanding and application of major concepts and principles in the study of culture and psychology, but with greater implementation support for the instructor, both in terms of course content and classroom dynamics.

The remainder of this Introduction discusses the central aims of teaching students about culture and psychology, explains the major approaches scholars have taken to research in this area, and outlines the content and structure of this book.

WHY TEACH CULTURE AND PSYCHOLOGY

There are numerous benefits to teaching about culture and psychology. Doing so facilitates student engagement and inclusion, teaches critical thinking as students contend with important questions about human nature and social problems, fosters intercultural competence and global citizenship, and perhaps most importantly, provides students with a more accurate understanding of human behavior (Akimoto, 2016; Keith, 2016; Morling, 2015). As discussed below, the content of this book was developed with these multiple objectives in mind.

Psychology Is WEIRD

A 2008 study by Jeffrey Arnett shined a spotlight on the limited cultural perspective of psychological research. He analyzed authors' institutional affiliations and the location of research samples in articles from six flagship journals representing major psychology subdisciplines. Arnett found that 73% of the first authors and 68% of the samples were based in the United States, a country that only accounts for approximately 5% of the world's population. Furthermore, in some areas, social psychology in particular, the majority of research participants were U.S. Americans enrolled in undergraduate psychology courses. A decade later, a follow-up study of the same six journals found little meaningful change (Thalmayer et al., 2021). Although fewer authors and samples were located in the United States (just over 60%), this change was primarily due to increased publications from Western European nations. The authors noted that 89% of the world's population remains unrepresented in psychology's most prominent research outlets.

This overrepresentation of North American and Western European researchers and participants would be less of a concern if the research findings could be generalized across the globe. However, as Henrich and colleagues (2010) have demonstrated, the behavior of individuals in WEIRD (Western, Educated, Industrialized, Rich, and Democratic; Henrich et al., 2010) nations is not universal.

These authors not only identified psychological differences between Western and non-Western nations (e.g., in self-concept, conformity, analytic vs. holistic reasoning), but also among WEIRD nations, such as between U.S. Americans and members of other Western nations (e.g., related to individualism), as well as within the U.S., such as between university undergraduates and non-students (e.g., in autonomy, social influence, intergroup attitudes). Beyond these overgeneralized findings, psychology as a discipline is also WEIRD in that its priorities, concepts, and methods are shaped by the social, cultural, political, historical, environmental, economic, and religious contexts in which they originated and developed. The activities and instructional support material in this book are designed to help students understand the nature and implications of this WEIRD bias, step outside of the WEIRD perspective, and consider the ethical dilemmas involved in efforts to make psychology more inclusive of non-WEIRD research.

The Need for Intercultural Competence

Universities, professional associations, and national governments across the globe have recognized the need to prepare students to live and work effectively in an increasingly intercultural and international context (de Wit & Altbach, 2021). Skrefsrud (2021, p. 63) explained, "As the speed and scale of migration and globalization changes societies, students need to develop the capacity to analyse and comprehend global issues, and learn how to interact respectfully with one another despite their cultural differences." This aim is reflected in the curricular guidelines of several psychology professional associations, particularly those from Western nations seeking to address a historically ethnocentric approach to the discipline (e.g., American Psychological Association, British Psychological Society, Canadian Psychological Association). For example, a stated goal of the American Psychological Association (APA; 2013, p. 18) is for psychology majors to "Examine the sociocultural and international contexts that influence individual differences (e.g., personality traits, abilities) and address applicability of research findings across societal and cultural groups."

Interculturally competent individuals – those who possess the "cognitive, affective, and behavioral skills and characteristics that support effective and appropriate interaction in a variety of cultural contexts" (Bennett, 2008, p. 97) – are better prepared to search internationally for solutions to local problems, collaborate in diverse work environments, and serve as practitioners when clients' backgrounds differ from their own. On a broader, global level, a cross-culturally informed understanding of human behavior is needed to address such critical issues as climate change, refugee resettlement, poverty, health disparities,

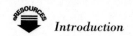

and international conflict and peacemaking. Teaching about culture and psychology can contribute to this goal of supporting and enhancing students' intercultural competence (Wei et al., 2021).

APPROACHES TO STUDYING CULTURE AND PSYCHOLOGY

Researchers and practitioners have taken a variety of approaches to studying the role of culture in human behavior, although in recent years there has been greater overlap and synthesis of these schools of thought. As you will see in the descriptions that follow, the primary differences in emphasis deal with these four interrelated questions:

- Is the focus on identifying human universals or understanding culture-specific forms of behavior?
- Should the concepts and methods studied arise from within or outside of the culture(s) of interest?
- Is it appropriate to make cross-cultural comparisons or does the act of comparison itself inescapably involve the imposition of culture-bound constructs?
- Are the culture(s) of interest domestic or international?

Cross-Cultural Psychology

Cross-cultural psychology focuses on comparing specific behaviors across cultures, often with the goal of identifying universal principles of human behavior. For example, based on research with children from 56 low- and middle-income countries, Julie Ma and colleagues (2022) found that spanking was associated with a significantly heightened risk of physical abuse. Cross-cultural psychologists work within a wide variety of research areas, such as social, developmental, cognitive, clinical, and organizational psychology. Rather than embodying a distinct content area, cross-cultural psychology is characterized by the unique methods used to make comparisons across cultures, methods that strive toward identifying culturally equivalent constructs, samples, and research instruments.

Cultural Psychology

Cultural psychology focuses on detailing the interrelationships among forms of behavior within a specific culture and is significantly less concerned with cross-cultural comparisons. Cultural psychology has been described as a bridge between anthropology and cognitive sciences in that while the focus is on understanding human functioning, the research tends to emphasize qualitative methods and take an insider perspective (Fryberg, 2012). From a purely cultural psychology standpoint, cross-cultural comparisons would not be valid because the concepts and methods of psychology are themselves culture-bound. An example of this approach is Barbara Rogoff's in-depth investigations of the knowledge and skills Mayan children learn through family and community interactions (e.g., Rogoff et al., 2017). Cultural psychologists often use observational techniques as well as interviews to gather information about the beliefs and practices of a specific group.

Multicultural Psychology

Multicultural psychology, which grew from what is sometimes termed *ethnic psychology*, is concerned with the use of culturally appropriate methods to understand the behavior and experiences of people in culturally diverse environments and has focused primarily on historically marginalized groups in North America. For example, Christina Cross and colleagues detailed the family social support networks of African American and Black Caribbean adolescents (Cross et al., 2018).

Indigenous, Decolonial, and Transnational Psychologies

The *indigenous psychologies* approach utilizes concepts and methods that arise from within the culture of interest (Kim et al., 2006). Although some scholars advocate for the inclusion of indigenous approaches within the dominant Western psychology framework, others increasingly link indigenous psychology to efforts toward decolonization – that is, challenging European American claims on what constitutes an intellectually valid understanding of human behavior and recognizing the historical and current power relations that shape the discipline of psychology (Pickren & Taşçı, 2022). For example, Bhatia (2019, p. 110) has advocated for a *decolonial psychology* with greater relevance to the needs of communities within the Global South which "embed[s] its understanding of identity, selfhood, organizations, social relationships, traditions, world views, and practices within the context of work, poverty, hunger, education, and the struggle for earning a decent livelihood." An emerging *transnational psychology* approach (Collins et al., 2019) applies the collaborative, community-level strategies of transnational feminist psychology to highlight indigenous knowledge and interrogate the colonialist and capitalist forces that accompany Western psychology.

Geographical and Latitudinal Psychology

Geographical psychology uses aggregate data to investigate how various psychological phenomena are spatially distributed, such as across neighborhoods, cities, states, and countries, and how they are shaped by the social and physical environment (Chen et al., 2020). For example, Peter Rentfrow and colleagues (e.g., Rentfrow, 2020; Rentfrow & Gosling, 2021) have mapped the Big Five personality traits across and within nations. Relatedly, Van de Vliert and Van Lange (2019) coined the term *latitudinal psychology*, which investigates changes in psychological variables associated with distance from the equator (due to cold vs. heat exposure). These authors reported that creativity, life satisfaction, and individualism increase whereas aggression decreases as one moves closer to the North or South Pole.

Evolutionary Psychology

Much cross-cultural research has emerged from an *evolutionary psychology* perspective, which seeks to identify species-specific psychological mechanisms that evolved in response to environmental conditions (Apicella & Barrett, 2016). For example, Cari Pick and over 50 colleagues from around the world investigated possible changes to the evolutionarily relevant motives of Affiliation and Kin Care due to the Covid-19 pandemic. Samples from 42 countries indicated that during the pandemic, such family-related motives were prioritized over motives associated with mating as well as over those associated with disease avoidance (Pick et al., 2022).

Although distinctions between these approaches are highlighted where relevant in this book, "cross-cultural" will often be used as an umbrella term to refer to taking a cultural perspective, as has been a common practice in the field (see, for example, Dasen, 2022; Keith, 2011).

THE CONTENT AND STRUCTURE OF THIS BOOK

It is not easy for instructors to create active learning experiences exploring cultural perspectives in psychology. Unlike many other areas of psychology, one cannot easily ask students to replicate cross-cultural studies. The 90 activities in this book encourage students to think critically about culture and human behavior by exploring their own cultural background, interviewing others with specific cross-cultural experiences, making cross-cultural comparisons using a broad interpretation of culture, and reading about cultures different from their own in scholarly sources and the materials included within activities. The activities provided revolve around case studies, self-administered scales, mini-experiments, and the collection of content-analytic, observational, and interview data. Background material is included for any concepts not commonly addressed in introductory texts. I have chosen to use a broad conceptualization of culture, inclusive of groups identified on a variety of dimensions in addition to nationality or ethnicity. This expanded view of culture and psychology reflects current thinking among cross-cultural scholars and allows for a discussion of culture in a context more relevant to the lives of many students.

This book is designed to support courses specifically focusing on culture and human behavior, such as a cultural or cross-cultural psychology course, as well as efforts to integrate cultural perspectives into an introductory psychology course. The nine sets of activities represent the topics addressed in most cross-cultural psychology textbooks and correspond to the organization of most introductory psychology texts as well.

The book is organized in three parts. Part One explores a range of pedagogical challenges faced by psychology instructors seeking to provide a cross-cultural perspective and details specific suggestions and resources for addressing these challenges. Part Two consists of instructor materials designed to support the activities. In this section you will find a variety of lecture and discussion ideas and detailed suggestions for tailoring the activity to your course. For example, there are suggestions for adapting the activities to challenge more advanced students and for expanding the writing component of activities to include techniques drawn from the literature on writing across the curriculum, such as free writing, journaling, and peer review. Part Three contains the student handouts in condensed form.

The large number of activities included in this book allows you to select those best suited to your course. Each of the activities may be assigned independently and out of sequence. Several of the activities would be appropriate as small group projects. Activities that require work outside of the classroom are indicated as such. Most of the activities are easily adapted for courses taught partially or entirely online. The nine sections include ten activities each, representing major content areas in research on culture and psychology, both classic and contemporary.

- Chapter 1: The Concept of Culture addresses the definition of culture and dimensions of cultural variability and universality.
- Chapter 2: Culture and Psychological Research explores major issues and techniques in the conduct of cross-cultural research.
- Chapter 3: Culture and Basic Processes brings a cross-cultural perspective to cognitive processes, and includes activities on intelligence, creativity, memory, perception, and language.

- Chapter 4: Culture and Developmental Processes focuses on socialization in cultural context and cultural variation in human development.
- Chapter 5: Personality, Emotion, and the Self in Cultural Context addresses the impact of culture on the construal of self, the expression of emotion across cultures, and the cross-cultural relevance of Western personality theory.
- Chapter 6: Health, Stress, and Coping Across Cultures deals with key cultural issues in research and practice related to physical and mental well-being.
- Chapter 7: Culture and Social Behavior explores major research findings in the areas of norms and values, conflict resolution, work-related behavior, close interpersonal relationships, and gender roles.
- Chapter 8: Intergroup Relations explores the phenomena of prejudice, discrimination, stereotyping, and marginalization across cultures.
- Chapter 9: Intercultural Interaction deals with research on intercultural adjustment, communication, and training for intercultural competence.

I invite you to contact me with any feedback about your experiences with the activities. I hope you will find this book to be a helpful tool in guiding students through an exploration of the role of culture in human behavior.

Susan B. Goldstein, Ph.D.
Department of Psychology, University of Redlands
1200 East Colton Avenue, P.O. Box 3080
Redlands, CA 92373, U.S.A.
Email: susan_goldstein@redlands.edu

References

Akimoto, S. (2016). Teaching cross-cultural psychology: Insights from an internationalized on-campus course. In D. Gross, K. Abrams, & C. Z. Enns (Eds.), *Internationalizing the undergraduate psychology curriculum: Practical lessons learned at home and abroad* (pp. 181–197). American Psychological Association.

American Psychology Association. (2013). *APA guidelines for the undergraduate psychology major: Version 2.0.* www.apa.org/ed/psymajor_guideline.pdf

Apicella, C. L., & Barrett, H. C. (2016). Cross-cultural evolutionary psychology. *Current Opinion in Psychology, 7,* 92–97. https://doi.org/10.1016/j.copsyc.2015.08.015

Arnett, J. J. (2008). The neglected 95%: Why American psychology needs to become less American. *American Psychologist, 63*, 602. https://doi.org/10.1037/0003-066X.63.7.602

Bennett, J. M. (2008). Transformative training: Designing programs for culture learning. In M. A. Moodian (Ed.), *Contemporary leadership and intercultural competence: Understanding and utilizing cultural diversity to build successful organizations* (pp. 95–110). Sage.

Bhatia, S. (2019). Searching for justice in an unequal world: Reframing indigenous psychology as a cultural and political project. *Journal of Theoretical and Philosophical Psychology, 39*(2), 107–114. https://doi.org/10.1037/teo0000109

Chen, H., Lai, K., He, L., & Yu, R. (2020). Where you are is who you are? The geographical account of psychological phenomena. *Frontiers in Psychology, 11*, 536. https://doi.org/10.3389/fpsyg.2020.00536

Collins, L. H., Machizawa, S., & Rice, J. K. (2019). *Transnational psychology of women: Expanding international and intersectional approaches.* American Psychological Association.

Cross, C. J., Taylor, R. J., & Chatters, L. M. (2018). Family social support networks of African American and Black Caribbean adolescents. *Journal of Child and Family Studies, 27*, 2757–2771. https://doi.org/10.1007%2Fs10826-018-1116-2

Dasen, P. R. (2022). Culture and cognitive development. *Journal of Cross-Cultural Psychology, 53*(7–8), 789–816. https://doi.org/10.1177/00220221221092409

de Wit, H., & Altbach, P. G. (2021). Internationalization in higher education: Global trends and recommendations for its future. *Policy Reviews in Higher Education, 5*(1), 28–46. https://doi.org/10.1080/23322969.2020.1820898

Fryberg, S. A. (2012). Cultural psychology as a bridge between anthropology and cognitive science. *Topics in Cognitive Science, 4*(3), 437–444. https://doi.org/10.1111/j.1756-8765.2012.01205.x

Henrich, J., Heine, S. J., & Norenzayan, A. (2010). The weirdest people in the world? *Behavioral and Brain Sciences, 33*, 1–75. https://doi.org/10.1017/s0140525x0999152x

Keith, K. D. (2011). Introduction to cross-cultural psychology. In K. D. Keith (Ed.), *Cross-cultural psychology: Contemporary themes and perspectives* (pp. 3–19). Wiley-Blackwell.

Keith, K. D. (2016). Culture and psychology: Evolution of a discipline. In W. D. Woody, R. L. Miller, & W. J. Wozniak (Eds.) *Psychological specialties in historical context: Enriching the classroom experience*

for teachers and students. (pp. 273–288). Society for the Teaching of Psychology.

Kim, U., Yang, K.-S., & Hwang, K.-K. (Eds.). (2006). *Indigenous and cultural psychology: Understanding people in context.* Springer.

Lonner, W. J. (2018). The continuing growth of cross-cultural psychology. In K. Keith (Ed.), *Elements of Psychology and Culture Series.* Cambridge University Press. [monograph]

Ma, J., Grogan-Kaylor, A., Pace, G. T., Ward, K. P., & Lee, S. J. (2022). The association between spanking and physical abuse of young children in 56 low- and middle-income countries. *Child Abuse & Neglect, 129*, 1–11. https://doi.org/10.1016/j.chiabu.2022.105662

Morling, B. (2015). Teaching cultural psychology. In D. S. Dunn (Ed.), *Oxford Handbook of the Teaching of Psychology* (pp. 599–611). Oxford University Press.

Norcross, J. C., Hailstorks, R., Aiken, L. S., Pfund, R. A., Stamm, K. E., & Christidis, P. (2016). Undergraduate study in psychology: Curriculum and assessment. *American Psychologist, 71*(2), 89–101. https://doi.org/10.1037/a0040095

Pick, C. M., Ko, A., Wormley, A. S., et al. (2022). Family still matters: Human social motivation across 42 countries during a global pandemic. *Evolution and Human Behavior.* https://doi.org/10.1016/j.evolhumbehav.2022.09.003

Pickren, W. E., & Taşçı, G. (2022). Indigenous psychologies: Resources for future histories. In D. McCallum (Ed.), *The Palgrave handbook of the history of human sciences* (pp. 1–22). Palgrave Macmillan. https://doi.org/10.1007/978-981-15-4106-3_80-2

Rentfrow, P. J. (2020). Geographical psychology. *Current Opinion in Psychology, 32*, 165–170. https://doi.org/10.1016/j.copsyc.2019.09.009

Rentfrow, P. J., & Gosling, S. D. (2021). Putting personality in its place: A geographical perspective on personality traits. In O. P. John & R. W. Robins (Eds.), *Handbook of personality: Theory and research* (pp. 824–836). The Guilford Press.

Rogoff, B., Coppens, A. D., Alcalá, L., Aceves-Azuara, I., Ruvalcaba, O., López, A., & Dayton, A. (2017). Noticing learners' strengths through cultural research. *Perspectives on Psychological Science, 12*(5), 876–888. https://doi.org/10.1177/1745691617718355

Skrefsrud, T.-A. (2021). Why student mobility does not automatically lead to better understanding: Reflections on the concept of intercultural learning. In D. Cairns (Ed.), *The Palgrave handbook of youth mobility and educational migration* (pp. 63–73). Springer. https://doi.org/10.1007/978-3-030-64235-8_7

Summers, N. M., & Poelker, K. E. (2017). Cultural expertise in U.S. psychology departments: An analysis of faculty profiles. *Scholarship of Teaching and Learning in Psychology*, *3*(1), 15–27. https://doi.org/10.1037/stl0000074

Thalmayer, A. G., Toscanelli, C., & Arnett, J. J. (2021). The neglected 95% revisited: American psychology becoming less American? *American Psychologist*, *76*(1), 116–129. https://doi.org/10.1037/amp0000622

Van de Vliert, E., & Van Lange, P. A. M. (2019). Latitudinal psychology: An ecological perspective on creativity, aggression, happiness, and beyond. *Perspectives on Psychological Science*, *14*(5), 860–884. https://doi.org/10.1177/1745691619858067

Wei, Y., Spencer-Rodgers, J., Anderson, E., & Peng, K. (2021). The effects of a cross-cultural psychology course on perceived intercultural competence. *Teaching of Psychology*, *48*(3), 221–227. https://doi.org/10.1177/0098628320977273

Part One

Pedagogical Strategies

Cultural and cross-cultural psychology courses are among the most exciting to teach. These courses have no shortage of content to spark student interest and critical thinking, enhance intercultural competence, and facilitate classroom inclusivity. What is more, these courses may provide students with a dramatically new perspective on the discipline of psychology as a whole. Yet, teaching about culture and psychology involves multiple challenges, many of which instructors may not have encountered in teaching other psychology courses. These include teaching as a cultural outsider, creating a classroom environment conducive to discussing diversity, making cross-cultural comparisons without creating or reinforcing stereotypes, raising awareness of power and privilege within cross-cultural psychology, and avoiding the marginalization of cross-cultural perspectives within the course or curriculum. Part One addresses strategies that I and others have found to be effective in dealing with these challenges. Interestingly, the teaching of culture and psychology itself varies with culture. For example, cross-cultural studies indicate significant variability in classroom norms and expectations for student engagement (e.g., Shcheglova, 2018). Therefore, I recognize the need to select from and tailor these recommendations to fit your own institutional and cultural context.

A SOCIAL JUSTICE APPROACH

Publications in journals addressing cross-cultural psychology indicate a marked interest in matters of social justice in terms of research topics. Yet, there has been little attention to how we might apply a social justice perspective to the *teaching* of courses on culture and psychology. In addition, although we might expect otherwise, gaining a social justice perspective is not necessarily an

 DOI: 10.4324/9781003356820-2

outcome of taking a cross-cultural psychology course. Students may acquire a fact-based knowledge of cultural variability without gaining an understanding of systems of oppression (Prieto, 2009). This may be particularly true for dominant group students in WEIRD (Western, Educated, Industrialized, Rich, and Democratic; Henrich et al., 2010) nations.

According to Hackman (2005), social justice education involves striving for greater inclusivity of students' voices and experiences, providing equitable access to learning opportunities and the distribution of resources, empowering student learners to enact social change, raising awareness about systems of power and privilege, and preparing students to approach real-world problems from multiple perspectives. As will become clear in the following sections, taking this perspective opens up a range of strategies for addressing the challenges of teaching about culture and psychology. In addition, teaching cross-cultural psychology from a social justice perspective may increase the likelihood that students will develop a sense of global citizenship, which involves not only global awareness and valuing diversity, but a sense of responsibility to take action toward a more sustainable and just world (Reysen & Katzarska-Miller, 2013). Nearly all of the activities and topics in this book can be approached from a social justice perspective. For example, in teaching about the concept of "culture" we can facilitate equal access by conceptual-izing – and explicitly discussing – the university or academia as a culture with a hidden curriculum and unspoken rules and expectations.

TEACHING AS A CULTURAL OUTSIDER

In recent years, there has been considerable debate about the legitimacy of teaching as an outsider, or what Mayberry (1996) called "teaching what you're not." This occurs, for example, when White faculty teach courses on race and ethnicity, men teach women's studies courses, or heterosexual faculty teach courses on LGBTQIA+ issues. Students often express a preference for instruc-tors whose identity aligns with the subject matter (Morgan Consoli & Marin, 2016), but in teaching cross-cultural psychology, being an outsider is inevitable, at least to some extent, given the vast number of cultural identities represented in the research literature, and typically in a single course. In fact, it could be argued that teaching beyond one's identity is desirable if we are to construct courses that are inclusive of the diversity of student backgrounds and experiences. In addition, this broader perspective is essential in educating future psychologists to reduce the focus on WEIRD societies in the discipline.

Yet, it is challenging to effectively discuss the diverse cultures we have not experienced ourselves without speaking on behalf of cultural insiders

(Peterson, 1996). This is particularly difficult when there are significant power disparities between outsider and insider cultures or individuals (for a detailed discussion of teaching as an outsider from a position of privilege, see Goldstein, 2021a). Two strategies that may ease the difficulty of teaching as an outsider include bringing insider voices into the classroom and being transparent about the limits of one's own cultural knowledge.

Inviting the Voices of Cultural Insiders

There is a wide range of options for inviting insider voices into the classroom, but in each case, students should be cautioned that individual perspectives and experiences, including their own, should not be assumed to generalize to all members of a cultural group or to independently refute research findings. Instructors may use films, first-person narrative accounts, as well as guest speakers to bring students an insider perspective (Yoon et al., 2014). Because insider voices may also enter class discussions indirectly through university-wide speakers or events, instructors might dedicate a few minutes of each class session to student announcements about such opportunities when relevant to the course content.

Students may also be exposed to insider voices through intercultural partnership opportunities. For example, Wickline et al. (2021) developed the Crossing Borders program, a series of empirically validated, shared cultural experiences and dialogues that paired domestic and international students at a Midwestern U.S. university. Insider voices may emerge through online inter-cultural discussions as well. Recently, several opportunities for virtual exchange have become available as a result of a combination of factors, including efforts to make student mobility more accessible and inclusive, particularly during the Covid-19 pandemic, as well as increasing concern about the carbon footprint associated with air travel. For example, in the Collaborative Online International Learning program (COIL; see Rubin, 2015, for a detailed description), faculty from institutions in different countries work jointly to develop an experiential curriculum that brings their students together in a virtual platform. There is a growing research literature supporting the ability of such virtual exchange programs to enhance students' intercultural awareness and sensitivity (e.g., Asojo et al., 2019; Chu & Torii, 2021; Gwillim & Karimova, 2021).

Insider voices may also come to light through service learning, although multiple authors have stressed the importance of approaching volunteering from a justice-oriented rather than charity-oriented motivation (Steckley & Steckley, 2021; Williams & Melchiori, 2013). On an international level, a number of programs have emerged around the practice of e-volunteering (Steckley & Steckley, 2021), in

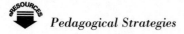

which students assist nonprofit organizations, often by conducting research to address jointly identified practical or policy concerns.

Student engagement with diverse voices may result from participatory action research, in which those most affected by the research outcomes become the central decision-makers regarding the research questions, design, and analysis. Fernandez (2022) described multiple examples of decolonizing participatory action to prioritize community knowledge, equitable collaboration, shared decision-making, and an interrogation of power dynamics.

Finally, students may wish to share their own experiences as cultural insiders and can make a valuable contribution to class discussion by doing so as long as care is taken not to overgeneralize from an individual case. However, it is critical to avoid placing students in the position of spokespersons for a specific cultural group. In addition to the potential for causing students discomfort or embarrassment, this action makes assumptions about the student's background and knowledge and creates a disparate classroom dynamic in which students from underrepresented groups become responsible for educating their peers in addition to working toward their own academic goals.

Being Transparent About Limits to Your Cultural Knowledge

Along with bringing the voices of insiders into the classroom, you may find it helpful to be transparent with students about the limits to your own cultural knowledge and perspectives. This approach might best be viewed within the framework of *cultural humility*, a term first coined by Tervalon and Murray-García (1998) in reference to multicultural training for health care professionals, and one which has more recently been applied to multicultural training for psychotherapists. These authors advocated transitioning from an emphasis on mastering specific multicultural content areas to a lifelong learning model of engagement with diversity and self-reflection. Power dynamics are a central component of the self-reflection associated with cultural humility in terms of interrogating the source of one's own potentially ethnocentric or biased standards of comparison. Applying this model to the teaching of psychology, Abbott et al. (2019, p. 5) suggested that:

> Although lifelong learning does not guarantee an absence of cultural missteps, it makes mistakes and dissemination of misinformation by educators less likely. In this way, cultural humility's emphasis on the lifelong nature of cultural learning, and the inability to ever achieve a state of sufficient knowledge, facilitates cultural competence while increasing the

likelihood that educators remain competent over time and as they encounter novel diversity and operate in everchanging systems.

In addition to aiding the instructor's efficacy, transparency on the part of the instructor also provides students with a model for how they might acknowledge limits to their own knowledge or awareness in a nondefensive manner. *Activity 2.2: Insiders and Outsiders* paves the way for a classroom discussion of the instructor's and students' own positionality relative to the course material.

CREATING A CLASSROOM ENVIRONMENT CONDUCIVE TO DISCUSSING DIVERSITY

Several studies have found that both instructors and students value class participation and an interactive educational experience (Rocca, 2010). Indeed, empirical research indicates that an inclusive and participatory classroom fosters student motivation, confidence, critical thinking, communication skills, and memory for course content (Rocca, 2010; Weaver & Qi, 2005). In cross-cultural psychology courses, however, both students and instructors may have some trepidation about participating in discussions. Students may be concerned about expressing opinions or asking questions that appear ethnocentric or otherwise biased in some respect. Instructors who teach about diversity may experience anxiety about encountering strong and at times unpredictable student responses (Miller et al., 2019). These behaviors are disproportionately experienced by faculty from minoritized groups, who tend to have greater responsibility for teaching diversity courses (Prieto, 2009). Both students and instructors may feel more comfortable and supported in discussing issues of diversity by setting ground rules for discussion and implementing other practices that facilitate equitable access to the course materials and educational experiences.

Setting Ground Rules for Discussion

Boysen (2012) described the use of discussion ground rules as central to an inclusive classroom. These guidelines generally seek to ensure that classroom interactions are respectful, tolerant, and confidential, the latter a growing concern given social media use. Ideally, discussion ground rules help create a collaborative and supportive learning environment that facilitates the exploration of conflicting views on complex topics (Pasque et al., 2013). Courses taught partially or entirely online can also benefit from employing discussion ground

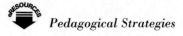
rules, given the potential for anonymity and lack of visual feedback to result in rude or hostile interactions (Suler, 2004).

There are multiple benefits to having students take the lead in constructing the ground rules for their own class (Goldstein, 2021b, p. 22).

> First, the discussion of potential ground rules may itself contribute to raising awareness of social justice issues, a key first step given the nonconscious nature of much bias (Boysen, 2012). Second, this activity gives students the opportunity to get to know each other, and, as a result, they are more likely to participate in class, are better able to communicate with each other, and are less likely to engage in unproductive conflict (Fournier-Sylvester, 2013; Rocca, 2010). Third, involving students in the development of ground rules facilitates the power-sharing that is fundamental to a learner-centered classroom (Spencer, 2015), and finally, taking primary responsibility for developing ground rules creates buy-in and builds trust among students (Landis, 2008).

Instructors have taken several different approaches to involving students in the development of discussion ground rules (for a detailed discussion of strategies for setting discussion ground rules, see Goldstein, 2021b).

Equitable Access

A central feature of a classroom environment conducive to discussing diversity is equitable access to course materials and educational experiences. To some extent, actions toward this goal apply across cultures and across courses in the curriculum. These actions include: (1) providing all students access to course materials, technology, and delivery methods, which involves a consideration of the cost of books and materials; (2) adhering to universal design principles, for example, using accessibility checkers for course materials and slide presentations; (3) creating syllabi and assessments that foster inclusivity and reduce stereotype threat (e.g., Fuentes et al., 2021; Taylor et al., 2019); (4) offering flexible requirements for outside activities and assignments; and (5) developing course evaluations that assess equitable access to materials and experiences.

Yet, creating a classroom environment with equitable access to educational experiences may also require consideration of students' cultural backgrounds (Goldstein, 2009). In fact, it may be valuable to explicitly discuss with students how culture may impact course policies and practices and, thus, classroom-related behavior and participation. For example, cultural psychologist Hazel

Markus (Markus & Conner, 2014) described an interaction in one of her classes that caused her to re-examine the assumption that speaking in class discussions indicates knowledge of the course material when one of her most capable, but quiet, students pointed out that this belief was culture-bound. This student, Heejung Kim, later demonstrated this in her doctoral dissertation, which was conducted in the U.S. For her East Asian student participants, talking was viewed as interfering – and in fact, did interfere – with the ability to think clearly. This was not the case for European American student participants, who viewed talking as a means of clarifying thoughts (Kim, 2002). Thus, instructors may want to avoid mandating that students speak in class as a way to earn participation credit.

Allowing students to have a range of participation options, including contributing in writing during class or on an online discussion forum, may result in greater inclusion of diverse student voices. Cultural norms and values may also impact how views are expressed in the classroom. For example, some instructors recommend the use of first person ("I statements") to indicate ownership of thoughts and feelings, reduce tension, and thus facilitate the inclusion of diverse perspectives (e.g., Souza, 2017). Yet, this form of speech may be viewed as unusually egocentric in some cultures, particularly those with a more collectivist orientation (Kashima & Kashima, 1998).

MAKING CROSS-CULTURAL COMPARISONS WITHOUT CREATING OR REINFORCING STEREOTYPES

Although courses dealing with issues of culture and psychology are often designed with the goal of dispelling stereotypes, you may find it is difficult for students – and instructors – to discuss such issues without creating or reinforcing stereotypical notions. Bronstein and Quina (1988) stated that the risk of creating stereotypes is particularly high when people are labeled on the basis of a single dimension and placed in opposition to other labeled groups for the purpose of comparison. This is precisely the format in which cross-cultural findings are typically presented. Avoiding stereotyping is relevant to both the presentation of cross-cultural research findings and the facilitation of class discussions. There are several strategies that may reduce the likelihood of creating or reinforcing stereotypes. These include educating students about the cognitive processes involved in stereotype formation and maintenance, presenting a balance of cultural differences and similarities, emphasizing within-group variability and intersectionality, attending to ethnocentric language, and focusing on the cultural context.

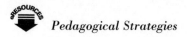

Teaching About the Stereotype Formation Processes

An effective strategy for addressing the tendency to stereotype is to educate students about the mechanics of the social categorization process. By regarding stereotyping as a result of human information processing, it is possible to separate stereotyping from prejudice and enable participants in discussions to point out stereotypic comments without making personal attacks. Activities 8.6: Cognition and Stereotype Formation and 8.7: The Content of Stereotypes are designed to help students learn to examine the source and nature of specific stereotypes, explore errors involved in attention, categorization, memory, and attributional processes, and seek stereotype-disconfirming information. The instructor content accompanying Activity 8.7 also provides information on some of the cognitive biases that may fuel stereotyping, such as confirmation bias and the outgroup homogeneity effect. For a more complete understanding of the process of stereotyping, students should also learn about the motivational and affective aspects of this phenomenon (e.g., Devos, 2014).

Presenting a Balance of Cultural Differences and Similarities

Despite an increasing tendency in culture and psychology publications to report and address cultural similarities (Brouwers et al., 2004), the field continues to overemphasize cultural differences. This is common in the classroom as well. Cultural differences seem to generate more interest than similarities and are certainly easier to communicate in terms of statistical results. Yet, this focus on differences increases the likelihood of stereotyping.

In reviewing cross-cultural research reports with students, you might encourage them to note the extent to which differences and similarities are each addressed in the results and discussion sections. They will likely find both differences and similarities detailed in the results section, but greater attention to differences than to similarities in the discussion section. To put research findings in a broader context, it may be helpful to share with students the concern that authors are more likely to undertake research on cultural differences than cultural similarities, and that studies subsequently reporting differences may be overrepresented due to the "file drawer effect" (Ferrin & Gillespie, 2009).

Additionally, Morling (2015) suggests discussing with students the types of differences identified and distinguishing between outcomes that differ in *direction* as opposed to those that differ in *degree*. For example, Castelo and Sarvary (2022) reported a difference in direction in their cross-cultural research on comfort with robots. They found that U.S. Americans were more comfortable with robots low in human-like emotion, but less comfortable with robots high in human-like emotion, whereas the opposite was true for Japanese participants. This may be explained in part by a finding in the same study that is a cross-cultural difference in degree – Japanese participants perceived robots in general to be more animate and to have more of a consciousness than did the U.S. American participants.

Discussions of cultural differences may also be contextualized by an exploration of human universals. Activity 1.3: Human Universals, based on Brown's (1991) concept of the *Universal People*, encourages students to identify commonalities across a wide range of behaviors and to consider the criteria for determining that a phenomenon is, in fact, universal.

Emphasizing Within-Group Variability and Intersectionality

Perhaps the most important strategy to avoid stereotyping is to help students stay aware of the diversity within any cultural group. Bronstein and Quina (2003) suggested carefully examining research results in order to help students clearly understand that within-group variability is generally greater than between-group variability. The diversity within groups can also be reinforced by clearly specifying characteristics of research participants and by highlighting intersectional identities. For example, Betancourt and López (1993) noted that culture, race, and ethnicity are frequently confounded with socioeconomic variables. Cross-cultural research should thus be discussed in terms of the specific characteristics of the research participants (such as social class, gender, and education level), and efforts should be made not to generalize these findings to all members of that cultural group.

Students can also be asked to monitor their readings for instances where cross-cultural research has ignored or minimized within-group diversity. Data gathered from small, typically more highly educated, samples from a specific country are often presented as representing the culture as a whole. In addition, findings about these research participants may then be generalized to discussions of entire ethnic groups or geographical regions. In more extreme instances, though less common in recent publications, data from a single country are framed as representing entire continents or regions. Studies of South Korean or Malaysian participants, for example, have inaccurately been presented as representing "Asian behavior." Similarly, data collected from predominantly White, North American college populations has been used as the basis for conclusions about "Western values" or "American behavior." Activity 1.7 provides an opportunity to discuss various forms of overgeneralization in cross-cultural psychology in that it focuses on how

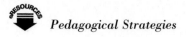

the use of broad ethnic group labels in academic research (what Trimble, 1990, termed "ethnic gloss") obscures important within-category variability.

Attending to Ethnocentric Language

The language we use to discuss cultural variability may unintentionally create stereotypes by setting ethnocentric standards of comparison. For example, cross-cultural psychologists frequently use a Western/non-Western classification in describing cultural differences in behavior. This dichotomy may reinforce the notion that what is Western is central, and thus the standard of comparison, and that members of all other cultures are less significant or are exotic "others" to be contrasted with what is portrayed as typical or normal.

Recently, some scholars (e.g., Kagitcibasi, 2002; Thalmayer et al., 2021) have shifted this dynamic by using the term "majority world" as opposed to "non-Western" to reflect the fact that most of the world's population is located in Asia, Africa, and Latin America. When possible, it may be preferable to discuss cross-cultural findings in terms of the specific cultural groups involved (such as European Americans and Japanese) or in terms of the relevant variables underlying the comparison (such as individualism and collectivism). Ethnocentric standards of comparison may also be implicit in what is *not* said. For example, Pillay (2017, p. 135) asked "Why is Western psychology innocently labeled 'psychology' but African psychology geographically located?"

In addition to conventions for labeling groups of people, ethnocentric language may also be a concern in regard to comparisons between objects or phenomena that are functionally equivalent and need not be described using separate terms. According to Pareek and Rao (1980, p. 131), "functional equivalence of a behaviour exists when the behaviour in question has developed in response to a problem shared by two or more social/cultural groups, even though the behaviour in one society may be superficially quite different from the behavior in another society." For example, Moore (1988) noted the unnecessary practice of referring to the homes of African people as huts, and that the word tribe, although frequently used to refer to human communities within African nations, is rarely used to refer to human communities within European nations. It may be useful to have students consider whether language contributes to describing relevant cross-cultural differences, or if it serves only an evaluative purpose. For example, an interesting class discussion might focus on various healing practices across cultures which might be considered "psychotherapy." Activity 3.10: Language and Thought provides an opportunity to discuss the ways in which the language of cross-cultural psychology may affect how we view the discipline and its content. Warner (2021) recommends framing any discussion of language use in the classroom in terms of accuracy in representation to avoid veering into disputes over freedom of speech or "political correctness."

Focusing on the Cultural Context

An additional strategy for avoiding stereotypes is to focus on the cultural context. Morling and Lamoreaux (2008) made an important distinction between culture inside-the-head (e.g., emotions, attitudes, self-perceptions) and culture outside-the head (e.g., laws, norms, media, traditions, languages). Morling (2015, p. 15) suggested that focusing on the latter component of culture can reduce the tendency to overgeneralize cultural differences. She recommended discussing cultural differences as an outcome of culturally different settings rather than individuals. For example, "instead of talking about 'Mexicans,' we should talk about 'people who are participating in the meanings and practices that are prevalent in Mexican cultural contexts.'"

A related approach is to introduce students to the method of priming cultural context. In these studies, specific tasks, such as writing an essay about the ways one is similar to family members (a collectivist prime) as opposed to the ways one is different from family members (an individualist prime), are used to experimentally activate cultural orientations. Although the effects of priming may be less straightforward than once thought (e.g., Yang & Vignoles, 2020), discussing this methodology is another way to illustrate to students that the cultural setting is distinct from attributes of the individual and that altering the setting can shift behavioral responses.

RAISING AWARENESS OF POWER AND PRIVILEGE WITHIN CROSS-CULTURAL PSYCHOLOGY

In addition to teaching as an outsider, creating a classroom conducive to discussing diversity, and making cross-cultural comparisons without stereotyping, instructors of courses on culture and psychology may find it challenging to raise students' awareness of the power dynamics within cross-cultural psychology itself. Doing so is important in facilitating an understanding of how the cultural context shapes academic disciplines and in enabling students to become active participants in efforts toward developing a more inclusive cross-cultural psychology and psychology as a whole.

As you discuss various topics and research areas in class, you may find students intrigued by making the content of cross-cultural psychology itself a topic for discussion. It is important for students to understand that academic disciplines are not fixed entities, but that their content and methods vary across time and place, and are shaped by social, cultural, political, historical, environmental, economic, and religious factors. We can encourage students, as Kessi and Kiguwa (2015, p. 1.4) suggested regarding efforts toward decolonizing psychology, to consider the motivation underlying psychological research and practice, and ask,

> Who does it benefit and in what ways? Who does it marginalise and in what ways? Who has the power to assign meaning to people's experiences? Who has the power to represent the lives and the minds of others? What behaviours are considered acceptable and normal and which ones are not?

Students can be encouraged to consider why some cultures (including many located in the Global South) and communities (including LGBTQIA+ individuals) are underrepresented in cross-cultural research. They can also explore why specific topics have had a significant presence in cross-cultural psychology. For example, we can look at the enormous number of cross-cultural studies on achievement motivation as compared with other forms of motivation, such as affiliation motives, and recognize – as Estrada-Villalta and Adams (2018) pointed out – the influence of individualistic conceptions of European and American economic development and dominance on academic disciplines. Students might also consider whether research questions and findings within the field are sufficiently contextualized. For example, Bhatia (2019, p. 110) observed that "The field of psychology has a tendency to reframe problems related to structural inequality as individual problems ..."

Finally, students might be asked to identify the vantage point from which various topics are investigated and to recognize generalizations based on the perspective of the dominant group. For example, we can explore ways that the intercultural competence literature tends to reflect the intergroup contact experience of those in the majority group within a society (Punti & Dingel, 2021). More advanced students might even investigate some of the structural inequities of the discipline including the historical and current gatekeepers, such as the continued domination of North American and European academics in journal authorship and editorial board membership (Arnett, 2008; Thalmayer et al., 2021). Please note that this may lead to some interesting discussions about which sources should be considered legitimate for use in student assignments!

AVOIDING THE MARGINALIZATION OF CROSS-CULTURAL PERSPECTIVES

Although for the most part we have moved on from the days when cultural perspectives in psychology were literally marginalized – in supplementary materials, in the "boxes" of primary texts, in separate diversity chapters, or in a single class session – conscious effort is still needed to communicate to students that culture is central to an understanding of human behavior. In structuring our courses across the psychology curriculum, we can do this by including cross-cultural phenomena in exam questions, class discussions, and key assignments. The placement of a cross-cultural psychology course within department offerings also makes an important statement to faculty and students. Departments where cultural perspectives are valued tend to list these courses in the course catalog, schedule them regularly, designate them as required rather than electives, assign them a regular course number, and include them in the criteria for evaluating student and instructor performance (Goldstein, 2005).

The challenges of teaching about culture and psychology are significant, but these need not be the instructor's alone. Asking students to join you as active change agents in working toward seeking the voices of insiders, creating an inclusive and supportive classroom environment, dispelling stereotypes, interrogating the power dynamics of cross-cultural psychology as an academic discipline, and positioning cross-cultural perspectives as central to the psychology curriculum creates a rich learning opportunity for fostering an expansive, culturally sensitive, and socially just world view.

References

Abbott, D. M., Pelc, N., & Mercier, C. (2019). Cultural humility and the teaching of psychology. *Scholarship of Teaching and Learning in Psychology*, *5*(2), 169. https://psycnet.apa.org/doi/10.1037/stl0000144

Arnett, J. J. (2008). The neglected 95%: Why American psychology needs to become less American. *American Psychologist*, *63*(7), 602–614. https://doi.org/10.1037/0003-066X.63.7.602

Asojo, A., Kartoshkina, Y., Amole, D., & Jaiyeoba, B. (2019). Multicultural learning and experiences in design through the Collaborative Online International Learning (COIL) framework. *Journal of Teaching and Learning with Technology*, *8*, 5–16. https://doi.org/10.14434/jotlt.v8i1.26748

Betancourt, H., & López, S. R. (1993). The study of culture, ethnicity, and race in American psychology. *American Psychologist, 48*(6), 629–637. https://psycnet.apa.org/doi/10.1037/0003-066X.48.6.629

Bhatia, S. (2019). Searching for justice in an unequal world: Reframing indigenous psychology as a cultural and political project. *Journal of Theoretical and Philosophical Psychology, 39*(2), 107–114. https://doi.org/10.1037/teo0000109

Boysen, G. A. (2012). Teachers' responses to bias in the classroom: How response type and situational factors affect student perceptions. *Journal of Applied Social Psychology, 42*(2), 506–534. https://doi.org/10.1111/j.1559-1816.2011.00784.x

Bronstein, P., & Quina, K. (1988). Perspectives on gender balance and cultural diversity in the teaching of psychology. In P. Bronstein & K. Quina (Eds.), *Teaching a psychology of people: Resources for gender and sociocultural awareness* (pp. 3–11). American Psychological Association.

Bronstein, P., & Quina, K. (Eds.). (2003). *Teaching a psychology of people: Resources for gender and sociocultural awareness* (2nd ed.). American Psychological Association.

Brouwers, S. A., van Hemert, D. A., Breugelmans, S. M., & van de Vijver, F. J. R. (2004). A historical analysis of empirical studies published in the *Journal of Cross-Cultural Psychology: 1970–2004. Journal of Cross-Cultural Psychology, 35*, 251–262. https://psycnet.apa.org/doi/10.1177/0022022104264121

Brown, D. E. (1991). *Human universals.* Temple University Press.

Castelo, N., & Sarvary, M. (2022). Cross-cultural differences in comfort with humanlike robots. *International Journal of Social Robotics.* https://doi.org/10.1007/s12369-022-00920-y

Chu, C., & Torii, Y. (2021). Communicating across cultures online: Introducing and comparing the implementation of three virtual study abroad programs. *The JACET International Convention Proceedings: The JACET 60th Commemorative International Convention*, 57–58.

Devos, T. (2014). Stereotypes and intergroup attitudes. In F. T. L. Leong, L. Comas-Díaz, G. C. Nagayama Hall, V. C. McLoyd & J. E. Trimble (Eds.), *APA handbook of multicultural psychology*, Vol. 1: Theory and research (pp. 341–360). American Psychological Association.

Estrada-Villalta, S., & Adams, G. (2018). Decolonizing development: A decolonial approach to the psychology of economic inequality. *Translational Issues in Psychological Science, 4*(2), 198–209. https://doi.org/10.1037/tps0000157

Fernandez, J. S. (2022). Decolonizing participatory action research in community psychology. In S. Kessi, S. Suffla, & M. Seedat (Eds.), *Decolonial enactments in community psychology* (pp. 29–51). Springer.

Ferrin, D. L., & Gillespie, N. A. (2009). Cultural differences and universals in the development of trust. *International Association for Conflict Management Conference*, Kyoto, Japan. https://ssrn.com/abstract= 1484885

Fournier-Sylvester, N. (2013). Daring to debate: Strategies for teaching controversial issues in the classroom. *The College Quarterly*, *16*(3), 1–7. http://collegequarterly.ca/2013-vol16-num03-summer/fournier-sylvester.html

Fuentes, M. A., Zelaya, D. G., & Madsen, J. W. (2021). Rethinking the course syllabus: Considerations for promoting equity, diversity, and inclusion. *Teaching of Psychology*, *48*(1), 69–79. https://doi.org/10. 1177/0098628320959979

Goldstein, S. B. (2005). Cross-cultural perspectives across the psychology curriculum: Moving beyond "add culture and stir." In B. Perlman, L. McCann, & W. Buskist (Eds.). *Voices of experience: Memorable talks from the National Institute on the Teaching of Psychology* (pp. 45–57). American Psychological Society.

Goldstein, S. B. (2009). Enlisting the participation of students in diversifying the curriculum. In R. A. R. Gurung & L. R. Prieto (Eds.), *Getting culture: Incorporating diversity across the curriculum* (pp. 201–212). Stylus.

Goldstein, S. B. (2021a). Outsiders teaching insiders: How instructors from privileged groups can effectively teach about diversity. In M. Kite, K. Case, & W. R. Williams (Eds.), *Navigating difficult moments in teaching diversity and social justice: Perseverance and resilience* (pp. 211–221). American Psychological Association. https://doi.org/ 10.1037/0000216-015

Goldstein, S. B. (2021b). Ground rules for discussing diversity: Complex considerations. In M. Kite, K. Case, & W. R. Williams (Eds.), *Navigating difficult moments in teaching diversity and social justice: Perseverance and resilience* (pp. 17–25). American Psychological Association.

Gwillim, T. D., & Karimova, I. I. (2021). Virtual exchanges: Fake mobility or unique experiences. *Universal Journal of Educational Research*, *9*(2), 373–379. http://dx.doi.org/10.13189/ujer.2021.090213

Hackman, H. W. (2005). Five essential components for social justice education. *Equity & Excellence in Education*, *38*(2), 103–109. http:// dx.doi.org/10.1080/10665680590935034

Henrich, J., Heine, S. J., & Norenzayan, A. (2010). The weirdest people in the world? *Behavioral & Brain Sciences, 33*(2–3), 61–83. https://doi.org/10.1017/s0140525x0999152x

Kagitcibasi, C. (2002). A model of family change in cultural context. *Online Readings in Psychology and Culture, 6*, 1. http://dx.doi.org/10.9707/2307-0919.1059

Kashima, E., & Kashima, Y. (1998). Culture and language: The case of cultural dimensions and personal pronoun use. *Journal of Cross-Cultural Psychology, 29*(3), 461–486. https://doi.org/10.1177/0022022198293005

Kessi, S., & Kiguwa, P. (2015). Social psychology and social change: Beyond Western perspectives. *Papers on Social Representations, 24*, 1–11. https://psr.iscte-iul.pt/index.php/PSR/article/view/119

Kim, H. (2002). *Speech and silence: A cultural analysis of the effect of talking on psychology* (Order No. AAI3026847). [Doctoral Dissertation, Stanford University].

Landis, K. (Ed.). (2008). *Start talking: A handbook for engaging difficult dialogues in higher education.* The University of Alaska Anchorage and Alaska Pacific University.

Markus, H. R., & Conner, A. (2014). *Clash! How to thrive in a multicultural world.* Plume.

Mayberry, K. J. (Ed.). (1996). *Teaching what you're not: Identity politics in higher education.* New York University Press.

Miller, R. A., Struve, L. E., & Howell, C. D. (2019). "Constantly, excessively, and all the time": The emotional labor of teaching diversity courses. *International Journal of Teaching and Learning in Higher Education, 31*(3), 491–502.

Moore, R. B. (1988). Stereotyping in the English language. In P. S. Rothenberg (Ed.), *Racism and sexism: An integrated study* (pp. 270–271). St. Martin's Press.

Morgan Consoli, M. L., & Marin, P. (2016). Teaching diversity in the graduate classroom: The instructor, the students, the classroom, or all of the above? *Journal of Diversity in Higher Education, 9*(2), 143–157. https://doi.org/10.1037/a0039716

Morling, B. (2015). Teaching cultural psychology. In D. S. Dunn (Ed.), *Oxford Handbook of the Teaching of Psychology* (pp. 599–611). Oxford University Press.

Morling, B., & Lamoreaux, M. (2008). Measuring culture outside the head: A meta-analysis of individualism – collectivism in cultural products. *Personality and Social Psychology Review, 12*(3), 199–221. https://psycnet.apa.org/doi/10.1177/1088868308318260

Pareek, U., & Rao, T. V. (1980). Cross-cultural surveys and interviewing. In H. C. Triandis & J. W. Berry (Eds.), *Handbook of cross-cultural psychology*: Vol. 2. Methodology (pp. 127–179). Allyn and Bacon.

Pasque, P. A., Chesler, M. A., Charbeneau, J., & Carlson, C. (2013). Pedagogical approaches to student racial conflict in the classroom. *Journal of Diversity in Higher Education*, *6*(1), 1–16. https://doi.org/10.1037/a0031695

Peterson, N. J. (1996). Redefining America: Literature, multiculturalism, and pedagogy. In K. J. Mayberry (Ed.), *Teaching what you're not: Identity politics in higher education* (pp. 23–46). New York University Press.

Pillay, S. R. (2017). Cracking the fortress: Can we really decolonize psychology? *South African Journal of Psychology*, *47*(2), 135–140. https://doi.org/10.1177/0081246317698059

Prieto, L. R. (2009). Teaching about diversity: Reflections and future directions. In R. A. R. Gurung & L. R. Prieto (Eds.), *Getting culture: Incorporating diversity across the curriculum* (pp. 23–39). Stylus.

Punti, G., & Dingel, M. (2021). Rethinking race, ethnicity, and the assessment of intercultural competence in higher education. *Education Sciences*, *11*(3), 110–127. https://doi.org/10.3390/educsci11030110

Reysen, S., & Katzarska-Miller, I. (2013). A model of global citizenship: Antecedents and outcomes. *International Journal of Psychology*, *48*(5), 858–870. http://dx.doi.org/10.1080/00207594.2012.701749

Rocca, K. A. (2010). Student participation in the college classroom: An extended multidisciplinary literature review. *Communication Education*, *59*(2), 185–213. https://doi.org/10.1080/03634520903505936

Rubin, J. (2015). *Faculty guide for collaborative online international learning course development*. www.ufic.ufl.edu/UAP/Forms/COIL_guide.pdf

Shcheglova, I. (2018). A cross-cultural comparison of the academic engagement of students. *Russian Education & Society*, *60*(8–9), 665–681. https://doi.org/10.1080/10609393.2018.1598163

Souza, T. (2017). Managing hot moments in the classroom: Concrete strategies for cooling down tension. *Diversity and Inclusion in the College Classroom*, p. 4. www.academia.edu/31355266/Article_1_Managing_Hot_Moments_in_the_Classroom_Concrete_Strategies_for_Cooling_Down_Tension_Paper_2_Microaggressions_and_Microresistance_Supporting_and_Empowering_Students

Spencer, L. G. (2015). Engaging undergraduates in feminist classrooms: An exploration of professors' practices. *Equity & Excellence in Education, 48*(2), 195–211. https://doi.org/10.1080/10665684.2015.1022909

Steckley, M., & Steckley, J. (2021). E-volunteering as *international experiential learning: student and community perspectives. Canadian Journal of Development Studies / Revue canadienne d'études du eveloppement.* https://doi.org/10.1080/02255189.2021.1952856

Suler, J. (2004). The online disinhibition effect. *Cyberpsychology & Behavior, 7*(3), 321–326. https://doi.org/10.1089/1094931041291295

Taylor, S. D., Veri, M. J., Eliason, M., Hermoso, J. C. R., Bolter, N. D., & van Olphen, J. E. (2019). The social justice syllabus design tool: A first step in doing social justice pedagogy. *Journal Committed to Social Change on Race and Ethnicity, 5*(2), 132–166. https://doi.org/10.15763/issn.2642-2387.2019.5.2.132-166

Tervalon, M., & Murray-García, J. (1998). Cultural humility versus cultural competence: A critical distinction in defining physician training outcomes in multicultural education. *Journal of Health Care for the Poor and Underserved, 9*(2), 117–125. https://doi.org/10.1353/hpu.2010.0233

Thalmayer, A. G., Toscanelli, C., & Arnett, J. J. (2021). The neglected 95% revisited: Is American psychology becoming less American? *American Psychologist, 76*(1), 116–129. https://doi.org/10.1037/amp0000622

Trimble, J. E. (1990). Ethnic specification, validation prospects and future of drug abuse research. *International Journal of the Addictions, 25*, 149–169. https://doi.org/10.3109/10826089009071038

Warner, L. R. (2021). When students frame prejudicial speech as "freedom of speech": Classroom and institutional implications. In M. Kite, K. Case, & W. R. Williams (Eds.), *Navigating difficult moments in teaching diversity and social justice: Perseverance and resilience* (pp. 223–234). American Psychological Association.

Weaver, R. R., & Qi, J. (2005). Classroom organization and participation: College students' perceptions. *The Journal of Higher Education, 76*(5), 570–601. https://doi.org/10.1353/jhe.2005.0038

Wickline, V., Wiese, D. L., & Aggarwal, P. (2021). Increasing intercultural competence among psychology students using experiential learning activities with international student partners. *Scholarship of Teaching and Learning in Psychology.* https://doi.org/10.1037/stl0000288

Williams, W. R., & Melchiori, K. J. (2013). Class action: Using experiential learning to raise awareness of social class privilege. In K. A. Case (Ed.). *Deconstructing privilege: Teaching and learning as allies in the classroom* (pp. 169–187). Routledge.

Yang, S., & Vignoles, V. (2020). Self-construal priming reconsidered: Comparing effects of two commonly used primes in the UK and China. *Open Science Journal, 5*(3). http://dx.doi.org/10.23954/osj.v5i3.2418

Yoon, E., Jérémie-Brink, G., & Kordesh, K. (2014). Critical issues in teaching a multicultural counseling course. *International Journal for the Advancement of Counseling, 36*(4), 359–371. https://doi.org/10.1007/s10447-014-9212-5

Part Two

Instructor Resources

The Concept of Culture

DOI: 10.4324/9781003356820-4

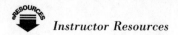

ACTIVITY 1.1
IS PSYCHOLOGY CULTURE-BOUND?

Activity Summary:

Seven major psychological concepts from across psychology's subfields are briefly described (e.g., the serial-position effect, social loafing, secure attachment) and students are asked to assess the universality of these concepts. Though often presented in psychology texts as universal, students will learn that each of the phenomena listed varies with culture.

Answers to Activity 1.1:

Although there is evidence that many psychological findings are universal, cross-cultural research has challenged each of the seven psychological concepts listed in this activity.

1. *Susceptibility to visual illusions* – A set of classic studies (Segall et al., 1966) demonstrated cultural differences in susceptibility to certain visual illusions. Explanations for these findings focused on differences in exposure to (a) angular structures (the "carpentered world theory"; increasing susceptibility to the Müller-Lyer illusion), (b) parallel lines extending into the distance (the "front-horizontal foreshortening theory"), and (c) two-dimensional representations of actual objects (the "symbolizing three dimensions in two theory").

2. *The serial position effect (primacy and recency)* – Although this effect may reflect an underlying universal tendency (even among nonhuman primates; Castro & Larsen, 1992), culture seems to influence whether it is expressed. Studies suggest that the serial position effect may be strengthened by specific memory strategies developed through formal schooling (Wagner, 1980). In addition, narrative memory strategies such as story-telling, used in primarily nonliterate societies, may override or diminish the serial position effect. Michael Cole and Sylvia Scribner (1974), for example, found no evidence of a serial position effect in studying memory among non-schooled Kpelle children in Liberia. Finally, there is evidence that the serial position effect may be linked to the sentence structure of specific languages which cues the listener to devote more attention to information at the beginning or end of the sentence (Amici et al., 2019).

3. *Social loafing* – Although research with men in individualist cultures has tended to demonstrate social loafing, studies with women across cultures and with men in collectivist cultures have had more mixed results, with

some studies indicating that being in a group may actually enhance individual performance (e.g., Karau & Williams, 1993; Klehe & Anderson, 2007; Simms & Nichols, 2014).

4. *Secure attachment* – Studies indicate a great deal of cultural variability in what is viewed as the ideal form of attachment between children and caregivers. In many cultures, stable multiple caregivers are seen as essential for raising well-adjusted children, such as among the Agta forager community in the Philippines (Mesman et al., 2016). In other communities, for example in many Zambian households, attachment to sibling caregivers is common (Mooya et al., 2016). In addition, the cross-cultural validity of Ainsworth's attachment styles and the primary method used to assess them, the Strange Situation Procedure, have been called into question (Keller, 2017; Otto et al., 2014). These studies challenge the notion that a secure mother-child relationship, as defined by Mary Ainsworth and colleagues, is the key to well-being.

5. *Delusions and hallucinations* – Much research indicates that criteria for normality are culture-bound. Although World Health Organization data (Jablensky et al., 1992) indicated that visual and auditory hallucinations are found cross-culturally as symptoms of schizophrenia, these are also forms of acceptable behavior in a variety of cultures that include altered states of consciousness as part of specific rituals or healing practices (Ward, 1989). Moreover, even when delusions and hallucinations accompany mental illness, the content of these experiences may differ across cultures. For example, individuals with schizophrenia in California, United States reported hearing disturbing, intrusive voices whereas those in Chennai, India heard voices that provided useful guidance, and individuals in Accra, Ghana often described the voices as those of relatives and morally good (Luhrmann et al., 2015). Mzimkulu and Simbayi (2006) described the phenomenon of *thwasa* in South African Xhosa culture which involves auditory and visual hallucinations but is viewed as a call to become a divine healer.

6. *Self-serving bias* – Several studies seem to indicate that members of Western societies are more likely than members of East Asian societies to exhibit a self-serving bias (e.g., Heine & Hamamura, 2007). However, there is also considerable variation among East Asian societies (which does not seem to be sufficiently explained by levels of individualism and collectivism). For example, a meta-analysis by Mezulis et al. (2004) found evidence of self-serving bias among Chinese and Korean participants, but not among Japanese and Pacific Islander participants. These findings may be due in part to cultural differences in motivation for and expression of self-enhancement.

7. *The similarity-attraction effect* – The magnitude of this effect appears to vary with culture. Heine et al. (2009) found the similarity-attraction effect to be weaker among Japanese as compared with Canadian participants. Their analyses indicated that level of self-esteem, which was higher among the Canadians, may influence interest in spending time with others who are similar to oneself. Bahns et al. (2019) reported that U.S. American relationship partners were more similar to each other than were Korean relationship partners. Their findings, while not entirely consistent across several studies, focused attention on the role of relational mobility in shaping the similarity-attraction effect. Relational mobility refers to the ease with which one can form or terminate relationships. Their findings suggest similarity-seeking may be associated with perceived ease of entry into relationships. Bahns and colleagues made the important point that relationship similarity should not be equated with relationship quality. They noted that the stability associated with low relationship mobility may facilitate satis-faction and closeness between partners.

Lecture/Discussion Suggestion:

What are the primary approaches taken in addressing psychology and culture? Adamopoulos and Lonner (1994) described three major theoretical orienta-tions in the study of culture and behavior that vary in emphasis on the cultural context and on commonalities in human experience: *Absolutism* (emphasizes commonalities and de-emphasizes the cultural context), *Relativism* (empha-sizes the cultural context and de-emphasizes commonalities), and *Universalism* (emphasizes both the cultural context and commonalities in human experi-ence). The field of psychology has historically taken an *absolutist* approach in which cultural factors are viewed as interfering with the search for universal aspects of human behavior. Researchers of culture and psychology have questioned the validity of this approach. For example, anthropologists and cultural psychologists have tended to emphasize a more *relativist* perspective in which observations of human behavior are viewed as meaningless apart from the cultural context. Cross-cultural psychologists generally advocate a *univer-salist* perspective in which an understanding of cultural variation is viewed as critical in searching for universal aspects of human behavior. This activity asks students to consider several major psychological findings that are frequently described in absolutist terms and consider whether these findings might be culture-bound.

Variation:

Have students use the list of research findings in Activity 1.1 to survey others. They can then pool their results to determine which behaviors are most likely to be viewed as universal. They will likely find that the behaviors involving basic psychological processes (memory and perception) are less likely to be viewed as culture-bound. Discussion can focus on explaining these findings, identifying other psychological processes that are culture-bound, and determining the implications of the culture-bound nature of psychological research findings for the field of psychology.

Writing Application:

Have students select one of the concepts listed in this activity or another concept that appears in an introductory psychology text, research the concept's universality, and write about their findings in a brief report, citing sources.

References:

Adamopoulos, J., & Lonner, W. J. (1994). Absolutism, relativism, and universalism in the study of culture and human activity. In W. J. Lonner & R. Malpass (Eds.), *Psychology and culture* (pp. 129–134). Allyn and Bacon.

Amici, F., Sánchez-Amaro, A., Sebastián-Enesco, C., Cacchione, T., Allritz, M., Salazar-Boney, J., & Rossano, F. (2019). The word order of languages predicts native speakers' working memory. *Scientific Reports*, 9(1124). https://doi.org/10.1038/s41598-018-37654-9

Bahns, A. J., Lee, J., & Crandall, C. S. (2019). Culture and mobility determine the importance of similarity in friendship. *Journal of Cross-Cultural Psychology*, 50(6), 731–750. https://doi.org/10.1177/0022022119852424

Castro, C. A., & Larsen, T. (1992). Primacy and recency effects in nonhuman primates. *Journal of Experimental Psychology: Animal Behavior Processes*, 18(4), 335–340. https://doi.org/10.1037//0097-7403.18.4.335

Cole, M., & Scribner, S. (1974). *Culture and thought: A psychological introduction*. Wiley.

Heine, S. J., Foster, J. B., & Spina, R. (2009). Do birds of a feather universally flock together? Cultural variation in the similarity-attraction effect. *Asian Journal of Social Psychology*, 12(4), 247–258. https://doi.org/10.1111/j.1467-839X.2009.01289.x

Heine, S. J., & Hamamura, T. (2007). In search of East Asian self-enhancement. *Personality and Social Psychology Review, 11*(1), 4–27. https://doi.org/10.1177/1088868306294587

Jablensky, A., Sartorius, N., Ernberg, G., Anker, M., Korten, A., Cooper, J. E., Day, R., & Bertelsen, A. (1992). Schizophrenia: Manifestations, incidence, and course in different cultures. A World Health Organization ten-country study. *Psychological Medicine, 20*, 1–97. https://doi.org/10.1017/s0264180100000904

Karau, S. J., & Williams, K. D. (1993). Social loafing: A meta-analytic review of social integration. *Journal of Personality and Social Psychology, 65*, 681–706. https://psycnet.apa.org/doi/10.1037/0022-3514.65.4.681

Keller, H. (2017). Culture and development: A systematic relationship. *Perspectives on Psychological Science, 12*(5), 833–840. https://doi.org/10.1177/1745691617704097

Klehe, U., & Anderson, N. (2007). The moderating influence of personality and culture on social loafing in typical versus maximum performance situations. *International Journal of Selection and Assessment, 15*(2), 250–262. http://dx.doi.org/10.1111/j.1468-2389.2007.00385.x

Luhrmann, T. M., Padmavati, R., Tharoor, H., & Osei, A. (2015). Hearing voices in different cultures: A social kindling hypothesis. *Topics in Cognitive Science, 7*(4), 646–663. https://doi.org/10.1111/tops.12158

Mesman, J., Minter, T., & Angnged, A. (2016). Received sensitivity: Adapting Ainsworth's scale to capture sensitivity in a multiple-caregiver context. *Attachment & Human Development, 18*(2), 101–114. https://doi.org/10.1080/14616734.2015.1133681

Mezulis, A. H., Abramson, L. Y., Hyde, J. S., & Hankin, B. L. (2004). Is there a universal positivity bias in attributions? A meta-analytic review of individual, developmental, and cultural differences in the self-serving attributional bias. *Psychological Bulletin, 130*(5), 711–747. https://doi.org/10.1037/0033-2909.130.5.711

Mooya, H., Sichimba, F., & Bakermans-Kranenburg, M. (2016). Infant–mother and infant–sibling attachment in Zambia. *Attachment & Human Development, 18*(6), 618–635. https://doi.org/10.1080/14616734.2016.1235216

Mzimkulu, K. G., & Simbayi, L. C. (2006). Perspectives and practices of Xhosa-speaking African traditional healers when managing psychosis. *International Journal of Disability, Development and Education, 53*, 417–431. https://doi.org/10.1080/10349120601008563

Otto, H., Potinius, I., & Keller, H. (2014). Cultural differences in stranger–child interactions: A comparison between German middle-class and Cameroonian Nso stranger–infant dyads. *Journal of Cross-Cultural Psychology, 45*(2), 322–334. https://doi.org/10.1177/0022022113509133

Segall, M. H., Campbell, D. T., & Herskovits, M. J. (1966). *The influence of culture on visual perception.* Bobbs-Merrill.

Simms, A., & Nichols, T. (2014). Social loafing: A review of the literature. *Journal of Management Policy and Practice, 15*(1), 58–67.

Wagner, D. A. (1980). Culture and memory development. In H. Triandis & A. Heron (Eds.), *Handbook of cross-cultural psychology,* Vol. 4: *Developmental psychology* (pp. 187–232). Allyn & Bacon.

Ward, C. (Ed.). (1989). *Altered states of consciousness and mental health: A cross-cultural perspective.* Sage.

ACTIVITY 1.2
WHAT IS CULTURE?

Activity Summary:

This activity encourages the student to explore the meaning of culture by applying several criteria to determine whether a specific group they select could, in fact, be considered a culture.

Lecture/Discussion Suggestions:

Do animals have culture? Students might be asked to consider how one would demonstrate that animals have culture. According to Whiten (2021) there are two types of phenomena that would need to be observed. First, animals would need to show social learning. That is, they would manifest a specific behavior after witnessing another animal perform that behavior. According to Whiten, there is clear evidence that this occurs in animals ranging from insects to whales. As an example, he cites research by Alem et al. (2016) in which bumblebees were trained to pull an artificial flower, which contained nectar, within reach. Once this behavior was observed by other bees, the practice spread throughout the hive. Whiten explained that there is far less evidence for the second criterion for animal culture, which deals with positive change in a behavior across generations. He cites two possible findings in support of this aspect of animal culture, one involving increased speed among homing pigeons and the other focusing on improved ability to identify good areas for grazing among generations of sheep.

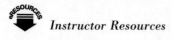

Variation:

Provide students with a list of different social groups and ask them to determine whether each is a culture by applying the criteria listed. These might include such social groups as, for example, members of the military, women, country music fans, cosplayers, Canadians, or people experiencing poverty.

Writing Application:

Have students write a one-page essay in which they develop their own definitions of culture.

References:

Alem, S., Perry, C. J., Zhu, X., Loukola, O. J., Ingraham, T., Søvik, E., & Chittka, L. (2016). Associative mechanisms allow for social learning and cultural transmission of string pulling in an insect. *PLoS Biology, 14*(10), e1002564. https://doi.org/10.1371/journal.pbio. 1002564

Whiten, A. (2021). The psychological reach of culture in animals' lives. *Current Directions in Psychological Science, 30*(3), 211–217. https://doi.org/10.1177/0963721421993119

ACTIVITY 1.3
HUMAN UNIVERSALS

Activity Summary:

In this activity, students are asked to identify human universals and write a description of, in Donald E. Brown's (1991) terms, the Universal People or "UPs." Brown's list of human universals is readily available online.

Lecture/Discussion Suggestion:

What are the different types of universals? As mentioned in the Activity 1.3 Handout, Norenzayan and Heine (2005) differentiated between types of universals. They used the analogy of the mind as a toolbox, and asked the following questions:

> First, are the tools in the cognitive toolboxes the same or different across cultures? Second, even if the tools are the same or nearly the same, are different tools used in the same situations? In other words, do people rely on the same tools to solve a given problem? Third, even if the tools are the same, and the same tools are used to solve a given problem, is the tool accessed with the same facility or frequency? (p. 772)

These questions resulted in the following four types of universals (listed in order of increasing strength):

- Nonuniversals (different tools)
- Existential universals (same tool but differential functions)
- Functional universals (same tool and same function or use but differential accessibilities)
- Accessibility universals (same tool, use, and degree of accessibility)

Brown (2004) also distinguished between, and provided examples of, five types of universals:

- *Absolute universals* – Found among all identified groups of people (e.g., child rearing).
- *Near universals* – Have a few known exceptions but are otherwise considered universal (e.g., using fire, keeping domestic dogs).
- *Conditional universals* – Present whenever a specific condition is met (e.g., if there is a preference for one hand over the other, it will be the right hand).
- *Statistical Universals* – Occurs in unrelated societies at a rate that is above chance (e.g., people who speak different and unrelated languages call the pupil of the eye something that means little person).
- *Universal pools* – A limited set of options reduces variation (e.g., all languages selecting from a limited set of possible speech sounds).

Variation:

Have students work in small groups to identify human universals in a specific area assigned to them, such as communication, family, social structure, or daily activities.

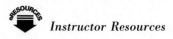

Writing Application:

Ask students to find a poem or song lyrics that illustrate a universal aspect of human behavior and then write a brief essay explaining how it does so.

References:

Brown, D. E. (1991). *Human universals.* Temple University Press.
Brown, D. E. (2004). Human universals, human nature & human culture. *Daedalus, 133*(4), 47–54. http://dx.doi.org/10.1162/0011526042365645
Norenzayan, A., & Heine, S. J. (2005). Psychological universals: What are they and how can we know? *Psychological Bulletin, 131*(5), 763–784. https://psycnet.apa.org/doi/10.1037/0033-2909.131.5.763

ACTIVITY 1.4
CROSS-CULTURAL PSYCHOLOGY'S DEATH WISH

Activity Summary:

Students investigate the degree to which cultural perspectives have been integrated into a psychological subdiscipline of their choice. [Requires work outside of the classroom.]

Lecture/Discussion Suggestion:

Why infuse culture across the psychology curriculum? Isn't a separate course on culture and psychology sufficient? Kite and Littleford (2015) discussed several reasons why diversity should be infused in non-diversity courses:

1. Unless diversity is infused across the curriculum, students will emerge from psychology courses with an inaccurate and incomplete view of human behavior.
2. Lack of exposure to diversity may result in ethnocentrism, or the view that one's own group is superior to others.
3. Isolating diversity in a separate course leads students and faculty to minimize the importance of diversity to psychology as a whole.
4. When all instructors discuss diversity issues, the topic no longer becomes associated with the presumed motivation of specific (often minority group) faculty who teach stand-alone diversity courses.

5. Infusing diversity provides more instructors with the satisfaction that results from facilitating the emotional, cognitive, and psychological growth students experience as a result of learning about diversity.

Kite and Littleford pointed out that when infusing diversity across the curriculum, enough time needs to be devoted to diversity issues to avoid conveying a superficial understanding or perpetuating misinformation about social groups.

Variation and Writing Application:

Students can follow this assignment with a task similar to the one described in Activity 4.10 and actually rewrite passages of the textbook that they find to lack attention to cultural perspectives.

Reference:

Kite, M. E., & Littleford, L. N. (2015). Teaching about diversity across the undergraduate psychology curriculum. *The Oxford handbook of undergraduate psychology education* (pp. 129–141). Oxford University Press.

ACTIVITY 1.5
A SEARCH FOR INDIVIDUALISM AND COLLECTIVISM

Activity Summary:

Students are asked to read the definitions of individualism and collectivism provided and then to identify one real-life example each of individualism and collectivism. [Requires work outside of the classroom.]

In completing Activity 1.5, students may find objects that exemplify both individualism and collectivism. For example, de Mooij (1998) mentioned that the Sony Walkman, a portable cassette tape player popular in the 1980s, was used in Western cultures to allow people to listen to music without being disturbed by others (an individualistic motive) although it was first designed by Akio Morita of Japan to allow people to listen to music without disturbing others (a collectivist motive).

Lecture/Discussion Suggestion:

Is it valid to describe cultures in terms of individualism and collectivism? The concepts of individualism and collectivism (IND/COL) have a long history in social science research, but first gained prominence in cross-cultural psychology as a result of Hofstede's (1980) study of work-related values. In Hofstede's study of IBM employees in 66 countries, Canada, Western European countries, and the United States tended to score high on individualism whereas the nations of Asian, African, and Latin American regions tended to be more collectivistic. Triandis (1995) expanded individualism and collectivism into a four-component construct by distinguishing between horizontal (preference for equality) and vertical (preference for hierarchy) types. According to Triandis (2001, p. 910), the four components are:

> Horizontal Individualism (HI), where people want to be unique and do 'their own thing'; Vertical Individualism (VI), where people want to do their own thing and also to be 'the best'; Horizontal Collectivism (HC), where people merge their selves with their in-groups; and Vertical Collectivism (VC), where people submit to the authorities of the in-group and are willing to sacrifice themselves for their in-group.

In the years since Hofstede's data was first published, the dimension of individualism and collectivism has been the focus of thousands of studies of individual behavior in such diverse areas as work-related confidence (Mellor, 2019), loneliness (Beller & Wagner, 2020), creativity (Nemeržitski, 2017), and Covid-19 transmission (Jiang et al., 2022).

There is empirical support for both the individualism-collectivism dichotomy and its more elaborate four-component form (Fatehi et al., 2020; Oyserman et al., 2002), however, some broad distinctions on these dimensions (such as the expectation that U.S. Euro-Americans are more individualist than Latinx or African Americans and that all East Asian countries are collectivist whereas Western nations are individualist) were challenged by Oyserman et al.'s, (2002) extensive meta-analysis. Additional criticisms of the IND/COL model include a lack of consensus on the definitions of individualism and collectivism, and inconsistency across measures of IND/COL, which vary widely in content, scope, and dimensionality (whether IND and COL are viewed as opposite poles on a continuum or are separate, orthogonal dimensions, such that one could score high on both or low on both; Wong et al., 2018). Given this lack of support for the expected group differences as well as much within-region (e.g., Asian nations) variability, students might discuss whether teaching practitioners about IND/

COL is a wise decision. Wong and colleagues suggested that the practice of labeling societies and racial/ethnic groups as collectivistic or individualistic, for example in multicultural counselor training, could amplify stereotyping and should be discontinued.

Finally, students should be aware of the ecological fallacy, which refers to the misapplication of national-level dimensions at the individual level. Brewer and Venaik (2014) detailed types of ecological fallacy and provided examples of how the Hofstede dimensions have been misapplied in research on organizational behavior.

Variation:

Ask students to search for objects that exemplify some of Hofstede's other dimensions: *Power Distance, Uncertainty Avoidance*, or *Masculinity/Femininity*. Please see the Activity 7.7 Handout for descriptions of these dimensions and the accompanying instructor materials for a discussion of Minkov and Kaasa's (2021) recent replication study of Hofstede's model.

Writing Application:

Have students write an advertisement for a specific product, first with an individualistic message and then with a collectivistic one.

References:

Beller, J., & Wagner, A. (2020). Loneliness and health: The moderating effect of cross-cultural individualism/collectivism. *Journal of Aging and Health, 32*(10), 1516–1527. https://doi.org/10.1177/0898264320943336

Brewer, P., & Venaik, S. (2014). The ecological fallacy in national culture research. *Organization Studies, 35*(7), 1063–1086. https://doi.org/10.1177/0170840613517602

de Mooij, M. K. (1998). *Global marketing and advertising: Understanding cultural paradoxes.* Sage.

Fatehi, K., Priestley, J. L., & Taasoobshirazi, G. (2020). The expanded view of individualism and collectivism: One, two, or four dimensions? *International Journal of Cross Cultural Management, 20*(1), 7–24. https://doi.org/10.1177/1470595820913077

Hofstede, G. (1980). *Culture's consequences: International differences in work-related values.* Sage.

Jiang, S., Wei, Q., & Zhang, L. (2022). Individualism versus collectivism and the early-stage transmission of Covid-19. *Social Indicators Research*. https://doi.org/10.1007/s11205-022-02972-z

Mellor, S. (2019). Confidence at work and individualism-collectivism: An empirical demonstration of the distinctiveness of American union employees. *Current Psychology: A Journal for Diverse Perspectives on Diverse Psychological Issues*, 38(2), 542–555. https://doi.org/10.1007/s12144-017-9636-2

Minkov, M., & Kaasa, A. (2021). A test of the Revised Minkov-Hofstede Model of Culture: Mirror images of subjective and objective culture across nations and the 50 US States. *Cross-Cultural Research*, 55(2–3), 230–281. https://doi.org/10.1177/10693971211014468

Nemeržitski, S. (2017). Implicit theories of creativity of secondary school students from Estonia and Russia: Effects of collectivism, individualism, and a bilingual educational environment. *Creativity Research Journal*, 29(1), 56–62. https://doi.org/10.1080/10400419.2017.1263510

Oyserman, D., Coon, H. M., & Kemmelmeier, M. (2002). Rethinking individualism and collectivism: Evaluation of theoretical assumptions and meta-analyses. *Psychological Bulletin*, 128, 3–72. https://psycnet.apa.org/doi/10.1037/0033-2909.128.1.3

Triandis, H. C. (1995). *Individualism and collectivism*. Westview Press.

Triandis, H. C. (2001). Individualism-collectivism and personality. *Journal of Personality*, 69(6), 907–924. https://doi.org/10.1111/1467-6494.696169

Wong, Y. J., Wang, S. Y., & Klann, E. M. (2018). The emperor with no clothes: A critique of collectivism and individualism. *Archives of Scientific Psychology*, 6(1), 251. http://dx.doi.org/10.1037/arc0000059

ACTIVITY 1.6
CLEANLINESS BELIEFS

Activity Summary:

A variety of cleanliness beliefs are presented in a self-administered question-naire format in order to challenge the common belief that cultures different from one's own are less concerned with cleanliness. Students will learn that cultures conceive of cleanliness in different ways and that some of the behaviors they take for granted might be viewed as of questionable cleanliness from the perspective of someone culturally different from themselves.

Lecture/Discussion Suggestion:

What factors contribute to cultural differences in cleanliness beliefs? Students may be interested in identifying the factors influencing cleanliness beliefs and practices in their culture(s). Some possibilities include:

- *Religion and religiosity* – Cleanliness is associated with purity of the soul in multiple religions.
- *Social class* – Cleanliness, and the means to maintain cleanliness, are stereotypically associated with wealth.
- *Social acceptance* – Cleanliness of the individual and household are associated with being liked and not offending others.
- *Science* – Cleanliness is viewed as the elimination of germs.

Speltini and Passini (2014) investigated the role of cleanliness beliefs in fomenting prejudice and stereotypes. Students might be asked to consider how this component of prejudice is manifested and toward whom. Students might also discuss why cleanliness-related beliefs appear to so strongly influence outgroup attitudes. According to these authors, an evolutionary explanation focuses on the tendency to associate outgroup members with increased vulnerability to disease.

Variation:

Have students use the items in this activity to survey others and then draw conclusions about their findings.

Writing Application:

Have students conduct an informal content analysis of ads for products that promote household or personal cleanliness. They should record claims used to sell these products and sort them into categories (such as "kills germs" and "promotes social acceptance of the user").

Reference:

Speltini, G., & Passini, S. (2014). Cleanliness/dirtiness, purity/impurity as social and psychological issues. *Culture & Psychology*, *20*(2), 203–219. https://doi.org/10.1177/1354067X14526895

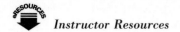

ACTIVITY 1.7
ETHNIC GLOSS

Activity Summary:

In this activity, students analyze three cross-cultural research articles to assess the presence and extent of *ethnic gloss* (Trimble, 1990), a term which refers to the use of overgeneralized ethnocultural labels that obscure important within-group differences.

Lecture/Discussion Suggestion:

Is there a similar, problematic "gloss" in labeling other dimensions of identity? In addition to the problem of ethnic gloss, students may be interested in discussing the extent to which other identity-related category labels, such as those referring to age group, gender, physical disability, religion, sexual orientation, and social class, mask important within-group differences as well as the possible implications of this lack of differentiation for psychological research and practice. This discussion could also include the concept of *intersectionality*, as students consider the within-social identity group differences that may result in disparate treatment and experiences. In contrast, students may also be interested in discussing the ways that broad social categories may facilitate organizing for social change.

Variation:

Have students analyze three articles using the "A Dimensions" categories of the Personal Dimensions of Identity Model, which include age, gender, culture, ethnicity, race, language, physical disability, sexual orientation, and social class (see Munley et al., 2002 for an example of a content analysis of psychology publications based on these criteria).

Writing Application:

Following this activity and using examples from the articles they identified, have students write a brief essay in response to the assertion that ethnic gloss "can generate biased and flawed scientific research outcomes and may promote stereotypes" (Trimble & Bhadra, 2013, p. 501).

References:

Munley, P. H., Anderson, M. Z., Baines, T. C., Borgman, A. L., Briggs, D., Dolan, J. P., Jr., & Koyama, M. (2002). Personal dimensions of identity and empirical research in APA journals. *Cultural Diversity and Ethnic Minority Psychology*, *8*(4), 357–365. https://doi.org/10.1037/1099-9809.8.4.358

Trimble, J. E. (1990). Ethnic specification, validation prospects, and the future of drug use research. *International Journal of the Addictions*, *25*(supp 2), 149–170. https://doi.org/10.3109/10826089009071038

Trimble, J. E., & Bhadra, M. (2013). Ethnic gloss. In K. Keith (Ed.), *The Encyclopedia of Cross-Cultural Psychology*, Vol. 2 (pp. 500–504). Wiley-Blackwell.

ACTIVITY 1.8
ETHNOCENTRISM, CULTURAL RELATIVISM, AND UNIVERSAL HUMAN RIGHTS

Activity Summary:

This activity encourages students to explore the concepts of ethnocentrism, cultural relativism, and universal human rights. A series of cultural practices are presented that challenge students to balance cultural relativism with human (or animal) rights (e.g. gender segregation, bullfighting, wearing religious symbols).

Lecture/Discussion Suggestion:

How do cross-cultural researchers balance cultural relativism with concerns about human rights? Professional associations for anthropologists throughout the world have begun to address the balance of cultural relativism and human rights. The American Anthropological Association (AAA; 1995) Commission to Review the AAA Statements on Ethics Final Report stated:

> What moral authority does AAA have to create a code of ethics if espousal of cultural relativism leads to the position that the moral codes of different cultures are morally equal? The Commission took the view that cultural relativism is an important intellectual stance enabling a researcher to study how and why people act as they do. To prejudge the

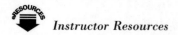

morality of people, to be concerned with how people ought to act before finding out how they do act, would skew the research ...

However, acceptance of 'cultural relativism' as a research and/or teaching stance does not mean that a researcher or a teacher automatically agrees with any or all of the practices of the people being studied or taught about, any more than any person is required to accept each practice of his or her own culture as morally acceptable. Segregation in the US was an accepted practice even though many US residents found it morally corrupt, and the institution of slavery is worthy of study even if the practice is considered immoral.

In addition, the 2020 update to the AAA Declaration on Anthropology and Human Rights includes the following statement:

Upholding human rights in the world-at-large, and in anthropological research and practice, requires more than the obligation to "do no harm." ... our position on human rights in 2020 demands forms of research and engagement that contribute to decolonization and help redress histories of oppression and exploitation.

Students might discuss how one might reconcile these seemingly contradictory goals and apply them in conducting research on culture and behavior.

Variation:

This activity can be structured as a debate. For each of the scenarios listed in this activity, assign one group of students to develop an argument supporting cultural relativism and a second group to develop an argument supporting a human rights rationale. For more advanced classes, students could be required to support their arguments with information from scholarly sources.

Writing Application:

Instruct students to write a statement from a fictional cross-cultural research professional association with recommendations about how researchers might balance human rights and cultural relativism.

References:

American Anthropological Association. (1995). *Final report of the Commission to Review the AAA Statements on Ethics.* https://americananthro.org/about/committees-and-task-forces/final-report-of-the-commission-to-review-the-aaa-statements-on-ethics/

American Anthropological Association. (2020). *2020 statement on anthropology and human rights.* https://americananthro.org/news-advocacy/2020-statement-on-anthropology-and-human-rights/

ACTIVITY 1.9
EXPLORING THE WORLD VILLAGE

Activity Summary:

Based on a concept promoted by the now defunct World Village Project, students are asked to imagine a village of 100 people that proportionately represents the population of the Earth. They then try to estimate the number of people who would fall into a variety of categories. For example, of the 100 people in the World Village, how many have access to clean drinking water?

Answers to Activity 1.9:

Of the 100 inhabitants:

1. *Gender*
   50 are male
   50 are female

2. *Age*
   25 are under age 15
   10 are over age 65

3. *Places of Origin*
   15 are Africans
   60 are Asians
   10 are Europeans
   6 are South Americans
   8 are North Americans
   1 is Oceanian (Australia, New Zealand, Papua New Guinea)

4. *Primary Language*
   5 speak Arabic
   3 speak Bengali
   5 speak English
   12 speak Mandarin
   3 speak Portuguese
   1 speaks Punjabi

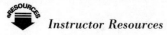
4 speak Hindi
2 speak Japanese

2 speak Russian
6 speak Spanish

5. *Religion*
2 are atheists
7 are Buddhists
31 are Christians
15 are Hindus

25 are Muslims
16 are non-religious
11 are other religions

6. *Education*
86 will be able to read and write
66 complete high school
7 hold a college degree

7. *Technology*
85 have a cell phone
60 have internet access
18 have cars

8. *Health and Well-Being*
74 have access to clean drinking water
54 have access to basic sanitation
16 are food insecure
56 live in urban areas
13 live in substandard housing

20 are affected by mental health problems
16 live with a disability
85 live in regions affected by climate change
1 is a refugee

9. *Wealth*
9 live below the internationally defined poverty line
1 controls half of all wealth

Lecture/Discussion Suggestion:

Saving Disappearing Languages. Although Activity 1.9 lists only ten languages, there are currently over 7000 living languages, according to the Ethnologue (n.d.) directory. Approximately a third of the world's languages have fewer than 1,000 speakers, and sadly one of these languages is lost approximately every two weeks (Strochlic, 2018). According to the Linguistic Society of America (n.d.), "When a language dies, a world dies with it, in the sense that a community's connection with its past, its traditions and its base of specific knowledge are all typically lost as the vehicle linking people to that knowledge is abandoned." Fortunately, the internet has been helpful in preserving rare languages. For example, a nonprofit called Wikitongues was established to document the world's languages. Students can explore the many oral histories and dictionaries posted on Wikitongues.[1]

---

[1] https://wikitongues.org

Variation:

Students can administer the items in this activity to others in order to assess the accuracy of their peers' perceptions of world demographics.

Writing Application:

Ask students to research and write about one of the categories addressed in this activity. For example, they might investigate access to school and the culture-specific variables that affect education among different populations (such as gender equity).

References:

Ethnologue. (n.d.). *Languages of the world.* www.ethnologue.com
Linguistic Society of America. (n.d.). *How many languages are there in the world?* www.linguisticsociety.org/content/how-many-languages-are-there-world
Strochlic, N. (2018) The race to save the world's disappearing languages. *National Geographic*, April 16.

Sources:

Callaghan, M., Schleussner, C.F., Nath, S. et al. (2021). Machine-learning-based evidence and attribution mapping of 100,000 climate impact studies. *Nature Climate Change, 11*, 966–972. https://doi.org/10.1038/s41558-021-01168-6
Central Intelligence Agency. (2023) *The world factbook.* www.cia.gov/the-world-factbook/
Ethnologue. (n.d.). *Languages of the world.* www.ethnologue.com
Population Reference Bureau. (2022). *2022 world population data sheet.* https://2022-wpds.prb.org/
United Nations. (2023). *United Nations world water development report.* www.unesco.org/reports/wwdr/2023/en
United Nations Educational, Scientific and Cultural Organization. (2021). *Global education monitoring report 2021/2.* United Nations.
United Nations High Commissioner for Refugees. (2022). *Refugee statistics.* www.unhcr.org/
World Bank. (2022). *Annual report 2022.* www.worldbank.org/en/about/annual-report

World Health Organization. (2022). World health statistics 2022: Monitoring health for the SDGs, sustainable development goals. www.who.int/publications/i/item/9789240051157

World Health Organization. (2023). *Disability and health fact sheet.* www.who.int/news-room/fact-sheets/detail/disability-and-health

ACTIVITY 1.10
A GLOBAL VIEW OF PSYCHOLOGY

Activity Summary:

Students learn about forms of psychology throughout the world by searching for information about the field of psychology in a country other than their own. They are then asked to consider the sociocultural factors that have shaped the research focus of the form of psychology they investigated as well as "Western" psychology. [Requires work outside of the classroom.]

Lecture/Discussion Suggestion:

What is the role of psychology in sustainable development across the globe?

Di Fabio and Rosen (2020) described a new direction for psychological research that is tied to the 17 United Nations' Sustainable Development Goals (SDGs; see https://sdgs.un.org/goals). In 2015, 193 countries who sit in the UN General Assembly adopted the SDGs, which were designed to be relevant worldwide. Students may be interested in discussing how psychology can contribute to reaching each of these goals and after completing Activity 1.10, they can report on the goals addressed by the form of psychology they investigated and the conditions that may have led to prioritizing those goals. In addition, students can complete an inventory developed and validated by Di Fabio and Rosen to assess their own interest, motivation, and self-efficacy associated with each of the goals (see the Appendix of Di Fabio & Rosen, 2020).

The United Nations' Sustainable Development Goals include:

1. No Poverty – End poverty in all its forms, everywhere.
2. Zero Hunger – End hunger, achieve food security and improved nutrition, and promote sustainable agriculture.

3. Good Health and Wellbeing – Ensure healthy lives and promote wellbeing for all, at all ages.

4. Quality Education – Ensure inclusive and equitable quality education and promote lifelong learning opportunities for all.

5. Gender Equality – Achieve gender equality and empower all women and girls.

6. Clean Water and Sanitation – Ensure availability and sustainable management of water and sanitation for all.

7. Affordable and Clean Energy – Ensure access to affordable, reliable, sustainable, and modern energy for all.

8. Decent Work and Economic Growth – Promote sustained, inclusive, and sustainable economic growth, full and productive employment, and decent work for all.

9. Industry, Innovation and Infrastructure – Build resilient infrastructure, promote inclusive and sustainable industrialization, and foster innovation.

10. Reduced Inequalities – Reduce inequality within and among countries.

11. Sustainable Cities and Communities – Make cities and human settlements inclusive, safe, resilient, and sustainable.

12. Responsible Consumption and Production – Ensure sustainable consumption and production patterns.

13. Climate Action – Take urgent action to combat climate change and its impacts.

14. Life Below Water – Conserve and sustainably use the oceans, seas, and marine resources for sustainable development.

15. Life on Land – Protect, restore, and promote sustainable use of terrestrial ecosystems, manage forests, combat desertification and biodiversity loss, and halt and reverse land degradation.

16. Peace, Justice, and Strong Institutions – Promote peaceful and inclusive societies for sustainable development, provide access to justice for all, and build effective, accountable, and inclusive institutions.

17. Partnerships – Strengthen the means of implementation and revitalize the global partnership for sustainable development.

Variation:

Ask students to work in pairs or small groups to identify and analyze a form of psychology in a country other than their own. Once the students have responded to the activity based on their reading, use the jigsaw technique (Aronson et al., 1978) described in Activity 8.10, so that each student is exposed to each other's findings.

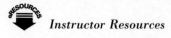

Writing Application:

Instruct students to write an essay based on the Thinking Further question in this activity, "Consider the theories, methods, and priorities of Western psychology. What do you conclude about the social, cultural, political, historical, environmental, economic, and/or religious factors that may have shaped its research focus?" More advanced students could address this issue in greater depth in the form of a term paper.

References:

Aronson, E., Blaney, N. Stephan, C., Sikes, J., & Snapp, M. (1978). *The jigsaw classroom*. Sage.

Di Fabio, A., & Rosen, M. A. (2020). An exploratory study of a new psychological instrument for evaluating sustainability: The sustainable development goals psychological inventory. *Sustainability*, *12*(18), 7617. http://dx.doi.org/10.3390/su12187617

Culture and Psychological Research

DOI: 10.4324/9781003356820-5

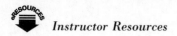
ACTIVITY 2.1
FUNCTIONS OF CROSS-CULTURAL RESEARCH

Activity Summary:

Students are provided with brief descriptions of several fictional cross-cultural research projects and are then asked to determine the specific functions illustrated by each.

Answers to Activity 2.1:

The following functions of cross-cultural research correspond to the project descriptions in Activity 2.1 (see project numbers in parentheses below) although each may fulfill additional functions as well.

a. Identifying culture-specific values, cognitive categories, or forms of behavior. (Project 5)
b. Unconfounding variables. Two variables that may be linked in one culture may be unrelated in another culture. (Project 3)
c. Expanding the range of variables. (Project 2)
d. Understanding the relationship between ecological and psychological variables. (Project 4)
e. Investigating possible human universals. (Project 7)
f. Testing the generality of psychological models or theories. (Project 1)
g. Studying the effect of cultural change. (Project 6)

Lecture/Discussion Suggestions:

What are some additional functions of cross-cultural research? Lonner and Adamopoulos (1997) mentioned two less direct functions of cross-cultural research that could also be discussed. Information gathered through cross-cultural research can be used to expand our worldmindedness and thus reduce ethnocentrism. In addition, this information can be used by cross-cultural trainers to assist sojourners and members of multicultural communities in increasing their levels of intercultural competence. Of course, the overarching function of cross-cultural psychology is to develop a more accurate and inclusive understanding of human behavior.

What are the different types of cross-cultural comparisons? Matsumoto & Juang (2023) identified three ways to distinguish between types of cross-cultural comparisons:

1. Exploratory vs. hypothesis testing – Exploratory studies are typically a preliminary form of research and investigate *whether* cultural differences exist, whereas hypothesis testing studies examine the relationship between variables to investigate *why* cultural differences exist. Hypothesis testing studies may include manipulated variables. Researchers also need to rule out the possibility that context variables play a role in any observed differences between cultural groups. These include characteristics of the participants (e.g., education level, gender) as well as of the culture (e.g., level of economic development, demographic diversity).

2. Structure- vs. level-oriented – Structure-oriented studies investigate whether a specific construct (e.g., creativity) is conceptualized similarly across cultures, whereas level-oriented studies examine cultural differences in the degree to which the amount of a construct is present (e.g., level of creativity as indicated by a score on a creativity test).

3. Individual vs. ecological (cultural) level – In individual-level studies, each participant's data serves as the unit of analysis, whereas in ecological-level studies, the country or culture serves as the unit of analysis (often by aggregating individual scores).

Variation:

With more advanced students, this activity could be used as an information literacy exercise. First, complete Activity 2.1 to familiarize students with the seven functions outlined. Then divide students into teams and have them search – scavenger hunt style – for articles that illustrate each of these functions of cross-cultural research.

Writing Application:

Have students work individually or in teams to develop their own examples of project ideas that fit the seven functions outlined in Activity 2.1, and then describe each project idea in a paragraph.

References:

Lonner, W. J., & Adamopoulos, J. (1997). Culture as antecedent to behavior. In J. W. Berry, Y. H. Poortinga, & J. Pandey (Eds.), *Handbook of cross-cultural psychology*: Vol. 1. Theory and method (2nd ed., pp. 43–83). Allyn & Bacon.

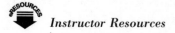

Matsumoto, D., & Juang, L. (2023) *Culture and psychology* (7th ed.). Cengage.

ACTIVITY 2.2
INSIDERS AND OUTSIDERS

Activity Summary:

Students are asked to interview two people (one an insider and one an outsider) using the same set of questions about a club or organization that is well known on or off of their campus. Interview questions deal with such matters as the criteria for membership, goals and success of the organization, and the public image of the organization. By comparing the responses of insiders and outsiders, students will learn about the relative advantages and disadvantages of being a cultural insider (characteristic of anthropology) vs. an outsider (characteristic of Western psychology) in conducting cross-cultural research. [Requires work outside of the classroom.]

Lecture/Discussion Suggestion:

What is the potential for error or distortion in information gathered by cultural outsiders? A classic article that still makes for great discussion is Miner's (1956) "Body ritual among the Nacirema." This "ethnography" illustrates the distortion that can occur when a naive outsider is drawing conclusions about a social group. Students are often appalled by the behavior of the Nacirema until they realize exactly who they are (Nacirema and several other key words are spelled backward). This article provides a good starting point for discussing ways to increase the validity of cross-cultural accounts and invariably leads to suggestions about collaboration between cultural insiders and outsiders. This activity can also serve as an introduction to discussions of outgroup homogeneity and ingroup favoritism.

Variation:

Have more advanced students develop a detailed interview schedule for gathering additional information from the insider and the outsider. Additional questions can focus on the specifics of the group selected. Students can keep written records of the insider's and outsider's responses and use these notes in answering the questions in this activity about the advantages and disadvantages of each approach.

Writing Application:

Instruct students to take the perspective of a naive outsider (from another planet, perhaps) in an account of a cultural ritual with which they are familiar (e.g., fraternity party, wedding ceremony). Have students read their accounts to each other and try to identify the ritual each has described.

> ### Reference:
>
> Miner, H. M. (1956) Body ritual among the Nacirema. *American Anthropologist, 58,* 503–507.

ACTIVITY 2.3
EMIC AND ETIC PERSPECTIVES

Activity Summary:

This activity familiarizes students with the distinction between emics and etics. Students generate etics and then identify associated emic phenomena. [May require work outside of the classroom.]

Lecture/Discussion Suggestion:

More on emics, etics, imposed etics, and derived etics. Pike (1954) first used the words *emic* and *etic* to describe approaches to the study of language and culture. The term emic originated from phonemics (sounds specific to a particular language) and is used to describe culture-specific phenomena. The term etic originated from phonetics (universal speech sounds) and is used to describe phenomena that are universal across cultures.

Berry (1990), who is credited with applying the emic/etic distinction to cross-cultural psychology, proposed two additional concepts: *imposed etics* and *derived etics.* As mentioned in the introduction to the Activity 2.3 Handout, imposed etic research occurs when researchers use concepts or instruments from their own culture as a basis for studying some phenomenon in another culture, without evaluating the methodological appropriateness of doing so. Often these imported concepts or instruments are used as the basis of cross-cultural comparison. In contrast, when researchers conduct, or have access to emic research, a *derived etic* is possible. A derived etic emerges from commonalities among emic phenomena. As Berry (1990) noted, a derived etic need not be universal in the sense that it applies to *all* cultures, rather, it is universal in terms of the cultures from which it is derived. An example of derived etic research comes from the efforts of Ursu and colleagues (2020) to identify conditions resulting in relational hurt and anger. These researchers collected data from young Romanians and Spaniards involved in romantic relationships to find culturally unique (emic) as well as common (derived etic) response categories. For example, emic sources of hurt feelings included injustice (for Spaniards) and infidelity (for Romanians), whereas criticism (the derived etic) emerged as a source of hurt feelings for both samples.

Variation/Writing Application:

After generating the list of etic categories required for Activity 2.3, divide students into small groups. Have each group choose an etic concept, then ask each individual student to identify an emic associated with the group's etic concept. Have students write a one-page description of the emic they investigated based on a literature search (the demands of which can vary with the level of the students). Finally, ask the students to share their findings within each group to see if a derived etic emerges from their findings. The group can then write a page describing the derived etic and submit that page along with the individual students' descriptions of an emic.

References:

Berry, J. W. (1990). Imposed etics, emics, and derived etics: Their conceptual and operational status in cross-cultural psychology. In T. N. Headlands, K. L. Pike, & M. Harris (Eds.), *Emics and etics: The insider/outsider debate* (pp. 84–99). Sage.

Pike, K. L. (1954). *Language in relation to a unified theory of the structure of human behavior*. Summer Institute of Linguistics.

Ursu, A., Turliuc, M. N., & Pavlopoulos, V. (2020). Hurt and anger in romantic relationships: A derived-etic approach of situational categories eliciting emotions in Romania and Spain. *Agathos, 11*(1), 243–279.

ACTIVITY 2.4
CULTURAL DISTANCE

Activity Summary:

Students read about the concept of cultural distance and then are asked to evaluate the relative importance of 12 different dimensions of cultural difference in creating a sense of cultural distance.

Lecture/Discussion Suggestion:

Are cultural distances shrinking? Kaasa and Minkov (2020) investigated this question using two sets of data from the World Values Survey (1995–1998 and 2010–2014). They compared 18 countries on variables assessing (1) ideal qualities in children, (2) moral ideologies, and (3) personal values to identify changes between the two time periods. Kaasa and Minkov concluded that over time parents' attitudes about the ideal qualities in children have become more similar across the globe (less cultural distance) with greater preference for children's independence and responsibility as opposed to religiosity and obedience. However, moral ideologies regarding such issues as sexual orientation, abortion, divorce, and suicide have become less similar (greater cultural distance) over the same time period. For personal values, such as the relative prioritization of religion, work, family, friends, and leisure, cultural distance has remained stable, despite an overall decrease in the importance allotted to religion and work and increase in that allotted to family, friends, and leisure.

Variation:

This activity can be used as the basis of a group discussion with the goal of generating consensus on the ranking of components.

Writing Application:

Have students read a story or watch a film about an intercultural interaction and then analyze the interaction from the perspective of cultural distance.

Reference:

Kaasa, A., & Minkov, M. (2020). Are the world's national cultures becoming more similar? *Journal of Cross-Cultural Psychology, 51*(7–8), 531–550. https://doi.org/10.1177/0022022120933677

ACTIVITY 2.5
WRITING TRANSLATABLE ITEMS

Activity Summary:

Students use scholarly sources to locate a set of questionnaire items that they rewrite or revise using Brislin, Lonner, and Thorndike's (1973) guidelines for writing translatable items. [Requires work outside of the classroom.]

Lecture/Discussion Suggestions:

Are there some words that cannot be translated? Despite efforts to rewrite material to facilitate translation, some words or phrases are almost impossible to translate, requiring entire paragraphs in one language to explain what can be said in a single word in a different language. Rheingold (2000) suggested that by seeking out and learning about these words we can expand our worldview and alter the way we think about the people and events in our lives (this view is based on the concept of linguistic relativity – see Activity 3.10). Some of the words Rheingold has identified as difficult to translate into English include:

- *Mokita* (Kilivila, Papua New Guinea) – A truth that everyone knows, but nobody speaks.
- *Uovo di Colombo* (lit. Columbus's egg, Italian) – A brilliant idea that seems obvious after the fact.
- *Wabi* (Japanese) – A flawed detail that creates an elegant whole.

Students who are bilingual will likely be able to identify words or phrases that are difficult to translate and may report switching between languages to express certain ideas or emotions.

Writing Application:

An additional translation problem comes from words that originate in one language and become integrated into another language, or what are sometimes called *loanwords*. These words often undergo substantial changes in sound and meaning as they become a part of another language (Sheperd, 1996). For example, Sowers (2017, p. 2) stated:

I was surprised to learn that サービス/saabisu or service means free of charge in Japanese. One of my favorite ramen restaurants in Mizonokuchi used to offer サービスチキン/*saabisu chikin* (service chicken), where customers were invited to top off their bowls from endless amounts of plates of fried chicken that were provided at the countertop. While *saabisu* is a borrowing from English, the semantic properties of this word are quite different in Japan.

For this writing application, have students identify a loanword in any language and discuss in a short essay what the existence of that loan word indicates about the culture or language that adopted it.

References:

Rheingold, H. (2000). *They have a word for it: A lighthearted lexicon of untranslatable words and phrases* (2nd ed.). Sarabande Books.

Sheperd, J. (1996). Loanwords: A pitfall for all students. *The Internet TESL Journal.* http://iteslj.org/Articles/Shepherd-Loanwords.html

Sowers, A. M. (2017). *Loanwords in context: Lexical borrowing from English to Japanese and its effects on second-language vocabulary acquisition.* [Unpublished master's thesis, Portland State University].

ACTIVITY 2.6
BACK-TRANSLATION

Activity Summary:

Students are guided through the process of back-translation using question-naire items and the help of two friends studying or fluent in the same two languages. This activity demonstrates the potential problems with using typical one-way translation methods in cross-cultural research. [Requires work outside of the classroom.]

Lecture/Discussion Suggestion:

How can translation efforts be improved? Behr (2017) explained that back-translation may fail to identify some flaws in the translation process that could only be identified through examination by native speakers. Brislin (1970,

p. 186), credited with the back-translation technique, also noted several factors that must be considered when using this process:

1. Translators may have a shared set of rules for translating certain nonequivalent words and phrases (e.g., "*amigo*" and "friend" are not always equivalent).
2. Some back-translators may be able to make sense out of a poorly written target language version.
3. The bilingual individual translating from the source language to the target may retain many of the grammatical forms of the source. This version would be easy to back-translate, but worthless for the purpose of asking questions of target-language monolinguals since its grammar is that of the source, not the target.

Ji (2019) described two other approaches that are sometimes used in addition to or instead of back-translation:

- *De-centering* – Words for concepts that are culture-specific or difficult to translate are removed or rewritten in the original to allow for smoother and more accurate translation.
- *Multiple-forward translation* (also called the "committee method") – A group of bilingual individuals pool areas of expertise and work cooperatively for a more accurate translation. Van de Vijver and Leung (2021) explained that this is the approach typically used for large-scale international comparative assessments.

Triandis (1976) introduced an alternative to translation. In his approach, research teams within the cultures of interest write emic items in response to the same etic concepts. Triandis and colleagues (1965) used this technique in developing a social distance measure used in Germany, Japan, and the United States. Ji (2019) proposed a more elaborate, sequenced version of this research-team-based strategy called the "dual-focus" approach" which additionally involves seeking feedback from members of the community of interest.

More recently, cross-cultural researchers have experimented with using artificial intelligence (AI) to translate materials. Although not identical in quality to human translations currently, AI-supported translation shows promise as a method for creating valid instruments for cross-cultural use (Kunst & Bierwiaczonek, 2023).

Variation:

Rather than having students seek out people to perform the translation and back-translation required for Activity 2.6, have them use two different internet translation programs. They should be able to readily identify flaws in this process.

Writing Application:

Brislin (1980) suggested that information from the back-translation process may help researchers generate new research questions. He gave the example of trying to translate the word "gossip" into Chamorro and learning that there are terms for both male gossip and female gossip. Have students write a one-page essay discussing a research question based on information that emerged from their back-translation experience.

References:

Behr, D. (2017). Assessing the use of back-translation: The shortcomings of back-translation as a quality testing method. *International Journal of Social Research Methodology: Theory & Practice*, 20(6), 573–584. https://doi.org/10.1080/13645579.2016.1252188

Brislin, R. W. (1970). Back-translation for cross-cultural research. *Journal of Cross-Cultural Psychology*, 1(3), 185–216. https://doi.org/10.1177/135910457000100301

Brislin, R. W. (1980). Translation and content analysis of oral and written materials. In H. Triandis & J. Berry (Eds.), *Handbook of cross-cultural psychology*, Vol. 2: Methodology (pp. 389–444). Allyn & Bacon.

Ji, M. (Ed.). (2019). *Cross-cultural health translation: Exploring methodological and digital tools*. Routledge.

Kunst, J. R., & Bierwiaczonek, K. (2023). Utilizing AI questionnaire translations in cross-cultural and intercultural research: Insights and recommendations. *PsyArXiv*. https://doi.org/10.31234/osf.io/sxcyk

Triandis, H. (1976). Approaches toward minimizing translation. In R. Brislin (Ed.), *Translation: Applications and research* (pp. 229–243). Wiley.

Triandis, H., Davis, E., & Takezawa, S. (1965). Some determinants of social distance among American, German, and Japanese students. *Journal of Personality and Social Psychology*, 2, 540–551. https://doi.org/10.1037/h0022481

Van de Vijver, F. J. R., & Leung, K. (2021). *Methods and data analysis for cross-cultural research* (2nd ed.). Cambridge University Press.

ACTIVITY 2.7
PAGTATANONG-TANONG: AN INDIGENOUS RESEARCH METHOD

Activity Summary:

A scenario portrays the typical Western psychological interview technique as inadequate in some cross-cultural settings. Students are asked to modify character-istics of the Western standard research methodology to increase the likelihood of successfully collecting data in the situation portrayed in the scenario. *Pagtatanong-tanong*, an indigenous social science research method in the Philippines (Pe-Pua, 1989, 2006) is introduced as an alternative to Western methods.

Lecture/Discussion Suggestion:

What other issues in addition to those addressed by pagtatanong-tanong should be considered in conducting cross-cultural interviews? van de Vijver and Leung (2021) explained that the mere presence of an interviewer from another culture might significantly affect the behavior being observed or measured. One strategy they suggest is to include attributes of the interviewer as variables in the study. That way, it is easier to determine the effect of characteristics such as interviewer gender or age. Another consideration in cross-cultural inter-viewing is cultural differences in ideas about property and ownership and how these views may be relevant to interviewee responses. For example, these differences affect both physical property and intangibles, such as dreams, historical accounts, and ideas (for a student-friendly discussion of culture and property, see Rudmin, 1994).

Writing Application:

Have students write a brief essay expanding on the Thinking Further item to discuss the degree to which a study using *pagtatanong-tanong* would be effective in their own culture and how it might be perceived.

References:

Pe-Pua, R. (1989). Pagtatanong-tanong: A cross-cultural research method. *International Journal of Intercultural Relations, 13,* 147–163. https://doi.org/10.1016/0147-1767(89)90003-5

Pe-Pua, R. (2006). From decolonizing psychology to the development of a cross-indigenous perspective in methodology: The Philippine experience. In U. Kim, K.-S. Yand, & K.-K. Hwang (Eds.), *Indigenous and cultural psychology: Understanding people in context* (pp. 109–137). Springer.

Rudmin, F. W. (1994). Property. In W. J. Lonner, & R. S. Malpass (Eds.), *Psychology and culture* (pp. 55–58). Allyn & Bacon.

van de Vijver, F. & Leung, K. (2021). *Methods and data analysis for cross-cultural research* (2nd ed.). Sage.

ACTIVITY 2.8
ETHICS IN CROSS-CULTURAL RESEARCH

Activity Summary:

A scenario depicts a cross-cultural research project wrought with ethical flaws. Students are asked to identify and remedy the ethical concerns, which focus on such topics as research collaboration with cultural insiders, compensation of research participants, credit and authorship, respect for the host culture, impact on the culture studied, presentation of research findings, and confidentiality.

Lecture/Discussion Suggestion:

What ethical issues should be considered in cross-cultural research? The scenario in Activity 2.8 illustrates a variety of ethical concerns discussed in greater detail by Broesch et al. (2020), Leach and Horne (2018), and Leong and Lyons (2010).

- *The research may be irrelevant, inappropriate, or disruptive to the community in which the research is being conducted* – The study is based on issues conceptualized outside of the country where it was conducted. Furthermore, the study may disrupt the local community by singling out those skilled at deceiving others. Ideally, the community should be included in decisions about the research questions, study design, implementation, and the presentation and housing of research results.
- *The researcher must maintain confidentiality and consider how the culture of interest is represented outside of that community* – The researcher documented the study with written and video records and presented his findings at a conference using the video materials as illustration.
- *The research should not alter the power structure within the culture of interest* – The researcher collaborated with a teacher and may have altered

his role in the community. Furthermore, the participants are being compensated at a rate that is a large amount in terms of the local economy and may thus alter the power structure or be coercive.

- *Individuals who act as research assistants or informants may contribute to the research as much or more than the outside investigator and should be given credit for doing so* – The researcher published his findings as the sole author of a journal article.
- *Participants may not understand the concept of informed consent* – The participants' education level is not mentioned in the scenario, so it is not clear if the participants can give true informed consent, particularly in written form.
- *Participants may not have the means or language ability needed to contact the researcher with questions or concerns* – The researcher provided an email address as the form of contact.
- *Poorly designed studies may result in inaccurate conclusions or cultural stereotypes* – In this scenario, the difference in sparse/enriched environments may be confounded with cultural or regional differences. The fact that both environments exist within the same country does not guarantee cultural uniformity or even similarity. In addition, the use of convenience sampling (the researcher was vacationing in Mexico) indicates that sufficient thought may not have been put into the choice of research location. Finally, the assumption that the desert is sparse in comparison to the tropical environment is a matter of opinion and not an objective fact.

Variation:

After they discuss the scenario in Activity 2.8, have students write a set of guidelines for conducting cross-cultural research that outlines potential areas of ethical concern and provides recommendations for addressing ethical dilemmas.

Writing Application:

After completing Activity 2.8, have students locate a journal article involving cross-cultural research and write a critique of the ethical aspects of the design.

References:

Broesch, T., Crittenden, A. N., Beheim, B. A., et al. (2020). Navigating cross-cultural research: Methodological and ethical considerations.

Proceedings of the Royal Society B: Biological Sciences. https://doi.org/10.1098/rspb.2020.1245

Leach, M. M., & Horne, S. G. (2018). Ethical issues in international research. In M. M. Leach & E. R. Welfel (Eds.), *The Cambridge handbook of applied psychological effects* (pp. 493–510). Cambridge University Press.

Leong, F. T. L., & Lyons, B. (2010). Ethical challenges for cross-cultural research conducted by psychologists from the United States. *Ethics & Behavior, 20*(3–4), 250–264. https://doi.org/10.1080/10508421003798984

ACTIVITY 2.9
TOWARD A MORE INCLUSIVE PSYCHOLOGY

Activity Summary:

Students are presented with a number of research scenarios which involve forms of bias based on gender, sexual orientation, disability, race/ethnicity, and age, and are then asked to identify these biases.

Lecture/Discussion Suggestion:

What are some of the ways forms of bias have affected psychological research? Each of the issues depicted by the project descriptions in Activity 2.9 has been discussed in terms of bias in psychological research (the articles cited in conjunction with these descriptions deal with a large number of additional forms of bias as well. Although some of these articles are not recent, the issues they describe remain pertinent):

1. Cowan and Cowan (2019) pointed out that many child development studies have been influenced by the notion of the mother-child bond to the point where fathers and other significant members of a household may be excluded from the research design.
2. Barnett and colleagues (2019) wrote about the degree to which LGBTQIA+ individuals are excluded or ignored in most psychological research.
3. Fine and Asch (1988) criticized the use of nondisabled individuals as confederates in research on disability. They pointed out that nondisabled people have not developed the same skills as disabled people in negotiating social interactions involving disability.

4. Buchanan et al. (2021) pointed out that research focusing on People of Color often requires a White comparison group if it is to be published in high-impact journals and that this practice perpetuates the positioning of Whiteness as normative.

5. Schaie (1988) compared age designations such as "over 60" to using the category of "under 12" in that it fails to recognize the developmental diversity within that age group.

Variation:

Assign a group of students to each of the five scenarios. Have each group also read the article associated with each scenario (see the reference list below) or others on bias in psychological research. Students can then present the key points of each article to the class using the scenario as an illustration. These articles can also be presented in class using the jigsaw technique (see the description of this technique in the Instructor Materials for Activity 8.10).

Writing Application:

Have students choose one of the scenarios included in Activity 2.9 and write a proposal for a research design that eliminates the biases in that scenario.

References:

Barnett, A. P., del Río-González, A. M., Parchem, B., Pinho, V., Aguayo-Romero, R., Nakamura, N., Calabrese, S. K., Poppen, P. J., & Zea, M. C. (2019). Content analysis of psychological research with lesbian, gay, bisexual, and transgender people of color in the United States: 1969–2018. *American Psychologist, 74*(8), 898–911. https://doi.org/10.1037/amp0000562

Buchanan, N. T., Perez, M., Prinstein, M. J., & Thurston, I. B. (2021). Upending racism in psychological science: Strategies to change how science is conducted, reported, reviewed, and disseminated. *American Psychologist, 76*(7), 1097–1112. https://doi.org/10.1037/amp0000905

Cowan, P. A., & Cowan C. P. (2019). Introduction: Bringing dads back into the family. *Attachment & Human Development, 21*(5), 419–425. https://doi.org/10.1080/14616734.2019.1582594

Fine, M., & Asch, A. (1988). Disability beyond stigma: Social interaction, discrimination, and activism. *Journal of Social Issues, 44*, 3–21. https://doi.org/10.1111/j.1540-4560.1988.tb02045.x

Schaie, K. W. (1988). Ageism in psychological research. *American Psychologist, 43*, 179–183. https://doi.org/10.1037/0003-066X.43.3.179

ACTIVITY 2.10
DESIGNING CROSS-CULTURAL RESEARCH

Activity Summary:

Students locate a psychological research report and then, focusing on issues of equivalence, describe the series of modifications that would be needed if the study were to be replicated in a cross-cultural context. [Requires work outside of the classroom.]

Lecture/Discussion Suggestion:

How are cultures selected for study in cross-cultural research? Before embarking on any proposal for cross-cultural study, students will need to consider how to select the culture(s) of interest. It is important to note that although countries are often used as a proxy for cultures, this is problematic in that doing so obscures within-country diversity. van de Vijver and Leung (2021) discussed four different methods used for selecting cultures:

6. *Convenience sampling* – Unfortunately, much cross-cultural research involves the selection of cultures based on such arbitrary reasons as the nationality of potential collaborators or the location of a planned sabbatical leave. van de Vijver and Leung suggested that when convenience sampling is used researchers do not generally approach the research with well-thought-out hypotheses but do more exploratory research and explain their findings after the fact.

7. *Systematic sampling* – In systematic sampling, cultures are selected based on the degree to which they vary on some dimension of interest. For example, Fernández et al. (2021) selected countries from which to sample based on income level. They investigated differences in the likelihood of completing mental health treatment in low-, middle-, and high-income countries. van de Vijver and Leung noted that problems may arise when

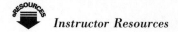

only two very different cultures are selected because so many alternative explanations for findings are possible.

8. *Random sampling* – In this technique, typically used in exploring the universality of some phenomenon, participants are randomly selected from a large number of countries (though the countries are not randomly chosen). van de Vijver and Leung explained that while this technique is difficult to implement, several large-scale studies include selections that approximate a random sample. For example, Meinck et al. (2020) administered a child abuse screening tool to a random sample of 42,194 school children from nine Balkan countries to better understand the frequency of children's exposure to physical and psychological violence and neglect across countries.

9. *Sampling from cultural zones* – In this technique, regions of the world are mapped based on theoretically significant psychological dimensions and then countries are selected to represent these regions. For example, Rescorla et al. (2019) sampled 45 societies from within the Global Leadership and Organizational Behavior Effectiveness (GLOBE) taxonomy to investigate the effect of culture on parents' ratings of children's mental health problems. The empirically derived GLOBE taxonomy groups nations into ten cultural clusters – Anglo, Latin Europe, Nordic Europe, Germanic Europe, Eastern Europe, Latin America, sub-Saharan Africa, Middle East, Southern Asia, and Confucian Asia.

Variation/Writing Application:

Rather than modifying an existing study to make it cross-culturally applicable, have more advanced students develop their own cross-cultural research proposal as a major project or term paper. Have students submit the proposal in three installments (introduction, methods, and expected results and discussion) and submit these installments to both the instructor and a classmate who serves as a peer reviewer. Both the proposal author and reviewer may be graded for each installment. Some questions for the peer reviewer are listed below. It may be helpful to have peer reviewers make comments on the draft installments of the paper as well.

Introduction:

1. In a sentence or two, state the primary goal of this study.
2. Map the logic of the literature review by listing each assertion made and the supporting source.

3. List any assertions that are not adequately supported by the literature reviewed.
4. Describe any material that should be removed from the literature review, such as nonessential details of the studies reviewed.
5. State the hypothesis of this study.
6. Identify the independent variable(s) and explain how they are operationalized.
7. Identify the dependent variable(s) and explain how they are operationalized.
8. Describe any information that should be added to the literature review in order to support the formation of this hypothesis.
9. Discuss the background required of the reader in order to understand this introduction.
10. List any grammatical, spelling, or citation errors.

Methods:

1. What culture(s) will be the focus of this study?
2. Explain the rationale for the selection of culture(s).
3. Explain how the culture(s) to be studied are defined.
4. Describe the research participants in terms of demographics.
5. Indicate any additional information that is needed regarding the demographics of research participants.
6. Describe the treatment of the research participants in terms of selection, assignment to conditions, and compensation.
7. Evaluate the author's choice and treatment of research participants in terms of adequately testing the hypothesis.
8. List any instruments to be used in this study and evaluate the evidence provided for the reliability and validity of these measures.
9. Discuss the degree to which the measures specified are an appropriate test of the hypothesis.
10. List the events that comprise the procedure in this study (in order of occurrence).
11. If you were to replicate this study, what additional information would you need to have?
12. Evaluate the methods in terms of the following forms of equivalence: (a) construct, (b) sampling, (c) items/tasks, (d) test situation, and (e) language.
13. Evaluate the proposed study in terms of research ethics (Are the contributions of the participants appropriately recognized and compensated? Does the research design involve the community in decision-making and benefit the cultures involved? Does the study provide for the

confidentiality of the participants? Is there a culturally appropriate method of informed consent?)

Results and Discussion:

1. Describe how the data are to be analyzed. Specify the independent and dependent variables as well as the statistical tests to be used.
2. Evaluate the degree to which the statistical methods proposed actually test the stated hypothesis.
3. Describe the expected outcome of the statistical tests in terms of the expected relationships between variables.
4. Explain the stated significance of obtaining the expected results (the "So what?" question).
5. Describe any implications of this study that the author may not have considered.
6. List all stated limitations in the design of this study.
7. Describe any limitations the author may not have considered.
8. List the author's recommendations for future research.
9. Provide any additional recommendations for future research that the author may not have considered.
10. List any additional comments or suggestions.

References:

Fernández, D., Vigo, D., Sampson, N. A., et al. (2021). Patterns of care and dropout rates from outpatient mental healthcare in low-, middle- and high-income countries from the World Health Organization's world mental health survey initiative. *Psychological Medicine, 51*(12), 2104–2116. https://doi.org/10.1017/S0033291720000884

Meinck, F., Murray, A. L., Dunne, M. P., et al. (2020). Measuring violence against children: The adequacy of the international society for the prevention of child abuse and neglect (ISPCAN) child abuse screening tool – Child version in 9 Balkan countries. *Child Abuse & Neglect, 108*, 15. https://doi.org/10.1016/j.chiabu.2020.104636

Rescorla, L. A., Althoff, R. R., Ivanova, M. Y., & Achenbach, T. M. (2019). Effects of society and culture on parents' ratings of children's mental health problems in 45 societies. *European Child & Adolescent Psychiatry, 28*(8), 1107–1115. https://doi.org/10.1007/s00787-018-01268-3

van de Vijver, F. J. R., & Leung, K. (2021). *Methods and data analysis for cross-cultural research* (2nd ed.). Sage.

Culture and Basic Processes

DOI: 10.4324/9781003356820-6   79

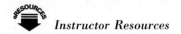

ACTIVITY 3.1
MAGICAL THINKING

Activity Summary:

Traditional cultures have sometimes been described as using forms of magical thinking that defy rules of logic and reason. Highly educated individuals, on the other hand, tend to assume that their thought processes are rational. A questionnaire based on the work of Rozin, Millman, and Nemeroff (1986; Rozin & Nemeroff, 2002) exposes the magical thinking of educated people. For example, these authors found that a laundered shirt previously worn by a disliked person is less desirable than one previously worn by a liked or neutral person. [Requires work outside of the classroom.]

Lecture/Discussion Suggestion:

Are members of highly industrialized societies rational thinkers? Psychologists have identified a number of ways that thinking may be irrational, based on studies of individuals from such societies (particularly in North America and Europe):

- *Hindsight bias* – The tendency to think that we "knew it all along" even if we did not.
- *Confirmation bias* – The tendency to search for information that validates our existing beliefs.
- *Illusion of control* – The tendency to perceive events (such as gambling) as more controllable than they are.
- *False consensus* – The tendency to assume that others hold the same beliefs that we do.
- *Illusory correlation* – The tendency to see two events that co-occur as related.
- *The sunk-cost fallacy* – The tendency to stay the course even when faced with negative outcomes.
- *Optimism bias* – The tendency to believe that we are less likely to experience a negative event than is, in fact, the case.
- *Availability heuristic* – The tendency to overestimate the likelihood of vivid events.

Variation:

An illustration of the law of similarity may be used to introduce this activity. Pass around a tray with gummy candy pieces shaped like pleasant (cute bears, fruit slices, fish) and unpleasant (spiders, centipedes) objects. The number of pleasant and unpleasant shapes should *each* equal the class size. Students should be told to take one that they will eat later. Once each student has selected a gummy candy, check to see which shapes are more numerous among those remaining on the tray. If more unpleasant shapes remain, the law of similarity may be operating. This demonstration is a milder version of Rozin et al.'s (1986) study in which participants were more likely to select a round piece of chocolate fudge than one in the shape of dog feces.

Writing Application:

Have students keep a week-long record of any instances of magical thinking they experience. After the week is over, have them turn in their notes along with a one-page essay addressing the question "What is the impact of magical thinking in daily life?"

References:

Rozin, P., Millman, L., & Nemeroff, C. (1986). Operation of the laws of sympathetic magic in disgust and other domains. *Journal of Personality and Social Psychology*, *50*(4), 703–712. https://doi.org/10.1037/0022-3514.50.4.703

Rozin, P., & Nemeroff, C. (2002). Sympathetic magical thinking: The contagion and similarity "heuristics." In T. Gilovich, D. Griffin, & D. Kahneman (Eds.), *Heuristics and biases: The psychology of intuitive judgment* (pp. 201–215). Cambridge University Press.

ACTIVITY 3.2
IMPLICIT THEORIES OF INTELLIGENCE

Activity Summary:

Students respond to open-ended questions on intelligence and giftedness and to an adjective checklist in order to explore implicit theories of intelligence. Follow-up questions will help students understand how the concepts of intelligence and giftedness vary across cultures with many cultures focusing on social intelligence and practical competencies over abstract problem-solving ability and verbal expression.

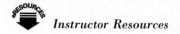

Lecture/Discussion Suggestion:

What is dynamic testing? In his research on culture and cognition, Sternberg (2004) administered tests *dynamically* rather than statically, which he argued more fully reveals children's intellectual potential. In dynamic testing, children receive feedback about their performance during the course of the test, often between repeated trials. This strategy, credited to Vygotsky (1962), is in line with the view that intelligence reflects the ability to learn from experience. Rahbardar et al. (2014, p. 48) explained that:

> The goals of [dynamic testing] are to: (a) assess the capacity of the child to grasp the principle underlying an initial problem and to solve it, (b) assess the nature and amount of investment (teaching) that is required to teach a child a given rule or principle, and (c) identify the specific deficient cognitive functions (i.e., systematic exploratory behavior) and non-intellective factors (i.e., need for mastery) that are responsible for failure in performance and how modifiable they are as a result of teaching. In contrast, the term static test (ST) generally refers to a standardized testing procedure in which an examiner presents items to examinees without any attempt to intervene to change, guide, or improve the child's performance.

According to Sternberg (2004, p. 333), "What a dynamic test does is directly measure processes of learning in the context of testing rather than measuring these processes indirectly as the product of past learning. Such measurement is especially important when not all children have had equal opportunities to learn in the past." This is illustrated by a study in low-income areas of Dar es Salaam, Tanzania (Humble et al., 2018). Findings indicated a significantly greater pre-post change in cognitive ability test scores for the dynamic testing group than for the static testing group. Additional examples of dynamic testing include the assessment of children's cognitive abilities in culturally diverse schools (Stevenson et al., 2016) and reading skills in multilingual adults (Pye & Chan, 2023).

Variation:

Students can collect definitions of intelligence and giftedness from others (Items 1 and 2 of Activity 3.2; see handout) and use these definitions to complete the remaining sections of the activity.

Writing Application:

After students have completed Activity 3.2, ask them to work individually or in groups to write a cross-culturally appropriate (or etic) definition of intelligence. (They may decide, along the lines of cultural psychology, that intelligence can only be defined in terms of emic constructs.)

References:

Humble, S., Dixon, P., & Schagen, I. (2018). Assessing intellectual potential in Tanzanian children in poor areas of Dar es Salaam. *Assessment in Education: Principles, Policy & Practice, 25*(4), 399–414. https://doi.org/10.1080/0969594X.2016.1194257

Pye, R. E., & Chan, H. H. (2023). Dynamic tests as a language-free method for assessing reading in a multilingual setting. *Journal of Cultural Cognitive Science.* https://doi.org/10.1007/s41809-023-00120-8

Rahbardar, H., Abbasi, M. A., & Talaei, A. (2014). Dynamic assessment (DA) and evaluation of problem-solving skills in children. *International Journal of Pediatrics, 2*(3–3), 47–54. https://doi.org/10.22038/ijp.2014.3150

Sternberg, R. J. (2004). Culture and intelligence. *American Psychologist, 59*(5), 325–338. https://doi.org/10.1037/0003-066X.59.5.325

Stevenson, C. E., Heiser, W. J., & Resing, W. C. M. (2016). Dynamic testing: Assessing cognitive potential of children with culturally diverse backgrounds. *Learning and Individual Differences, 47*, 27–36. https://doi.org/10.1016/j.lindif.2015.12.025

Vygotsky, L. S. (1962). *Thought and language.* MIT Press.

ACTIVITY 3.3
RACE AND IQ: INTERROGATING THE ASSUMPTIONS

Activity Summary:

Students use at least two scholarly sources to aid them in writing essays that critically evaluate one of several assumptions underlying controversial studies of race and IQ. [Requires work outside of the classroom.]

Lecture/Discussion Suggestion:

Are "culture-free" intelligence tests possible? One assumption of studies of race and IQ is that tests of cognitive abilities are not culturally biased. A culture-free test would be devoid of cultural influences and be able to measure some human capacity equally well across diverse groups of individuals (Frijda & Jahoda, 1966). Such a test does not seem possible because it would have to consist of items, materials, and procedures that are equally familiar – or equally unfamiliar – to test takers across cultures. Most attempts to develop culture-free intelligence tests use nonverbal tasks based on the assumption that, as opposed to verbal tests, these are less imbued with cultural content. However, as Gonthier (2022) details, multiple studies have shown just the opposite, with higher performance on verbal than nonverbal measures, particularly for members of groups that are culturally distant from the West. For example, the Raven's Progressive Matrices, a nonverbal intelligence test, was originally promoted as "culture-free," but is now recognized as culturally biased due, in part, to the advantage gained by those with formal schooling and thus familiarity with such depictions as well as with timed tests (Gonthier, 2022).

In addition to cultural bias surrounding the test itself, cross-cultural and cross-ethnic comparisons with this measure have often used culturally inappropriate norms for assessing performance. For example, Lozano-Ruiz et al. (2021) pointed out that most of the studies in the Arab world using the Raven's measures interpreted scores based on norms from the United Kingdom. These authors administered the Raven's Colored Progressive Matrices to children in Morocco and reported that when British norms were used, up to 62.5% of Moroccan children were categorized as "below average."

Variation/Writing Application:

Have students take a version of the Raven's Progressive Matrices test and write a brief essay discussing aspects of the content and testing procedure that could be sensitive to cultural influences.

References:

Frijda, N., & Jahoda, G. (1966). On the scope and methods of cross-cultural research. *International Journal of Psychology*, *1*, 110–127. https://doi.org/10.1080/00207596608247118

Gonthier, C. (2022). Cross-cultural differences in visuo-spatial processing and the culture-fairness of visuo-spatial intelligence tests: An integrative review and a model for matrices tasks. *Cognitive Research: Principles and Implications*, *7*(11). https://doi.org/10.1186/s41235-021-00350-w

Lozano-Ruiz, A., Fasfous, A. F., Ibanez-Casas, I., Cruz-Quintana, F., Perez-Garcia, M., & Pérez-Marfil, M. N. (2021). Cultural bias in intelligence assessment using a culture-free test in Moroccan children. *Archives of Clinical Neuropsychology, 36*(8), 1502–1510. https://doi.org/ 10.1093/arclin/acab005

ACTIVITY 3.4
MEASURING CREATIVITY ACROSS CULTURES

Activity Summary:

In this activity, based on the work of Greenfield (1997), students answer a series of questions to explore a cultural psychologist's (as opposed to a cross-cultural psychologist's) approach to studying creativity across cultures.

Lecture/Discussion Suggestion:

What assumptions are involved in using tests of abilities across cultures? Greenfield (1997) identified several assumptions involved in taking tests developed in one culture and using them to assess abilities in a different culture. These assumptions deal with three areas – values, knowing, and communicating – and, according to Greenfield, are likely to be unmet in the conduct of cross-cultural research. Some of these assumptions include:

Values:

- *There is agreement between participants and experimenters on the value of a given response.* Greenfield cited the example of a study by Cole and colleagues (1971) where Kpelle participants were asked to group objects. The participants unexpectedly grouped the objects by function. For example, a potato and a knife were grouped together because you can cut the potato with the knife. The researchers had expected the knife to be placed in the tools category and the potato to be placed in the food category. When asked why they sorted the objects as they did, the participants responded that this was the way a wise person would perform the task. When Cole and colleagues asked the participants to sort as a fool would do it, the participants came up with perfect taxonomic groupings – the knife in the tools category and the potato in the food category.
- *The same test items mean the same things in different cultures once linguistic translation has been made.* There is substantial evidence that a variety of words considered translation equivalents may not be so. For example,

Russell and Sato (1995) demonstrated the lack of equivalence of emotion words (such as *disgusting* and *exciting*) when translated across languages.

Knowing:

- *The knower is always an individual.* Greenfield drew a distinction between an individualistic and a collectivistic model of knowing in that societies characterized by the latter model may think of knowing as a group process in which knowledge is constructed collaboratively through dialogue. In such cases it would be inappropriate to interview or test people on an individual basis.
- *People across cultures make a distinction between the process of knowing and the object of knowledge.* In some cultures, there is no distinction made between one's thoughts about something and the thing itself. Greenfield (p. 1118) presented an example from her Piagetian research in Senegal. When she asked participants (in Wolof language), "Why do you *think* the amount of water is the same?" they had no response, but when she asked them, "Why *is* the water the same?" they responded in a manner similar to that of Piaget's research participants in Geneva.

Communication:

- *The function of questions is the same across cultures.* Greenfield explained that testing typically involves a questioner who already has the relevant information asking the test taker for that same piece of information. This situation is unusual across cultures in that it runs counter to typical forms of questioning in which questioners are asking for information that they are lacking.
- *Communication with strangers is acceptable.* In the typical psychological research situation, the researcher and the research participants are strangers to each other. However, in many cultures, it is unusual for people to be involved in interpersonal interactions of this type.

References:

Cole, M., Gay, J., Glick, J., & Sharp, D. W. (1971). *The cultural context of learning and thinking.* Basic Books.

Greenfield, P. M. (1997). You can't take it with you: Why ability assessments don't cross cultures. *American Psychologist, 52,* 1115–1124. https://doi.org/10.1037/0003-066X.52.10.1115

Russell, J. A., & Sato, K. (1995). Comparing emotion words between languages. *Journal of Cross-Cultural Psychology*, *26*, 384–391. https:// doi.org/10.1177/0022022195264004

ACTIVITY 3.5
CULTURAL NEUROSCIENCE

Activity Summary:

After reading a description and examples of cultural neuroscience research, students are asked to find a research article that takes a neuroscience approach to investigating emotions, cognition, personality, or social behavior across cultures and then answer a series of questions about that study. [Requires work outside of the classroom.]

Lecture/Discussion Suggestion:

How do genes and culture interact? According to Sasaki and Kim (2017, p. 7), "The basic idea of the gene-culture interaction perspective is that genetic influences shape psychological and behavioral predispositions, and cultural influences shape how these predispositions are manifested in the form of social behaviors and psychological outcomes." One theory is that genes may predispose people to be more or less susceptible to cultural influences, such as norms and expectations. According to Sasaki and Kim, often researchers will identify a documented cross-cultural behavioral difference and then investigate genetic contributions to that behavior. For example, several studies indicate that in general, attention to social cues of approval and disapproval, such as changes in others' facial expressions, is more critical in the Japanese cultural context than in the U.S. In line with this finding, Ishii et al. (2014) reported that Japanese, but not U.S. American (both Asian American and European American), carriers of a specific variant of the 5-HTTLPR genotype associated with environmental sensitivity, showed increased attention to changes in others' facial expressions involving the disappearance of smiles. Sasaki and Kim noted that studies focusing on the interaction of genes and culture may add a third, bicultural, group of participants that shares a similar genetic heritage with one group and cultural context with the other group (Asian Americans in the above example).

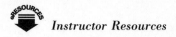

Variation/Writing Application:

Advanced students could be asked to find a cross-cultural study using non-neuroscience methods and then write a brief research proposal describing how they could take a neuroscience approach to studying the same phenomenon.

References:

Ishii, K., Kim, H. S., Sasaki, J. Y., Shinada, M., & Kusumi, I. (2014). Culture modulates sensitivity to the disappearance of facial expression associated with serotonin transporter polymorphism (5-HTTLPR). *Culture and Brain, 2,* 72–88. https://doi.org/10.1007/s40167-014-0014-8

Sasaki, J. Y., & Kim, H. S. (2017). Nature, nurture, and their interplay: A review of cultural neuroscience. *Journal of Cross-Cultural Psychology, 48*(1), 4–22. https://doi.org/10.1177/0022022116680481

ACTIVITY 3.6
CULTURE AND MEMORY STRATEGIES

Activity Summary:

Students are encouraged to think about the sociocultural context for their own memory strategies. Students are asked to recall material they have memorized in different ways (e.g., a list of words, planets in the solar system, the layout of their campus or neighborhood) in order to demonstrate that cross-cultural research on memory must consider the context in which these skills are used.

Lecture/Discussion Suggestion:

How does culture affect memory for childhood events? MacDonald and colleagues (2000) studied the recall of childhood memories in New Zealand European, Maori, and Asian men and women. They found that across cultures women reported more detailed memories than men. However, Maori adults reported significantly earlier memories than adults from the other two groups. These authors suggested that this finding may be due to the Maori traditional culture's strong emphasis on the past.

Additional insight into childhood memory comes from a series of studies by Wang and colleagues (e.g., Ross & Wang, 2010; Wang, 2021) investigating cultural differences in autobiographical memory. These authors found that self-goals influenced the memories participants recalled. European American adults and children, as a result of cultural values emphasizing autonomy, recalled more and earlier memories focused on their own roles and perspectives than did Asians and Asian Americans, who recalled more information about social interactions and group activities. In addition, when these researchers manipulated self-goals by priming participants to think about themselves as either unique individuals or as members of social groups, they were able to elicit more self-focused memories in the former group and socially focused memories in the latter group, regardless of the participants' cultural background.

Variation/Writing Application:

Have students keep a journal for one week noting instances of recalling information. Have them record how the information was recalled and what strategies (such as mnemonic devices, clustering) and memory tools (such as a telephone contact list, or calendar) were used, and how these strategies were learned. Finally, based on these journal entries, have students write a brief essay discussing the cultural context and its effect on memory processes.

References:

MacDonald, S., Uesiliana, K., & Hayne, H. (2000). Cross-cultural and gender differences in childhood amnesia. *Memory, 8,* 365–376. https://doi.org/10.1080/09658210050156822

Ross, M., & Wang, Q. (2010). Why we remember and what we remember: Culture and autobiographical memory. *Perspectives on Psychological Science, 5*(4), 401–409. https://psycnet.apa.org/doi/10.1177/1745691610375555

Wang, Q. (2021). The cultural foundation of human memory. *Annual Review of Psychology, 72,* 151–179. https://doi.org/10.1146/annurev-psych-070920-023638

ACTIVITY 3.7
CULTURE AND AESTHETIC PREFERENCES

Activity Summary:

Students have others rank various stimuli in order to explore the relationship between complexity and aesthetic appeal. Complexity is one of the most

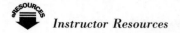

investigated variables in cross-cultural studies of aesthetic preferences. [Requires work outside of the classroom.]

Lecture/Discussion Suggestions:

Complexity is complex! Although there is evidence for a universal, inverted U-shaped relationship between complexity and aesthetic appreciation (greater appreciation at moderate levels of complexity), there are also studies with conflicting findings. Van Geert and Wagemans (2020) explained that this may be due in part to the fact that stimulus complexity has been defined in a wide variety of ways. For example, these authors state that it is important to distinguish between objective and subjective complexity. There are many different measures of objective complexity, some of which include the number of elements, the level of image compression, the predictability of forms within an image, the degree of similarity between the object as a whole and its parts, and the magnitude of changes in luminance or color in an image. Subjective complexity has also been measured in different ways, including forced-choice tasks and rating scales. Furthermore, perceptions of complexity may change over time with exposure to the image. Finally, individual differences such as personality traits, education level, creativity, and need for cognitive structuring may shape perceptions of complexity. In addition to complexity, Van Geert and Wagermans argued that aesthetic appeal also depends on the level of order within a stimulus, which is separate from, but may interact with, complexity. Order refers to "the structure and organization of the information (in the stimulus)" (p. 12). For example, an image may involve a large or small number of different shapes (complexity) that could be arranged randomly or grouped by shape (order).

How might attention to context influence aesthetic preferences? Based on their previous research (mentioned in the handout for Activity 3.6) demonstrating that East Asians were more attentive to contextual information than Westerners, Masuda and colleagues (Masuda, 2017; Masuda et al., 2008) investigated whether these differences might be correlated with differences in aesthetic preference in landscapes and photographs. Their studies found that:

- Among museum pieces, traditional East Asian portraits and landscapes emphasized context whereas Western art pieces emphasized the focal object. For example, the location of the horizon was significantly higher in East Asian than in Western art, allowing for the inclusion of more background detail.
- When asked to take photos or draw landscapes, research participants from East Asian countries (international students from Taiwan, Korea,

Japan, and China in the U.S.) and the U.S. (European Americans and African Americans) demonstrated these orientations. For example, the East Asian students included more of the background when asked to take a photographic portrait of a peer than did the U.S. Americans. Illustrations of these differences are available in the Masuda et al. (2008) article.

These results were attributed in part to differences in the built environments of these two regions in that the authors referred to research indicating that brief exposure to Japanese scenes (priming) caused both Japanese and Westerners to notice more context than did exposure to American scenes (Miyamoto et al., 2006).

Variation:

More advanced students might repeat the procedure outlined in Activity 3.7 with pieces of music, poems, or photos of buildings that vary on three levels of complexity.

Writing Application:

Have students seek out a piece of music or art from a culture with which they are unfamiliar. Have them write a brief essay describing their aesthetic reaction to the piece and speculating on the reason for this reaction.

References:

Masuda, T. (2017). Culture and attention: Recent empirical findings and new directions in cultural psychology. *Social and Personality Psychology Compass, 11*(12), 1–16. https://doi.org/10.1111/spc3.12363

Masuda, T., Gonzalez, R., Kwan, L., & Nisbett, R. E. (2008). Culture and aesthetic preference: Comparing the attention to context of East Asians and Americans. *Personality and Social Psychology Bulletin, 34*(9), 1260–1275. https://doi.org/10.1177/0146167208320555

Miyamoto, Y., Nisbett, R. E., & Masuda, T. (2006). Culture and physical environment: Holistic versus analytic perceptual affordances. *Psychological Science, 17*, 113–119. https://doi.org/10.1111/j.1467-9280.2006.01673.x

Van Geert, E., & Wagemans, J. (2020). Order, complexity, and aesthetic appreciation. *Psychology of Aesthetics, Creativity, and the Arts, 14*(2), 135–154. https://doi.org/10.1037/aca0000224

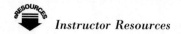

ACTIVITY 3.8
INTERPLANETARY PERCEPTION

Activity Summary:

Students are asked to evaluate the potential usefulness of a message that was inscribed on an American satellite in the 1970s. The message took the form of a line drawing of a naked male and female, a chart drawing the 14 pulsars of the Milky Way, and a diagram of the solar system. It was hoped that the satellite would be intercepted by intelligent beings who would "read" the message and decipher the return address. Students are expected to learn that the cognitive and perceptual processes required to comprehend the message are not universal across cultures ... let alone planets!

Lecture/Discussion Suggestion:

How does culture affect pictorial perception? According to Russell et al. (1997, p. 110), "Perception of what a picture depicts, and indeed the perception that it depicts anything at all, depends on both the picture and the perceiver." The most relevant characteristic of the perceiver is previous exposure to pictorial depictions. For example, Deregowski et al. (1972) reported that when Me'en people in Ethiopia, who had no previous exposure to pictures on paper, were presented with paper coloring book pages they ignored the pictures and instead tried to smell, taste, and examine the pages. In the case presented in Activity 3.8, one can only speculate about the characteristics of the extra-terrestrial perceiver, but it is possible to identify characteristics of the depiction (the *Pioneer 10* plaque) that could potentially result in cross-cultural misunderstanding. These include:

- *The familiarity of the materials used* – Deregowski and colleagues further reported that when the Me'en people were presented with depictions of familiar animals on a familiar cloth material the majority attended to and correctly identified the image.
- *The representation of three-dimensional objects in two-dimensional form* – People who attend school gain more exposure to two-dimensional depictions of three-dimensional objects than do unschooled individuals. The ability to perceive two-dimensional depth cues has been demon-strated to increase with training (Leach, 1975) and vary considerably with the nature of the task. For example, U.S. American college students had difficulty perceiving depth cues when presented with the African version of the Hudson Pictorial Depth Perception Test (Hagen & Johnson, 1977).

- *The use of symbols as representations of common objects or events* – A study by Wendy Winter (1963) provided an example of cultural differences in the interpretation of symbols. Winter explored the perception of safety posters by Bantu industrial workers. This study identified several instances in which the artist's symbolic meanings were not interpreted as intended, particularly when the perceiver had not attended school or was from a rural area. For example, a red star intended as an indication that someone was hit by an object was often thought to represent fire.

Many of the lessons from these early studies have been applied to improve the design of computer interfaces (e.g., Bühler et al., 2022) and warning signs (e.g., Wogalter et al., 2006), areas where several components of images – such as icons, symbols, colors, gestures, and facial expressions – have been erroneously assumed to be universal across cultures.

Variation:

Once students have completed this activity, have them try a new form of picture perception as a way to further illustrate that picture perception is to some extent learned. One option is the stereogram embedded images, such as those from "Magic Eye, Inc." A second option is to bring in an older (not high resolution) ultrasound picture and ask students to identify the features of the fetus pictured. Both types of images are readily available online.

Writing Application:

Have students write a letter as if for NASA explaining their concerns about the potential for communicating with extraterrestrials through the *Pioneer 10* plaque. Students could be required to cite sources from cross-cultural research to support their assertions.

References:

Bühler, D., Hemmert, F., Hurtienne, J., & Petersen, C. (2022). Designing universal and intuitive pictograms (UIPP) – A detailed process for more suitable visual representations. *International Journal of Human-Computer Studies, 163*, 1–18. https://doi.org/10.1016/j.ijhcs.2022.102816

Deregowski, J. B., Muldrow, E. S., & Muldrow, W. F. (1972). Pictorial recognition in a remote Ethiopian population. *Perception, 1*, 417–425. https://doi.org/10.1068/p010417

Hagen, M. A., & Johnson, M. M. (1977). Hudson Pictorial Depth Perception Test: Cultural content and question with a Western sample. *Journal of Social Psychology, 101,* 3–11. https://doi.org/10.1080/00224545.1977.9923978

Leach, M. L. (1975). The effect of training on the pictorial depth perception of Shona children. *Journal of Cross-Cultural Psychology, 6,* 457–470. https://doi.org/10.1177/002202217564008

Russell, P. A., Deregowski, J. B., & Kinnear, P. R. (1997). Perception and aesthetics. In J. W. Berry, P. R. Dasen, & T. S. Saraswathi (Eds.), *Handbook of cross-cultural psychology*: Vol. 2. Basic processes and human development (2nd ed., pp. 107–142). Allyn & Bacon.

Winter, W. (1963). The perception of safety posters by Bantu industrial workers. *Psychologia Africana, 10,* 127–135.

Wogalter, M. S., Silver, N. C., Leonard, S. D., & Zaikina, H. (2006). Warning symbols. In M. S. Wogalter (Ed.), *Handbook of warnings* (pp. 159–176). Lawrence Erlbaum Associates.

ACTIVITY 3.9
SOUND SYMBOLISM

Activity Summary:

As in the protocol for many sound symbolism (once called phonetic symbolism) studies, students are given a series of word pairs in several different languages and are asked to match meanings to the words. For example, they are asked to determine which word means "dark" and which means "bright" in Mandarin, Czech, and Hindi word pairs. Students generally find that they can correctly guess the word meaning at a level better than chance despite a lack of previous experience with the language. These results are explained in terms of sound symbolism theory.

Answers to Activity 3.9:

English	Mandarin	Czech	Hindi
1. beautiful (b) ugly (u)	mei (b) chǒu (u)	osklivost (u) krasa (b)	badsurat (u) khubsurat (b)
2. blunt (b) sharp (s)	kuài (s) dùn (b)	tupy (b) spicaty (s)	tez (s) gothil (b)

3. bright (b)	liang (b)	tmavy (d)	chamakdar (b)
dark (d)	an (d)	svetly (b)	andhera (d)
4. fast (f)	man (s)	rychly (f)	tez (f)
slow (s)	kuài (f)	pomaly (s)	sust (s)
5. hard (h)	ying (h)	mekky (s)	sakht (h)
soft (s)	ruǎn (s)	tvrdy (h)	narm (s)
6. light (l)	zhòng (h)	tezky (h)	wazani (h)
heavy (h)	qīng (l)	lehky (l)	halka (l)
7. warm (w)	nuan (w)	teply (w)	thanda (c)
cool (c)	liang (c)	chladny (c)	garam (w)
8. wide (w)	zhǎi (n)	siroky (w)	chaura (w)
narrow (n)	kuān (w)	uzky (n)	sankara (n)

Lecture/Discussion Suggestion:

Why does sound symbolism occur? Research seems to support the existence of sound symbolism in that speech sounds have similar connotations across languages (O'Boyle et al., 1987). Students may be interested in discussing possible sources of this universality. One explanation is that the tones represent naturally occurring qualities of our sensory world. For example, when heavy things fall they make a lower tone than when light things fall. Tarte and O'Boyle (1982) suggested that the speed, as well as the frequency of speech sounds, may be responsible for sound symbolism. Lev-Ari et al. (2021) proposed that sound symbolism is helpful in overcoming communication barriers. In support of this claim, they found that participants were better able to identify which word meant "big" and which meant "small" in unfamiliar languages that were widely spoken (such as Russian, Korean, and Swahili), but significantly less so in more uncommon languages (such as Icelandic, Korwa, or Alamblak). They reasoned that widely spoken languages would be under greater pressure to facilitate ease of understanding. A new direction in research on sound symbolism focuses on features of articulating the sound rather than hearing the sound (e.g., Körner & Rummer, 2022).

Variation:

Have more advanced students use the measure of sound symbolism in Activity 3.9 to collect data from others and compile the results. Students can then determine an overall proportion of correct to incorrect responses.

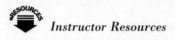

Writing Application:

Have students write a brief essay addressing the following question: *Evidence indicates that speech sounds may themselves carry some universal meaning, regardless of the language in which they are found. What are the implications of this finding for intercultural communication?*

References:

Körner, A., & Rummer, R. (2022). Articulation contributes to valence sound symbolism. *Journal of Experimental Psychology: General, 151*(5), 1107–1114. https://doi.org/10.1037/xge0001124

Lev-Ari, S., Kancheva, I., Marston, L., Morris, H., Swingler, T., & Zaynudinova, M. (2021). "Big" sounds bigger in more widely spoken languages. *Cognitive Science, 45*(11), 1–15. https://doi.org/10.1111/cogs.13059

O'Boyle, M., Miller, D. A., & Rahmani, F. (1987). Sound-meaning relationships in speakers of Urdu and English: Evidence for a cross-cultural phonetic symbolism. *Journal of Psycholinguistic Research, 16*, 273–288.

Tarte, R. & O'Boyle, M. (1982). Semantic judgments of compressed monosyllables: Evidence for phonetic symbolism. *Journal of Psycholinguistic Research, 11*, 183–196. https://doi.org/10.1007/bf01067562

ACTIVITY 3.10
LANGUAGE AND THOUGHT

Activity Summary:

An explanation and an example of linguistic relativity are provided. Students are asked to gather subcultural terms as a basis for exploring the validity of linguistic relativity and determinism. [Requires work outside of the classroom.]

Lecture/Discussion Suggestions:

How can we reconcile the seemingly inconsistent findings in the research on linguistic relativity? Students (and instructors!) may find it challenging to sort through the seemingly inconsistent findings in studies of linguistic relativity. Gleitman and Papafragou (2013) discussed conflicting outcomes in studies of language and thought in a wide variety of domains, including color perception, grammatical distinctions between objects and substances, spatial relationships and orientation, expression of motion, and number systems. One pattern that emerged was that linguistic differences seemed to affect how concepts were processed, but not the concepts themselves. In addition, these authors suggested that the strongest effects are found when the task requires the use of language, such as when participants are asked to produce a verbal label.

A series of studies on color illustrate Gleitman and Papafragou's supposition. Winawer et al. (2007) demonstrated that speakers of Russian were able to distinguish between lighter and darker shades of blue more quickly than speakers of English. Unlike English, the Russian language has a specific term for lighter blues (*goluboy*) and darker blues (*siniy*). Despite this difference in processing, speakers of Russian and English similarly subdivided the blue stimuli into dark and light shades. In addition, for the Russian speakers (but not the English speakers), the processing advantage was disrupted by verbal interference (participants silently rehearsed digit strings while simultaneously completing the color discrimination trials) but not nonverbal interference (participants maintained a spatial pattern in memory while completing color discrimination trials).

Additional support for the importance of verbal processing in linguistic relativity effects comes from cognitive neuroscience. These studies found that linguistic relativity effects occur when the stimuli are presented in the right visual field of the perceiver (which is processed by the more language-specialized left hemisphere), but not if presented to the left visual field (which is processed by the more spatially specialized right hemisphere; Gilbert et al., 2006; Roberson et al., 2008).

Does the English language dominance in cognitive psychology shape its content? To engage students on the issue of language and thought at a more "meta" level, discuss how the dominance of English language in the conduct of cognitive research could potentially shape the content of this field. Blasi et al. (2022) presented a strong argument for the inappropriateness of generalizing from studies overwhelmingly conducted by English speakers using English language research stimuli. They detailed some of the significant ways that spoken English (a limited dialect of which dominates academic research) differs from many of the world's approximately 7000 spoken or signed languages, including the absence of tonal features, an alphabetic writing system, the presence of mirrored graphs (e.g., b vs. d and p vs. q), left to right written format, grammatically rigid word order, sentence constructions embedded with cause and effect and theory of mind content, as well as language-specific conventions for social interaction. These authors convincingly argue that the overreliance on English results in a limited understanding of such cognitive processes as memory, social cognition, perception, and decision-making.

Writing Application:

More advanced students might write a term paper investigating language and thought in greater depth. Because of the complexity of this literature, one way to structure this term paper is to have students work in teams, with each member of the team investigating the evidence on a specific dimension of research related to linguistic relativity. Students can then work collaboratively to write the final paper. This form of collaborative writing, sometimes called hierarchical collaborative writing (Atwood, 1992), allows students to divide tasks and be evaluated for their separate contributions as well as the group effort (see Rice-Bailey, 2018, for an explanation of and resources for teaching collaborative writing).

John Lucy (1997, 2016) identified classic topics in studies of linguistic relativity, including:

- Temporal marking studies, such as Whorf's original comparisons of tenses in Hopi and English grammar (Whorf, 1956).
- Number marking studies, such as Lucy's (1992) research on number systems and cognition among speakers of English and Yucatec Maya.
- Color category research, such as Berlin and Kay's (1969) work on basic color terms.
- Spatial orientation studies, Brown and Levinson's (1993) research on spatial terms and cognition.

Some more recent research areas of importance include:

- Grammatical gender (e.g., Mecit et al., 2022; Samuel et al., 2019).
- Time perception (e.g., Bylund & Athanasopoulos, 2017).
- Musical pitch (Dolscheid et al., 2013).
- Linguistic priming (Gendron et al., 2012).

References:

Atwood, J. (1992). Collaborative writing: The "other" game in town. *The Writing Instructor, 12*, 13–26.

Berlin, B., & Kay, P. (1969). *Basic color terms: Their universality and evolution.* University of California Press.

Blasi, D. E., Henrich, J., Adamou, E., Kemmerer, D., & Majid, A. (2022). Over-reliance on English hinders cognitive science. *Trends in Cognitive Science, 26*(12), 1153–1170. https://doi.org/10.1016/j.tics.2022.09.015

Brown, P., & Levinson, S. C. (1993). "Uphill" and "downhill" in Tzeltal. *Journal of Linguistic Anthropology, 3*, 46–74. www.mpi.nl/publications/item_66672

Bylund, E., & Athanasopoulos, P. (2017). The Whorfian time warp: Representing duration through the language hourglass. *Journal of Experimental Psychology: General, 146*(7), 911–916. https://doi.org/10.1037/xge0000314

Dolscheid, S., Shayan, S., Majid, A., & Casasanto, D. (2013). The thickness of musical pitch: Psychophysical evidence for linguistic relativity. *Psychological Science, 24*(5), 613–621.

Gendron, M., Lindquist, K. A., Barsalou, L., & Barrett, L. F. (2012). Emotion words shape emotion percepts. *Emotion, 12*(2), 314–325. https://doi.org/10.1037/a0026007

Gilbert, A. L., Regier, T., Kay, P., & Ivry, R. B. (2006). Whorf hypothesis is supported in the right visual field but not the left. *Proceedings of the National Academy of Sciences of the USA, 103*, 489–238. https://doi.org/10.1073/pnas.0509868103

Gleitman, L., & Papafragou, A. (2013). Relations between language and thought. In D. Reisberg (Ed.), *The Oxford handbook of cognitive psychology* (pp. 504–523). Oxford University Press.

Lucy, J. A. (1992). *Grammatical categories and cognition: A case study of the linguistic relativity hypothesis.* Cambridge University Press.

Lucy, J. A. (1997). Linguistic relativity. *Annual Review of Anthropology, 26*, 291–312. www.jstor.org/stable/2952524

Lucy, J. A. (2016). Recent advances in the study of linguistic relativity in historical context: A critical assessment. *Language Learning, 66*(3), 487–515. https://doi.org/10.1111/lang.12195

Mecit, A., Shrum, L. J., & Lowrey, T. M. (2022). COVID-19 is feminine: Grammatical gender influences danger perceptions and precautionary behavioral intentions by activating gender stereotypes. *Journal of Consumer Psychology, 32*(2), 316–325. https://doi.org/10.1002/jcpy.1257

Rice-Bailey, T. (2018). *Student collaboration.* Council for Programs in Technical and Scientific Communication. http://cptsc.org/wp-content/uploads/2018/02/Student-Collaboration-Rice-Bailey-final-WORD.pdf

Roberson, D., Pak, H. S., & Hanley, J. R. (2008). Categorical perception of colour in the left and right hemisphere is verbally mediated: Evidence from Korean. *Cognition, 107*, 752–762. https://doi.org/10.1016/j.cognition.2007.09.001

Samuel, S., Cole, G., & Eacott, M. J. (2019). Grammatical gender and linguistic relativity: A systematic review. *Psychonomic Bulletin & Review, 26*(6), 1767–1786. https://doi.org/10.3758/s13423-019-01652-3

Whorf, B. L. (1956). The relation of habitual thought and behavior to language. In J. B. Carroll (Ed.), *Language, thought, and reality: Selected writings of Benjamin Lee Whorf* (pp. 134–159). MIT Press.

Winawer, J., Witthoft, N., Frank, M. C., Wu, L., Wade, A. R., & Boroditsky, L. (2007). Russian blues reveal effects of language on color discrimination. *Proceedings of the National Academies of Sciences, 104*, 7780–7785. https://doi.org/10.1073/pnas.0701644104

Culture and Developmental Processes

DOI: 10.4324/9781003356820-7   *101*

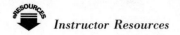

ACTIVITY 4.1
PARENTAL ETHNOTHEORIES

Activity Summary:

A series of questions assists students in exploring their own cultural beliefs about parenting and the degree to which these beliefs are culturally relative. For example, in some cultures, the practice of putting an infant to sleep in a crib in a room separated from the parents is regarded as cruel and neglectful behavior. In addition to sleeping practices, questions deal with such topics as responding to crying, praise, the role of extended family, sibling relationships, feeding practices, and cognitive development.

Lecture/Discussion Suggestion:

How do parental ethnotheories differ across cultures? One parental ethnotheory on which there are significant cultural differences deals with spanking children. In 1979, Sweden became the first country to make spanking illegal. By 2023, similar bans had been enacted in 65 countries. Speaking in regard to such legislation in France, Dr. Giles Lazimi, a leader of the anti-spanking campaign for the Foundation for Childhood, stated, "Above all, it removes the notion of a threshold: there is no small or big violence. There is violence, full stop" (Samuel, 2017). Cross-cultural research supports anti-spanking bans. For example, Elgar et al. (2018) reported that the 30 countries with full bans (at school and home) experienced 69% of the rate of fighting in males and 42% in females of the 20 countries without bans.

Parental ethnotheories have important implications for how "normal" childhood development is assessed. Karasik and Robinson (2022) argued that the developmental milestones used by parents and health care professionals (such as when a child is expected to crawl, walk, or talk) are based on Western standards and do not account for the diverse ethnotheories that shape the age at which these behaviors emerge. For example, they detail the use of *gahvora* cradling in Tajikistan and much of Central Asia, which is associated with a significantly later onset of walking as compared with Western norms. The *gahvora* is a carved cradle which greatly restricts the child's movement and is used for much of the day, often until age two or beyond. In terms of walking and other motor skills, Tajik babies seem to catch up to their Western peers by about age 4 with no indication of long-term repercussions.

At times the parental ethnotheories of one culture may conflict with those of another culture. In 1997, a Danish couple was arrested in New York for leaving their 14-month-old daughter in a stroller just outside of a restaurant where the couple was dining (Harden, 1997). The parents had positioned the stroller inside a chained off area of tables and chairs on the other side of a plate-glass window from where they were sitting. The police were called, and the couple spent two nights in jail while the baby was put in foster care. The mother later explained that this was a common practice in Denmark.

Variation:

Have students use these 12 items to collect data from their peers or parents. This data can be analyzed to assess gender, generational, or cultural differences.

Writing Application:

Have students take field notes on children's behavior in a public setting, such as a playground or toy store, and then formulate a parental ethnotheory based on their observations. The field notes should document their observations as well as reflections on those observations.

References:

Elgar, F. J., Donnelly, P. D., Michaelson, V., Gariépy, G., Riehm, K. E., Walsh, S. D., & Pickett, W. (2018). Corporal punishment bans and physical fighting in adolescents: An ecological study of 88 countries. *BMJ Open, 8*(9). https://doi.org/10.1136/bmjopen-2018-021616

Harden, B. (1997). Parking tot outside cafe is normal in Denmark, but couple arrested in New York. *Seattle Times*, May 14.

Karasik, L. B., & Robinson, S. R. (2022). Milestones or millstones: How standard assessments mask cultural variation and misinform policies aimed at early childhood development. *Policy Insights from the Behavioral and Brain Sciences, 9*(1), 57–64. https://doi.org/10.1177/23 727322211068546

Samuel, H. (2017). France bans smacking, raising pressure on UK to follow suit. *The Telegraph*, January 3. www.telegraph.co.uk/news/2017/ 01/03/france-bans-smacking-raising-pressure-uk-follow-suit/

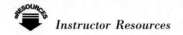

ACTIVITY 4.2
DEVELOPMENTAL NICHE

Activity Summary:

Students apply the three components of the developmental niche to their own experiences in order to better understand this concept. The three components are: (1) physical and social setting, (2) customs and practices of child-rearing, and (3) caretaker psychology. [Please note that on occasion students may reveal difficult family circumstances via this activity and instructors should be prepared to make appropriate referrals.]

Lecture/Discussion Suggestion:

What is the impact of poverty as part of a child's developmental niche? Studies throughout the world show that poverty (which is linked to poor housing conditions, inadequate nutrition, lack of access to education, and threats to personal safety) is associated with negative effects on the physical and mental health of children. For example:

- Research in the U.K. identified a link between persistent poverty and delays in the cognitive development of 3-, 5-, and 7-year-old children (Dickerson & Popli, 2016).
- In the U.S., even after controlling for child and family characteristics, neighborhood poverty levels were associated with low performance on measures of reading, math, and behavioral outcomes (Morrissey & Vinopal, 2018).
- Research in Germany found that poverty predicted delayed early language skills even when controlling for maternal education and frequency of joint picture book reading (Karwath et al., 2022).
- Among children of Latinx immigrants to the U.S., immigration stress interacted with economic hardship to result in internalizing (e.g., anxiety and depression) and externalizing (e.g., rule-breaking and aggression) behaviors (Mendoza et al., 2017).
- Poverty predicted levels of anxiety and depression in children from an economically depressed area of China (Li et al., 2017).
- Poverty was associated with social exclusion for children in Japan (Abe, 2012).

Variation:

Rather than report on their own developmental niche, students could gather information by observing the developmental niche of a young child and interviewing her or his parents or caregivers.

Writing Application:

Have students read an autobiography and then write an assessment of the developmental niche of the subject of the book.

References:

Abe, A. (2012). Affluence and poverty: Relative poverty of children in Japan. *Japanese Journal of Developmental Psychology, 23*(4), 362–374. http://dx.doi.org/10.11201/jjdp.23.362

Dickerson, A., & Popli, G. K. (2016). Persistent poverty and children's cognitive development: Evidence from the UK millennium cohort study. *Journal of the Royal Statistical Society: Series A (Statistics in Society), 179*(2), 535–558. https://doi.org/10.1111/rssa.12128

Karwath, C., Attig, M., von Maurice, J., & Weinert, S. (2022). Does poverty affect early language in 2-year-old children in Germany? *Journal of Child and Family Studies.* https://doi.org/10.1007/s10826-022-02500-0

Li, C., Jiang, S., & Yin, X. (2017). Understanding the relationship between poverty and children's mental health in poverty-stricken area of China: Social causation or social selection? *Journal of Child and Family Studies, 27,* 1186–1192. https://doi.org/10.1007/s10826-017-0960-9

Mendoza, M. M., Dmitrieva, J., Perreira, K. M., Hurwich-Reiss, E., & Watamura, S. E. (2017). The effects of economic and sociocultural stressors on the well-being of children of Latino immigrants living in poverty. *Cultural Diversity and Ethnic Minority Psychology, 23*(1), 15–26. https://doi.org/10.1037/cdp0000111

Morrissey, T. W., & Vinopal, K. M. (2018). Neighborhood poverty and children's academic skills and behavior in early elementary school. *Journal of Marriage and Family, 80*(1), 182–197. https://doi.org/10.1111/jomf.12430

Instructor Resources

ACTIVITY 4.3
ETHNIC-RACIAL SOCIALIZATION

Activity Summary:

Students are guided in mapping their childhood ethnic-racial socialization (ERS) in terms of the agent and content of the messages. Follow-up questions address explicit vs. implicit messaging, intersectional identities, and changes through development in ERS. [Please note that on occasion students may reveal difficult experiences via this activity and instructors should be prepared to make appropriate referrals.]

Lecture/Discussion Suggestion:

What is the effect of a "colorblind" approach to race and ethnicity? Some parents and teachers, particularly White Americans, emphasize "colorblindness" in their ethnic-racial socialization messages (Hazelbaker & Mistry, 2021; Karras et al., 2021). Those incorporating a colorblind perspective into ERS often do so with the belief that this strategy reduces the development of racial bias. However, it is important to note that colorblindness has two different components. According to Kite et al. (2022, p. 632), "*Color evasion* reflects the belief that one should avoid recognizing, discussing, or otherwise engaging with issues related to race or ethnicity. *Equality orientation* reflects the belief that one should view outgroup members as individuals and focus on intergroup similarities rather than differences." Although color evasion is positively correlated with prejudice, equality orientation is negatively correlated with prejudice.

Variations:

Students can work in a small group to identify ERS messages that fill various cells in the chart. In classrooms with limited racial/ethnic diversity, students can explore online sources, such as blog posts, to identify various ERS messages.

Writing Application:

To better understand the complexities of ERS, have students investigate the research literature on either a specific agent of socialization (e.g., siblings, teachers, social media) or on a specific identity group (e.g., Latina Americans, Palestinians, transracial adoptees, multiethnic individuals) and then share their findings.

References:

Hazelbaker, T., & Mistry, R. S. (2021). "Being colorblind is one of the worst things": White teachers' attitudes and ethnic-racial socialization in a rural elementary school. *Journal of Social Issues*, *77*(4), 1126–1148. https://doi.org/10.1111/josi.12489

Karras, J. E., Niwa, E. Y., Adesina, F., & Ruck, M. D. (2021). Confronting Whiteness: Conceptual, contextual, and methodological considerations for advancing ethnic-racial socialization research to illuminate White identity development. *Journal of Social Issues*, *77*(4), 1305–1326. https://doi.org/10.1111/josi.12485

Kite, M. E., Whitley, B. E., & Wagner, L. S. (2022). *Psychology of prejudice and discrimination*. Routledge.

ACTIVITY 4.4
FORMAL AND INFORMAL LEARNING

Activity Summary:

Students generate a list of skills that they learned through formal education and through informal education. A series of follow-up questions help students distinguish between the two forms of learning and explore the values each supports and teaches. Finally, students consider how these two forms of learning might be integrated in order to teach specific skills more effectively.

Lecture/Discussion Suggestion:

How do formal and informal learning differ? Formal learning typically:

- Occurs in a specified setting and time period. (Item a)
- Holds emotions separate from the subject matter. (Item c)
- Views teachers of a specific subject as basically interchangeable. (Item e)
- Uses a fairly structured and predictable learning process. (Item h)

In contrast, informal learning typically:

- Occurs through observation. (Item b)
- Involves teachers who have a personal connection with the subject matter. (Item d)

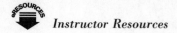

- Involves interaction between learners that is characterized by cooperation, rather than competition. (Item f)
- Involves subject matter closely tied to life experiences. (Item g)

A classic article by Scribner and Cole (1973) outlined some of the cognitive consequences of formal and informal education. According to these researchers and subsequent studies on this topic (see Cole, 2005; Preiss, 2022), schooling exerts a profound influence on cognition in that:

- Schooled children are more likely to generalize rules used to solve subsequent problems, whereas unschooled populations tend to solve each problem singly.
- Schooled children tend to use language to describe tasks and actions more than unschooled children. In fact, language is the primary mode of exchanging information for schooled children, whereas in informal learning children may utilize a variety of senses to a far greater extent.
- Schooled children learn abstract rules or concepts, often before they are linked to an actual event or object, whereas unschooled children learn rules or concepts in the context of everyday objects or events.
- Schooling involves becoming competent in symbol systems (such as letters and numbers) that may be used for a variety of tasks, whereas the tools with which one becomes competent in informal learning are typically linked to specific tasks.
- Schooled children learn to organize unrelated pieces of information (for example, lists of names and dates), whereas there is little need for this among unschooled children.

Variation:

Following this activity, divide students into groups and have each group choose a skill that can be taught through formal and informal means. Have half of each group develop a plan to teach the skill through formal learning and the other half develop a plan to teach the skill through informal learning. If time allows, have the groups demonstrate their lesson plans and then discuss similarities and differences between the two learning processes.

Writing Application:

Have students design an elementary school program that draws on the best qualities of formal and informal learning based on their knowledge of the characteristics and consequences of formal and informal education. Some of the issues they might address include:

- What would be the curriculum? What is the subject matter to be taught and how should it be categorized into subjects?
- What would be the method or mechanism for teaching and learning? Who would determine what is to be taught and how it is to be taught?
- What would the physical environment of the school be like?
- How will you group students (for example, by age or ability)?
- How will you assess the students' progress?
- What will be the school's policy on handling conflicts?
- Would you distinguish between curricular and extracurricular activities? If so, how?
- Would you use any symbols of school membership (such as insignia, school song, or uniform)?
- In what language(s) would instruction be conducted?

References:

Cole, M. (2005). Cross-cultural and historical perspectives on the developmental consequences of education. *Human Development*, *48*, 195–216. https://doi.org/10.1159/000086855

Preiss, D. D. (2022). Metacognition, mind wandering, and cognitive flexibility: Understanding creativity. *Journal of Intelligence*, *10*(3), 69–81. https://doi.org/10.3390/jintelligence10030069

Scribner, S., & Cole, M. (1973). Cognitive consequences of formal and informal education. *Science*, *182*, 553–559. https://doi.org/10.1126/science.182.4112.553

ACTIVITY 4.5
HOME CULTURE AND SCHOOL CULTURE FIT

Activity Summary:

In this activity, students read about efforts to create a fit between home and school cultures and then make observations in a classroom and respond to a set of questions to further explore this issue.

Lecture/Discussion Suggestion:

What barriers prevent access to school? Grigorenko and O'Keefe (2004) observed that psychological research conducted in the industrialized world has neglected the experiences of children who do not attend school. According to data from the United Nations Educational, Scientific and Cultural Organization (UNESCO; 2021/2022):

- Approximately 244 million children and youth between the ages of 6 and 18 worldwide are out of school.
- The Sub-Saharan African Region has the most children and youth out of school (98 million), and is the only region where this number is increasing. The region with the second highest out-of-school population is Central and Southern Asia (85 million).
- Globally, the gender gap in school attendance is closing. However, regional disparities persist. For example, since the 2021 Taliban takeover of Afghanistan, girls older than 12 have been prohibited from attending school.

The United Nations Office for the Coordination of Humanitarian Affairs (OCHA; 2020) has identified several barriers to school attendance, including:

- Attacks on schools – thousands of schools have been bombed or occupied by armed forces.
- Child labor – More than 150 million children, some as young as five, work in jobs that prevent them from attending school, often in physically or emotionally dangerous settings.
- Child marriage – Each year, about 12 million girls under the age of 18 are married.
- Climate change – Approximately 37 million children have their education disrupted each year because of environmental threats, including floods, typhoons, and droughts, which often result in migration.
- Wars and conflict – An estimated 48.5 million children in conflict zones throughout the world are unable to attend school.
- Disability – In low- and lower-middle-income countries, approximately 40% of children with disabilities have no access to primary school and 55% cannot attain a secondary education.

Writing Application:

Along with Activity 4.5, have students explore the data on UNESCO's Visualizing Indicators of Education for the World (VIEW) site for a specific country or region (https://education-estimates.org/). This interactive site provides data on the number of children out-of-school and on educational level completion rates in total and by gender. Students can then use scholarly sources to investigate possible variables associated with access to formal schooling.

References:

Grigorenko, E. L., & O'Keefe, P. A. (2004). What do children do when they cannot go to school? In R. J. Sternberg & E. L. Grigorenko (Eds.), *Culture and competence: Contexts of life success; culture and competence: Contexts of life success* (pp. 23–53). American Psychological Association.

United Nations Educational, Scientific and Cultural Organization. (2021/ 2022). *Global education monitoring report.* www.unesco.org/gem-report/en

United Nations Office for the Coordination of Humanitarian Affairs. (2020). *20 reasons why, in 2020, there are still 260 m children out of school* [Press release]. February 7. https://reliefweb.int/report/world/20-reasons-why-2020-there-are-still-260m-children-out-school

ACTIVITY 4.6
A CULTURALLY APPROPRIATE PIAGETIAN TASK

Activity Summary:

The issue of task familiarity in cognitive ability testing is outlined and examples are provided. Students are then asked to develop a Piagetian conservation task that would be appropriate for a specific culture or region with which they are familiar.

Lecture/Discussion Suggestion:

What findings have emerged from cross-cultural research on Piagetian theory? Cross-cultural researchers have conducted thousands of studies of Piagetian theory on children and adults throughout the world. These studies generally support the sequence of stages described by Piaget, although the age at which different stages are attained varies across cultures, often with people from more industrialized cultures outperforming people from less industrialized cultures. As was the case with early cognitive testing across cultures in general, findings of studies on Piagetian tasks were often framed in a biased manner. For example, Mishra (1997) observed that in the past, tests of Piagetian stages were used to describe groups of adults as having child-like abilities. In actuality, these differences were likely due to task familiarity (the focus of Activity 4.6) as well as an emphasis on verbal communication in Piagetian tasks, the use of standardized measures rather than Piagetian clinical interviews, and a failure to accurately gauge the ages of research participants (Kamara, 1971, cited in Gardiner, 1994). For example, Maynard and Greenfield (2003) compared U.S. American children from Los Angeles and Zinacantec Mayan children on two Piagetian tasks – one similar to those used by Piaget and one based on weaving practices, familiar to the Zinacantec Mayan children. They reported that the Zinacantec children were more advanced on the weaving problems, whereas U.S. children were more advanced on the Piagetian spatial problems. Dasen (2022) suggested that one use an ecocultural framework to explore how stages of Piagetian cognitive development may be adaptive in cultural context. For example, Dasen (1994) reported that for Australian Aboriginal children, the ability to perform spatial tasks develops sooner than the ability to perform conservation tasks. The reverse was true for the children Piaget tested in Geneva. Dasen suggested that these differences are adaptive considering the relative importance for the Australian Aboriginal child of learning to negotiate land areas as opposed to quantifying water or other substances.

Variation:

Students administer two Piagetian tasks, one using familiar materials and one using unfamiliar materials, to a child aged 5 to 7 years old and report the impact of task familiarity on performance.

Writing Application:

In a brief essay, students describe a task they attempted or completed that involved the use of unfamiliar materials and assess the impact of this lack of familiarity on their ability to perform the task.

References:

Dasen, P. R. (1994). Culture and cognitive development from a Piagetian perspective. In W. J. Lonner & R. S. Malpass (Eds.), *Psychology and culture* (pp. 145–147). Allyn & Bacon.

Dasen, P. R. (2022). Culture and cognitive development. *Journal of Cross-Cultural Psychology*, *53*(7–8), 789–816. https://doi.org/10.1177/00220221221092409

Gardiner, H. W. (1994). Child development. In L. L. Adler, & U. P. Gielen (Eds.), *Cross-cultural topics in psychology* (pp. 61–72). Praeger.

Maynard, A. E., & Greenfield, P. M. (2003). Implicit cognitive development in cultural tools and children: Lessons from Maya Mexico. *Cognitive Development*, *18*(4), 489–510. https://doi.org/10.1016/j.cogdev.2003.09.005

Mishra, R. C. (1997). Cognition and cognitive development. In J. W. Berry, P. R. Dasen, & T. S. Saraswathi (Eds.), *Handbook of cross-cultural psychology*, Vol. 2: Basic processes and human development (2nd ed., pp. 143–175). Allyn & Bacon.

ACTIVITY 4.7
GROWING UP AS A LANGUAGE BROKER

Activity Summary:

Students are presented with a description of language brokering and then are asked to consider the knowledge and intrapersonal, interpersonal, and intercultural skills likely to emerge from taking on this role. [Note that in multicultural university communities, classes may have one or more students who act as language brokers and may – or may not – wish to share their experiences].

Lecture/Discussion Suggestion:

What does research tell us about children and adolescents who act as language brokers? Researchers are just beginning to understand the effects of language brokering on children and their families. Some of the initial research findings (Crafter & Iqbal, 2020; Kim et al., 2017; Kobak et al., 2017; Rainey et al., 2017; Shen et al., 2019; Weisskirch, 2017) are listed below.

Knowledge:

- Domain-specific knowledge, such as medical terms or the content of rental agreements

- Increased exposure to and understanding of racism and anti-immigrant bias
- Greater knowledge about family members' work and personal lives

Intrapersonal skills:

- Increased self-confidence, self-efficacy, and empathy
- Greater understanding of ethnocultural heritage
- Greater executive functioning and ability to adapt to shifting tasks

Interpersonal skills:

- Conflict management skills
- Ability to navigate power dynamics

Intercultural skills:

- Negotiating cultural differences, such as being assertive on the family member's behalf while respecting the adults in various official positions
- Ability to explain cultural differences to family and nonfamily members
- Greater ability to retain one's heritage language as compared with non-brokering immigrant peers

Researchers have also identified risks of language brokering, though the level of harm seems to depend in part on the child's perception of the language brokering role, family dynamics and parenting style, and the sociopolitical context. These potential harms include:

- Unhealthy shifts in family dynamics
- Missing school
- Loss of opportunities to participate in childhood activities
- Significant stress in high-stakes situations, such as dealing with immigration matters

Language brokering may also interact with developmental stages – a phenomenon which may help explain some of the mixed findings about the outcomes of language brokering (Weisskirch, 2017). For example, language brokering appears to be associated with a boost to academic performance for younger children but may interfere with academic performance in college students.

Shen et al. (2019) note that increased funding for and implementation of professional translation services is an important strategy for minimizing any harmful effects of language brokering.

Writing Application:

Given that this is a relatively new research area with several conflicting findings, it may be interesting for students to develop a concept map of the variables that have been – and could be – helpful in understanding the outcomes of language brokering. This can be done on paper or students can use one of the many free online sites that allow one to create and download a concept map.

References:

Crafter, S., & Iqbal, H. (2020). The contact zone and dialogical positionalities in "non-normative" childhoods: How children who language broker manage conflict. *Review of General Psychology*, *24*(1), 31–42. https://doi.org/10.1177/1089268019896354

Kim, S. Y., Hou, Y., & Gonzalez, Y. (2017). Language brokering and depressive symptoms in Mexican-American adolescents: Parent–child alienation and resilience as moderators. *Child Development*, *88*, 867–881. https://doi.org/10.1111/cdev.12620

Kobak, R., Abbott, C., Zisk, A., & Bounoua, N. (2017). Adapting to the changing needs of adolescents: Parenting practices and challenges to sensitive attunement. *Current Opinion in Psychology*, *15*, 137–142. https://doi.org/10.1016/j.copsyc.2017.02.018

Rainey, V. R., Flores-Lamb, V. C., & Gjorgieva, E. (2017). Cognitive, socioemotional, and developmental neuroscience perspectives on language brokering. In R. S. Weisskirch (Ed.), *Language brokering in immigrant families: Theories and contexts* (pp. 205–223). Routledge.

Shen, Y., Kim, S. Y., & Benner, A. D. (2019). Burdened or efficacious? Subgroups of Chinese American language brokers, predictors, and long-term outcomes. *Journal of Youth and Adolescence*, *48*, 154–169. https://doi.org/10.1007/s10964-018-0916-4

Weisskirch, R. S. (2017). A developmental perspective on language brokering. In R. S. Weisskirch (Ed.), *Language brokering in immigrant families: Theories and contexts* (pp. 7–21). Routledge.

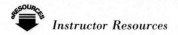

ACTIVITY 4.8
"EAST-WEST" DIFFERENCES IN AGEISM: MYTH OR REALITY?

Activity Summary:

Students survey three individuals to examine beliefs about the existence of cultural differences in age-related attitudes. Follow-up questions based on current cross-cultural research prompt students to take a more nuanced view of cultural variation in attitudes about older adults.

Lecture/Discussion Suggestion:

Is there a worldwide ageism crisis? According to the World Health Organization's (WHO; 2021) *Global Report on Ageism,* half of individuals surveyed worldwide expressed some ageism against older adults (juvenile ageism, focusing mainly on the negative stereotypes of children and teenagers, is also widespread, though not addressed here). The WHO report discussed ageism's threat to older adults' physical and psychological well-being, including mistreatment and abuse as well as discrimination in such areas as employment and health care.

Levy et al. (2022) presented detailed possible explanations for a "worldwide ageism crisis" which has been exacerbated by the Covid-19 pandemic. These authors make the following points:

- An assessment of ageism must consider both benign and malignant forms. Benign ageism views older adults as warm but incompetent and may be associated with patronizing treatment. Malignant ageism views older adults as of low value and is associated with hostility.
- The Covid-19 pandemic increased ageism in that older people were often portrayed as a burden and blamed for lockdowns and the economic downturn.
- Increased ageism during the pandemic was expressed in survey research and manifested in greater negativity and hate speech in social media posts.
- Ageism has intersectional effects, in that it interacts with other types of "isms" such as racism, sexism, heterosexism, classism, and ableism.
- There are multiple strategies for reducing ageism, including celebrating the contributions of older adults (such as when retired teachers and health care professionals returned to work during the pandemic), programs that promote positive intergenerational relations, and campaigns to raise awareness about the prevalence and detrimental effects of ageism.

Writing Application:

More advanced students can be asked to develop a research proposal to test their hypothesis from the Thinking Further section of Activity 4.8.

References:

Levy, S. R., Lytle, A., & Macdonald, J. (2022). The worldwide ageism crisis. *Journal of Social Issues.* https://doi.org/10.1111/josi.12568
World Health Organization. (2021). *Global Report on Ageism.* www.who. int/publications/i/item/9789240016866

ACTIVITY 4.9
ETHNOGRAPHIC STUDIES OF HUMAN DEVELOPMENT

Activity Summary:

Students locate and answer a series of questions about an ethnographic study of human development. Examples of ethnographic research findings and sources for ethnographic research reports are provided. [Requires work outside of the classroom.]

Lecture/Discussion Suggestion:

What specific techniques are used in ethnographic research? Kottak (2018) suggested that ethnography produces an "ethnopicture" (in the form of a book, article, or film) of a specific group or society. He outlined several techniques used in ethnographic study:

- *Observation* – Direct, firsthand observation of daily behavior, which one records in the form of field notes.
- *Interviews* – Structured or unstructured conversations with members of the groups studied.
- *Genealogical method* – Mapping kin relationships in order to trace historical events and understand current sociopolitical structures.
- *Cultural consultants* – Discussions with members of a society who are able to provide useful information about life in that society.

- *Life histories* – Case studies of particular individuals as a cultural portrait or as an illustration of diversity within a specific group.
- *Local individuals' and the ethnographer's beliefs/perceptions* – Understanding a group from both the insider (emic) and outsider (etic) perspectives.
- *Problem-oriented research* – Focuses on a particular societal problem rather than testing a theoretical position.
- *Longitudinal research* – The study of a society or group over time, typically through repeated visits.

Variation:

Have more advanced students identify two studies addressing a similar issue in human development – one study that is ethnographic and one that is more quantitative. They can then compare the two studies in order to more fully answer question 5 in Activity 4.9 (see handout) regarding the strengths and weaknesses of the ethnographic method.

Writing Application:

Have students identify a social group or setting related to issues of human development and write an ethnographic description of that group using observations, interviews, or a cultural consultant. Possible research settings include a childcare facility, a student activist organization, or a senior services center.

Reference:

Kottak, C. P. (2018). *Mirror for humanity: A concise introduction to cultural anthropology* (11th ed.). McGraw-Hill.

ACTIVITY 4.10
TEXTBOOK REWRITE

Activity Summary:

Students select a 1–2 paragraph segment of a developmental psychology chapter or textbook and rewrite the material so that it is more inclusive of research addressing diverse social groups (based on such dimensions as culture, race/

ethnicity, gender, social class, sexual orientation, and disability). [Requires work outside of the classroom.]

Lecture/Discussion Suggestion:

What are some of the barriers to infusing culture and diversity in psychology classes? Prieto (2018) surveyed 91 psychology instructors about the incorporation of diversity content in their courses and nearly one third viewed the lack of diversity in textbooks as a barrier to doing so. There is much agreement about the importance of diversity content in psychology textbooks (e.g., Gurung et al., 2016). Student texts shape course organization and lecture material (Slade et al., 2023), raise awareness and spur further inquiry, and may even influence the level of stereotype threat within the classroom (Fuentes & Shannon, 2016). Other barriers cited by the instructors in Prieto's study were time constraints (55%), lack of relevance to instructional material (32%), student apprehension about diversity issues (29%), and lack of preparation or training on the instructor's part (20%). More recently, an additional barrier to the infusion of diversity in psychology courses has emerged in the U.S. in the form of legislation prohibiting the discussion of race and LGBTQIA+-related issues in the classroom.

Variation/Writing Application:

The Textbook-Rewrite can be used as a major assignment or term paper in which students rewrite a larger portion of text. In addition, students can be asked to rewrite text material on areas of psychology other than developmental psychology.

References:

Fuentes, M. A., & Shannon, C. R. (2016). The state of multiculturalism and diversity in undergraduate psychology training. *Teaching of Psychology, 43*, 197–203. https://doi.org/10.1177/0098628316649315

Gurung, R. A., Hackathorn, J., Enns, C., Frantz, S., Cacioppo, J. T., Loop, T., & Freeman, J. E. (2016). Strengthening introductory psychology: A new model for teaching the introductory course. *American Psychologist, 71*, 112–124.

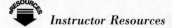

Prieto, L. R. (2018). Incorporating diversity content into courses and concerns about teaching culturally diverse students. *Teaching of Psychology*, *45*(2), 146–153. https://doi.org/10.1177/0098628318762875

Slade, J. J., Byers, S. M., & Gurung, R. A. R. (2023). Introductory psychology textbooks (still) more different than alike. *Scholarship of Teaching and Learning in Psychology*. https://doi.org/10.1037/stl0000365

Personality, Emotion, and the Self in Cultural Context

DOI: 10.4324/9781003356820-8

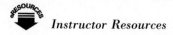

ACTIVITY 5.1
THE INTERDEPENDENT AND INDEPENDENT SELVES

Activity Summary:

Students complete a checklist that measures two concepts of self – one that emphasizes connectedness with others (interdependent) and one that focuses on the uniqueness of the individual (independent). Follow-up questions address the possibility of multiple self-construals and the implications of studies in which self-construal is elicited via priming.

Lecture/Discussion Suggestion:

How does our construal of self impact psychological processes? Markus and Kitayama (1991) introduced a model of two very different views of self. The *independent self* holds that the self is autonomous, self-contained, and behaves in accord with a unique configuration of internal attributes (such as traits, abilities, motives, and values). The *interdependent self* is a view of self in relation to others, and thus, behavior is dependent upon the social situation. Markus and Kitayama stated that most psychological research, a product of the West, is based upon the assumption of an independent self-construal. These authors proposed that such psychological processes as cognition, emotion, and motivation are strongly influenced by one's self-construal as follows:

Cognition:

- People with interdependent self-construals will have a greater need to attend to and understand the social situation.
- People with interdependent self-construals are more likely to process, categorize, and retrieve information about themselves and others in terms of the social situation rather than in terms of knowledge about the self in general or the other person in general.

Emotion:

- People with interdependent self-construals may more frequently express, and experience, other-focused emotions (such as sympathy, interpersonal communion, and shame), whereas people with independent self-construal may more frequently express and experience ego-focused emotions (such as guilt, anger, and pride).

- Emotional expression for those with independent self-construals may function to reveal inner feelings, whereas emotional expression for those with interdependent self-construals may depend on social needs and may or may not be directly related to inner feelings.

Motivation:

- People with interdependent self-construals will be motivated by more social needs.
- For people with an independent self-construal, personal choices will reflect one's internal needs as distinct from the needs of others, whereas for people with interdependent self-construals, choices will reflect an effort to be sensitive to the needs of others and restraint of one's inner desires in order to maintain the social dynamic.
- A focus on the unique personality characteristics associated with an independent self will result in a need to maintain consistency of actions and reactions across situations. For those with an interdependent self-construal, personal attributes are not a central aspect of self, and thus would not result in concern about consistency.
- A focus on the unique personality characteristics associated with an independent self will result in a need to maintain a positive view of self in terms of these attributes. For those with an interdependent self-construal, a positive view of self may be achieved through harmonious relationships with relevant others.

Subsequent research findings on self-construal have been somewhat inconsistent. Dean (2013a, 2013b), discussed two explanations for these findings:

1. The scales used to assess self-construal may be flawed. For example, some of these scales may be more appropriate for Western than East Asian participants in that the items fail to address some important aspects of interdependent self-construal such as "self-regulation of socially inappropriate thoughts and emotions" (Dean, 2013b, p. 753).
2. There may be a reference-group effect in that people from different cultural groups may use different standards to assess their level of agreement with the self-construal items. For example, Heine et al. (2002) found that Japanese respondents rated themselves as more independent if making comparisons with other Japanese people than if comparing themselves to people of other cultures. However, when participants were asked to make cross-cultural comparisons, the findings tended to support those predicted by self-construal theory.

Variation:

Ask more advanced students to look over the characteristics of interdependent and independent selves (listed in Activity 5.1) and think about the psychological processes linked to self-construal. For example, from the first pair of characteristics (Success depends on help from others / Success depends on my abilities) students may be able to discern that self-construal is linked to the process of attribution.

Writing Application:

Ask students to think about a significant decision they made in the past and write a brief essay about how this decision may have been affected by their independent or interdependent self-construal (or both).

References:

Dean, K. K. (2013a). Independent self-construal. In K. Keith (Ed.), *Encyclopedia of cross-cultural psychology* (pp. 691–695). Wiley-Blackwell.

Dean, K. K. (2013b). Interdependent self-construal. In K. Keith (Ed.), *Encyclopedia of cross-cultural psychology* (pp. 750–755). Wiley-Blackwell.

Heine, S. J., Lehman, D. R., Peng, K., & Greenholtz, J. (2002). What's wrong with cross-cultural comparisons of subjective Likert scales? The reference-group effect. *Journal of Personality and Social Psychology, 82*, 903–918. https://doi.org/10.1037/0022-3514.82.6.903

Markus, H. R., & Kitayama, S. (1991). Culture and the self: Implications for cognition, emotion, and motivation. *Psychological Review, 98*, 224–253. https://doi.org/10.1037/0033-295X.98.2.224

ACTIVITY 5.2
MULTIPLE AND SHIFTING IDENTITIES

Activity Summary:

Students are guided in delineating their multiple group identities (e.g., Puerto Rican, male, cyclist) in order to demonstrate that there is much within-culture variability, and that the importance of each identity group varies with the social context. A follow-up question introduces the concept of intersectionality. [This activity and the variation below may involve some sensitive issues of identity and should be used in a manner such that students are not required to reveal identity groups to the rest of the class.]

Lecture/Discussion Suggestion:

How do identity groups affect communication? Collier (2015, p. 56) suggested that in contrast to the social psychological approach which views identity as a product of personality and social roles, a communication approach views identity as emerging from "the messages exchanged between persons." According to Collier, "Who we are and how we are differs and emerges depending upon who we are with, the cultural identities that are important to us and others, the context, the topic of conversation, and our interpretations and attributions." Singer (1998) suggested that similarity in identity groups is associated with ease and quantity of communication. When there is little similarity in identity groups – and thus, in perception – communication becomes more difficult and infrequent. When students think about the people they communicate with most, are these the people with whom they share the greatest number of identity groups?

Variation:

Have students approach members of a single social group (such as computer science majors) and have them list their identity groups. This is a good way to make within-group variability clear and can be the basis for a discussion of stereotyping.

Writing Application:

Ask students to read a biographical or autobiographical account and then write an essay describing the subject's likely identity groups and discussing how these identity groups might interact and vary with the social context.

References:

Collier, M. J. (2015). Cultural identity and intercultural communication. In L. A. Samovar, R. E. Porter, E. R. McDaniel, & C. S. Roy (Eds.), *Intercultural communication: A reader* (pp. 53–64). Cengage.

Singer, M. R. (1998). *Perception & identity in intercultural communication.* Intercultural Press.

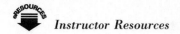

ACTIVITY 5.3
MULTIRACIAL IDENTITY

Activity Summary:

A series of questions require that students consider how a variety of factors (e.g., role of parents, personal appearance, gender, neighborhood identity, and experience with discrimination) may impact the ethnic identity of multiracial individuals.

Lecture/Discussion Suggestion:

What factors may influence the identity development of multiracial individuals? Maria P. P. Root has written extensively about issues of multiracial identity. Her ecological model of racial identity development (Root, 1998), the basis of much subsequent research, proposed that the experiences that influence identity development are filtered through the "macrolenses" of *gender, social class*, and *regional history of race*, as well as the "microlenses" of *inherited influences* (such as given names, languages spoken in the home, phenotype, cultural values, and sexual orientation), *traits* (such as temperament, talents, and coping skills), and *social environments* (such as home, school, and work). *Generational differences* are also relevant to each component of this model.

Root (1998) applied this model in a study of biracial siblings who identified differently despite the same ancestry. One type of experience that seemed to affect the racial identity development of the participants in the study was hazing. This hazing often took the form of "authenticity testing" in which multiracial individuals were forced to demonstrate their status as a racial insider (based on interests, language, friendships, or physical appearance). Sometimes these experiences became "color-coded" and shaped attitudes toward subsequent experiences with members of specific racial/ethnic groups.

Students may be interested in reading Root's (1996) *Bill of Rights for Racially Mixed People*, which is readily available online.

Variation:

After students complete this activity, have them work in groups or individually to develop their own models of multiracial identity development. It may be useful to have students also read about Cross' (1995), Helms' (1995), Poston's (1990), or Renn's (2008) models of multiracial identity development.

Writing Application:

Despite increases in the number of multiracial children born each year, there exist few resources to support parents of these children in the unique childrearing issues they may face. Have students write a research-based magazine article or blog post providing advice to parents on this topic.

References:

Cross, W. E. (1995). The psychology of Nigresence: Revising the Cross model. In J. G. Ponterotto, J. M. Casas, L. A. Suzuki, & C. M. Alexander (Eds), *Handbook of multicultural counseling* (pp. 93–122). Sage.

Helms, J. E. (1995). An update of Helms' White and people of color racial identity models. In J. G. Ponterotto, J. M. Casas, L. A. Suzuki, & C. M. Alexander (Eds), *Handbook of multicultural counseling* (pp. 181–198). Sage.

Poston, W. S. C. (1990). The biracial identity development model: A needed addition. *Journal of Counseling and Development, 67*, 152–155. https://doi.org/10.1002/j.1556-6676.1990.tb01477.x

Renn, K. A. (2008). Research on biracial and multiracial identity development: Overview and synthesis. *New Directions for Student Services, 123*, 13–21. https://doi.org/10.1002/ss.282

Root, M. P. P. (1996). A bill of rights for racially mixed people. In M. P. P. Root (Ed.), *The multiracial experience: Racial borders as the new frontier* (pp. 3–14). Sage.

Root, M. P. P. (1998). Experiences and processes affecting racial identity development: Preliminary results from the biracial sibling project. *Cultural Diversity and Ethnic Minority Psychology, 4*, 237–247. https://doi.org/10.1037/1099-9809.4.3.237

ACTIVITY 5.4
CULTURE AND SELF-CONSISTENCY

Activity Summary:

Students respond to items to explore their perceived self-consistency and consider how self-consistency may be related to dialectical thinking as well as to the focus of psychological research in different cultures.

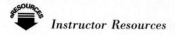

Lecture/Discussion Suggestion:

Are there actual differences in self-consistency across cultures? Activity 5.4 deals with cultural differences in *beliefs* about self-consistency, but are there actual *behavioral* differences in the extent to which individuals manifest consistent traits across time and situation? According to Locke and colleagues (2017, 2019) when studying the consistency of an individual's traits, it is critical to control for the influence of *trait injunctions* – the individual's beliefs about the behaviors that others will approve or disapprove of within a specific situation. If injunctions differ across situations, the traits expressed will likely be less consistent. Locke and colleagues (2017) asked students in nine countries (Australia, Canada, the United States, Ecuador, Mexico, Venezuela, Japan, Malaysia, and the Philippines) to report the traits they expressed, and the traits others wanted them to express (injunctions) in four different social situations (at home with parents, at home with siblings or close relatives of similar age, at college with friends, and at college with professors). Locke et al. (2019) used the same protocol to investigate self-consistency with Asian American, Asian Canadian, European American, and European Canadian students. Both studies found cultural differences in self-consistency, but that these differences could be explained to some extent by the degree to which injunctions were or were not consistent. For example, participants from Japan expressed lower self-consistency than participants from the other countries tested, yet this inconsistency disappeared when researchers controlled for differences in injunctions across situations, such as expected behavior with parents vs. peers (Locke et al., 2017). Similarly, Locke et al. (2019) found that Asian Canadians had lower self-consistency than European Canadians, but that the inconsistency was due in part to different injunctions for parent and peer interactions among the Asian Canadians.

Variation/Writing Application:

Have students keep a journal of their actions for a week and then write a brief report in which they review their own behavior to determine whether their traits appear to be consistent across time and situation. They can then discuss how cultural influences may have shaped their perceptions of – and their actual – self-consistency.

References:

Locke, K. D., Church, A. T., Mastor, K. A., et al. (2017). Cross-situational self-consistency in nine cultures: The importance of separating influences of social norms and distinctive dispositions. *Personality and Social Psychology Bulletin, 43*(7), 1033–1049. https://doi.org/10.1177/0146167217704192

Locke, K. D., Sadler, P., & McDonald, K. (2019). Cross-situational consistency of trait expressions and injunctive norms among Asian Canadian and European Canadian undergraduates. *Cultural Diversity and Ethnic Minority Psychology, 25*(2), 210–219. https://doi.org/10.1037/cdp0000195

ACTIVITY 5.5
RELIGION AND UNDERSTANDING CULTURE

Activity Summary:

In this activity, students are asked to consider the impact of religion on various aspects of culture, including values, child-rearing practices, health-related behaviors, prejudice and stereotyping, gender roles, the concept of the self, beliefs about interpersonal relationships, and beliefs about education and learning.

Lecture/Discussion Suggestion:

How does religiosity differ from religious identity? Although these terms are often used (and assessed) interchangeably, Zagumny (2013, p. 1094) defined religiosity as "a measure of one's commitment and corresponding actions in relation to religious tradition." In contrast, religious identity refers to "the tendency to form one's perceptions of self, at least in part, around the religious tradition to which the person currently, historically, and culturally subscribes." Measures of religiosity and of religious identity have taken both general and religion-specific approaches. For example, the Indic Religiosity Scale (Jayakumar & Verma, 2021) measures concordance with the beliefs of the major religions of India – Hinduism, Jainism, Sikhism, and Buddhism. An example of a more general measure is the Religious Orientation Scale (ROS; Allport & Ross, 1967), which has been translated into numerous languages and modified to fit various ages and religions as well as non-religious samples. Despite the fact that religion-related measures often merge the concepts of religiosity and religious identity, recent cross-cultural research (Leite et al., 2023) confirmed the distinction, but relatedness, of religious identity, religious practice, and religious beliefs in 27 countries throughout Asia, Europe, North America, Oceania, and South America.

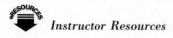

Variation:

Have each student (or small groups of students) investigate a different religion and then answer the questions in this activity focusing on the specific religion they investigated.

Writing Application:

Have students write a brief report summarizing statistical data illustrating the impact of religion on one aspect of human behavior.

References:

Allport, G. W., & Ross, M. J. (1967). Personal religious orientation and prejudice. *Journal of Personality and Social Psychology, 5,* 432–443. http://dx.doi.org/10.1037/h0021212

Jayakumar, T., & Verma, A. (2021). Indic religiosity scale: Developing and validating an Indian religiosity scale. *Journal of Management, Spirituality & Religion, 18*(1), 35–56. https://doi.org/10.1080/14766086.2020.1824801

Leite, Â., Nobre, B., & Dias, P. (2023). Religious identity, religious practice, and religious beliefs across countries and world regions. *Archive for the Psychology of Religion.* https://doi.org/10.1177/00846724221150024

Zagumny, M. J. (2013). Religious identity. In K. Keith (Ed.), *Encyclopedia of cross-cultural psychology* (pp. 1094–1095). Wiley-Blackwell.

ACTIVITY 5.6
PUTTING EMOTIONS INTO WORDS

Activity Summary:

Students look up emotion terms in a thesaurus to identify related somatic referents and then answer questions that address the functions and implications of such referents. [Requires work outside of the classroom.]

Lecture/Discussion Suggestion:

What is the role of somatic referents in assessing well-being? Dunnigan et al. (1993), in their efforts to construct an instrument appropriate for assessing the emotional well-being of Laotian Hmong youth, encountered a number of expressions focusing on the state of the liver (perhaps similar to some English language expressions about the heart, such as having a broken heart). They included these metaphors in their assessment tool, as in the following example (pp. 349–350; the translation appears in brackets; the numbered items in parentheses reflect the original English screening items):

During the past month, have there been times that …

- *Koj tau ntsib kev nyuaj siab thiab kev cov nyom hauv koj lub neej?* [you have encountered a difficult liver and troubles – rough terrain – in your life?] (1: strain, stress, or pressure?)
- *Koj xav tias koj tau chim, kho siab, los is tu siab?* [you have thought of yourself as angry, having a lonely liver, or a hurt liver?] (2: downhearted and blue?)
- *Koj txhawj siab txog lwm yam?* – [you have had a worried liver about a number of things?] (3: been moody or brooded about things?)
- *Koj kho siab* – [you have a lonely liver?] (4: felt depressed?)
- *Koj nyuaj siab los sis ntxhov siab heev?* [you have a difficult liver or a greatly obscured liver?] (5: in low or very low spirits?)

Variation:

Enlist the aid of bilingual students or other individuals to compare the frequency of somatic referents for emotion terms across several languages and discuss possible reasons for any differences in frequency discovered.

Writing Application:

Have students write an essay in which they invent a new somatic referent to express an emotion. Advanced students might discuss how the referent they developed is an expression of cultural values or conventions.

Reference:

Dunnigan, T., McNall, M., & Mortimer, J. T. (1993). The problem of metaphoric nonequivalence in cross-cultural survey research: Comparing the mental health statuses of Hmong refugee and general population adolescents. *Journal of Cross-Cultural Psychology, 24,* 344–365. https://doi.org/10.1177/0022022193243005

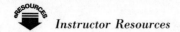

ACTIVITY 5.7
CULTURAL DISPLAY RULES

Activity Summary:

Students record ten instances in which they experienced an emotion noting the nature of the emotion, the setting, and the emotional expression. Based on this data, students answer a series of questions focusing on Ekman and Friesen's (Ekman, 1972) concept of cultural display rules. [Requires work outside of the classroom. Please note that on occasion students may reveal emotional distress via this activity and instructors should be prepared to make appropriate referrals.]

Lecture/Discussion Suggestions:

How do we learn culturally appropriate display rules? Emotion researchers agree that display rules are likely learned in childhood, to a large extent through direct statements and indirect messages (such as modeling) by parents and other family members (McDowell & Parke, 2005). Tsai and colleagues (2007) suggested that one other way we learn rules for emotional expression is through storybooks. Their research investigated the content of and reactions to best-selling children's books in the U.S. and Taiwan and found that as compared with Taiwanese storybooks, U.S. American storybooks emphasized excited (vs. calm) states, as indicated by the activities and expressions of the characters. A second phase of the research manipulated the level of excitement with children's books developed by the authors to have an excited (e.g., splashing in the water) vs. calm (e.g., floating in the water) version. Interestingly, after exposure to a specific state (excited or calm) in the storybook, preschoolers tended to prefer that state regardless of nationality, although the U.S. children were still more likely than the Taiwanese children to prefer the exciting activity over the calm one.

Does culture affect which facial cues we view as most important in assessing emotion? There is some evidence that this is the case. Yuki et al. (2007) conducted two studies, one using drawings of faces, and one using facial expressions from real people, in which they independently manipulated the emotional expression portrayed by the mouth and the eyes. As compared with U.S. Americans, Japanese participants place more importance on facial cues in the eyes. The Japanese participants rated happy eyed-faces as happier, and sad eyed-faces as sadder. In contrast, the American participants rated happy mouthed-faces as happier and sad-mouthed faces as sadder. The authors suggested that in cultures where greater emotional restraint is the norm (such as Japan) people would focus more on eyes, where emotional expression is more difficult to control. However, in cultures where overt emotional expression is the norm (such as the U.S.), people would tend to focus on the mouth, which is the most expressive part of the face.

Similar results were found with a study of emoticons – the early version of emojis that were formed from computer keyboard characters. Park et al. (2014) investigated emoticon usage patterns on Twitter in 78 countries and found that people in individualistic cultures were more likely to use mouth-oriented emoticons like:), whereas those in collectivistic cultures preferred eye-oriented emoticons like ^_^.

How might the focus on eyes or mouth affect the ability to read the emotions of masked individuals (a topic that gained interest among psychologists during the Covid-19 pandemic)? Saito et al. (2022) had U.S. American and Japanese participants judge emotional expressions (happy, fearful, angry, sad, disgust, and neutral) on faces with and without masks. The results indicated that masking decreased recognition of sadness and disgust for both groups and decreased recognition of happiness for the U.S. Americans but not the Japanese. In addition, masking increased recognition of anger for the Japanese participants and increased recognition of fear for the U.S. group. The authors suggested that the masks impeded the U.S. Americans' tendency to seek information about happiness from mouth-related cues, whereas masking drew their attention to the eyes, where fear cues may be more visible. Regarding the Japanese participants' improved ability to detect anger in masked faces, the authors cited research indicating that anger and disgust may be more similar in some Asian cultures as compared to those of the West. They suggested that masking may have helped to separate disgust cues (typically mouth-related) from anger cues.

Variation:

Instead of having students use the grid on the Activity 5.7 Handout to chart their own emotions, have them view a dramatic film, television drama, or telenovela and keep track of the emotional displays of a specific character and the settings in which these displays occur.

References:

Ekman, P. (1972). Universals and cultural differences in facial expressions of emotion. In J. Cole (Ed.), *Nebraska Symposium on Motivation*, Vol. 19. University of Nebraska Press.

McDowell, D. J., & Parke, R. D. (2005). Parental control and affect as predictors of children's display rule use and social competence with peers. *Social Development, 14*(3), 440–457. https://doi.org/10.1111/j. 1467-9507.2005.00310.x

Park, J., Baek, Y. M., & Cha, M. (2014). Cross-cultural comparison of nonverbal cues in emoticons on Twitter: Evidence from big data analysis. *Journal of Communication, 64*(2), 333–354. https://doi.org/ 10.1111/jcom.12086

Saito, T., Motoki, K., & Takano, Y. (2022). Cultural differences in recognizing emotions of masked faces. *Emotion.* https://doi.org/10.1037/ emo0001181

Tsai, J. L., Louie, J. Y., Chen, E. E., & Uchida, Y. (2007). Learning what feelings to desire: Socialization of ideal affect through children's storybooks. *Personality and Social Psychology Bulletin, 33*(1), 17–30. https://doi.org/10.1177/0146167206292749

Yuki, M., Maddux, W. W., & Masuda, T. (2007). Are the windows to the soul the same in the East and West? Cultural differences in using the eyes and mouth as cues to recognize emotions in Japan and the United States. *Journal of Experimental Social Psychology, 43*(2), 303–311. https://doi.org/10.1016/j.jesp.2006.02.004

ACTIVITY 5.8
DEAR SIGMUND (OR CARL)

Activity Summary:

Students are asked to write a letter either to Sigmund Freud or Carl Rogers explaining the need for a cross-cultural perspective in developing personality theory. Specific aspects of the Freudian and Rogerian theories are listed to aid students in making connections between cross-cultural psychology and Western personality theory.

Lecture/Discussion Suggestion:

In what ways are classic personality theories culture-bound? Specific issues concerning the cross-cultural applicability of Freudian and Rogerian personality theories are listed below:

In Rogerian theory:

• The focus is on the autonomous individual.

- It is assumed that you know yourself better than others know you.
- Part of being fully functioning is resisting the tendency to conform to societal demands.
- High levels of self-disclosure and emotional expression are an essential part of personal growth and client-centered therapy.
- Anxiety stems from experiences that are inconsistent with one's self-concept, which is assumed to have cross-situational consistency.

In Freudian theory:

- A nuclear family configuration with the mother as the primary caregiver is assumed.
- The competition between boys with their fathers is a central component of development.
- The impact of sociocultural factors, such as prejudice and gender roles, is ignored.
- Psychoanalysis involves high levels of disclosure as well as a long term time and financial commitment, which is not possible for all sociocultural groups.
- The interpretation of dreams and projective tests does not consider cultural variability in the interpretation of symbols.

An interesting example of cultural bias in Freudian theory comes from Bronislaw Malinowski's (1927) classic study of boys' dreams in the Trobriand Islands (frequently cited as an example of how cross-cultural psychology may unconfound variables). Malinowsi challenged Freud's theory that boys experience an Oedipal stage in which they are hostile toward their fathers due to jealousy over their father's sexual role with their mothers. Malinowski suggested that the hostility expressed by boys may be due to their father's disciplinary role rather than their role as mother's sexual partner. When he analyzed the dreams of boys from the Trobriand Islands – where, like some other Pacific societies, the mother's brother is the disciplinarian – the target of hostility was more often the uncle. Thus, Malinowski concluded that the hostility Freud explained in terms of an Oedipal stage was actually due to a reaction against being disciplined. Although questions have been raised about Malinowski's data analysis (see, for example, Spiro, 1988), and reasonable alternative explanations for Oedipal-like behavior have been proposed (e.g., Türkarslan, 2022), this study illustrates how culture-bound assumptions about family dynamics limit the cross-cultural generalizability of Freudian theory.

References:

Malinowski, B. (1927). *Sex and repression in savage society*. Kegan Paul.

Spiro, M. E. (1988). Is the Oedipus complex universal? In G. H. Pollock & J. M. Ross (Eds.), *The Oedipus papers: Classics in psychoanalysis, Monograph 6* (pp. 435–473). International Universities Press.

Türkarslan, K. K. (2022). Children's affectionate and assertive attitudes towards their parents: The Oedipus complex or parent–offspring conflict? *Integrative Psychological and Behavioral Science, 56*, 653–673. https://doi.org/10.1007/s12124-021-09624-w

ACTIVITY 5.9
THE CULTURE AND PERSONALITY SCHOOL – OLD AND NEW

Activity Summary:

After reading a brief description of Cora DuBois' (1944) culture and personality study of the Alorese, students evaluate five assumptions underlying this once popular school of psychological anthropology and then examine the reasoning behind new approaches linking culture to personality traits.

Lecture/Discussion Suggestion:

How might different regions develop different mean levels of personality traits? Rentfrow and Jokela (2016, 2019) drew on the field of *geographical psychology* to answer this question. Geographical psychology overlaps with cross-cultural psychology in its attention to the influence of the environment on psychological phenomena but focuses specifically on spatial organization. These authors identified three different mechanisms that could be responsible for geographic variation in psychological phenomena:

1. *Social influence* – The social norms in different regions shape the individual's thoughts, feelings, and behaviors. [In terms of personality, students might consider how regional norms shape the *expression* of personality traits.]
2. *Ecological influence* – Features of the natural and built environment result in some traits and behaviors being more adaptive than others. Rentfrow and Jokela explained, for example, that regions with high pathogen

prevalence favor personality traits associated with risk-averse behavior, such as low extraversion, low openness, and high conscientiousness.

3. *Selective migration* – Individuals move into or out of social groups to find one appropriate for their personality traits. For example, Hofstede and McCrae (2004) suggested that high power distance cultures would allow only a small number of people to be in leadership positions. Over time, more extraverts would leave the social group and more introverts would stay. [You may want to discuss with students how selective migration has been used to justify racist psychological models of intelligence in the past.]

Hofstede and McCrae (2004) posed an interesting question about the causal ordering of culture and personality traits. How would acculturation impact personality? If personality is based entirely on inherited traits, then moving to a new culture should have little impact on personality. However, if culture shapes traits, then over generations individual personalities should become more similar to that of the host culture.

Variation:

Have students read a study from the culture and personality school (such as Benedict, 1946 or DuBois, 1944) and use it as a basis for responding to the five assumptions outlined in the Activity 5.9 Handout. Students will likely have no difficulty challenging these assumptions. More advanced students could be asked to build a case against one or more of these assumptions through a search of the relevant literature.

Writing Application:

Based on the five assumptions outlined in Activity 5.9, have students write a brief (2–3 page) analysis of personality in a culture with which they are familiar.

References:

Benedict, R. (1946). *The chrysanthemum and the sword*. Houghton Mifflin.
DuBois, C. (1944). *The people of Alor*. Harper & Row.
Hofstede, G., & McCrae, R. R. (2004). Personality and culture revisited: Linking traits and dimensions of culture. *Cross-Cultural Research, 38*, 52–88. https://doi.org/10.1177/1069397103259443
Rentfrow, P. J., & Jokela, M. (2016). Geographical psychology: The spatial organization of psychological phenomena. *Current Directions*

in Psychological Science, 25(6), 393–398. https://doi.org/10.1177/0963
721416658446

Rentfrow, P. J., & Jokela, M. (2019). Geographical variation in the Big
Five personality domains. In D. Cohen & S. Kitayama (Eds.),
Handbook of cultural psychology (pp. 768–792). The Guilford Press.

ACTIVITY 5.10
ETIC AND EMIC APPROACHES TO PERSONALITY

Activity Summary:

This activity is based on Cheung et al.'s (2011) combined emic-etic approach in
which, in addition to testing the universality of FFM traits across cultures,
indigenously derived traits are tested for universality. Several steps are involved in
this activity, which explores the universality of a model specifying five underlying
dimensions of personality. First students generate a list of traits, then they use
descriptions of the Five Factor Model (FFM) to categorize these traits. Finally,
they read about three personality traits from a language other than English and
determine whether they can be classified as part of the FFM. A follow-up
question requires students to discuss how the combined etic-emic approach could
be used to investigate an area of psychology other than personality.

Lecture/Discussion Suggestion:

How can we more accurately measure personality traits? There has been much
criticism of the use of self-report methods in cross-cultural personality research
due to the risk of differences in response style (such as acquiescence response
bias, social desirability effects, and differences in the selection of extreme
scores on rating scales) and reference group effects (in which participants from
different cultures use different standards to evaluate their own traits; Oishi &
Roth, 2009). Costello et al. (2018) suggested that rather than using self-report
measures to assess personality, a more accurate strategy might focus on
revealed traits. In this technique, the traits of individuals or groups are assessed
based on the degree to which they perform actions that judges view as
indicative of a specific trait. According to these authors (p. 555):

> This technique can be used either by observing the individual's actual
> responses in a large number of situations or by surveying how the
> individual would be likely to respond to hypothetical situations. For

instance, "telling a stern professor that their answer is wrong in a large lecture class" might be characterized as a fairly *assertive* action. Then, rather than directly asking participants to rate how *assertive* they are, the revealed traits technique indirectly measures assertiveness by correlating one's likelihood of performing a wide range of actions such as these with the extent to which those actions have been judged by others to be *assertive*.

Using this technique, Costello et al. noted different results from that obtained on measures of self-reported traits, particularly in regard to the much researched finding of lower self-reported conscientiousness scores among participants from East Asian nations.

Variation:

Rather than having students categorize traits in terms of the FFM, have them list proverbs and categorize the traits promoted by those proverbs in terms of the FFM. Lists of proverbs from around the world are readily available online.

Writing Application:

Have more advanced students expand on the Thinking Further item in Activity 5.10 and write a detailed research proposal outlining the theoretical rationale, methods, and expected results of a study utilizing the combined etic-emic approach.

References:

Cheung, F. M., van de Vijver, F. J. R., & Leong, F. T. L. (2011). Toward a new approach to the study of personality in culture. *American Psychologist*, 66(7), 593–603. https://doi.org/10.1037/a0022389

Costello, C. K., Wood, D., & Tov, W. (2018). Revealed traits: A novel method for estimating cross-cultural similarities and differences in personality. *Journal of Cross-Cultural Psychology*, 49(4), 554–586. https://doi.org/10.1177/0022022118757914

Oishi, S., & Roth, D. P. (2009). The role of self-reports in culture and personality research: It is too early to give up on self-reports. *Journal of Research in Personality*, 43(1), 107–109. https://doi.org/10.1016/j.jrp.2008.11.002

Health, Stress, and Coping Across Cultures

   DOI: 10.4324/9781003356820-9

ACTIVITY 6.1
WHAT IS ABNORMAL?

Activity Summary:

A series of questions encourage students to consider how normality is situationally and culturally defined.

Lecture/Discussion Suggestions:

Are there universal criteria for identifying abnormal behavior? Across psychology texts, disordered behavior is generally described as determined by a combination of the following criteria:

- *Maladaptive behaviors* – Behaviors that are harmful to oneself or others or result in impaired day-to-day functioning.
- *Unjustifiable* – Behaviors that don't make sense to most people.
- *Atypical behaviors* – Behaviors that are rare or infrequent.
- *Disturbing* – Behaviors that most people find troubling.

Each of these criteria may be shaped by culture in that the behaviors that are maladaptive, unjustifiable, atypical, or disturbing vary depending on the cultural context. For example, "cutting," which is considered abnormal behavior in much of the world, is a normal part of coming-of-age rituals among some indigenous people along the Amazon River (Ayan & Calliess, 2005).

Does understanding behavior make it seem more normal? According to Ban et al. (2012, p. 290), this seems to depend on culture. For Euro-Australians, reading a causal explanation for a specific behavior (e.g., "J.K. was severely abused as a child. *Because of ongoing issues arising from this* he regularly gets drunk and is aggressive towards others") made the behavior seem less abnormal than when these facts were presented in isolation (e.g., "J.K. was severely abused as a child. He regularly gets drunk and is aggressive towards others"). This was not the case for Chinese-Singaporeans. The authors suggested that the Chinese-Singaporean participants may be less familiar than the Euro-Australians with the psychologizing language used in the causal explanations. In addition, it may be that in Singapore behavior that violates social norms is considered less acceptable regardless of whether it has an explanation (Vargas et al., 2019).

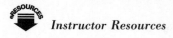

Variation:

Instruct students to administer items 1–5 in Activity 6.1 to others and record several responses to each item. Students can then meet in small groups to pool the responses they collected and develop answers to items 6 and 7.

Writing Application:

Have students choose a single behavior (such as reading, counting objects, or body piercing) and in a brief essay, explain the situational and cultural factors that might determine whether this behavior is considered normal or abnormal.

References:

Ayan, S. J., & Calliess, I. T. (2005). Abnormal as norm. *Scientific American Mind*, April 1.

Ban, L., Kashima, Y., & Haslam, N. (2012). Does understanding behavior make it seem normal? Perceptions of abnormality among Euro-Australians and Chinese-Singaporeans. *Journal of Cross-Cultural Psychology, 43*(2), 286–298.

Vargas, S. M., Dere, J., Garcia, L., & Ryder, A. G. (2019). The role of cultural values in the folk psychiatry explanatory framework: A comparison of Chinese- and Euro-Canadians. *Journal of Cross-Cultural Psychology, 50*(5), 703–707. https://doi.org/10.1177/0022022119836517

ACTIVITY 6.2
CULTURE AND HEALTH: THE NI HON SAN STUDY

Activity Summary:

A series of questions, based on the Ni Hon San study of cardiovascular disease, guide students in exploring research that compares the health outcomes of ethnic group members that do and do not migrate. Students are expected to gain an understanding of how such research attempts to isolate the effects of heredity and cultural environment.

Lecture/Discussion Suggestion:

How can we explain the findings of the Ni Hon San study? The finding of the Ni Hon San study that Japanese men living in Japan had the lowest rate of heart disease can be explained by the process of acculturation. According to Beardsley and Pedersen (1997), the process of acculturation involves changes in the physical environment, physiological factors (such as diet), cultural factors (such as religion and language), and psychological factors (such as values and beliefs). Of particular importance in the Ni Hon San study was diet. Japanese men living in Hawaii and California ate more high-fat foods, more processed meats, and less fish, complex carbohydrates, soy products, vegetables, and fruit than Japanese men in Japan.

A second interesting research design to consider is that of the Adventist Health Studies. Beardsley and Pedersen pointed out that these studies use a model opposite to that of the Ni Hon San study. Since there are large numbers of Seventh-Day Adventists throughout the world, and the religion dictates specific dietary and lifestyle patterns (avoiding meat, caffeine, tobacco, and alcohol), researchers can essentially hold lifestyle constant and look at variations among ethnic groups. For example, these studies have shown several benefits associated with the Adventist lifestyle, including delayed onset of dementia and lower incidence of lung cancer (even lower than non-Adventist nonsmokers, perhaps due to a protective function of fruit consumption). However, the benefits are not quite as great for Black Adventists, although health indices were better than for non-Adventist Black and White individuals (Fraser et al., 2020). This is most likely due to a combination of social (e.g., health disparities, racism, housing discrimination), physiological (e.g., higher BMI and blood pressure), and lifestyle factors (lower lifetime rates of vegetarianism).

Writing Application:

Have students write a brief essay speculating about the role of ethnic or sociocultural factors on their own health-related behaviors.

References:

Beardsley, L. M., & Pedersen, P. (1997). Health and culture-centered intervention. In J. W. Berry, M. H. Segall, & C. Kagitcibasi (Eds.), *Handbook of cross-cultural psychology*: Vol. 3 (2nd ed., pp. 413–448). Allyn & Bacon.

Fraser, G. E., Cosgrove, C. M., Mashchak, A. D., Orlich, M. J., & Altekruse, S. F. (2020). Lower rates of cancer and all-cause mortality in an Adventist cohort compared with a US Census population. *Cancer*, *126*(5), 1102–1111. https://doi.org/10.1002/cncr.32571

ACTIVITY 6.3
THE GLOBAL OBESITY EPIDEMIC

Activity Summary:

Students investigate how the global obesity crisis has manifested in a specific country other than their own and report on the statistics, causes, consequences, prevention efforts, and cultural factors involved. [Requires work outside of the classroom.]

Lecture/Discussion Suggestion:

What is the relationship between obesity and socioeconomic status? Much research has supported the *reversal hypothesis* – socioeconomic status (SES) and weight are positively correlated in lower-income countries but negatively correlated in higher-income countries. In other words, high SES individuals tend to weigh more than others in poor countries but weigh less than others in rich countries. Pampel et al. (2012) found support for the reversal hypothesis, particularly among women, using individual- and country-level data for 67 nations across the globe. Why might this occur? These authors suggested that the health costs of obesity are greater in wealthier nations since life span may be limited regardless of obesity-related health risks in poorer nations. Other explanations focus on cultural value differences. In poor countries, greater access to food and avoidance of physically demanding work may be associated with higher-status individuals. In wealthier nations, however, it may be the higher SES individuals who have the time and resources to eat more healthily and exercise.

Jaacks et al. (2019) outlined a stage model of the reversal process based on data from the 30 most populous countries, representing over two-thirds of the world's population.

Their model maps changes in obesity prevalence over time and across sub-populations within countries in order to "provide guidance to researchers and policymakers in identifying the current stage of the obesity transition in a population, anticipate sub-populations that will experience obesity in the future, and enact proactive measures to attenuate the transition, taking into consideration local contextual factors" (pp. 231–232).

Stage 1: Obesity is more prevalent among higher SES individuals, women, and adults. Jaacks et al. indicated that many countries in South Asia and sub-Saharan Africa are currently in this stage.

Stage 2: The prevalence of obesity significantly increases among adults, with a smaller increase among children. The gender and socioeconomic gap narrows. Jaacks et al. stated that many Latin American and Middle Eastern countries are currently at this stage, as are higher-income East Asian nations, though with a much lower prevalence of obesity.

Stage 3: The prevalence of obesity among lower SES individuals surpasses that of higher SES individuals. Prevalence of obesity in high SES women and children plateaus. Jaacks et al. indicated that most European countries are currently at this stage.

Stage 4: Obesity prevalence starts to decline. According to World Obesity Atlas (Lobstein et al., 2023), a non-governmental organization that files reports with the World Health Organization, at this point there is no country reporting a nation-wide decline in obesity prevalence.

Variation/Writing Application:

Have more advanced students write a paper investigating the obesity crisis in greater depth. Students can then work individually or in small groups to draft a list of recommendations for developing a culturally appropriate intervention.

References:

Jaacks, L. M., Vandevijvere, S., Pan, A., McGowan, C. J., Wallace, C., Imamura, F., Mozaffarian, D., Swinburn, B., & Ezzati, M. (2019). The obesity transition: Stages of the global epidemic. *Lancet Diabetes and Endocrinolology, 7*(3), 231–240. https://doi.org/10.1016%2FS2213-8587(19)30026-9

Lobstein, T., Jackson-Leach, R., Powis, J., Brinsden, H., & Gray, M. (2023). *World obesity atlas 2023.* World Obesity Federation. https://data.worldobesity.org/publications/?cat=19

Pampel, F. C., Denney, J. T., & Krueger, P. M. (2012). Obesity, SES, and economic development: A test of the reversal hypothesis. *Social Science & Medicine, 74*(7), 1073–1081. https://doi.org/10.1016/j.socscimed.2011.12.028

ACTIVITY 6.4
CULTURE AND MENTAL HEALTH QUIZ

Activity Summary:

A self-administered quiz encourages students to consider major research questions in the area of culture and mental health.

Answers to Activity 6.4:

1. TRUE. Several core symptoms of schizophrenia and depression have been found in cultures across Africa, Asia, Europe, North America, and South America, though there is significant variability in prevalence, etiology, symptoms, treatment, and outcomes (Bhugra, 2005; Kessler & Bromet, 2013; World Health Organization, 2022).
2. PROBABLY FALSE. The World Health Organization's International Studies of Schizophrenia concluded that schizophrenia may have a better prognosis in less industrialized nations due to such factors as support from extended family, opportunities for meaningful work, and the option to recover at one's own pace (Humphries et al., 2015; Lin & Kleinman, 1988). However, subsequent studies have challenged these findings and, in general, have found greater stigmatization, decreased family care, and poorer outcomes in non-industrialized nations (e.g. Patel et al., 2006; Pescosolido et al., 2015).
3. FALSE. Across cultures studied, boys are more likely than girls to meet the criteria for autism spectrum disorder (ASD). For example, a multinational comparison of Greece, Italy, Japan, Poland, and the United States found that 72% to 87% of those diagnosed with ASD in each sample were boys (Matson et al., 2017). However, there is evidence that girls and women engage in more "camouflaging" to hide behaviors associated with ASD and avoid stigmatization (Lundin Remnélius & Bölte, 2023). Interestingly, camouflaging itself appears to be a stressor and thus engaging in camouflaging does not increase indices of well-being (Perry et al., 2022).
4. TRUE. *Karoshi*, death by overwork, and *karo-jisatsu*, suicide by over-work, are recognized forms of mental illness in Japan (Kanai, 2009). In fact, *karoshi* hotline centers were established throughout Japan to assist workers and their families in dealing with the stress-related problems associated with working extremely long hours. In addition to the hotline, government efforts to reduce *karoshi* include clear regulations on work

hours and overtime pay, public awareness campaigns dealing with mental health and power-based harassment of workers, and specialized training for counselors and medical doctors (Ministry of Health, Labour and Welfare, 2017).

5. FALSE. Anorexia nervosa has been documented in every region of the world (e.g., GBD 2019 Mental Disorders Collaborators, 2022) although there are cultural differences in etiology. For example, Rodrigues (2017) identified acculturation as a risk factor for the development of eating disorders among Latina girls. Bulimia nervosa, however, may be culture-bound in that it requires private access to large quantities of food (Keel & Klump, 2003).

6. FALSE. Therapists' views of controlled drinking treatments (as opposed to abstinence) vary significantly across nations, with the frequency of use and evidence for the effectiveness of controlled drinking programs increasing over the past several decades (Henssler et al., 2021; Körkel, 2015).

7. TRUE. However, the impact of matching clients and counselors by race/ethnicity on treatment outcomes varies depending on such factors as the client's race/ethnicity, reason for seeking counseling, history of discrimination, and whether cultural issues are discussed (Cabral & Smith, 2011; Joiner et al., 2022; Kim & Kang, 2018; Presley & Day, 2019; Swift et al., 2015).

8. FALSE. Studies carried out in different cultural settings throughout the world, including North America, Western Europe, China, India, Israel, Brazil, Chile, Puerto Rico, Australia, Indonesia, Nigeria, and Thailand, have found remarkable similarities in the cluster of behaviors characteristic of ADHD (Bauermeister et al., 2010). Differences do exist, however, in the prevalence rate (Castaldelli-Maia & Bhugra, 2022), which is likely due to cultural differences in the consequences for such behavior. Chan et al. (2022) shed light on this latter issue by comparing Hong Kong and United Kingdom parents' ratings of ADHD-associated behaviors. The authors also used an actometer to measure children's actual activity during tasks that required waiting. What they found was that although the children in Hong Kong were less active than the children in the U.K., their parents rated them as more hyperactive. Chan et al. attributed this to cultural norms in Hong Kong that call for compliance and restraint.

9. TRUE and FALSE. Presenting depression in terms of somatic symptoms is common in many different cultures (Lara-Cinisomo et al., 2020). In one study, Chinese outpatients reported significantly higher levels of *typical* somatic symptoms, as compared to the Euro-Canadians, such as weight loss, decreased appetite, insomnia, psychomotor problems, and fatigue. However, Euro-Canadians reported greater levels of *atypical* somatic symptoms, such as weight gain, appetite gain, and hypersomnia,

as compared to the Chinese. Furthermore, contrary to the belief that somatic symptoms are reported due to discomfort with discussing psychological symptoms, Chinese outpatients reported "depressed mood" at similar levels as the Euro-Canadians (Dere et al., 2013). The authors stated, "it is worth noting ... that the very concept of somatization rests on the cultural assumption that psychological symptoms are more central to depression than somatic symptoms. It is equally as legitimate to study the phenomenon of 'Western psychologization' as it is to study 'Chinese somatization'" (p. 3).

10. TRUE. Elizabeth Page-Gould (2010) summarized research showing that those who view diversity as a threat are more likely to respond to intergroup contact with stress reactions that are detrimental to physical and psychological health.

Lecture/Discussion Suggestion:

Which aspects of mental health are culture-specific? Even in the case of more "universal" forms of mental disorder, cultural factors are critical in that they influence:

- *The prevalence of the disorder* – Prina et al. (2011) investigated anxiety among older adults using a geriatric anxiety measure in seven countries (China, India, Cuba, Dominican Republic, Venezuela, Mexico, and Peru). They found marked differences in prevalence, ranging from very low rates in China to substantially higher rates in Peru. Predictors of prevalence included age, gender, socioeconomic status, and comorbid physical illnesses.
- *The way symptoms are manifested* – Nguyen et al. (2016) investigated symptoms of postnatal distress among new mothers in Ethiopia, India, and Vietnam. Although there were several similarities, there were also significant differences in how distress was manifested. For example, respondents from Ethiopia reported "depressive thoughts" at a rate significantly greater than did individuals from India or Vietnam.
- *The circumstances related to the onset of the disorder* – Bhugra et al. (1997) found family conflicts, as opposed to other psychosocial factors, associated with the onset of depression in north India. These authors attributed this finding to cultural factors influencing family responsibilities and expectations. In another example of cultural differences in the circumstances related to the onset of disorders, U.S. drone strikes on Pakistan

were associated with an increase in anxiety, depression, and other psychiatric conditions (Ullah et al., 2015).

Variation:

This quiz may be administered to others and the results compiled as a basis for class discussion.

References:

Bauermeister, J. J., Canino, G., Polanczyk, G., & Rohde, L. A. (2010). ADHD across cultures: Is there evidence for a bidimensional organization of symptoms? *Journal of Clinical Child and Adolescent Psychology, 39*(3), 362–372. https://doi.org/10.1080/15374411003691743

Bhugra, D. (2005). The global prevalence of schizophrenia. *PLoS Medicine, 2*(5). https://doi.org/10.1371/journal.pmed.0020151

Bhugra, D., Gupta, K. R., & Wright, B. (1997). Depression in North India – comparison of symptoms and life events with other patient groups. *International Journal of Psychiatry in Clinical Practice, 1*, 83–87. https://doi.org/10.3109/13651509709024708

Cabral, R. R., & Smith, T. B. (2011). Racial/ethnic matching of clients and therapists in mental health services: A meta-analytic review of preferences, perceptions, and outcomes. *Journal of Counseling Psychology, 58*(4), 537–554. https://doi.org/10.1037/a0025266

Castaldelli-Maia, J. M., & Bhugra, D. (2022). Analysis of global prevalence of mental and substance use disorders within countries: Focus on sociodemographic characteristics and income levels. *International Review of Psychiatry, 34*(1), 6–15. https://doi.org/10.1080/09540261.2022.2040450

Chan, W. W. Y., Shum, K. K., & Sonuga-Barke, E. J. S. (2022). Attention-deficit/hyperactivity disorder (ADHD) in cultural context: Do parents in Hong Kong and the United Kingdom adopt different thresholds when rating symptoms, and if so why? *International Journal of Methods in Psychiatric Research, 12*. https://doi.org/10.1002/mpr.1923

Dere, J., Sun, J., Zhao, Y., et al. (2013). Beyond "somatization" and "psychologization": Symptom-level variation in depressed Han Chinese and Euro-Canadian outpatients. *Frontiers in Psychology, 4*, 377. https://doi.org/10.3389/fpsyg.2013.00377

GBD 2019 Mental Disorders Collaborators. (2022). Global, regional, and national burden of 12 mental disorders in 204 countries and territories,

1990–2019: A systematic analysis for the global burden of disease study 2019. *The Lancet Psychiatry, 9*(2), 137–150. https://doi.org/10.1016/S2215-0366(21)00395-3

Henssler, J., Müller, M., Carreira, H., Bschor, T., Heinz, A., & Baethge, C. (2021). Controlled drinking – non-abstinent versus abstinent treatment goals in alcohol use disorder: A systematic review, meta-analysis and meta-regression. *Addiction, 116*(8), 1973–1987. https://doi.org/10.1111/add.15329

Humphries, S. H., King, R. J., Dunne, M. P., & Cat, N. H. (2015). Psychiatrists' perceptions of what determines outcomes for people diagnosed with schizophrenia in Vietnam. *ASEAN Journal of Psychiatry, 16*(2), 181–192.

Joiner, T. E., Robison, M., Robertson, L., Keel, P., Daurio, A. M., Mehra, L. M., & Millender, E. (2022). Ethnoracial status, intersectionality with gender, and psychotherapy utilization, retention, and outcomes. *Journal of Consulting and Clinical Psychology, 90*(10), 837–849. https://doi.org/10.1037/ccp0000726

Kanai, A. (2009). "Karoshi (work to death)" in Japan. *Journal of Business Ethics, 84*, 209–216. www.jstor.org/stable/40294785

Keel, P. K., & Klump, K. L. (2003). Are eating disorders culture-bound syndromes? Implications for conceptualizing their etiology. *Psychological Bulletin, 129*, 747–769. https://doi.org/10.1037/0033-2909.129.5.747

Kessler, R. C., & Bromet, E. J. (2013). The epidemiology of depression across cultures. *Annual Reviews Public Health, 34*, 119–138. https://doi.org/10.1146/annurev-publhealth-031912-114409

Kim, E., & Kang, M. (2018). The effects of client-counselor racial matching on therapeutic outcome. *Asia Pacific Education Review, 19*(1), 103–110. https://doi.org/10.1007/s12564-018-9518-9

Körkel, J. (2015). Controlled drinking as a treatment goal for at-risk drinking and alcohol use disorders: A systematic review. *Sucht: Zeitschrift Für Wissenschaft Und Praxis, 61*(3), 147–174. https://doi.org/10.1024/0939-5911.a000367

Lara-Cinisomo, S., Akinbode, T. D., & Wood, J. (2020). A systematic review of somatic symptoms in women with depression or depressive symptoms: Do race or ethnicity matter? *Journal of Women's Health, 29*(10), 1273–1282. https://doi.org/10.1089/jwh.2019.7975

Lin, E., & Kleinman, A. (1988). Psychopathology and clinical course of schizophrenia: A cross-cultural perspective. *Schizophrenia Bulletin, 14*, 555–567. https://doi.org/10.1093/schbul/14.4.555

Lundin Remnélius, K., & Bölte, S. (2023). Camouflaging in autism: Age effects and cross-cultural validation of the Camouflaging Autistic Traits

Questionnaire (CAT-Q). *Journal of Autism and Developmental Disorders.* https://doi.org/10.1007/s10803-023-05909-8

Matson, J. L., Matheis, M., Burns, C. O., et al. (2017). Examining cross-cultural differences in autism spectrum disorder: A multinational comparison from Greece, Italy, Japan, Poland, and the United States. *European Psychiatry, 42,* 70–76. https://doi.org/10.1016/j.eurpsy.2016.10.007

Ministry of Health, Labour and Welfare. (2017). *White paper on measures to prevent karoshi.* Ministry of Health, Labour and Welfare.

Nguyen, A. J., Haroz, E. E., Mendelson, T., & Bass, J. (2016). Symptom endorsement and sociodemographic correlates of postnatal distress in three low income countries. *Depression Research and Treatment, 2016,* 11. https://doi.org/10.1155/2016/1823836

Page-Gould, E. (2010). The unhealthy racist. In J. Marsh, R. Mendoza-Denton, & J. A. Smith (Eds.), *Are we born racist? New insights from neuroscience and positive psychology* (pp. 41–44). Beacon Press.

Patel, V., Cohen, A., Thara, R., & Gureje, O. (2006). Is the outcome of schizophrenia really better in developing countries? *Brazilian Journal of Psychiatry, 28*(2), 149–152. https://doi.org/10.1590/s1516-44462006000200014

Perry, E., Mandy, W., Hull, L., & Cage, E. (2022). Understanding camouflaging as a response to autism-related stigma: A social identity theory approach. *Journal of Autism and Developmental Disorders, 52,* 800–810. https://doi.org/10.1007/s10803-021-04987-w

Pescosolido, B. A., Martin, J. K., Olafsdottir, S., Long, J. S., Kafadar, K., & Medina, T. R. (2015). The theory of industrial society and cultural schemata: Dows the "cultural myth of stigma" underlie the WHO schizophrenia paradox? *American Journal of Sociology, 121*(3). https://doi.org/10.1086/683225

Presley, S., & Day, S. X. (2019). Counseling dropout, retention, and ethnic/language match for Asian Americans. *Psychological Services, Psychological Services, 16*(3), 491–497. https://doi.org/10.1037/ser0000223

Prina, A. M., Ferri, C. P., Guerra, M., Brayne, C., & Prince, M. (2011). Prevalence of anxiety and its correlates among older adults in Latin America, India and China: Cross-cultural study. *The British Journal of Psychiatry, 199*(6), 485–491. https://doi.org/10.1192/bjp.bp.110.083915

Rodrigues, M. (2017). Do Hispanic girls develop eating disorders? A critical review of the literature. *Hispanic Health Care International, 15*(4), 189–196. https://doi.org/10.1177/1540415317744500

Swift, J. K., Callahan, J. L., Tompkins, K. A., Connor, D. R., & Dunn, R. (2015). A delay-discounting measure of preference for racial/ethnic matching in psychotherapy. *Psychotherapy*, *52*(3), 315–320. https://doi.org/10.1037/pst0000019

Ullah, M., Shah, R., Ayaz, M., Faqir, K., Khan, I., & Khan, M. S. (2015). Identification of drone attacks psychotrauma effects on 10th class students in North Waziristan Agency. *Gomal University Journal of Research*, *31*(1), 111–119.

World Health Organization. (2022). *World mental health report.* www.who.int/publications/i/item/9789240049338

ACTIVITY 6.5
SUBJECTIVE WELL-BEING ACROSS CULTURES

Activity Summary:

Students survey three individuals on their beliefs about subjective well-being (SWB) across cultures regarding the role of life stage, income, and self-esteem. They then answer a series of questions to better understand sources of cultural differences in SWB. [Requires work outside of the classroom.]

Lecture/Discussion Suggestion:

What are some challenges in defining SWB across cultures? Deiner and colleagues (2017) discussed some of the difficulties in defining "happiness" cross-culturally:

- The threshold for being "happy" varies by language. For example, English speakers use the word "happy" in more trivial circumstances than do speakers of many other languages.
- In many languages, "happiness" has more of a meaning of good luck and fortune than well-being.
- In some cultures, there is a concern that too much happiness will elicit negative consequences (good luck followed by bad luck).

An additional challenge in cross-cultural comparisons of SWB is reflecting critical within-nation differences. For example, Rööts-Ausmees and Realo (2016) documented the lower levels of life satisfaction for members of ethnic minority, as compared with majority, groups in the European Social Survey of 29 nations. This lower level of life satisfaction was predicted by perceived discrimination, current unemployment, perceived social support, and subjective health.

Variation:

After surveying others, students can compare quality of life indices across countries using the OECD Life Satisfaction Index: www.oecdbetterlifeindex. org/topics/life-satisfaction/

Writing Application:

Have students survey a larger group of individuals on their beliefs about SWB and write up their findings in an APA formatted research report.

References:

Diener, E., Heintzelman, S. J., Kushlev, K., Tay, L., Wirtz, D., Lutes, L. D., & Oishi, S. (2017). Findings all psychologists should know from the new science on subjective well-being. *Canadian Psychology/Psychologie Canadienne, 58*(2), 87–104. https://doi.org/10.1037/cap0000063

Kööts-Ausmees, L., & Realo, A. (2016). Life satisfaction among ethnic minorities in Europe. *Journal of Cross-Cultural Psychology, 47*(3), 457–478. https://doi.org/10.1177/0022022116628671

ACTIVITY 6.6
CLIMATE CHANGE AND MENTAL HEALTH

Activity Summary:

Students are asked to search a psychology database (such as PsycINFO) to locate a journal article reporting research on climate change and mental health and then to identify variables that could help us to understand this relationship in countries across the globe. [Requires work outside of the classroom.]

Lecture/Discussion Suggestion:

Is climate change skepticism universal or culture-specific? Although climate change skepticism is found all over the world, researchers have identified some predictors of these beliefs. For example, Nartova-Bochaver et al. (2022) recruited participants from Armenia, China, Cuba, Estonia, India, Poland, Russia, Turkey, and Ukraine and surprisingly found a weak, negative correlation between climate change denial and the countries' level of individualism. Predictors of climate denial may vary by culture. For example, Jylhä et al. (2021) reported that in Hong Kong, climate denial was best predicted by acceptance of human dominance over nature and animals, whereas in New Zealand and Sweden, Social Dominance Orientation was the best predictor. The authors suggested that climate change denial in Asian societies may be motivated more by hierarchical attitudes related to nature than to social groups. Beiser-McGrath and Bernauer (2021) cautioned that social desirability bias results in an underreporting of climate skepticism, particularly among the high-income individuals they studied in the U.S. and the conservative political party members they studied in Germany.

Regarding more traditional societies, Rudiak-Gould (2013) argued that climate change beliefs vary with the degree to which members of a culture view the weather as controlled by supernatural figures or as retaliation for moral or immoral behavior. Reflecting on his anthropological fieldwork in the Marshall Islands, Rudiak-Gould stated, "If bad weather is a punishment and good weather a reward, then the climate is under human influence, even if needing the intermediary of a deity" (p. 1709). According to Rudiak-Gould, a culture-specific orientation in Western nations that feeds climate skepticism is belief in a just world. Those who believe in a just world expect that in life people get what they deserve and deserve what they get. Thus, climate skeptics have difficulty accepting the idea of an unjust circumstance in which progress and technology would bring about an "unsustainable, declining world" (p. 1710).

Variation:

Students can pool their findings to develop a model of the direct and indirect pathways through which climate change may affect mental health.

Writing Application:

Have students write a summary of their findings and relate the variable they uncovered to others mentioned in Activity 6.6.

References:

Beiser-McGrath, L., & Bernauer, T. (2021). Current surveys may underestimate climate change skepticism evidence from list experiments in Germany and the USA. *PLoS ONE, 16*(7), 13. https://doi.org/10.1371/journal.pone.0251034

Jylhä, K. M., Tam, K., & Milfont, T. L. (2021). Acceptance of group-based dominance and climate change denial: A cross-cultural study in Hong Kong, New Zealand, and Sweden. *Asian Journal of Social Psychology, 24*(2), 198–207. https://doi.org/10.1111/ajsp.12444

Nartova-Bochaver, S., Donat, M., Kiral Ucar, G., et al. (2022). The role of environmental identity and individualism/collectivism in predicting climate change denial: Evidence from nine countries. *Journal of Environmental Psychology, 84.* https://doi.org/10.1016/j.jenvp.2022.101899

Rudiak-Gould, P. (2013). Cross-cultural insights into climate change skepticism. *Bulletin of the American Meteorological Society, 94*(11), 1707–1713. https://doi.org/10.1175/BAMS-D-12-00129.1

ACTIVITY 6.7
CULTURAL CONCEPTS OF DISTRESS

Activity Summary:

Students use scholarly sources to investigate a cultural concept of distress. Students then use Beardsley's (1994) method of mapping the emic and etic components of that syndrome and explore Draguns' (1973) concept of mental disorders as "exaggeration of the normal." [Requires work outside of the classroom.]

Lecture/Discussion Suggestion:

Could a cultural concept of distress become universal? Kato et al. (2018) suggested that this might be what is happening with *hikikomori*, a syndrome that affects about 1.2% of the Japanese population. These authors (p. 106) cited the Japan Ministry of Health, Labour, and Welfare definition for *hikikomori*, which translates as, "a situation where a person without psychosis is withdrawn into his/her home for more than six months and does not participate in society such as attending school and/or work." This problem primarily affects young men in their 20s and 30s and may be a function of the competitive Japanese education system and the rampant bullying it produces, current employment and economic conditions, as well as cultural norms for protective parenting (Teo et al., 2014). Kato and colleagues (2018) found that *hikikomori* is increasingly prevalent in countries outside of Japan, with cases identified in Hong Kong, Spain, Oman, India, South Korea, and the U.S. These authors attributed this internationalization of *hikikomori* to a growing virtual world in which face-to-face communication is more and more infrequent. There is evidence that cases of *hikikomori* became even more frequent and widespread during the Covid-19 pandemic, particularly for men. An online survey of participants in 45 countries may help to explain this gender difference. Although internet use increased regardless of gender during the pandemic, the risk of developing *hikikomori* was reduced by (non-gaming) social interaction online, an activity in which women may have been more likely than men to have engaged (Gavin & Brosnan, 2022).

Variation:

To use this activity within a single class period, provide groups of students with descriptions of a cultural concept of distress (from the DSM-5 or internet resources) and have them use these descriptions as a basis for completing the activity.

Writing Application:

Have students identify and write a brief description of a cultural concept of distress prevalent in their own culture. Some possibilities for more industrialized cultures include Type A behavior pattern and Problematic Internet Use.

References:

Beardsley, L. M. (1994). Medical diagnosis and treatment across cultures. In W. J. Lonner, & R. S. Malpass (Eds.), *Psychology and culture* (pp. 279–284). Allyn & Bacon.

Draguns, J. (1973). Comparison of psychopathology across cultures: Issues, findings, directions. *Journal of Cross-Cultural Psychology, 4,* 9–47. https://doi.org/10.1177/002202217300400104

Gavin, J., & Brosnan, M. (2022). The relationship between hikikomori risk and internet use during Covid-19 restrictions. *Cyberpsychology, Behavior, and Social Networking.* https://doi.org/10.1089/cyber.2021.0171

Kato, T. A., Kanba, S., & Teo, A. R. (2018). Hikikomori: Experience in Japan and international relevance. *World Psychiatry, 17*(1), 105–106. https://doi.org/10.1002%2Fwps.20497

Teo, A. R., Stufflebam, K. W., & Kato, T. A. (2014). The intersection of culture and solitude: The hikikomori phenomenon in Japan. In R. J. Coplan & J. C. Bowker (Eds.), *The handbook of solitude: Psychological perspectives on social isolation, social withdrawal, and being alone* (pp. 445–460). Wiley-Blackwell.

ACTIVITY 6.8
SELF-HELP AND CULTURAL IDEALS

Activity Summary:

Students visit a library or actual/virtual bookstore to explore the concept of well-being promoted by self-help books in the dominant culture. Questions address such issues as differences in self-help books marketed to males and females, the emphasis on individualist vs. collectivist goals, and the exclusion of diverse audiences for self-help books. [Requires work outside of the classroom.]

Lecture/Discussion Suggestion:

What values are conveyed in self-help books? Rimke (2020, p. 40) documented the "hyper-individualism" that characterizes much of the self-help literature, which simplifies "complex factors, relations, and processes by giving the appearance that the individual alone is responsible for problems and experiences in the world rather than dealing with the effects of the world itself" – a phenomenon she termed "responsibilization." According to Rimke, this minimization of social and structural factors is accompanied by "victim-blaming" in which difficulties are framed as a result of the reader's behavior or lack of behavior (e.g., bad choices, poor habits, failure to take action toward improvement). Thus, rather than boosting self-acceptance and self-efficacy, the end result may be that readers become increasingly self-critical. Riley et al. (2019) observed that the individualistic nature of the self-help industry positions women, who make up the majority of self-help readers, as particularly in need of improvement while often ignoring inequalities structured around gender, race, class, and sexuality.

Variation:

This activity can be modified for use with self-help podcasts, videos, websites, or apps rather than books.

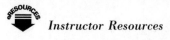

Writing Application:

After they complete this activity, have students write a table of contents for a self-help book that addresses an aspect of well-being relevant to a group that is underrepresented as the target of self-help books.

References:

Riley, S., Evans, A., Anderson, E., & Robson, M. (2019). The gendered nature of self-help. *Feminism & Psychology, 29*(1), 3–18. https://doi.org/10.1177/0959353519826162

Rimke, H. (2020). Self-help, therapeutic industries, and neoliberalism. In D. Nehring, O. J. Madsen, E. Cabanas, C. Mills, & D. Kerrigan (Eds.), *The Routledge handbook of global therapeutic cultures* (pp. 37–50). Routledge.

ACTIVITY 6.9
CLIENT'S AND COUNSELOR'S THOUGHTS

Activity Summary:

Based on Pedersen's (1994) Triad Model, a cross-cultural counseling scenario is presented first without – then with – the thoughts of the counselor and client. Students are then asked to develop a scenario of their own to illustrate misperceptions in a cross-cultural counseling context.

Lecture/Discussion Suggestion:

Does it make sense to try to match clients and counselors based on ethnicity or cultural background? Studies of ethnic or cultural matching have generally found clients are more likely to prefer and trust ethnolinguistically similar counselors (Meyer et al., 2011; Swift et al., 2015; Thompson et al., 2004; Wong et al., 2003) and that ethnolinguistic matching may increase client retention (Ibaraki & Hall, 2014). However, studies are mixed in terms of the effect of matching on therapeutic outcomes (Cabral & Smith, 2011; Gamst et al., 2001; Kim et al., 2005; Smith & Trimble, 2016). Meta-analytic research has indicated that an ethnic match did not have lasting effects on therapy after the initial sessions (Cabral & Smith, 2011). Furthermore, content analysis of client-counselor interactions found no significant differences in emotion-focused communication for clients in matched vs. unmatched conditions (Mujica et al., 2020). Often when ethnolinguistic matching is associated with positive outcomes, it is a weak predictor (e.g., Hung et al., 2023). Other qualities of the counselor (such as credibility and education level) and of the client (such as stage of acculturation) also figure into counselor preferences and therapeutic outcomes. For example, Zane and Ku (2014) found that (in terms of participants' reactions to a recorded statement by a counselor) matching clients and counselors on gender increased some forms of self-disclosure whereas matching on ethnicity had no significant effect on intent to disclose.

Despite the advantages of matching strategies, there are several concerns:

- Ethnicity or culture may not always be the most salient aspect of a client's identity. As Hays (2001) pointed out, determining the aspect(s) of identity most central to client's self-identification is a critical task for cross-cultural counselors. Hays' ADDRESSING model has focused on the overlapping identities associated with Age, Developmental and acquired Disability, Religion, Ethnicity, Social status, Sexual orientation, Indigenous heritage, National origin, and Gender.
- Matching may not always be logistically possible, particularly in the case of counseling with individuals in intercultural relationships or people with multicultural backgrounds. For example, in one survey of 60 substance use disorder treatment centers throughout the U.S., 39% of centers indicated that it was not possible to match a client with a racially similar counselor (Steinfeldt et al., 2020).
- Matching strategies assume that counselors will be familiar with ethnic cultural values and practices, which may not be the case (Smith & Trimble, 2016). Thus, some form of intercultural training for counselors should be required regardless of the counselor's cultural background.
- Sue (1998) also noted that at times research findings supporting ethno-linguistic matching have been used to justify segregation of mental health services and result in treatment disparities.
- Counselors, particularly members of smaller ethnic communities, may have to negotiate multiple relationships with their ethnolinguistically matched clients. (These multiple relationships, while highlighted by APA as an ethical concern, may be beneficial in terms of facilitating help-seeking behavior and establishing trust; Littleford, 2007.)

Variations:

Have students perform the scenarios for each other, first without the client's and counselor's thoughts and then, after a brief discussion of the possible cultural issues involved, have them perform the scenarios a second time with the client's and counselor's thoughts included. Alternatively, you can play a video of a simulated counseling session in class and have the students write a script for the counselor's and client's thoughts.

Writing Application:

Use the above variation, but prior to the discussion of cultural issues have the student complete a two-minute free write in response to the scenario (without the client's and counselor's thoughts) as a way to help students formulate their ideas prior to discussion.

References:

Cabral, R. R., & Smith, T. B. (2011). Racial/ethnic matching of clients and therapists in mental health services: A meta-analytic review of preferences, perceptions, and outcomes. *Journal of Counseling Psychology, 58*(4), 537–554. https://doi.org/10.1037/a0025266

Gamst, G., Dana, R. H., Der-Karabetian, A., & Kramer, T. (2001). Asian American mental health clients: Effect of ethnic match and age on global assessment and visitation. *Journal of Mental Health Counseling, 23,* 57–71.

Hays, P. A. (2001). *Addressing cultural complexities in practice: A framework for clinicians and counselors.* American Psychological Association.

Hung, Y., Linville, D., Janes, E., & Yee, S. (2023). Race matching in predicting relational therapy outcome: A machine learning approach. *International Journal of Systemic Therapy, 34*(2), 83–94. https://doi.org/10.1080/2692398X.2023.2169028

Ibaraki, A. Y., & Hall, G. C. N. (2014). The components of cultural match in psychotherapy. *Journal of Social and Clinical Psychology, 33*(10), 936–953. https://doi.org/10.1521/jscp.2014.33.10.936

Kim, B. S. K., Ng, G. F., & Ahn, A. J. (2005). Effects of client expectation for counseling success, client-counselor worldview match, and client adherence to Asian and European American cultural values on counseling process with Asian Americans. *Journal of Counseling Psychology, 52,* 67–76. https://doi.org/10.1037/0022-0167.52.1.67

Littleford, L. N. (2007). How psychotherapists address hypothetical multiple relationship dilemmas with Asian American clients: A national survey. *Ethics & Behavior, 17*(2), 137–162. https://doi.org/10.1080/10508420701378081

Meyer, O., Zane, N., & Cho, Y. (2011). Understanding the psychological processes of the racial match effect in Asian Americans. *Journal of Counseling Psychology, 58*, 335–345. https://doi.org/10.1037%2Fa0023605

Mujica, C., Alvarez, K., Tendulkar, S., Cruz-Gonzalez, M., & Alegría, M. (2020). Association between patient-provider racial and ethnic concordance and patient-centered communication in outpatient mental health clinics. *Journal of Psychotherapy Integration, 30*(3), 423–439. https://doi.org/10.1037/int0000195

Pedersen, P. (1994). Simulating the client's internal dialogue as a counselor training technique. *Simulation and Gaming, 25*, 40–50. https://doi.org/10.1177/1046878194251005

Smith, T. B., & Trimble, J. E. (2016). Matching clients with therapists on the basis of race or ethnicity: A meta-analysis of clients' level of participation in treatment. In *Foundations of multicultural psychology: Research to inform effective practice* (pp. 115–128). American Psychological Association.

Steinfeldt, J. A., Clay, S. L., & Priester, P. E. (2020). Prevalence and perceived importance of racial matching in the psychotherapeutic dyad: A national survey of addictions treatment clinical practices. *Substance Abuse Treatment, Prevention, and Policy, 15*, 8. https://doi.org/10.1186/s13011-020-00318-x

Sue, S. (1998). In search of cultural competence in psychotherapy and counseling. *American Psychologist, 53*, 440–448. https://doi.org/10.1037/0003-066X.53.4.440

Swift, J. K., Callahan, J. L., Tompkins, K. A., Connor, D. R., & Dunn, R. (2015). A delay-discounting measure of preference for racial/ethnic matching in psychotherapy. *Psychotherapy, 52*(3), 315–320. https://doi.org/10.1037/pst0000019

Thompson, V. L. S., Bazile, A., & Akbar, M. (2004). African Americans' perceptions of psychotherapy and psychotherapists. *Professional Psychology: Research and Practice, 35*, 19–26. https://doi.org/10.1037/0735-7028.35.1.19

Wong, E. C., Kim, B. S. K., Zane, N. W. S., Kim, J. K., & Huang, J. S. (2003). Examining culturally based variables associated with ethnicity: Influences on credibility perceptions of empirically supported interventions. *Cultural Diversity & Ethnic Minority Psychology, 9*, 88–96. https://doi.org/10.1037/1099-9809.9.1.88

Zane, N., & Ku, H. (2014). Effects of ethnic match, gender match, acculturation, cultural identity, and face concern on self-disclosure in counseling for Asian Americans. *Asian American Journal of Psychology, 5*(1), 66–74. https://doi.org/10.1037/a0036078

ACTIVITY 6.10
CULTURE AND PSYCHOTHERAPY

Activity Summary:

Students define therapy and state criteria for determining whether a treatment constitutes a therapy. They then read a brief description of Morita Therapy and respond to questions regarding their reaction to this form of therapy, and the degree to which it meets their criteria for being a therapy.

Lecture/Discussion Suggestions:

How do indigenous healers differ from psychotherapists? Lefley (1994) distinguished between the treatment techniques of indigenous healers and psychotherapists in that the former tend to focus on supernatural or other external causes, immediate precipitants, restoring harmony between forces, and performing rituals or appeasing gods, whereas the latter focus on internal causes and individual patterns of behavior over time. Traditional healers are less likely to differentiate between physical and mental concerns than psychotherapists, although Lefley suggested a trend in that direction in Western medicine as a result of the increase in health management organizations. Despite these differences between healers and psychotherapists, Lefley (1994, p. 179) observed that "Almost all cultures of the world, from tribal units to nation-states, acknowledge an officially sanctioned Western medical system as well as a traditional healing system. They also recognize the types of cases their respective practitioners are trained to serve." Researchers have documented the integration of these two forms of healing throughout the world. For example, Anishnawbe healing practices have been combined with Western therapeutic techniques to treat sexual trauma among indigenous peoples in Canada (Reeves & Stewart, 2014). Green and Colucci (2020) suggested that collaborations between biomedical and traditional practitioners could greatly improve access to mental health care in low- and middle-income nations.

How might psychologists' efforts to provide disaster aid across cultures do more harm than good? Wessells (2009) discussed ways that well-meaning psychologists who "parachute in" to aid in disaster situations may actually do more harm than good:

- Scare resources may go toward sustaining parachuters rather than toward the affected individuals or experienced humanitarian aid workers.
- Parachuters may violate cultural or social norms (such as drinking or inappropriate dress).

- The presence of parachuters may threaten security or shift the balance of power.
- By providing short-term care without follow-up available, parachuters raise expectations and may leave people feeling abandoned.
- Most parachuters are unprepared to coordinate their efforts with a broader humanitarian aid system, which may result in assessment fatigue and undermine trust among the affected individuals.
- Counseling methods focusing on individual self-disclosure and processing feelings associated with trauma are inappropriate – and possibly ineffective – in many cultural contexts.
- Informed consent may not be possible in emergencies due to language and communication issues and lack of autonomy in conflict situations, particularly in regard to interactions with outsiders.
- Unintentional stigmatization of specific populations may occur (for example, despite the need to assist child soldiers, programs targeting this group specifically may stigmatize them in the eyes of their community and result in a lack of support for other war-affected children).
- Parachuters often focus on an individual, clinical approach whereas experienced emergency practitioners understand the need for holistic interventions to address the interacting needs of families, communities, and societies.
- Parachuters tend to emphasize deficits (e.g., mental illness, post-traumatic stress, social isolation) which creates an often demeaning stereotype of the helpless victim and neglects sources of resilience (e.g., existing supports, coping strategies).
- Parachuters may shift residents toward dependence on outside – and temporary – sources of support rather than strengthening long-existing support systems.
- Parachuters often have inadequate training with little supervision or follow-up and tend to implement Western psychological approaches when indigenous healing practices may be more culturally appropriate and effective.
- A focus on crisis intervention shifts attention and resources away from disaster risk reduction and emergency preparation efforts.

Writing Application:

Have students investigate a traditional healing practice, such as *santeria* or *ayurveda*. In a brief essay, have them describe the treatment, its cultural underpinnings, and then discuss why they believe that the treatment is – or is not – a form of psychotherapy.

References:

Green, B., & Colucci, E. (2020). Traditional healers' and biomedical practitioners' perceptions of collaborative mental healthcare in low- and middle-income countries: A systematic review. *Transcultural Psychiatry, 57*(1), 94–107. https://doi.org/10.1177/13634615198943

Lefley, H. P. (1994). Mental health treatment and service delivery in cross-cultural perspective. In L. L. Adler, & U. P. Gielen (Eds.), *Cross-cultural topics in psychology* (pp. 179–199). Praeger.

Reeves, A., & Stewart, S. L. (2014). Exploring the integration of indigenous healing and Western psychotherapy for sexual trauma survivors who use mental health services at Anishnawbe Health Toronto. *Canadian Journal of Counselling and Psychotherapy, 49*(1). https://cjc-rcc.ucalgary.ca/article/view/61008

Wessells, M. G. (2009). Do no harm: Toward contextually appropriate psychosocial support in international emergencies. *American Psychologist, 64*(8), 842–854. https://doi.org/10.1037/0003-066X.64.8.842

Culture and Social Behavior

DOI: 10.4324/9781003356820-10   *165*

ACTIVITY 7.1
VIOLATING CULTURAL NORMS

Activity Summary:

The strength of even subtle cultural norms can be easily demonstrated through their violation. Questions guide students first in identifying cultural norms, and then in observing reactions to the violation of these norms. A final question explores the concept of tightness-looseness as it relates to the nature of social norms across cultures. [Requires work outside of the classroom.]

Lecture/Discussion Suggestion:

How did tightness-looseness affect behavior during the Covid-19 pandemic? Gelfand et al. (2021) investigated the relationship between cultural tightness-looseness and per capita Covid-related cases and deaths in 57 countries. Their measure of tightness-looseness assessed the strength of norms within a nation and the level of tolerance for people who violate norms. Stronger norms and lower tolerance indicated greater tightness (vs. looseness). Although there were some exceptions to this relationship between tightness-looseness and Covid, "the results indicated that, compared with nations with high levels of cultural tightness, nations with high levels of cultural looseness are estimated to have had 4.99 times the number of cases (7132 per million *vs* 1428 per million, respectively) and 8.71 times the number of deaths (183 per million *vs* 21 per million, respectively)" (Gelfand et al., 2021, p. e135). In addition, these results held when the authors controlled for various measures of under-reporting, wealth, inequality, population density, migration, government efficiency, collectivism, power distance, political authoritarianism, median age, non-pharmaceutical government interventions, spatial interdependence, climate, relational mobility, mandated vaccination, population size, and previous experience with SARS viruses. Gelfand and colleagues suggested that strong social norms around such behaviors as mask-wearing and social distancing, as well as greater fear of contracting Covid-19, may have contributed to the lower numbers of cases and deaths in tight vs. loose countries.

Studies by Talhelm and colleagues have linked rice cultivation to cultural tightness and looseness. Talhelm et al. (2022) found significantly fewer Covid-related deaths in rice-, as opposed to wheat-, farming prefectures within China. The authors reported that rice-farming nations have tighter social norms and lower social mobility, which are factors associated with better Covid outcomes.

Variation:

Have students complete this activity by violating a norm about gender-specific behavior. Discussion can address the issue of whether there are different levels of uncertainty avoidance for norms concerning male as opposed to female behavior.

Writing Application:

Ask students to write three questions for small group discussion based on their experiences with this activity.

References:

Gelfand, M. J., Jackson, J. C., Pan, X., Nau, D., Pieper, D., Denison, E., Dagher, M., Van Lange, P. A. M., Chiu, C., & Wang, M. (2021). The relationship between cultural tightness–looseness and COVID-19 cases and deaths: A global analysis. *The Lancet Planetary Health*, 5(3), e135–e144. https://doi.org/10.1016/S2542-5196(20)30301-6

Talhelm, T., Lee, C.-S., English, A. S., & Wang, S. (2022). How rice fights pandemics: Nature–crop–human interactions shaped COVID-19 outcomes. *Personality and Social Psychology Bulletin*. https://doi.org/10.1177/01461672221107209

ACTIVITY 7.2
SHOPPING FOR CULTURAL VALUES

Activity Summary:

Students are guided through a trip to their local supermarket to explore cultural values. They are asked to observe the types of products that are most plentiful, claims used to promote products, factors distinguishing less from more expensive products, the sizes in which items are available, the packaging of animal products, the distribution of items with different ethnic origins throughout the store, and the behavior of shoppers given the time of day. Students shopping in an American supermarket, for example, would likely see claims indicating the value of new as opposed to established items, many products available for people living alone (such as single-serving meals), products promoted as taking little time to prepare, meats and poultry labeled and packaged such that they have little resemblance to their original animal form, and often an "international" section which houses products from some ethnic groups while the products of other groups are shelved by product type. Follow-up questions allow observations such as these to be explored in terms of cultural values. [Requires work outside of the classroom.]

For a student-friendly discussion of Schwartz' Theory of Basic Values, see his article in the *Online Readings in Psychology and Culture* at https:// scholarworks.gvsu.edu/orpc

Lecture/Discussion Suggestions:

How do marketing strategies differ across cultures? Culture influences how consumers process marketing appeals and the emotions the messages elicit. For example, it is well known that advertisers must be aware of the connotations of specific symbols, colors, and numbers across cultures (de Mooij, 2021). Marketing research has also involved more complex analyses of cultural variability, often framed in terms of Hofstede's (2005) dimensions of culture (please see Activity 7.7 for detailed definitions of these dimensions). Here are some examples:

- Research comparing marketing strategies in collectivist and individualist societies has found a greater reliance on peer endorsements of products in the former than in the latter (Shavitt et al., 2019).
- Direct, persuasive communication is more common in individualist societies. These appeals focus on factual information and distinguishing products from the competition through scientific or logical reasoning. In contrast, advertisements focusing on creating an overall mood (often by associating a celebrity with the product) tend to be favored in collectivist societies (de Mooij, 2021; Pham, 2022).
- In countries with high Power Distance, consumers are more likely to make judgments about the quality of a product based on its price (Shavitt et al., 2019). High Power Distance is also associated with lower interest in DIY products, such as those marketed by IKEA, due to the expectation that others should provide assembly services (de Mooij, 2021).
- Hartati et al. (2021) suggested that the combined dimensions of Masculinity/Femininity and Uncertainty Avoidance could be used to explain car marketing strategies across cultures. They reported, for example, that in line with low uncertainty avoidance and high femininity, advertisements from the Netherlands emphasized high-value and eco- nomical cars, whereas those from the Arab world, consistent with high

Masculinity and high Uncertainty Avoidance, emphasized comfort, fastness, design, and excitement (Hartati et al., 2021).

• Shavitt et al. (2019) tied marketing appeals to Triandis and colleagues' elaboration of the Individualism/Collectivism dimension (Singelis et al., 1995). In this model, Vertical Collectivism (VC) refers to collectivist societies where there is an acceptance of inequality. Horizontal Collectivism (HC) refers to collectivist societies where equality is stressed. Correspondingly, Vertical Individualism (VI) refers to individualist societies where there is an acceptance of inequality and Horizontal Individualism (HI) refers to individualist societies with an emphasis on equality. According to Shavitt et al., VC marketing focuses on traditional values, VI on self-enhancement, HC on self-transcendence, such as supporting humanitarian values, and HI on openness to new experiences.

Variation:

Have students answer the questions in this activity through a visit to a grocery store of an unfamiliar culture. For a more in-depth project, please refer to an exercise by Kluver (1998), which involves developing an ethnographic account of a grocery store setting.

Writing Application:

Instruct students to write an advertisement for a product of their choice that targets the values of a specific culture. The advertisement need not make these values explicit. For example, depending on the culture you might emphasize that a product is new and improved or traditional and old fashioned.

References:

de Mooij, M. K. (2021). *Global marketing and advertising: Understanding cultural paradoxes* (6th ed.). Sage.

Hartati, R., Panah, E., & Matsom, H. (2021). A critical discourse analysis of the use of metaphor in online car advertisements. *SALTeL Journal (Southeast Asia Language Teaching and Learning)*, 4(2). http://dx.doi.org/10.35307/saltel.v4i2.77

Hofstede, G. H. (2005). *Cultures and organizations: Software of the mind.* McGraw-Hill.

Kluver, R. (1998). Grocery store ethnography. In T. M. Singelis (Eds.), *Teaching about culture, ethnicity, & diversity: Exercises and planned activities* (pp. 23–28). Sage.

Pham, T. (2022). Individualism and collectivism in advertising – An overview. *Journal of English Language Teaching and Applied Linguistics, 4*(1), 30–36. https://doi.org/10.32996/jeltal.2022.4.1.3

Shavitt, S., Cho, H., & Barnes, A. J. (2019). Culture and consumer behavior. In D. Cohen & S. Kitayama (Eds.), *Handbook of cultural psychology* (pp. 678–698). The Guilford Press.

Singelis, T. M., Triandis, H. C., Bhawuk, D. P. S., & Gelfand, M. J. (1995). Horizontal and vertical dimensions of individualism and collectivism: A theoretical and measurement refinement. *Cross-Cultural Research, 29*(3), 240–275. https://doi.org/10.1177/1069397195 02900302

ACTIVITY 7.3
CULTURE AND MORAL REASONING

Activity Summary:

Students respond to questions about the "trolley problem" to learn about emic and etic aspects of moral reasoning. The Thinking Further question asks students to consider why moral identity and moral behavior have been found to be more closely linked in Western than in Eastern cultures. (Jia and Krettenauer, 2017, suggested that for people in Western cultures moral identity is more individually oriented, whereas for people in Eastern cultures, moral identity tends to be societally oriented and thus more context-driven).

Lecture/Discussion Suggestion:

How does culture shape moral reasoning around vegetarianism? Although there are people all over the world who choose vegetarianism for moral reasons, those reasons have been found to vary with culture. For example, Ruby et al. (2013) reported the results of two studies on this topic, which compared vegetarians and omnivores from India and North America. The first study found that Euro-American vegetarians differed from their omnivore peers in their strength of concern about the impact of their food choices on the environment and animal welfare, whereas Indian vegetarians and omnivores did not differ significantly on these concerns. The second study found that Indian vegetarians differed from their omnivore peers in their strength of the belief that eating meat is polluting and in their endorsement of the conservative values of purity and respect for authority and tradition, values which did not distinguish between Euro-Canadian and Euro-American vegetarians and their omnivore peers.

Variation/Writing Application:

After they have completed this activity, have students discuss or write about the cross-cultural applicability of other moral reasoning scenarios. For example, they may be familiar with Kohlberg's Heinz dilemma, which involves a man who considers stealing a drug he cannot afford to save his dying wife. Much has been written about the need to broaden the criteria for high-level moral reasoning in response to this scenario, given cultural variability in communitarian values and religious concerns (e.g., Miller et al., 2019).

References:

Jia, F., & Krettenauer, T. (2017). Recognizing moral identity as a cultural construct. *Frontiers in Psychology, 8,* 412. https://doi.org/10.3389/fpsyg.2017.00412

Miller, J. G., Wice, M., & Goyal, N. (2019). Cultural psychology of moral development. In D. Cohen & S. Kitayama (Eds.), *Handbook of cultural psychology* (2nd ed., pp. 424–446). The Guilford Press.

Ruby, M. B., Heine, S. J., Kamble, S., Cheng, T. K., & Waddar, M. (2013). Compassion and contamination: Cultural differences in vegetarianism. *Appetite, 71,* 340–348. https://doi.org/10.1016/j.appet.2013.09.004

ACTIVITY 7.4
BARE BRANCHES

Activity Summary:

Students read about the significant gender imbalance in China and India and envision a hypothetical society that results from a disproportional number of men.

Lecture/Discussion Suggestion:

How did China's one-child policy affect family dynamics? China's one-child policy (1979–2016) created what has been called the 4-2-1 family configuration, in that a single child receives the attention of two parents and four grandparents. In addition to the attention, material goods, and opportunities that benefit these children, there is also an unprecedented level of pressure, parental expectations (Li et al., 2020), and concern about ensuring the care of parents and grandparents in old age (Huo et al., 2021). However, empirical studies in China comparing only children and peers with siblings have found few distinctions in terms of physical health, suicidal ideation (Hesketh et al., 2003), loneliness (Lin et al., 2021), or resilience (Morgan et al., 2020).

Variation/Writing Application:

This activity could be completed in small groups which then report back to the class. Alternatively, each student or small group could be responsible for considering and writing a report on the implications of gender imbalance for a specific domain (e.g., crime, education, status of women).

References:

Hesketh, T., Qu, J. D., & Tomkins, A. (2003). Health effects of family size: Cross-sectional survey in Chinese adolescents. *Archives of Disease in Childhood, 88,* 467–471. https://doi.org/10.1136/adc.88.6.467

Huo, C., Xiao, G., & Chen, L. (2021). The crowding-out effect of elderly support expenditure on household consumption from the perspective of population aging: Evidence from China. *Frontiers of Business Research in China, 15*(5). https://doi.org/10.1186/s11782-021-00099-5

Li, L., Shi, J., Wu, D., & Li, H. (2020). Only child, parental educational expectation, self-expectation and science literacy in Zhuang adolescents in China: A serial mediation model. *Children and Youth Services Review, 115.* https://doi.org/10.1016/j.childyouth.2020.105084

Lin, S., Falbo, T., Qu, W., Wang, Y., & Feng, X. (2021). Chinese only children and loneliness: Stereotypes and realities. *American Journal of Orthopsychiatry, 91*(4), 531–544. https://doi.org/10.1037/ort0000554

Morgan, T., Yang, S., Liu, B., & Cao, Y. (2020). A comparison of psychological resilience and related factors in Chinese firstborn and only children. *Asian Journal of Psychiatry*, *53*, 6. https://doi.org/10.1016/j.ajp.2020.102360

ACTIVITY 7.5
AGGRESSION ACROSS CULTURES: A QUIZ

Activity Summary:

A self-administered quiz encourages students to consider major research questions in the area of culture and aggressive behavior.

Answers to Activity 7.5:

1. FALSE. According to Fry (2017, p. 88), the vast majority of human conflicts are dealt with nonviolently, such as "through withdrawal of one or both opponents, toleration of a situation, discussion of the issues, reprimands, withdrawal of support, negotiation of agreements, payment of compensation, third-party processes such as mediation or adjudication, sulking, apologizing, forgiving, reconciling, and so forth."
2. TRUE. Fry (2017) stated that across cultures, male aggression tends to be more frequent and more damaging than female aggression. For example, in one study of 63 low- and middle-income nations, adolescent males were more than twice as likely as females to report having engaged in physical fighting over the previous year (Nivette et al., 2019). Interestingly these authors reported that sex differences in physical aggression decrease as societal gender inequality increases. Other studies suggest that whereas there is little difference between males and females in the frequency of verbal aggression, females are more likely than males to use indirect forms of aggression, such as cyberbullying or excluding someone from a group. Björkqvist (2018) observed that indirect aggression requires a level of social intelligence that girls may be more likely than boys to develop, particularly in adolescence.
3. FALSE. Although some previous findings of a link between violent media exposure and aggression failed to replicate with Latinx samples (a finding attributed to greater family support), a large study with data from diverse Latinx communities in Brazil, Mexico, and Southwest Texas U.S.

reported media exposure-to-aggression effect sizes comparable to those from previous studies with samples from other ethnicities and countries (Miles-Novelo et al., 2022). As in previous studies, additional risk factors for aggression were parental abuse and neighborhood violence.

4. FALSE. Light and Miller (2018) analyzed 24 years' worth of multiple criminological sources from all 50 states in the U.S. and Washington D.C. They concluded that – at least in the U.S. – the relationship between undocumented immigration and violent crime is generally negative. Furthermore, the authors investigated, but did not find evidence for, decreased reporting as an explanation for lower rates of violent crime committed by undocumented immigrants. In terms of victimization, both documented and undocumented immigrants in the U.S. are equally targeted (Caraballo & Topalli, 2023), though research with undocumented Latina immigrants found they were significantly less likely than their documented counterparts to seek help, such as medical care for an injury resulting from victimization (Zadnik et al., 2016).

5. TRUE. Douglas Fry (2017) pointed out that one of the most consistent findings in research on aggression across cultures is the correlation between aggression and social organization, with warfare more common in complex and hierarchical social systems as opposed to, for example, small-scale bands or tribal societies. Ferraro and Andreatta (2018) explained that warfare is more likely when it can be coordinated and financed by a centralized government, when food surpluses can be accumulated, when motivated by control of territorial boundaries, and when there are few familial ties between groups. All of these conditions are more likely in larger- than in smaller-scale societies.

6. FALSE. Ersan et al. (2020) identified cultural differences in the reports of drivers from five countries (Estonia, Greece, Kosovo, Russia, and Turkey) about their own and others' aggressive behaviors. For example, Russian drivers expressed significantly greater hostile aggression toward other drivers, were the only sample that reported more aggression on their part than that of the other driver, and were more likely to report physically attacking or threatening the other driver.

7. TRUE. Silva (2022) analyzed available data from mass shooting incidents worldwide that occurred between 1998 and 2019. Silva found that workplace locations were more likely to be a predictor of shootings in the U.S. as compared with other "developed" or "developing" nations (as categorized by the United Nations). The author indicated that employment/financial motives were more common for U.S. mass shooters than for those in other nations.

8. TRUE. Nearly 2000 studies across cultures have confirmed that parental rejection is positively correlated with aggression in children (Rohner et al., 2005). For example, children's perceptions of parental rejection in families from China, Colombia, Italy, Jordan, Kenya, the Philippines, Sweden, Thailand, and the United States predicted later internalizing (e.g., fear and anxiety), and externalizing (e.g., getting into fights) behavior problems (Rothenberg et al., 2022).

9. FALSE. In fact, the reverse is true. People from the southern United States are more likely than people from the northern United States to react to affronts to their dignity with violent behavior. According to Nisbett (1996), this "culture of honor" may stem from the herding heritage of the ethnic groups that settled in this region. Herding involves a livelihood dependent upon animals that could easily be stolen by others. Strong displays of aggression in response to any threat may have been used to protect one's property and deter any future threat. Behaviors targeting one's reputation and social status are particularly damaging to one's self-worth in honor cultures (Severance et al., 2013). Honor cultures have been identified in parts of Mediterranean Europe, North Africa, the Middle East, Latin America, and South Asia as well as the southern United States (Smith et al., 2013; Uskul & Cross, 2020). Although alternative explanations for higher rates of homicides in honor cultures have been posed focusing on greater economic inequality in those regions (Bond & Tedeschi, 2001), a measure of culture of honor was found to be a better predictor of homicide rates in a study of 49 countries than was a measure of economic inequality (Altheimer, 2013).

10. TRUE. Several different video games have been developed with the goal of reducing intimate partner and peer violence. For example, *Tsiunas* is a videogame to raise awareness about gender-based violence among adolescents in Colombia (Gonzalez et al., 2022). The game presents real-life conflicts in a fictional world called "New Town." Only by selecting options with non-sexist and anti-violence attitudes can the player advance. Pre-post surveys indicated a significant reduction in tolerance for gender-based violence.

Lecture/Discussion Suggestion:

What are the predictors of intimate partner violence across cultures? Ebbeler et al. (2017) investigated the frequency and extent of physical violence between heterosexual married partners in 34 countries using data gathered as part of a larger study of marital satisfaction. They found that intimate partner violence against women was associated with greater poverty, power distance and gender inequality in decision-making as well as lower individualism. However, the rate of aggression perpetrated by women against men was higher in countries with greater gender equality than in countries with low gender equality. Higher gender equality within the marriage predicted less aggression in general and a smaller sex difference in perpetrating aggression.

Kemp (2001) has written about the challenges of making cross-cultural comparisons of aggressive behavior. He noted that although most cultures agree that aggressive behavior is undesirable, there is little agreement across cultures about what constitutes an aggressive act. Ebbeler and colleagues (2017) dealt with this issue by asking participants about the frequency of specific aggressive behaviors rather than the presence or absence of domestic violence [students might be interested in discussing how the study of domestic violence relates to the issue of cultural relativism vs. universal human rights – see Activity 1.8].

Differences in domestic violence laws also contribute to the difficulty of investigating domestic violence across cultures. For example, in February 2017 the Russian government decriminalized certain forms of domestic violence such that violence committed against family members has been made an administrative offense. Only repeated instances of battery are now punishable by criminal law. If prosecuted, the perpetrators of domestic violence may be sentenced to only a small fine, which in some cases is required to be paid by the victims of abuse (Isajanyan, 2017).

Finally, rates of domestic violence may be masked by other outcomes. Devries and colleagues (2011) found that in Brazil, Ethiopia, Japan, Namibia, Peru, Samoa, Serbia, Thailand, and Tanzania, a primary predictor of suicidal behavior among women was domestic violence.

Variation:

This quiz can be used by students to collect data from their peers. They can then summarize the results to uncover common misperceptions about aggressive behavior.

Writing Application:

Ask students to imagine that they are preparing to conduct cross-cultural research on aggressive behavior. In a brief essay have them develop a definition of aggressive behavior that would be cross-culturally applicable. (Students may conclude that the use of emic definitions of aggressive behavior may be preferable to striving for a cross-culturally equivalent definition.)

References:

Altheimer, I. (2013). Cultural processes and homicide across nations. *International Journal of Offender Therapy and Comparative Criminology*, *57*(7), 842–863. https://doi.org/10.1177/0306624X12438756

Björkqvist, K. (2018). Gender differences in aggression. *Current Opinion in Psychology*, *19*, 9–42. https://doi.org/10.1016/j.copsyc.2017.03.030

Bond, M. H., & Tedeschi, J. T. (2001). Polishing the jade: A modest proposal for improving the study of social psychology across cultures. In D. Matsumoto (Ed.), *The handbook of culture and psychology* (pp. 309–324). Oxford University Press.

Caraballo, K., & Topalli, V. (2023). "Walking ATMs": Street criminals' perception and targeting of undocumented immigrants. *Justice Quarterly*, *40*(1), 75–105. http://dx.doi.org/10.1080/07418825.2021.2005819

Devries, K., Watts, C., Yoshihama, M., et al. (2011). Violence against women is strongly associated with suicide attempts: Evidence from the WHO multi-country study on women's health and domestic violence against women. *Social Science & Medicine*, *73*(1), 79–86. https://doi.org/10.1016/j.socscimed.2011.05.006

Ebbeler, C., Grau, I., & Banse, R. (2017). Cultural and individual factors determine physical aggression between married partners: Evidence from 34 countries. *Journal of Cross-Cultural Psychology*, *48*(7), 1098–1118. https://doi.org/10.1177/0022022117719497

Ersan, Ö., Üzümcüoğlu, Y., Azık, D., et al. (2020). Cross-cultural differences in driver aggression, aberrant, and positive driver behaviors. *Transportation Research Part F: Traffic Psychology and Behaviour*, *71*, 88–97. https://doi.org/10.1016/j.trf.2020.03.020

Ferraro, G., & Andreatta, S. (2018). *Cultural anthropology: An applied perspective* (11th ed.). Cengage.

Fry, D. P. (2017). Cross-cultural differences in aggression. In P. Sturmey (Ed.), *The Wiley handbook of violence and aggression*, Vol. 1. (pp. 81–92). Wiley.

Gonzalez, C., Mera-Gaona, M., Tobar, H., Pabón, A., & Muñoz, N. (2022). TSIUNAS: A videogame for preventing gender-based violence. *Games Health Journal*, *11*(2), 117–131. https://doi.org/10.1089/g4h.2021.0091

Isajanyan, N. (2017). *Russian Federation: Decriminalization of domestic violence*. The Law Library of Congress, Global Legal Research Center.

Kemp, G. (2001). Definitions of international aggression: Lessons for cross-cultural research. In M. J. Ramirez & D. S. Richardson, *Cross-cultural approaches to research on aggression and reconciliation* (pp. 51–58). Nova Science.

Light, M. T., & Miller, T. Y. (2018). Does undocumented immigration increase violent crime? *Criminology, 56*(2), 370–401. https://doi.org/10.1111%2F1745-9125.12175

Miles-Novelo, A., Groves, C. L., Anderson, K. B., et al. (2022). Further tests of the media violence–aggression link: Replication and extension of the 7 nations project with multiple Latinx samples. *Psychology of Popular Media, 11*(4), 435–442. https://doi.org/10.1037/ppm0000428

Nisbett, R. E. (1996). *Culture of honor: The psychology of violence in the South*. Westview.

Nivette, A., Sutherland, A., Eisner, M., & Murray, J. (2019). Sex differences in adolescent physical aggression: Evidence from sixty-three low-and middle-income countries. *Aggressive Behavior, 45*(1), 82–92. https://doi.org/10.1002/ab.21799

Rohner, R. P., Khaleque, A., & Cournoyer, D. E. (2005). Parental acceptance-rejection: Theory, methods, cross-cultural evidence, and implications. *Ethos, 33*, 299–334. https://doi.org/10.1525/eth.2005.33.3.299

Rothenberg, W. A., Ali, S., Rohner, R. P., et al. (2022). Effects of parental acceptance-rejection on children's internalizing and externalizing behaviors: A longitudinal, multicultural study. *Journal of Child and Family Studies, 31*(1), 29–47. https://doi.org/10.1007/s10826-021-02072-5

Severance, L., Bui-Wrzosinska, L., Gelfand, M. J., et al. (2013). The psychological structure of aggression across cultures. *Journal of Organizational Behavior, 34*(6), 835–865. https://doi.org/10.1002/job.1873

Silva, J. R. (2022). Global mass shootings: Comparing the United States against developed and developing countries. *International Journal of Comparative and Applied Criminal Justice.* https://doi.org/10.1080/01924036.2022.2052126

Smith, P. B., Fischer, R., Vignoles, V. L., & Bond, M. H. (2013). *Understanding social psychology across cultures: Engaging with others in a changing world* (2nd ed.). Sage.

Uskul, A. K., & Cross, S. E. (2020). Socio-ecological roots of cultures of honor. *Current Opinion in Psychology, 32*, 177–180. https://doi.org/10.1016/j.copsyc.2019.11.001

Zadnik, E., Sabina, C., & Cuevas, C. A. (2016). Violence against Latinas: The effects of undocumented status on rates of victimization and help-seeking. *Journal of Interpersonal Violence, 31*(6), 1141–1153. https://doi.org/10.1177/0886260514564062

ACTIVITY 7.6
CONFLICT COMMUNICATION STYLE

Activity Summary:

This self-administered, self-scored Conflict Communication Scale (Goldstein, 1999) provides students with a profile of their response to conflict situations on five dimensions that vary with culture: Confrontation, Emotional Expression, Public/Private Behavior, Self-Disclosure, and Conflict Approach/Avoidance. Follow-up questions link conflict communication style with the concept of high- and low-context cultures.

Lecture/Discussion Suggestion:

What are some indigenous methods of resolving disputes? One indigenous form of conflict resolution is Ho'oponopono, a traditional Hawaiian conflict resolution practice. Ho'oponopono means "to set right" and involves family members as well as the ancestors and 'aumakua (family gods). It may go on for hours or days until the process is complete. It first focuses on "untangling" the emotions each person is having in response to the problem and peeling through the layers of the problem until all of the concerns have been identified. The next stage involves seeking forgiveness. This is followed by working to unbind each person from the problem and then reunite the family as a group. For a detailed description, see Hurdle (2002).

Variation:

More advanced students might administer this scale to others, if possible analyzing the data for cultural or gender differences. As explained in Activity 7.6, people from low-context cultures tend to have higher levels of confrontation, public disputing behavior, self-disclosure, emotional expression, and tend to approach rather than avoid conflict as compared with members of high-context cultures. Among low-context culture individuals, females tend to have higher levels of emotional expression and self-disclosure than males.

Writing Application:

Have students write an account of a dispute they witnessed or experienced and then analyze the dispute based on the five Conflict Communication Scale dimensions.

References:

Goldstein, S. B. (1999). Construction and validation of a Conflict Communication Scale. *Journal of Applied Social Psychology, 29*(9), 1803–1832. https://doi.org/10.1111/j.1559-1816.1999.tb00153.x

Hurdle, D. E. (2002). Native Hawaiian traditional healing: Culturally based interventions for social work practice. *Social Work, 47*(2), 183–192. https://doi.org/10.1093/sw/47.2.183

ACTIVITY 7.7
WORK-RELATED VALUES

Activity Summary:

Students analyze a work setting of their choice using Hofstede's (1980, 2001) cultural dimensions as a framework.

Lecture/Discussion Suggestion:

What determines the importance people place on work? Early cross-cultural research on work centrality, the importance of work in one's life, by the Meaning of Working International Research Team (MOW 1987) found Japan to be the top scorer followed by (then) Yugoslavia, Israel, the United States, Belgium, the Netherlands, Germany, and Britain.

Researchers also explored cultural variation in work centrality based on the responses of employees from 45 nations to the World Values Survey. Lu and colleagues (2016) investigated the *relative* centrality of work (RCW) in that they measured the importance of work in comparison with other important aspects of life, including friends, leisure, politics, religion, and family. They found that RCW was best predicted by the employee's belief in "work as good" (or "beneficial to the individual's personal development and to societal progress," p. 280), particularly in countries where Self-Directedness (self-determination and independence) and Civility (tolerance and benevolence toward others) were stressed. This held for both male and female workers.

A follow-up study (Lu et al., 2019) with data from 33 nations investigated the relationship between RCW and life satisfaction. These authors reported that work centrality is associated with poorer life satisfaction when other major life domains (friends, leisure, politics, religion, and family) are neglected.

However, the strength of this relationship is reduced when the job itself is interesting, challenging, and provides an opportunity to use one's skills (*job complexity* – an individual-level variable), and in nations where workplace performance in general is valued and rewarded (*performance orientation* – a culture-level variable).

Students can use the MOW technique to measure their own work centrality. Ask them to divide a total of 100 points among five major domains (work, leisure, community, religion, and family) in their lives, based on their relative importance.

Variations:

Have students view a popular movie or a documentary about a workplace as the basis for applying the work-related values described in Activity 7.7.

Students can also make country comparisons and view maps of Hofstede's dimensions at: www.hofstede-insights.com/product/compare-countries/

Writing Application:

Have students write a brief essay describing their ideal workplace in terms of the dimensions listed in Activity 7.7.

References:

Hofstede, G. (1980). *Culture's consequences: International differences in work-related values*. Sage.

Hofstede, G. (2001). *Culture's consequences: Comparing values, behaviors, and organizations across nations* (2nd ed.). Sage.

Lu, Q., Huang, X., & Bond, M. H. (2016). Culture and the working life: Predicting the relative centrality of work across life domains for employed persons. *Journal of Cross-Cultural Psychology, 47*(2), 277–293. https://doi.org/10.1177/0022022115615235

Lu, Q., Huang, X., Bond, M. H., & Xu, E. H. (2019). Committing to work at the expense of other life pursuits: The consequence of individuals' relative centrality of work across job types and nations differing in performance orientation. *Journal of Cross-Cultural Psychology, 50*(7), 848–869. https://doi.org/10.1177/0022022119865614

MOW-International Research Team. (1987). *The meaning of work: an international view*. Academic Press.

ACTIVITY 7.8
CULTURAL INFLUENCES ON LEADERSHIP

Activity Summary:

To assist students in understanding how leadership styles vary across cultures, students are asked to rate qualities of a good leader. Next, a different cultural context is described, and the students are again asked to determine the ideal leader for that context. It is expected that students will shift their preference for leadership style with the shift in culture. Follow-up questions help students link specific leadership and cultural attributes.

Lecture/Discussion Suggestion:

What themes have emerged from the study of leadership in Africa? Fourie et al. (2017) reviewed 60 years of research on leadership in various African nations (from 1950–2009). They concluded that:

- Scholarship on leadership in Africa is now more likely to be written by scholars from Africa than by scholars from other countries. Yet, a disproportionately large number of articles continue to originate from outside of Africa.
- Within Africa a disproportionately large number of articles focus on the nation of South Africa (likely due to a more developed research infrastructure and greater access to journals, and incentives for publishing peer-reviewed research). Nearly one-third of leadership research in Africa was produced by South Africa, Egypt, and Nigeria.
- There has been a dramatic increase in publications on leadership (particularly on gender and leadership) by female authors. Fourie and colleagues found no gender and leadership articles during the 60-year period produced by male authors.
- Legitimacy is a central theme in the scholarship on leadership, with a specific focus on the role of colonial forces in illegitimate forms of political leadership. Fourie and colleagues stated, for example, that whereas pre-colonial Somalia had a cooperative social structure, based on the household, shared religion, and kinship, Somali chieftainship was created by colonialists, and resulted in leaders who derived their power from the resources and coercive power of the Colonialists.

- An additional theme of leadership scholarship in Africa focuses on attempts to identify forms of leadership based on traditional African religions, ethnic identity, and values. For example, there have been a large number of publications addressing the role of *ubuntu* in leadership behavior (translated from Zulu as compassion and humanity).

To understand the perspective of future leaders in Africa, Lerutla and Steyn (2021) surveyed participants in the Young African Leaders Initiative, a University of South Africa leadership development program. This study identified the following elements of African business leadership: Leadership was viewed as:

> unique to leaders on the continent (Afrocentric), as an act of service to the community (Ubuntu), operating in challenging and resource-deprived environments (because of the legacy of colonialism) and providing hope for creating a better future. African business leadership is further seen as being dominated by those in positions of (political) authority, who engage in entrepreneurial activities, and yet as still requiring development because many leaders are corrupt (brokenness), which seems to be legitimised by post-colonial sentiments (Afrocentric). (p. 1)

Writing Application:

Have students work individually or in small groups to write an employment ad for a fictional leadership position of their choice. The ad should specify the required and preferred characteristics of the candidate.

References:

Fourie, W., van der Merwe, S. C., & van der Merwe, B. (2017). Sixty years of research on leadership in Africa: A review of the literature. *Leadership, 13*(2), 222–251. https://doi.org/10.1177/1742715015580665

Lerutla, M., & Steyn, R. (2021). African business leadership: Perspectives from aspiring young leaders. *SA Journal of Human Resource Management / SA Tydskrif vir Menslikehulpbronbestuur, 19*. http://dx.doi.org/10.4102/sajhrm.v19i0.1467

ACTIVITY 7.9
CHOOSING A LIFE PARTNER

Activity Summary:

Based on the work of Buss and colleagues (Buss et al., 1990) students complete a set of items to indicate the importance they place on various characteristics in a life partner. They then answer questions dealing with research findings on mate selection.

Lecture/Discussion Suggestion:

Are there cultural differences in verbal expressions of love? Wilkins and Gareis (2006; Gareis & Wilkins, 2011) investigated the circumstances under which (if at all) people in various cultures would verbalize, "I love you." Across cultures, people were most likely to report saying "I love you" to romantic partners (62%), followed by parents (40%), grandparents (38%), and then children or grandchildren. Men were less likely to say "I love you" than women, and of men who did so, they were more likely than women to do so only occasionally or rarely.

These authors cited several instances in which nonverbal expressions of love were more appropriate. For example, a Chinese American woman reported, "Every time when I go back home, my father always goes to kitchen and asks me what I want to eat. He doesn't say anything but make food for me quietly. It is very touching every time when I see my father does it. Love doesn't have to be express verbally. I completely agree with it. Love my Dad!" (Wilkins & Gareis, 2006, p. 62). In other cases, verbalizing "I love you" was viewed as unnecessary, immature, or overly emotional. Some respondents reported that there was no way to easily say "I love you" in their native language. In fact, non-native speakers of English reported using the phrase "I love you" more in English than in their native languages.

Variation:

The questions that make up the first part of Activity 7.9 may be administered by students to their peers in survey form. You can then tally the answers in class and have students work in groups to respond to the questions that follow.

Writing Application:

Assign students the task of reading a love story (you can specify the quality of the material you will allow, ranging from classic fiction to romance novels) or ask them to view a love story (ranging from classic films to telenovela), preferably from a culture other than their own. In a brief essay, have them discuss the criteria that the characters appeared to value in their mate selection choices.

References:

Buss, D. M., Abbott, M., Angleitner, A., et al. (1990). International preferences in selecting mates: A study of 37 cultures. *Journal of Cross-Cultural Psychology, 21,* 5–47.   http://dx.doi.org/10.1177/00220221 90211001

Gareis, E., & Wilkins, R. (2011). Love expression in the United States and Germany. *International Journal of Intercultural Relations, 35*(3), 307–319. https://doi.org/10.1016/j.ijintrel.2010.06.006

Wilkins, R., & Gareis, E. (2006). Emotion expression and the locution "I love you": A cross-cultural study. *International Journal of Intercultural Relations, 30*(1), 51–75. https://doi.org/10.1016/j.ijintrel.2005.07.003

ACTIVITY 7.10
INTERCULTURAL PARTNERSHIPS

Activity Summary:

Students conduct an interview with someone involved in an intercultural dating relationship, marriage, or committed partnership. Interview data is analyzed based on the work of Mayer (2023) and Romano (2001). Follow-up questions explore the concept of intercultural partnerships and compare the challenges of these unions with those of intracultural relationships. [Requires work outside of the classroom.]

Lecture/Discussion Suggestion:

What questions are psychologists asking about intercultural partnerships? There is a substantial research literature on intercultural romantic relationships. Some of the main psychological research questions include.

Are there differences between intercultural and intracultural partnerships in relationship satisfaction? Responses to this question have been mixed. Based on a scoping review, Calderon et al. (2022) reported poorer psychological well-being and higher rates of intimate partner violence among those in interracial relationships. In contrast, two recent meta-analyses found no significant difference between interracial and intra-racial relationships in terms of relationship satisfaction (Brooks, 2021; Henderson & Braithwaite, 2021). That said, there is a great deal of variability in divorce rates *among* intercultural couples depending on the specific combination of ethnic/racial/national backgrounds. Brooks suggested that the inconsistencies across studies may be due in part to publication bias favoring studies reporting group differences.

Do intercultural couples experience stigma? Although attitudes about intercultural relationships have generally become more positive, inter-cultural couples continue to report experiences with stigmatization, ranging from more severe forms of prejudice and discrimination to microaggressions (Greif, 2023). One of the primary concerns of inter-cultural couples is the reactions of family and society (Harris & Kalbfleisch, 2000). Rosenthal et al. (2019) noted that stigma from friends and family may be more harmful than stigma stemming from the larger society. These authors reported relationship stigma from family was associated with greater anxiety and depressive symptoms for individuals in heterosexual, but not same-sex, interracial relationships. They suggested that partners in same-sex interracial relationships may have dealt with family stigma prior to the relationship and/or may have put an alternative support system in place.

In the U.S., attitudes toward intercultural romantic relationships vary by ethnicity and generation, with European American and Latinx families more open to intercultural partnerships than Asian American families and third generation families more open to intercultural partnerships than second or first generation families (Shenhav et al., 2017). One cross-cultural study of dating preferences in the U.S., the U.K., and India found that participants were less willing to date individuals from religious outgroups than individuals from other race/culture/ethnic or socio-economic status outgroups (Allen & Uskul, 2019).

Does being a member of an intercultural partnership facilitate the development of intercultural competence? Interview studies of intercultural partners have identified a range of skills and new areas of awareness gleaned over time in the relationship. For example, Kuramoto (2018, p. 558) described how interracial couples in Japan learned new skills as they transitioned to parenthood, such as improved communication skills "that were not typical behaviors in their countries," respect for cultural differences, increased flexibility and open-mindedness.

How can mental health practitioners best assist clients in intercultural partnerships? Many communities are underserved in terms of culturally appropriate counseling services, particularly for intercultural partners. For example, Shaji (2023) documented the need for practitioners to understand the multiple challenges faced by members of the Indian diaspora, including the collectivist and family expectations of South Asian Indian culture and the stigmatization of intermarried individuals from within the Indian community. Greif (2023) proposed that clinicians approach intercultural relationships from a position of cultural humility and that they emphasize a strengths-based perspective that builds on the skills the couple has developed for coping with negative experiences.

There are several limitations to the research in this area including data largely from North American samples, the exclusion of multiethnic/multiracial individuals, and the use of panethnic categories (e.g. Asian) that may mask ethnic group differences (see Activity 1.7 on ethnic gloss). de Guzman and Nishina (2017) suggested that this latter issue could be addressed by having the research participants themselves determine whether their relationship is intra- or intercultural. Finally, the intercultural partnership research overwhelmingly focuses on heterosexual couples. Jones et al. (2021) reported that same-sex couples are more likely to be in a White/Black interracial pairing than different-sex couples.

Writing Application:

Ask students to write a dialogue illustrating one of the challenges identified in Activity 7.10 (see Thinking Further question 1).

References:

Allen, C. K., & Uskul, A. K. (2019). Preference for dating out-group members: Not the same for all out-groups and cultural backgrounds.

International Journal of Intercultural Relations, 68, 55–66. https://doi.org/10.1016/j.ijintrel.2018.11.002

Brooks, J. E. (2021). Differences in satisfaction? A meta-analytic review of interracial and intraracial relationships. *Marriage & Family Review.* https://doi.org/10.1080/01494929.2021.1937443

Calderon, P. S. P., Wong, J. D., & Hodgdon, B. T. (2022). A scoping review of the physical health and psychological well-being of individuals in interracial romantic relationships. *Family Relations: An Interdisciplinary Journal of Applied Family Studies, 71*(5), 2011–2029. https://doi.org/10.1111/fare.12765

de Guzman, N. S., & Nishina, A. (2017). 50 years of loving: Interracial romantic relationships and recommendations for future research. *Journal of Family Theory & Review, 9*(4), 557–571. https://doi.org/10.1111/jftr.12215

Greif, G. L. (2023). Long-term interracial and interethnic marriages: What can be learned about how spouses deal with negativity from others. *Journal of Ethnic & Cultural Diversity in Social Work: Innovation in Theory, Research & Practice.* https://doi.org/10.1080/15313204.2023.2173697

Harris, T. M., & Kalbfleisch, P. J. (2000). Interracial dating: The implications of race for initiating a romantic relationship. *Howard Journal of Communications, 11,* 49–64. https://doi.org/10.1080/106461700246715

Henderson, E. K., & Braithwaite, S. R. (2021). Cross-group relationship satisfaction: A meta-analysis. *Marriage & Family Review, 57*(7), 621–646. https://doi.org/10.1080/01494929.2021.1887046

Jones, N. E., Malone, D. E. Jr., & Campbell, M. E. (2021). Same-sex and different-sex interracial couples: The importance of demographic and religious context. *Race and Social Problems, 13*(4), 267–278. https://doi.org/10.1007/s12552-021-09340-5

Kuramoto, M. (2018). Strength of intercultural couples in the transition to parenthood: A qualitative study of intermarried parents in Japan. *Marriage & Family Review, 54*(6), 549–564. https://doi.org/10.1080/01494929.2017.1403995

Mayer, C. (2023). Challenges and coping of couples in intercultural romantic love relationships. *International Review of Psychiatry, 35*(1), 4–15. https://doi.org/10.1080/09540261.2023.2173000

Romano, D. (2001). *Intercultural marriage: Promises and pitfalls* (2nd ed.). Nicholas Brealey.

Rosenthal, L., Deosaran, A., Young, D. L., & Starks, T. J. (2019). Relationship stigma and well-being among adults in interracial and same-sex relationships. *Journal of Social and Personal Relationships*, *36*(11–12), 3408–3428. https://doi.org/10.1177/0265407518822785

Shaji, D. (2023). Negotiating the challenges of an interracial marriage: An interpretive phenomenological analysis of the perception of diaspora Indian partners. *Family Relations*. https://doi.org/10.1111/fare.12888

Shenhav, S., Campos, B., & Goldberg, W. A. (2017). Dating out is intercultural: Experience and perceived parent disapproval by ethnicity and immigrant generation. *Journal of Social and Personal Relationships*, *34*(3), 397–422.

–8–

Intergroup Relations

DOI: 10.4324/9781003356820-11

ACTIVITY 8.1
DISCRIMINATION INCIDENTS

Activity Summary:

This activity introduces interpersonal, institutional, and cultural forms of discrimination and provides a mechanism for eliciting definitions of these terms. Students write a description of an instance of prejudice or discrimination. Based on this description students extract characteristics of prejudice and discrimination. The event described need not be something the student has directly experienced. [Please note that on occasion students may reveal difficult experiences via this activity and instructors should be prepared to make appropriate referrals.]

Lecture/Discussion Suggestion:

Does the experience of being stereotyped affect one's academic achievement? A fascinating area of research pioneered by Steele and Aronson (1995) deals with how the expectation of being stereotyped, which they term *stereotype threat*, interferes with performance on cognitive tasks and may ultimately cause students to distance themselves from the threatened abilities in order to protect their self-concept. Stereotype threat occurs when one expects to be judged negatively based on stereotypes of one's social group and feels at risk of confirming these stereotypes (Steele et al., 2002). In their original study, Steele and Aronson administered a difficult test of verbal aptitude to African American and European American undergraduates with comparable SAT scores. Half of each group was told that the test was measuring their verbal ability (the diagnostic condition), whereas the other half was told that the test was to be used to better understand the psychology of problem-solving (the nondiagnostic condition). The results indicated that the African American and European American students performed equally well in the nondiagnostic condition (without stereotype threat), but the African Americans performed significantly lower than the European Americans in the diagnostic condition (where stereotype threat was presumed to be operating). Another example of stereotype threat comes from Yopyk and Prentise's (2005) study of student-athletes in which those primed to focus on their identity as athletes performed worse on a challenging math test than those primed to focus on their identity as students. Stereotype threat has been demonstrated based on a wide variety of social identities in addition to race/ethnicity, including gender, age, socioeconomic level, and immigration status. Stereotype threat has even been found among U.S. students on study abroad programs who expected to be viewed negatively (as Americans) and feared confirming the negative stereotypes (Goldstein, 2017). Many of these students enacted strategies to achieve what Block et al. (2011, p. 575) called "fending off the stereotype" such as *distancing* by altering their appearance and behavior to appear less American.

Stereotype threat seems to be a factor in "positive stereotypes" as well. Shih et al. (1999) administered a test of mathematical ability to two groups of Asian American women. One group was primed to focus on their identity as women, the other group was primed to focus on their identity as Asians. When gender was made salient, math performance declined (women are stereotyped as poor at math). When ethnicity was made salient, math performance increased (Asians are stereotyped as good at math).

It is not entirely clear how stereotype threat occurs, but it may be that focusing on the stereotype depletes the working memory needed for the task at hand (Dong et al., 2022). Strategies for reducing stereotype threat include self-affirmation and building resilience, activating multiple identities, promoting social belonging and reducing distinctiveness, describing the task to participants in a less threatening manner, educating individuals about stereotype threat and appropriate coping strategies, and by creating "identity-safe environments," for example by providing role models from the targeted group or having members of the targeted group administer the test (Liu et al., 2021; Spencer et al., 2016).

Variation:

Introduce this activity by asking students to write about an incident of prejudice or discrimination (the first task of Activity 8.1) that they would be willing to share with other students. Once the students have completed the activity, have them meet in small groups to read the incidents to the group and discuss their answers to the reaction questions. In a larger class, you might collect the incidents and then read them aloud to the class maintaining the anonymity of the authors or have students post them anonymously to a class online discussion forum.

Writing Application:

Use one of the variations above in which students are provided with an opportunity to listen to each other's incidents. Then have students do a two-minute free write about what these incidents have in common. This is a good lead-in to talking about the definitions or characteristics of prejudice and discrimination.

References:

Block, C. J., Koch, S. M., Liberman, B. E., Merriweather, T. J., & Roberson, L. (2011). Contending with stereotype threat at work: A model of long-term responses. *The Counseling Psychologist, 39*(4), 570–600. https://doi.org/10.1177/0011000010382459

Dong, T., Tong, W., & He, W. (2022). Effects of meta-stereotype threat on working memory: The mechanisms of emotion and core self-evaluations. *Current Psychology,* 1–11. https://doi.org/10.1007/s12144-022-03701-y

Goldstein, S. B. (2017). Stereotype threat in U.S. students abroad: Negotiating American identity in the age of Trump. *Frontiers: The Interdisciplinary Journal of Study Abroad, 29*(2), 94–108. https://doi.org/10.36366/frontiers.v29i2.395

Liu, S., Liu, P., Wang, M., & Zhang, B. (2021). Effectiveness of stereotype threat interventions: A meta-analytic review. *Journal of Applied Psychology, 106*(6), 921–949. https://doi.org/10.1037/apl0000770

Shih, M., Pittinsky, T., & Ambady, N. (1999). Stereotype susceptibility: Identity salience and shifts in quantitative performance. *Psychological Science, 10*, 80–83. https://doi.org/10.1111/1467-9280.00111

Spencer, S. J., Logel, C., & Davies, P. G. (2016). Stereotype threat. *Annual Review of Psychology, 67*, 415–437. https://doi.org/10.1146/annurev-psych-073115-103235

Steele, C. M., & Aronson, J. (1995). Stereotype threat and the intellectual test performance of African Americans. *Journal of Personality and Social Psychology, 69*, 797–811. https://doi.org/10.1037//0022-3514.69.5.797

Steele, C. M., Spencer, S. J., & Aronson, J. (2002). Contending with group image: The psychology of stereotype and social identity threat. In M. Zanna (Ed.), *Advances in experimental social psychology*, Vol. 34 (pp. 379–440). Academic Press.

Yopyk, D. J. A., & Prentise, D. A. (2005). Am I an athlete or a student? Identity salience and stereotype threat in student-athletes. *Basic and Applied Social Psychology, 27*, 329–336. https://psycnet.apa.org/doi/10.1207/s15324834basp2704_5

ACTIVITY 8.2
EXPLORING PRIVILEGE

Activity Summary:

Students develop items to illustrate privilege based on race, gender, sexual orientation, physical disability, and social class, and then answer a series of questions addressing the link between privilege and discrimination. While not explicitly mentioned in this activity, the topic of intersectionality could be introduced as part of the discussion of student responses.

Lecture/Discussion Suggestion:

Is everyone prejudiced? The Museum of Tolerance in Los Angeles has two entrances. One is for people who are prejudiced, the other is for people who are not prejudiced. The door for people who are not prejudiced cannot be opened. Tatum (1997) suggested that we are all prejudiced because we are continually exposed to misinformation (stereotypes, omissions, and distortions) about each other. Tatum distinguished between prejudice and racism in that racism includes a power or privilege component, whereas prejudice does not. (This is true for the other "isms" as well, such as sexism, classism, and heterosexism.) Tatum (1997) made the following suggestions about racism:

- It is easier to become aware of discrimination than it is to become aware of privilege.
- Acknowledging one's own privilege may elicit emotions ranging from pain to anger and guilt, since this view runs counter to traditional notions of meritocracy.
- Active racism (such as the behavior of White supremacist groups) should be distinguished from passive racism (such as failing to challenge a racist joke). Tatum used the analogy of a moving sidewalk to describe passive racist behavior – unless one is actively antiracist – walking in the opposite direction – one will be carried along with everyone else in supporting a racist system.

Variation:

Have students read aloud the items they developed for this activity a category at a time (White skin privilege, male privilege, etc.). Let students privately keep tallies of the privileges they personally receive. Afterward, ask for volunteers to report any conclusions or realizations. McIntosh (1988) offered an extensive list of privileges associated with being White that could be read to or read by the class as well. There are also many lists of privileges associated with other forms of dominant group membership that are readily available online.

Writing Application:

Have students keep a journal for at least one week in which they record any forms of privilege they can identify. Students should focus on the ways in which they, themselves, are privileged (few students will be unable to find at least one form of privilege they receive).

References:

McIntosh, P. (1988). White privilege and male privilege. In M. L. Andersen & P. H. Collins (Eds.), *Race, class, and gender: An anthology* (pp. 70–81).Wadsworth.

Tatum, B. D. (1997). *"Why are all the Black kids sitting together in the cafeteria?" And other conversations about race.* Basic Books.

ACTIVITY 8.3
INSTITUTIONAL DISCRIMINATION

Activity Summary:

Six policies are presented for students to evaluate in terms of the degree to which they are discriminatory. An argument can be made for each of the policies as a form of institutional discrimination. This activity is expected to demonstrate that discrimination is perpetuated in ways other than individual prejudices.

Lecture/Discussion Suggestions:

Is it possible to discriminate without individual prejudice? Students often have difficulty distinguishing between prejudice on an individual level and institutional forms of discrimination that systematically exclude or marginalize specific groups. Jones (1997) stated that whether a policy was *intended* to be discriminatory or not is irrelevant. He explained that "bias-free" policies may result in inequality due to a history of discrimination. For example, seniority policies, though not overtly biased, are often ultimately discriminatory due to the history of excluding specific groups from the job market.

It can be argued that each of the six policies stated in Activity 8.3 represents some form of institutional discrimination. Some of the groups of people excluded or marginalized by these policies are listed below:

1. A government issued ID card is required to vote. Rigorous studies indicate that this practice tends to disproportionately impact older adults, college students, and People of Color (Darrah-Okike et al., 2021; D'Ercole, 2021; Kuk et al., 2022).
2. Children of alumni receive preference for admission into some colleges and universities. These policies, sometimes referred to as "legacy admissions," exclude applicants who are the first generation to attend college, often people from lower income or immigrant families.
3. A retail company seeks to hire people with a specific "look." This may exclude people with a variety of ethnic backgrounds or body types. Among some employment agencies, the term "All-American" has been used as a code term to recruit blond and blue eyed candidates.
4. Persons accused of a crime who cannot post bail remain in jail while awaiting trial. This discriminates against people of lower socioeconomic status. As a result of pretrial incarceration, individuals may lose their jobs and thus the ability to feed and house their families.
5. A corporation decides to fill a position opening "in-house" rather than advertise. This may exclude members of groups not well represented in the corporation – often women and People of Color.
6. White actors are chosen to play the part of People of Color. This may exclude actors of color due to the already limited roles available. Until recent decades, for example, White people were frequently cast in lead Asian roles in American films.

How do individual and institutional forms of bias interact? Students might be asked to consider individual psychological processes that could contribute to institutional bias. For example, outgroup homogeneity could result in assumptions about an entire group and thus failure to include members of certain groups in an organization. They can also be asked to identify ways that institutional discrimination could shape individual-level bias. For example, unequal representation in an organization could result in stereotype threat, internalized oppression, and possibly self-fulfilling behaviors on the individual level. Payne et al. (2017) discussed possible mechanisms for connections between individual and institutional forms of bias. These authors suggested that implicit bias on the individual level is in part a function of the degree to which the social environment (such as the presence of Confederate monuments) increases the accessibility of concepts that cue such biases.

Variation:

Assign students to argue either for or against one of the policies so that a brief debate can be presented to the class before students answer the corresponding questions in Activity 8.3.

Writing Application:

Have students write a position paper on one of the policies, arguing that the policy is – or is not – a form of discrimination. More advanced students could be assigned the creation of a formal policy brief. There are multiple internet sites with templates for and examples of policy briefs.

References:

Darrah-Okike, J., Rita, N., & Logan, J. R. (2021). The suppressive impacts of voter identification requirements. *Sociological Perspectives*, *64*(4), 536–562. https://doi.org/10.1177/0731121420966620

D'Ercole, R. (2021). Fighting a new wave of voter suppression: Securing college students' right to vote through the Twenty-Sixth Amendment's enforcement clause. *Washington and Lee Law Review*, 78. https://scholarlycommons.law.wlu.edu/wlulr/vol78/iss4/9/

Jones, J. M. (1997). *Prejudice and racism* (2nd ed.). McGraw-Hill.

Kuk, J., Hajnal, Z., & Lajevardi, N. (2022). A disproportionate burden: Strict voter identification laws and minority turnout. *Politics, Groups, and Identities*, *10*(1), 126–134. https://doi.org/10.1080/21565503.2020.1773280

Payne, B. K., Vuletich, H. A., & Lundberg, K. B. (2017). The bias of crowds: How implicit bias bridges personal and systemic prejudice. *Psychological Inquiry*, *28*(4), 233–248. https://doi.org/10.1080/1047840X.2017.1335568

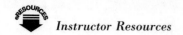

ACTIVITY 8.4
GEOGRAPHIC KNOWLEDGE AND INTERGROUP ATTITUDES

Activity Summary:

Students conduct an informal test of the connection between geographic knowledge and intergroup attitudes. First, they identify a current issue involving the relationship between their own and another country. Then they write two questions to gauge attitudes about the issue and those involved. Finally, they ask ten people to find the country they have selected on an outline map and respond to the two questions. [Requires work outside of the classroom.]

Lecture/Discussion Suggestion:

Why do U.S. Americans score so poorly on tests of Geographical Knowledge? The National Geographic Society's 2002 cross-cultural comparison of geographic knowledge found that 18 to 24 year olds in the U.S. came in next to last among nine countries in the *National Geographic–Roper 2002 Global Geographic Literacy Survey*, which quizzed more than 3000 young adults in Canada, France, Germany, Great Britain, Italy, Japan, Mexico, Sweden, and the United States. The top scorers were young adults in Sweden, Germany, and Italy. A more recent survey conducted by members of the tourist industry similarly found that Europeans far outperformed U.S. Americans on the ability to identify countries of the world on a blank map (Newton, 2018). Also in 2018, only 25% of U.S. eighth-grade students reached the level of proficiency on the National Assessment of Educational Progress geography assessment.

In 2016 and 2019, the Council on Foreign Relations and the National Geographic Society administered a global literacy survey to college students in the U.S. Their findings included:

- On average, just over half of the questions were answered correctly.
- Only 49% correctly selected Mandarin Chinese as the most spoken language.
- 49% incorrectly believed that more people are entering the U.S. from Mexico than are leaving.
- Fewer than half could identify Iraq or Iran on a map.
- Only 12% correctly identified the percentage of the U.S. federal budget spent on foreign aid (1%).

- 37% overestimated the percentage of the world's population that lives in the U.S. (4–5%).

On a positive note, the majority of respondents indicated that they believed it is important to be knowledgeable about geography, world history, foreign cultures, and world events.

One topic for discussion might be the causes and implications of this lack of geographic knowledge among Americans. Why was knowledge of geography relatively advanced in Sweden? Why was it intermediate in Canada? One reason might be the lack of geography courses required for American children. Other causes may have to do more with intergroup attitudes. For example, Uhlmann (2012, p. 381) coined the term *American psychological isolationism* to refer to "a distinctive cultural mindset characterized by a lack of regard for and even lack of awareness of the perspectives of other countries, coupled with a passionate desire to spread American values throughout the world."

Variation/Writing Application:

Have students take one or more interactive world geography quizzes (readily available online) and then write a reflection paper about this experience.

References:

Council on Foreign Relations/National Geographic Society. (2016). *What college-aged students know about the world: A survey on global literacy*. Author.

Council on Foreign Relations/National Geographic Society. (2019). *U.S. adults' knowledge about the world*. Author.

National Geographic Society. (2002). *National Geographic–Roper 2002 Global Geographic Literacy Survey*. Author.

Newton, J. (2018). The U.S. vs Europeans interactive test that shows that Americans really aren't very good at geography. *Daily Mail*, October 18.

Uhlmann, E. L. (2012). American psychological isolationism. *Review of General Psychology*, *16*(4), 381–390. https://doi.org/10.1037/a0027702

ACTIVITY 8.5
INTERNALIZED OPPRESSION

Activity Summary:

Students read a list of behaviors and determine which they believe indicate internalized oppression.

Lecture/Discussion Suggestion:

How might attributions for discrimination affect well-being? Crocker and Major (1989) proposed that because prejudice may be expressed in subtle ways, members of stigmatized groups often experience attributional ambiguity, in which there is uncertainty as to whether they are personally responsible for specific outcomes (such as not being selected for a job) or if these outcomes are due to prejudice based on social identity group. When this occurs, members of stigmatized groups may blame themselves or may attribute the outcome to prejudice and discrimination. Feasel et al. (2022) investigated the health effects of attributions for setbacks during college in a sample of Latinx college students attending a majority-White university in the U.S. They proposed that self-blame and discrimination-related attributions may co-occur. Their results indicated that levels of discrimination and self-blame attributions each uniquely predicted poorer mental health. In addition, these two types of attributions interacted such that students who frequently made both discrimination attributions and self-blame attributions reported the highest levels of anxiety and depressive symptoms as well as the worst physical health one year later. Feasel et al. suggested high levels of both discrimination and self-blame attributions may indicate greater uncertainty about the cause of personal setbacks, and the experience of uncertainty itself is distressing. Furthermore, as demonstrated in previous studies, health effects were significantly reduced when setbacks were attributed to discrimination in the absence of self-blame.

Writing Application:

Have students write a position paper on one of the policies, arguing that the practice is – or is not – a form of internalized oppression.

References:

Crocker, J., & Major, B. (1989). Social stigma and self-esteem: The self-protective properties of stigma. *Psychological Review, 96*(4), 608–630. https://doi.org/10.1037/0033-295X.96.4.608

Feasel, S. H., Dover, T. L., Small, P. A., & Major, B. (2022). Effects of discrimination versus self-blame attributions on health: A longitudinal study. *Stigma and Health, 7*(3), 289–299. https://doi.org/10.1037/sah0000393

ACTIVITY 8.6
COGNITION AND STEREOTYPE FORMATION

Activity Summary:

Students enlist the aid of four volunteers who evaluate stimulus persons varying by age and gender. Follow-up questions guide the interpretation of these responses in terms of the cognitive processes of categorization, memory, and attribution. [Requires work outside of the classroom.]

Lecture/Discussion Suggestion:

Can stereotypes influence our evaluations of song lyrics and songwriters? This activity was designed to illustrate the impact of stereotypes on information processing. Fried (1996) provided an additional example of how stereotypes can influence the way we process new information. Fried asked research participants to read song lyrics from the American folk song, "Bad Man's Blunder," recorded by the Kingston Trio in the 1960s. In one study, the lyrics were presented to White participants as either a folk song, a country music song, or a rap song. In a second study, participants were told that the lyrics were recorded by either a White artist or a Black artist. In both studies, participants were asked to rate the lyrics on a series of items dealing with the offensiveness of the lyrics. Fried's results indicated that when the lyrics were represented as a rap song or were associated with a Black artist, they were rated as more objectionable.

In two more recent studies, Dunbar and colleagues replicated and expanded on Fried's work. As in the original study, Dunbar et al. (2016) found that song lyrics labeled as "rap" were judged to be more negative than when the same lyrics were labeled "country," yet no effect was found for the race of the songwriter. Dunbar and Kubrin (2018) randomly assigned participants to evaluate music lyrics labeled as either a country, heavy metal, or rap song and asked them to make judgments about the 12 characteristics of the songwriter (e.g., honesty, criminality, intelligence, violence). Results indicated that writers were perceived to have more negative characteristics when portrayed as the author of rap as opposed to country or heavy metal lyrics. Although there was no effect of the manipulated race of the songwriter, when no information about race was provided, participants who inferred the songwriter was Black judged him more negatively than those who inferred he was White. Dunbar and colleagues caution that these findings have implications for racial disparities in the criminal justice system given the use of defendant-authored rap music by prosecutors as evidence of the defendant's violent character or criminal intent.

Variation:

The data collected by the class for this activity can be compiled and analyzed during class. Divide the class into four groups – one for each of the stimulus persons (Participants A–D). Then have each group categorize and tally responses for that stimulus person in an informal content analysis and write their answers on the board. You will likely see a clear distinction between the descriptors associated with the young and older, and male and female stimulus persons. To take a sampling of responses, it may be easiest to categorize and tally responses to items 2 (what courses), 3 (what kind of work), 5 (type of pet), 7 (type of exercise), 9 (what is cooked), and 10 (hobbies).

In a large class, you could assign a different one of the four scenarios to a quarter of the students.

Writing Application:

Have students investigate an area of stereotyping research and develop an annotated bibliography including annotations for approximately 8–10 of the studies they identify. The research area might focus on a specific target of stereotypes (for example, stereotypes of the elderly), a specific aspect of the stereotyping process (such as stereotype threat), or the measurement of stereotypes.

References:

Dunbar, A., & Kubrin, C. E. (2018). Imagining violent criminals: An experimental investigation of music stereotypes and character judgments. *Journal of Experimental Criminology, 14*(4), 507–528. https://doi.org/10.1007/s11292-018-9342-6

Dunbar, A., Kubrin, C. E., and Scurich, N. (2016). The threatening nature of "rap" music. *Psychology, Public Policy, and Law, 22*(3), 280–292. https://doi.org/10.1037/law0000093

Fried, C. B. (1996). Bad rap for rap: Bias in reactions to musical lyrics. *Journal of Applied Social Psychology, 26,* 2135–2146.

ACTIVITY 8.7
THE CONTENT OF STEREOTYPES

Activity Summary:

Students identify a specific social group that they know to be stereotyped, then plot it on the dimensions of the stereotype content model (warmth and competence).

Lecture/Discussion Suggestion:

Is the stereotype content model universal across cultures? Cuddy and colleagues (2009) investigated the cross-cultural universality of the stereotype content model. They found nearly uniform application of the model in ten countries, with one exception – in Western nations people categorized their ingroup as warm and competent, but people in Asian nations did not. According to the authors, members of more collectivist cultures did not locate reference groups (in-groups and societal prototype groups) in the most positive cluster (high competence / high warmth), in contrast to members of individualist cultures. According to the authors, these findings are consistent with "collectivist modesty" in which one's own group is placed in "a more moderate, humble location instead of the in-group-enhancing high–high quadrant, as in the western within-country samples" (p. 24). The Stereotype Content Model has been used to describe perceptions of social groups in over 50 nations, yet the placement of groups along the two dimensions appears to vary depending on the level of income equality as well as on the level of peace or conflict (Fiske, 2018). In countries with greater income inequality, more groups were placed in the ambivalent quadrants (low competence / high warmth or high competence / low warmth) whereas in countries with greater income equality, groups were more often perceived as all positive (high warmth / high competence) or all negative (low warmth / low competence). Fiske (p. 69) suggested that "Income inequality apparently generates more complicated lay theories (e.g., we have deserving and undeserving poor, deserving and undeserving rich).” In terms of peace and conflict, it seems that in nations with high levels of conflict, groups are also more likely to be characterized at the extremes, whereas nations with lower levels of conflict tend to place groups in the more ambivalent quadrants.

Variation/Writing Application:

Students can be asked to think (and write) about how they themselves (or someone close to them) may have been stereotyped, plot this stereotype on the two dimensions, and then discuss the implications of this stereotype for how they (or the close friend/relative) have been treated.

References:

Cuddy, A. J. C., Fiske, S. T., Kwan, V. S. Y., et al. (2009). Stereotype content model across cultures: Towards universal similarities and some differences. *British Journal of Social Psychology, 48*(1), 1–33. https://doi.org/10.1348/014466608x314935

Fiske, S. T. (2018). Stereotype content: Warmth and competence endure. *Current Directions in Psychological Science, 27*(2), 67–73. https://doi.org/10.1177/0963721417738825

ACTIVITY 8.8
CULTURE AND THE STIGMA OF MENTAL ILLNESS

Activity Summary:

Students are asked to use journal articles and other scholarly sources to read about mental illness stigma in a particular culture, country, or region, and then answer questions about the universal and culture-specific components of the stigmatization. [Requires work outside of the classroom.]

Lecture/Discussion Suggestion:

How does the stigmatization of mental illness vary across cultures? The stigmatization of mental illness appears to be a worldwide phenomenon. For instance, studies have not supported the assumption that people hold more positive attitudes about mental illness in Northern and Western Europe.

Hellström et al. (2022), for example, reported that levels of mental illness-related stigma in Nordic countries closely resembled global findings.

Yet, the form that stigma takes does seem to vary across cultures. Several cross-cultural studies have applied Jones et al.'s (1984) six dimensions to understand stigmatized conditions. These dimensions (defined in the handout for this activity) include origin, disruptiveness, peril, stability, aesthetics, and concealability. For example, Gavan et al. (2022) reviewed 93 studies on stigma from countries in Africa, the Western Pacific, the Eastern Mediterranean, Europe, and the Americas and reported that origin (controllability) and disruptiveness appear to be most frequently highlighted across cultures. Additional dimensions of stigmatization identified by these authors (p. 3) included:

- Worth – To what extent does the stigma influence the value of a person?
- Immorality – To what extent is the stigmatized individual perceived to be going against the morality standards … of their culture?
- Positive discrimination – To what extent is the person with the stigma perceived to receive too much support and attention?

One way to explore cultural variability in mental illness stigma is to look within each of Jones et al.'s (1984) dimensions. For example, research has documented cultural differences in "peril" – the degree to which people with mental illnesses are viewed as dangerous (Mirza et al., 2019). There are also significant cultural differences in terms of origin (and thus, controllability). For example, mental illness stigmatization may vary depending on whether one views the condition as stemming from external stressors as opposed to past misdeeds (Ran et al., 2021) or spiritual weakness (Alattar et al., 2021).

We might also investigate the dimension of disruptiveness and explore, within a specific culture, what aspects of life are most disrupted. Eghaneyan and Murphy (2020), for example, observed the ways that disruption of family roles is related to stigma for Latinx families where there are often strong values around fulfilling family obligations; these family roles may be closely linked to gender (Mascayano et al., 2016).

In addition, it is useful to consider the target of stigmatization in cross-cultural perspective. In more collectivist societies, for example, there may be little distinction between the stigmatization of the individual dealing with mental illness and their entire family, as Alattar et al. (2021) observed in Saudi culture and Ran et al. (2021) noted in a review of studies from Pacific Rim nations.

Finally, several authors have discussed what Turan et al. (2019) termed "intersectional stigma" – the finding that various forms of stigma interact. For example, Eylem et al. (2020) explained that the consequences of mental health-related stigma tend to be more severe for individuals with other minoritized identities, such as members of the LGBTQIA+ community.

Variation:

Have students share their findings in small groups and then work together to identify etic (universal) and emic (culture-specific) aspects of mental illness stigma.

References:

Alattar, N., Felton, A., & Stickley, T. (2021). Mental health and stigma in Saudi Arabia: A scoping review. *The Mental Health Review*, *26*(2), 180–196. https://doi.org/10.1108/MHRJ-08-2020-0055

Eghaneyan, B. H., & Murphy, E. R. (2020). Measuring mental illness stigma among Hispanics: A systematic review. *Stigma and Health*, *5*(3), 351–363. https://doi.org/10.1037/sah0000207

Eylem, O., de Wit, L., Annemieke, V. S., et al. (2020). Stigma for common mental disorders in racial minorities and majorities a systematic review and meta-analysis. *BMC Public Health*, *20*, 1–20. https://doi.org/10.1186/s12889-020-08964-3

Gavan, L., Hartog, K., Koppenol-Gonzalez, G. V., Gronholm, P. C., Feddes, A. R., Kohrt, B. A., Jordans, M. J. D., & Peters, R. M. H. (2022). Assessing stigma in low- and middle-income countries: A systematic review of scales used with children and adolescents. *Social Science & Medicine*. https://doi.org/10.1016/j.socscimed.2022.115121

Hellström, L., Gren Voldby, K., & Eplov, L. F. (2022). Stigma towards people with mental illness in the Nordic countries – a scoping review. *Nordic Journal of Psychiatry*. https://doi.org/10.1080/08039488.2022.2105946

Jones, E. E., Farina, A., Hastorf, A. H., Markus, H. R., Miller, T., & Scott, R. (1984). *Social stigma: The psychology of marked relationships*. W. H. Freeman.

Mascayano, F., Tapia, T., Schilling, S., Alvarado, R., Tapia, E., Lips, W., & Yang, L. H. (2016). Stigma toward mental illness in Latin America and the Caribbean: A systematic review. *Brazilian Journal of Psychiatry*, *38*(1), 73–85. https://doi.org/10.1590/1516-4446-2015-1652

Mirza, A., Birtel, M. D., Pyle, M., & Morrison, A. P. (2019). Cultural differences in psychosis: The role of causal beliefs and stigma in White

British and South Asians. *Journal of Cross-Cultural Psychology*, *50*(3), 441–459. https://doi.org/10.1177/0022022118820168

Ran, M. S., Hall, B. J., Su, T. T., Prawira, B., Breth-Petersen, M., Xu-Hong, L., & Tian-Ming, Z. (2021). Stigma of mental illness and cultural factors in Pacific Rim region: A systematic review. *BMC Psychiatry*, *21*, 1–16. https://doi.org/10.1186/s12888-020-02991-5

Turan, J. M., Elafros, M. A., Logie, C. H., et al. (2019). Challenges and opportunities in examining and addressing intersectional stigma and health. *BMC Medicine*, *17*, 7. http://dx.doi.org/10.1186/s12916-018-1246-9

ACTIVITY 8.9
UNDERSTANDING ANTI-IMMIGRANT PREJUDICE

Activity Summary:

Students cite specific news and social media sources to respond to questions applying the Integrated Threat Model to anti-immigrant attitudes. [Requires work outside of the classroom.]

Lecture/Discussion Suggestion:

How can we best reduce our own stereotypes? Devine (1996) suggested that stereotyping is like a habit that can be broken once one decides to do so. Devine distinguished between automatic and controlled processes in prejudice. Research conducted by Devine and colleagues indicated that for both high- and low-prejudiced individuals, stereotyping is an automatic process. In other words, once learned, stereotypes will come to mind spontaneously. One difference between low- and high-prejudiced people, according to Devine is that, when time allows, low-prejudiced people will reject responses based on the stereotype and instead respond based on internalized standards for nonprejudiced ways to treat others. In contrast, high-prejudiced people are likely to accept the stereotype. In addition, low-prejudiced people experience guilt feelings when they become aware of their own stereotyped beliefs, but high-prejudiced people do not. Devine suggested that these feelings of compunction are helpful in breaking the "prejudice habit" in that they help us to focus on using controlled processes to reject our own stereotyped beliefs. These guilt feelings are associated with "decreased stereotype activation, less self-reported prejudice, and greater compensatory behavior" (Chaney & Wedell, 2022, p. 2). Monteith and colleagues (2016) suggested that over time people can become sensitized to

the environmental cues that are present in situations where they are likely to become prejudiced and then learn to replace prejudiced responses with nonprejudiced ones.

Variation/Writing Application:

Have students rewrite the news or media sources so that rather than perpetrating realistic threats, symbolic threats, intergroup anxiety, or negative stereotypes they support positive messages.

The UNHCR website includes pictorial representations of statistics on refugees worldwide. See www.unhcr.org/figures-at-a-glance.html

---

References:

Chaney, K. E., & Wedell, E. (2022). How lay theories of prejudice shape prejudice confrontations: Examining beliefs about prejudice prevalence, origins, and controllability. *Social and Personality Psychology Compass*, *16*(4). https://doi.org/10.1111/spc3.12658

Devine, P. G. (1996). Breaking the prejudice habit. *Psychological Science Agenda*, Jan/Feb, 10–12.

Monteith, M. J., Parker, L. R., & Burns, M. D. (2016). The self-regulation of prejudice. In T. D. Nelson (Ed.), *Handbook of prejudice, stereotyping, and discrimination* (2nd ed., pp. 409–432). Psychology Press.

ACTIVITY 8.10
THE CONTACT HYPOTHESIS

Activity Summary:

A brief description of the contact hypothesis is presented along with information on the conditions that lead to favorable and unfavorable contact situations. Students use this information to respond to a scenario depicting an interethnic conflict situation in a high school setting.

Lecture/Discussion Suggestion:

How can we facilitate intergroup contact in the schools? Several cooperative learning-based interventions were developed in response to the failure of school desegregation efforts to create the conditions necessary to reduce prejudice through contact. One such intervention is the *jigsaw technique* (Aronson et al., 1978). In a class of 30 students, one might use this technique by dividing the students into five groups of six people each. The material to be learned would then be divided into six sections – one for each student in the group. In the first phase, students are reconfigured into six *expert groups –* one for each section of the material to be learned. Students within these groups are responsible for the same content and consult with each other in order to become experts on their section of the material. Once the material has been mastered, students return to their original jigsaw groups (five groups of six persons each) to teach their peers about the section of the material they have mastered. Each student becomes an expert on one section of the material such that they must depend upon each other if all of them are to master all of the material. Because each student holds an important part of the whole, students must cooperate if they are all to succeed. The jigsaw technique creates a situation that is sanctioned by school authorities, and involves equal status contact, superordinate goals, intimate and pleasant interaction, and coopera- tion and interdependence. (This technique is applicable to any age group and seems to be quite successful with, and well-liked by, college students.)

Other strategies for facilitating positive contact and intergroup friendships have involved such projects as mural painting, playground design, gardening, organizing community events, and recycling and sustainability programs (Tropp et al., 2022).

Writing Application:

Have students write a brief essay describing intergroup relations in their high school and analyzing this situation in terms of the contact hypothesis.

References:

Aronson, E., Blaney, N., Stephan, C., Sikes, J., & Snapp, M. (1978). *The jigsaw classroom*. Sage.

Tropp, L. R., White, F., Rucinski, C. L., & Tredoux, C. (2022). Intergroup contact and prejudice reduction: Prospects and challenges in changing youth attitudes. *Review of General Psychology, 26*(3), 342–360. https:// doi.org/10.1177/10892680211046517

Intercultural Interaction

   DOI: 10.4324/9781003356820-12

ACTIVITY 9.1
CULTURE MIXING

Activity Summary:

Students create an example of culture mixing and then gather reactions to their example from at least three people. They then consider different factors that could shape reactions to a culturally mixed image. [Requires work outside of the classroom.]

Lecture/Discussion Suggestion:

What are some of the factors that affect an individual's reactions to culture mixing? Aspects of the culturally mixed image and characteristics of the respondent have been found to influence reactions.

The image:

- Participants' reactions depended in part on their evaluation of the source country (Cheon & Hong, 2020).
- Foreign images that appear to have been modified by an image from one's home culture tended to be viewed more favorably than home-culture images that appear to have been modified by an image from a foreign culture (Cui et al., 2016).
- Research participants responded more negatively to a fusion between a home culture and foreign image than they did to a fusion of two different foreign images (Cheon et al., 2016).

The respondent:

- Low openness to experience (Chen et al., 2016), and in some cases, patriotism (Cheon & Hong, 2020), were found to be associated with more negative responses to culture mixing.
- People with a high need for closure responded less favorably to culture mixing than did those with a low need for closure. This relationship between need for closure and attitudes toward culture mixing was mediated by Right-Wing Authoritarianism and was explained by the authors in terms of threat to security needs in the form of one's understanding of the world (De Keersmaecker et al., 2016).

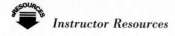

Variation:

Rather than create an example of culture mixing, students could be asked to find an example and bring it to class.

Writing Application:

Ask students to write a brief essay detailing their own reaction to an instance of culture mixing and to discuss possible reasons for and implications of this reaction.

References:

Chen, X., Leung, A. K., Yang, D. Y., Chiu, C., Li, Z., & Cheng, S. Y. Y. (2016). Cultural threats in culturally mixed encounters hamper creative performance for individuals with lower openness to experience. *Journal of Cross-Cultural Psychology*, *47*(10), 1321–1334. https://doi.org/10.1177/0022022116641513

Cheon, B. K., Christopoulos, G. I., & Hong, Y. (2016). Disgust associated with culture mixing: Why and who? *Journal of Cross-Cultural Psychology*, *47*(10), 1268–1285. https://doi.org/10.1177/0022022116667845

Cheon, B. K., & Hong, Y. (2020). Aversive response towards culture fusion is moderated by the source of foreign cultural inflow. *Journal of Cross-Cultural Psychology*, *51*(5), 370–386. https://doi.org/10.1177/0022022120919994

Cui, N., Xu, L., Wang, T., Qualls, W., & Hu, Y. (2016). How does framing strategy affect evaluation of culturally mixed products? The self–other asymmetry effect. *Journal of Cross-Cultural Psychology*, *47*(10), 1307–1320. https://doi.org/10.1177/0022022116670513

De Keersmaecker, J., Van Assche, J., & Roets, A. (2016). Need for closure effects on affective and cognitive responses to culture fusion. *Journal of Cross-Cultural Psychology*, *47*(10), 1294–1306. https://doi.org/10.1177/0022022116666375

ACTIVITY 9.2
NONVERBAL COMMUNICATION

Activity Summary:

Through a comparison of verbal and nonverbal communication, this activity clarifies the reasons why nonverbal behavior presents great difficulty for sojourners. Students first list words or meanings they are able to express nonverbally and then develop a dictionary entry for a particular nonverbal behavior.

Lecture/Discussion Suggestions:

What are the correlates of interpersonal distance preferences throughout the world? Sorokowska and 80 co-authors (2017) investigated the preferred interpersonal space of nearly 9,000 individuals in 42 countries. Saudi Arabia, Hungary, and Romania had the greatest preferred distance when approaching a stranger and Bulgaria, Peru, and Argentina had the smallest distance. Variability in preferred distance was predicted by participants' gender and country's average temperature, in that women and people in colder countries preferred greater distance toward strangers.

What are the similarities and differences between verbal and nonverbal communication? Gudykunst and Kim (2003) and Martin and Nakayama (2005) have identified the following similarities and differences in their comparisons of verbal and nonverbal communication:

Similarities:

- Both nonverbal cues and verbal language are discrete. Nonverbal cues can be separated from one another just as one can identify words or phrases.
- Both nonverbal cues and verbal language are based on agreed upon meanings.
- Both nonverbal and verbal communication are governed by rules that vary with the context.

Differences:

- Verbal language can be used to refer to events or things that are not present, whereas nonverbal cues are restricted to the present.
- Verbal language may be learned explicitly (through grammar or spelling lessons, for example), whereas nonverbal communication is generally learned implicitly.

- Verbal and nonverbal communication carry different weights for the perceiver in that nonverbal communication is generally assigned more weight than verbal communication in determining meaning.

Alternatively, the "embodied communication" approach views verbal and nonverbal communication as more enmeshed. Wachsmuth et al. (2008, p. 3) define embodied communication as "any exchange of information among members in a social group that depends on the presence of an expressive body and its relation to objects and other expressive bodies." From this perspective, gestures, facial expressions, gaze, posture, interpersonal distance, and other bodily movements interact with each other and with speech. These components of communication as well as the ways in which they interact will vary across cultures. Students might consider turn-taking in a conversation, for example, and try to identify the verbal and nonverbal components involved and how these interact.

Variation:

After this activity has been completed, ask students to investigate the sign languages used as a form of communication within Deaf Culture. In what ways is sign language like a verbal language? In what ways is it like gestures? Students can also explore the sign languages used in different cultures. To what extent do signs have universal meanings? To what extent do they vary with culture? Monaghan and colleagues (2003) pointed out that sign languages are shaped by the wealth, power, and relative isolation of the countries in which they develop. The internet contains sites for a variety of sign languages.

Writing Application:

Prior to assigning this activity, send students to an area where there is much social interaction (the campus cafeteria, perhaps) to observe and take notes on various forms of nonverbal communication. Or ask students to watch 15–30 minutes of a dramatic television show or film with the sound turned off and make similar observations. The field notes can then be typed and submitted with Activity 9.2.

References:

Gudykunst, W. B., & Kim, Y. Y. (2003). *Communicating with strangers.* McGraw-Hill.

Martin, J. N., & Nakayama, T. K. (2005). *Experiencing intercultural communication* (2nd ed.). McGraw-Hill.

Monaghan, L., Schmaling, C., Nakamura, K., & Turner, G. H. (2003). *Many ways to be deaf: International variation in deaf communities.* Gallaudet University Press.

Sorokowska, A., Sorokowski, P., Hilpert, P., et al. (2017). Preferred interpersonal distances: A global comparison. *Journal of Cross-Cultural Psychology, 48*(4), 577–592. https://doi.org/10.1177/0022022117698039

Wachsmuth, I., Lenzen, M., & Knoblich, G. (2008). *Embodied communication in humans and machines.* OUP Oxford.

ACTIVITY 9.3
DISNEYLAND PARIS: AN INTERCULTURAL CONFLICT

Activity Summary:

Students read a summary of the Disneyland Paris case in which there were multiple intercultural errors. After reading a list of the Disney Company's erroneous assumptions, students identify areas of cultural difference and then write a training talk designed to prevent the misunderstandings that occurred. [May require work outside of the classroom.]

Answers to Activity 9.3:

Analyses of the intercultural conflict in the Disneyland Paris case point to the Disney officials' failure to acknowledge or adapt to cultural differences (including use of the metric system!) and their expectation that policies and practices from the U.S. could be transported to Europe without modification.

Here is an explanation of some of the *invalid assumptions* on which the Disney Company operated:

1. *Visitors would spend four or five days in the park on vacation rather than a day or two.* Theme parks were not a preferred destination for an extended vacation.

2. *Fewer visitors would come on Mondays and more would come on Fridays.* People were actually more likely to visit attractions on Mondays and less likely to visit on Fridays. This assumption resulted

in Disneyland Paris being overstaffed on Fridays and understaffed on Mondays.

3. *Visitors would view Disneyland as an acceptable activity for cold or rainy days.* Disney underestimated the effect of the gray, cold winters and rainy weather in the Paris area on park attendance. People tended to prefer attending destinations in sunny weather if possible.

4. *Most visitors would arrive in cars.* Large parking lots – designed for cars with little room for the buses that brought most of the visitors – remained relatively empty.

5. *Families would take children out of school to go to Disneyland.* Families were not likely to take children out of school to go to Disneyland and thus attendance was lower than expected during the 10-month school year.

6. *Visitors would be enthusiastic about American culture.* In Tokyo Disneyland the majority of signs are in English, most restaurants do not serve Japanese food, and visitors embrace American pop culture; European visitors were not enthusiastic about this approach.

7. *Alcohol must be banned from the park to prevent behaviors associated with intoxication.* Visitors expected to have wine with their meal, a practice not associated with drunkenness.

8. *Dogs must not be allowed in restaurants.* Dogs are welcome in restaurants, cafes, and bars in much of Europe.

9. *Visitors would eat at various times, with many visitors snacking as they walked throughout the park.* The visitors expected to sit down around noon for a meal lasting an hour or more.

10. *The restrictions on the behavior of cast members (staff) that were implemented in the U.S. and Japan would also be appropriate in France. These included a dress code specifying acceptable clothing, hair length and dye colors, facial hair, make-up, and nail polish. Cast members were also prohibited from smoking, eating, or drinking in public and were expected to smile and be consistently polite when interacting with visitors.* French workers, coming from a system that emphasizes self-reliance rather than teamwork, viewed the dress and conduct codes as overreach. In addition, the excessively cheerful and solicitous approach to customer service is not expected in France.

By 1994 the Disney Company had changed its strategy. Euro-Disney was renamed Disneyland Paris to strengthen the park's identity, the "no alcohol policy" was reversed, dogs were allowed in much of the park, and designated smoking areas were added. French-style restaurants were opened. Customer service expectations were modified to provide a culturally appropriate version of the "Disney experience." Packman and Casmir (1999) referred to this resolution as a form of "third culture building." An interactive process that allows for the two parties to develop a third culture that has meaning beyond the additive process of combining the two.

Despite closures during the Covid-19 pandemic and a major employee strike in 2023, Disneyland Paris continues to be one of the top vacation destinations in Europe. Disney moved on to open theme parks in Hong Kong and Shanghai.

Variation:

Have teams collaborate to write the training talks and then each team can choose a representative to perform the talk for the class.

Sources:

Aupperle, K., & Karimalis, G. (2001). Using metaphors to facilitate cooperation and resolve conflict: Examining the case of Disneyland Paris. *Journal of Change Management*, *2*(1), 23–32. https://doi.org/10.1080/714042489

King, T. R. (July 9, 1993). Euro Disney 3rd quarter loss to spur study of woes by U.S. concern. *Wall Street Journal*, A3.

Newell, L. A. (2013). Mickey goes to France: A case study of the Euro Disneyland negotiations. *Cardozo Journal of Conflict Resolution*, *15*, 193–221.

Packman, H., & Casmir, F. L. (1999). Learning from the Euro Disney experience. *Gazette*, *61*, 473–489. https://doi.org/10.1177/0016549299061006002

Spencer, E. P. (1995). Educator insights: Euro Disney – What happened? What next? *Journal of International Marketing*, *3*(3), 103–114. https://doi.org/10.1177/1069031X9500300308

Reference:

Packman, H., & Casmir, F. L. (1999). Learning from the Euro Disney experience. *Gazette*, *61*, 473–489. https://doi.org/10.1177/0016549299061006002

ACTIVITY 9.4
CLOCK TIME AND EVENT TIME

Activity Summary:

Students spend a day altering their time orientation in order to understand the role of temporal differences in cross-cultural adjustment. [Requires work outside of the classroom.]

Lecture/Discussion Suggestion:

What factors influence the pace of life across cultures? Robert Levine (1997) suggested that apart from mastering a new language, the greatest difficulty experienced by sojourners is adjusting to a different pace of life, or tempo. Levine took three measures of tempo in 31 countries:

- The average walking speed of randomly selected pedestrians over a distance of 60 feet.
- The average time it took postal workers to fulfill a request for a standard stamp.
- The accuracy of 15 bank clocks in a downtown area.

Across the 31 countries, pace of life was quicker in places with a strong economy, a high degree of industrialization, larger populations, cooler climates, and an individualistic cultural orientation. Levine recommended that we all learn to live in a "multitemporal" society, in which we are able to comfortably move back and forth across time orientations. In a 2006 follow up study across 32 nations, Wiseman (n.d.) found that pace of life has increased 10% since Levine's data was collected. A more recent strategy for measuring pace of life is the General Acceleration Scale (Jens & Tilman, 2021) which has four components: performing activities faster, multitasking, replacing time-consuming by time-saving activities, and filling breaks or waiting times with productive activities.

Variation:

As a two-day activity, students (who are typically on clock time) spend one day recording any decisions or behaviors guided by the clock, and then follow this with Activity 9.4, spending the day on event time.

Writing Application:

Have students keep a journal of their day on the alternate time perspective. Ask them to record any changes in their behavior, their feelings, and the reactions of others.

References:

Jens, B., & Tilman, S. (2021). A pace of life indicator. development and validation of a general acceleration scale. *Time & Society*, *30*(3), 273–301. https://doi.org/10.1177/0961463X20980645

Levine, R. (1997). *A geography of time: The temporal misadventures of a social psychologist*. Basic Books.

Wiseman, R. (n.d.). Pace of life. Retrieved from www.richardwiseman. com/quirkology/pace_method.htm

---

ACTIVITY 9.5
ACCULTURATION STRATEGIES

Activity Summary:

Students are asked to describe a time when they faced an adjustment to a new environment. Questions help them to analyze their own adjustment process and coping strategies using Berry's (2001) revised model of acculturative stress.

Lecture/Discussion Suggestion:

How important is the acculturation strategy of the host culture? The acculturation strategy of the host culture is a critical determinant in the outcome of culture contact. The case of the Roma, Europe's largest ethnic minority, illustrates the difficulty of acculturating when the larger society adopts a strategy of segregation or exclusion. The Roma community has experienced widespread dehumanization, discrimination, and violence primarily in Eastern European countries such as Czechia, Hungary, Poland, and the Slovak Republic. Crimes against Roma individuals are rarely prosecuted, the Roma are allocated inferior housing and are vulnerable to eviction, a very high proportion of Roma children are assigned to lower tracks in school, and Roma families have shorter life expectancies and higher infant mortality rates than the majority population (Bobakova et al., 2022; Civitillo et al., 2022; Molnar, 2023). As Schmitz and Schmitz (2022) observed, depending on the immigration policies and practices of the host culture, preferences for acculturation strategy and actual acculturation behavior may differ significantly.

Variation:

Have students work in pairs to ask each other about an acculturation experience using the questions in Activity 9.5 as an interview schedule.

Writing Application:

Ask students to work in groups to write a short vignette illustrating one of Berry's four modes of acculturation. Have the students perform the vignette while the class tries to identify the mode portrayed.

References:

Berry, J. W. (2001). A psychology of immigration. *Journal of Social Issues*, *57*, 615–631. https://doi.org/10.1111/0022-4537.00231

Bobakova, D. F., Chovan, S., Bosakova, L., Koky, R., de Kroon, M. L. A., & Veselska, Z. D. (2022). Desirable but not feasible: Measures and interventions to promote early childhood health and development in marginalized Roma communities in Slovakia. *Frontiers in Public Health*, *10*. https://doi.org/10.3389/fpubh.2022.942550

Civitillo, S., Ialuna, F., Lieck, D., & Jugert, P. (2022). Do infrahumanization or affective prejudice drive teacher discrimination against Romani students? A conceptual replication of Bruneau et al. (2020) in Germany. *Peace and Conflict: Journal of Peace Psychology*, *28*(3), 340. https://doi.org/10.1037/pac0000609

Molnar, L. (2023). The imperative need for criminological research on the European Roma: a narrative review. *Trauma, Violence, & Abuse*, *24*(2), 1016–1031. https://doi.org/10.1177/15248380211048448

Schmitz, P. G., & Schmitz, F. (2022). Correlates of acculturation strategies: Personality, coping, and outcome. *Journal of Cross-Cultural Psychology*, *53*(7–8), 875–916. https://doi.org/10.1177/00220221221109939

ACTIVITY 9.6
A SOJOURNER INTERVIEW

Activity Summary:

Students conduct an interview with someone who has sojourned to a culture other than their own. Interview questions are provided. Follow-up questions ask students to draw conclusions about the cross-cultural adjustment process. [Requires work outside of the classroom.]

Lecture/Discussion Suggestion:

What do students believe to be the causes of culture shock?

Goldstein and Keller (2015) investigated college students' thinking about the causes of culture shock (their "lay theories"). Findings indicated that students tended to attribute culture shock to differences in the external environment, such as language, communication, and surroundings, rather than to internal affective or cognitive factors, such as poor stress management, identity confusion, or prejudice. The tendency to attribute culture shock to internal causes was greater for those with higher levels of cultural competence, whereas low travel experience and low interest in foreign language learning predicted the tendency to attribute culture shock to external causes. Given the importance of congruence between expectations and experience for intercultural adjustment, it may be helpful for students preparing for study abroad to become acquainted with both internal and external sources of acculturative stress.

Variation:

Instead of conducting an interview, many of these questions may be applied to fictional cases of crossing cultures. Multiple lists of novels and short stories about crossing cultures are available online.

Writing Application:

After completing the interview, have students write a letter to a real or fictional friend who will be taking a sojourn in the near future. This letter should provide the friend with information about what to expect about the intercultural adjustment experience and offer some sound advice on how to ease the transition to the new culture. Alternatively, students who are planning a sojourn in the near future can write a letter to themselves to be opened upon their arrival in the host culture.

Reference:

Goldstein, S. B., & Keller, S. R. (2015). U.S. college students' lay theories of culture shock. *International Journal of Intercultural Relations, 47,* 187–194. https://doi.org/10.1016/j.ijintrel.2015.05.010

ACTIVITY 9.7
INTERCULTURAL COMPETENCE: A SELF-ASSESSMENT

Activity Summary:

A self-assessment questionnaire helps students identify strengths and weaknesses in their intercultural skills and develop a plan to increase their competence in handling intercultural situations.

Lecture/Discussion Suggestion:

Is it valid to assess one's own level of intercultural competence? A criticism of much of the research on intercultural competence (ICC) stems from the use of self-report scales. Some of the concerns include:

- Social desirability bias – Kealey (2015, p. 14) observed that "most individuals in responding to questionnaire items will easily know the 'right answer,' i.e. how to look culturally sensitive and knowledgeable."
- Deardorff and Jones (2012) distinguished between the "effectiveness" and the "appropriateness" components of ICC. They suggested that while an individual may be able to determine whether specific behaviors were effective (for example, in asking for assistance in an unfamiliar country), whether the behavior was done in a culturally appropriate manner can only be determined by members of that culture. Thus, Koester and Lustig (2015) suggested that questions of appropriateness, often included in assessments of ICC, may not be a valid area for self-report.
- Much of the relevant information about one's own intercultural interactions may not be accessible to the individual. Recent neuroscience studies indicate that some cultural differences may occur on a level that is beyond the individuals' conscious awareness (Chang, 2017).

Several decades ago, William Howell (1982) described four levels of inter-cultural competence that incorporate the idea that we are not always able to assess our own ICC. These are listed below from least to most effective:

1. *Unconscious incompetence* – The individual is not aware of cultural differences and does not alter their behavior in intercultural situations.
2. *Conscious incompetence* – The individual is aware that intercultural misunderstandings have occurred but cannot understand or explain these misunderstandings.
3. *Conscious competence* – Intercultural interaction goes smoothly for individuals at this level as long as they make an intentional effort to anticipate and respond to cultural differences.
4. *Unconscious competence* – Intercultural interaction goes smoothly for individuals at this level without intentional processing of thoughts and behaviors.

Deardorff (2015) observed that ICC assessment strategies are beginning to shift from self-report inventories to measures focusing on observable behavior in real-life situations. For example, Chi and Suthers (2015) proposed a strategy for assessing ICC based on a measure of social connectivity with members of the host community. These authors reasoned that it is not one's cultural knowledge per se that results in effective intercultural interaction and adjustment, but one's ability to access relevant knowledge through relational networks. Finally, Deardorff (2015) pointed out that the value of self-report measures of ICC is greatly dependent upon their intended use. For example, rather than predicting behavior in intercultural interactions, these instruments may be more useful as a tool for self-reflection and mentoring.

Variation:

Students can have others close to them (friends or relatives) rate them on the components of intercultural competence listed in this activity.

Writing Application:

Assign students the task of developing and writing up a lesson plan to teach others one of the intercultural competence components. More advanced students can be asked to research methods of assessing and enhancing specific competencies.

References:

Chang, W.-W. (2017). Approaches for developing intercultural competence: An extended learning model with implications from cultural neuroscience. *Human Resource Development Review*, *16*(2), 158–175. https://doi.org/10.1177/1534484317704292

Chi, R., & Suthers, D. (2015). Assessing intercultural communication competence as a relational construct using social network analysis. *International Journal of Intercultural Relations*, *48*, 108–119. https://doi.org/10.1016/j.ijintrel.2015.03.011

Deardorff, D. K. (2015). Intercultural competence: Mapping the future research agenda. *International Journal of Intercultural Relations*, *48*, 3–5. https://doi.org/10.1016/j.ijintrel.2015.03.002

Deardorff, D. K., & Jones, E. (2012). Intercultural competence: An emerging focus in international higher education. In D. K. Deardorff, H. de Wit, J. D. Heyl, & T. Adams (Eds.), *The SAGE handbook of international higher education* (pp. 283–304). Sage.

Howell, W. S. (1982). *The empathic communicator*. Wadsworth.

Kealey, D. J. (2015). Some strengths and weaknesses of 25 years of research on intercultural communication competence: Personal reflections. *International Journal of Intercultural Relations*, *48*, 14–16. https://doi.org/10.1016/j.ijintrel.2015.03.00

Koester, J., & Lustig, M. W. (2015). Intercultural communication competence: Theory, measurement, and application. *International Journal of Intercultural Relations*, *48*, 20–21. https://doi.org/10.1016/j.ijintrel.2015.03.006

ACTIVITY 9.8
THE PSYCHOLOGY OF TOURISM

Activity Summary:

Students make observations about tourist behavior and then answer questions about the potential for tourism to promote intercultural understanding. [Requires work outside of the classroom.]

Lecture/Discussion Suggestion:

What are the different categories of tourists? Colleen Ward and colleagues (2001) noted that there are very different motivations involved in various forms of tourism. Here are some examples of tourism types:

- Adventure tourism – Travel that includes physical activities that are actually, or perceived to be, risky.
- Agritourism: Sometimes called "farm stays," aims to give travelers an experience with rural life.
- Backpacker tourism – A form of independent travel, generally low cost. Ward and colleagues suggested that backpackers may have the most personal and genuine intercultural interactions of all tourist types.
- Culinary tourism – Travel with the goal of experiencing unique and memorable eating, drinking, and sometimes cooking experiences.
- Cultural tourism – Focuses on visiting festivals, museums, musical events, and ethnocultural events and communities.
- Disaster tourism – Travel to the sites of natural or human-made disasters.
- Ecotourism – Currently the fastest growing form of tourism, involves travel to sites that are ecologically sustainable and aid environmental understanding.
- First contact tourism – Purports to allow travelers to meet individuals from "stone age" cultures that are isolated from the rest of the world. Questions have been raised about the ethics and legitimacy of this form of tourism.
- Genealogy tourism – Travel to the location of one's ancestral heritage.
- Medical tourism – Travel to a country other than one's own to obtain medical treatment.
- Sex tourism – Typically involves travel packages that include contact with sex workers.
- Shopping tourism – Travel to obtain items or brands that are not available locally.
- Sport tourism – Travel which involves either observing or participating in sporting events.
- Volunteer tourism (or "voluntourism") – Travel that involves volunteer work, often with nonprofit organizations.

Variation:

Students can interview others about their tourism experiences and use those accounts as the basis for their analysis.

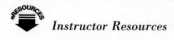
Writing Application:

Have students create their own, culturally and ecologically sensitive, travel brochures for a specific location of their choice.

Reference:

Ward, C., Bochner, S., & Furnham, A. (2001). *The psychology of culture shock* (2nd ed.). Taylor & Francis.

ACTIVITY 9.9
CROSSING CULTURES WITH CRITICAL INCIDENTS

Activity Summary:

Students are provided with an example of a critical incident (often used in intercultural training) and are asked to develop their own critical incident and explanation.

Lecture/Discussion Suggestion:

What is the history of intercultural training? The use of critical incidents has its roots in a long history of intercultural training as a professional activity. Paige and Martin (1996) and Pusch (2004) provided excellent historical accounts of the development of intercultural training. The major events outlined in their discussions are summarized and updated briefly below. Please note that this field is also called *cross-cultural training*, though as Raver and Van Dyne (2017, p. 411) observed, there is a "current shift toward using the term intercultural training because many intercultural (and cross-cultural) interactions take place within one's home country and many workplace interactions are culturally diverse."

The field of intercultural training emerged following World War II when the United States government established the Foreign Service Institute in 1946 to conduct pre-departure orientation for government and business personnel. Staffed with such distinguished social scientists as Edward T. Hall and Ray L. Birdwhistell, the training emphasized practical knowledge as well as verbal and nonverbal communication skills.

In the 1960s, intercultural training efforts expanded. Paige and Martin noted that although there was much need for attention to domestic concerns with intergroup relations in the United States at that time, the field of intercultural training was concerned primarily with international issues. In the 1960s, the *university model* became the dominant training method and was widely used to train Peace Corp volunteers. Trainees were presented with information about the host culture in a lecture-style format. According to Paige and Martin, Peace Corp trainers quickly learned that this country-specific information was of little use in preparing trainees for intercultural communication and adjustment.

In the 1970s, several professional associations developed divisions focusing on intercultural training and the Society for Intercultural Education, Training, and Research (SIETAR) was formed with the express purpose of promoting the field of intercultural training. The *human relations sensitivity model* gained popularity during this period. The focus of this approach was to provide trainees with experiential activities that would aid them in understanding their own value system and the perspectives of others. Paige and Martin explained that this approach soon failed due to its highly confrontational nature and the learning-inhibiting resistance that resulted, the lack of trainers skilled in processing the emotions elicited, and the lack of a sound conceptual base.

In the 1980s, intercultural training as a field became increasingly professionalized and globalized (with discussions of certification within professional organizations). The expansion of intercultural training was fueled by the growth of international business and the need to prepare expatriate individuals and families to be interculturally competent. The increasingly diverse U.S. workforce resulted in the emergence of the field of diversity training and intercultural trainers increasingly began to attend to domestic issues. The dominant method of training became an integration of cognitive and experiential approaches. According to Taras et al. (2020, p. 520), "cognitive methods involve passive listening, reading, writing, or Socratic discussion, whereas experiential methods entail 'learning by doing.'" One form of cognitive training uses critical incidents to assist trainees in learning to make attributions for events that are congruent with those made by members of the host culture. Experiential training methods typically use role plays and simulations to aid the development of intercultural skills.

During the 1990s intercultural trainers began identifying ethical concerns, primarily in terms of trainer competencies. This period of time also brought greater collaboration between researchers and practitioners. Currently, approaches to intercultural training tend to integrate cognitive and experiential components. Increasingly these efforts are grounded in empirical research and attend to the social context of the interaction, such as power differentials (see

Fowler & Yamaguchi, 2020, for an overview of the specific methods used in intercultural training).

More recent publications have highlighted the lack of attention to diversity within the intercultural training literature. For example, in an integrative review of the intercultural training research literature, Nam et al. (2014) found that the majority of intercultural training programs and research focused on the adjustment of North American and European sojourners and expatriates, neglecting the growing number of Asian companies sending employees on international assignments. They suggested that to be more culturally inclusive, future efforts in this area should consider cultural perspectives on how diversity is defined, the role of family members in expatriate intercultural adjustment, and methods for assessing intercultural effectiveness. In the years since, there have been several publications addressing best practices for the use of intercultural training with trainees from countries throughout the world. For example, the 2020 edition of the *Handbook of Intercultural Training* (Landis & Bhawuk, 2020) includes chapters on intercultural training in Brazil, Russia, India, China, and Japan. An emerging area of scholarship challenges the dominant culture vantage point characterizing much of the assessment of and training for intercultural competence (e.g., Lieberman & Gamst, 2015).

Variation:

Depending upon the level of the students in terms of their background in research methods, one can vary the rigor with which students construct a critical incident. For example, more advanced students can systematically elicit responses to their incident from people viewed as insiders and outsiders to the target culture and then develop a more elaborate critical incident in the form of a culture assimilator item. Culture assimilator items are critical incidents with several possible explanations that vary in terms of cultural congruence (see Bhawuk & Brislin, 2000).

References:

Bhawuk, D. P. S., & Brislin, R. W. (2000). Cross-cultural training: A review. *Applied Psychology*, *49*(1), 162–191. https://doi.org/10.1111/1464-0597.00009

Fowler, S. M., & Yamaguchi, M. (2020). An analysis of methods for intercultural training. In D. Landis & D. P. S. Bhawuk (Eds.), *The Cambridge handbook of intercultural training* (pp. 192–257). Cambridge University Press. https://doi.org/10.1017/9781108854184.008

Landis, D., & Bhawuk, D. P. S. (2020). *The Cambridge handbook of intercultural training*. Cambridge University Press.

Lieberman, D. A., & Gamst, G. (2015). Intercultural communication competence revisited: Linking the intercultural and multicultural fields. *International Journal of Intercultural Relations*, *48*, 17–19. https://doi.org/10.1016/j.ijintrel.2015.03.007

Nam, K.-A., Cho, Y., & Lee, M. (2014). West meets East? Identifying the gap in current cross-cultural training research. *Human Resource Development Review*, *13*(1), 36–57. https://doi.org/10.1177/1534484313500143

Paige, R. M., & Martin, J. N. (1996). Ethics in intercultural training. In D. Landis & R. S. Bhagat (Eds.), *Handbook of intercultural training* (2nd ed., pp. 41–60). Sage.

Pusch, M. (2004). Intercultural training in historical perspective. In D. Landis, J. M. Bennett, & M. J. Bennett (Eds.), *Handbook of intercultural training* (3rd ed., pp. 13–36). Sage.

Raver, J., & Van Dyne, L. (2017). Developing cultural intelligence. In K. Brown (Ed.), *The Cambridge handbook of workplace training and employee development* (Cambridge Handbooks in Psychology, pp. 407–440). Cambridge University Press.

Taras, V., Liu, Y., Mehta, A., Stackhouse, M. R. D., & Gonzalez-Perez, M. A. (2020). Cross-cultural training: History, developments, future directions. In B. Szkudlarek, L. Romani, D. V. Caprar, & J. S. Osland (Eds.), *Sage handbook of contemporary cross-cultural management* (pp. 519–535). Sage.

ACTIVITY 9.10
A DIVERSITY TRAINING INVESTIGATION

Activity Summary:

Using the questions provided, students interview a representative of an organization that conducts some form of diversity training.[1] Responses are then analyzed to assess the goals, content, and process of diversity training. [Requires work outside of the classroom.]

---

[1] At the time of this writing, several states in the U.S. have passed legislation to limit the use of diversity and inclusion training programs. As an alternative, students may be able to address many of the interview questions on the handout using internet sources (see the Writing Application section for Activity 9.10).

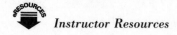

Lecture/Discussion Suggestion:

What are some informal sources of diversity training? Cortés (2004) made a compelling argument that for many people, media serves the function of intercultural trainer. According to Cortés, the media provides intercultural training in the following ways:

- Presenting and organizing information about cultural groups
- Transmitting values and forming expectations about cultures and intercultural contact
- Providing models for how to behave in intercultural situations

Students may be able to easily generate examples of these three functions of intercultural training by the media and evaluate their usefulness.

Variation:

It may be helpful to coordinate students and sites or organize groups of students to examine the diversity training program or organizations you select to avoid any one organization being deluged by calls from your class. An alternative is to invite a speaker and have the class as a whole conduct the interview. More advanced students can research the techniques reported and write a program evaluation.

Writing Application:

Investigate one of the hundreds of diversity training (or "cross-cultural training") sites on the internet. Write a report describing the training program offered including the goals, process, and emphases of the training.

Reference:

Cortés, C. E. (2004). Media and intercultural training. In D. Landis, J. M. Bennett, & M. J. Bennett (Eds.), *Handbook of intercultural training* (3rd ed., pp. 266–286). Sage.

Part Three

Student Activities

–1–

The Concept of Culture

ACTIVITY 1.1
HANDOUT

IS PSYCHOLOGY CULTURE-BOUND?

Psychology as a discipline strives to identify and describe universal principles of behavior. However, most psychological research has been conducted with undergraduate students in "WEIRD" (Western, educated, industrialized, rich, and democratic) societies, one of the least representative populations for drawing conclusions about human behavior (Henrich et al., 2010). Unfortunately, many psychology textbooks discuss these research findings as if they are universal, even in cases where cross-cultural studies indicate otherwise. This activity asks you to think about several concepts that appear in introductory psychology textbooks and consider the universality of each.

Directions: Read the description of each of the psychological concepts below. Then indicate in the space provided after each concept whether you believe it applies to people everywhere (universal) or believe it is limited to certain cultural groups (culture-specific). Write a brief rationale for your response. Your instructor can provide information on the possible universality of each concept.

1. Susceptibility to visual illusions – Although the two lines in the Müller-Lyer illusion below are the same length, the second line with the reverse arrowheads looks longer.

DOI: 10.4324/9781003356820-14   233

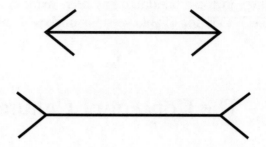

2. The serial-position effect (primacy and recency) – The first few items and the last few items in a list are remembered better than the items in the middle of the list.
3. Social loafing – The tendency for people to exert less effort when working as a group than when individually accountable.
4. Secure attachment – Mary Ainsworth and colleagues (1978) delineated three types of attachment: secure, avoidant, and ambivalent. Secure attachment is viewed as ideal in terms of the development of basic trust and other mental health indices (Waters et al., 2003).
5. Delusions and hallucinations – Delusions and hallucinations are signs of mental illness, specifically schizophrenia.
6. Self-serving bias – The tendency to use dispositional (internal) attributions when explaining our successes and situational (external) attributions when explaining our failures.
7. The similarity-attraction effect – The tendency for people to like others who they perceive to be similar to themselves.

References:

Ainsworth, M. D. S., Blehar, M. D., Waters, E., & Wall, S. (1978). *Patterns of attachment: A psychological study of the Strange Situation.* Lawrence Erlbaum.

Henrich, J., Heine, S. J., & Norenzayan, A. (2010). The weirdest people in the world? *Behavioral and Brain Sciences*, 33(2–3), 111–135. https://doi.org/10.1017/s0140525x0999152x

Waters, E., Merrick, S., Treboux, D., Crowell, J., & Albersheim, L. (2003). Attachment security in infancy and early adulthood: A twenty-year longitudinal study. In M. E. Herzig & E. A. Farber (Eds.), *Annual progress in child psychiatry and child development* (pp. 63–72). Brunner-Routledge.

ACTIVITY 1.2
HANDOUT

WHAT IS CULTURE?

Culture is not an easy concept to define. Even among those who study culture and human behavior, there are a large number of definitions in use. Perhaps the most straightforward definition is that of Melville Herskovits (1948) who proposed that culture is the human-made part of the environment. Harry Triandis and colleagues (1972) further suggested that culture has both physical components (such as tools, buildings, and works of art) and subjective components (such as roles, values, and attitudes). Recently, the term *culture* has been used more broadly to refer to the common values, beliefs, and behaviors within groups that share an ethnic heritage, disability, sexual orientation, or socioeconomic class, as well as to those who share a corporate identity, occupation, sport, or college campus. This activity encourages you to explore the meaning of culture by applying several commonly cited criteria (e.g., Baldwin et al., 2005; Matsumoto & Hwang, 2013) to determine whether a specific group is, in fact, a culture.

Directions: Identify a group that you think of as possibly having its own culture. First describe this group, then by answering the questions below, decide whether this group has the characteristics of a culture.

Group Name and Description:

1. Does the group hold shared perspectives, norms, values, or assumptions that direct the behavior of its members? Please give an example.
2. Is the information that is important to this group learned and handed down through generations (or cohorts) of its members? Please give an example.
3. Does this group have a common language, dialect, or set of terms? Please give an example.
4. Are the perspectives and practices of this group widely shared among its members? Please give an example.
5. Do members react strongly when the perspectives or practices of this group are not upheld? Please give an example.
6. Do the practices of this group contribute to its survival and the well-being of its members? Please give an example.
7. Discuss your conclusions about whether the group you chose to examine is a culture.

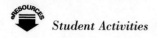

Thinking Further:

1. Is it helpful to distinguish cultures from subcultures (that is, smaller cultural groups within a larger culture)? Why or why not?
2. There has been criticism of cross-cultural research that equates culture with nationality and makes comparisons between members of different countries (e.g., Italians and Canadians). Why might there be concern about this approach?
3. How might culture be distinguished from race, ethnicity, and nationality?

References:

Baldwin, J. R., Faulkner, S. L., Hecht, M. L., & Lindsley, S. L. (Eds.). (2005). *Redefining culture: Perspectives across the disciplines.* Lawrence Erlbaum Associates.

Herskovits, M. J. (1948). *Man and his works: The science of cultural anthropology.* Knopf.

Matsumoto, D., & Hwang, H. S. (2013). Culture. In K. Keith (Ed.), *Encyclopedia of cross-cultural psychology* (pp. 345–347). Wiley-Blackwell.

Triandis, H. C., Vassiliou, V., Vassiliou, G., Tanaka, Y., & Shanmugam, A. V. (1972). *The analysis of subjective culture.* Wiley.

ACTIVITY 1.3
HANDOUT

HUMAN UNIVERSALS

One criticism of research on culture and psychology is that it focuses too much on cultural differences and neglects similarities. This may be due to several factors including the statistical methods used in psychological research, which are aimed at testing for differences, and an innate tendency of humans to categorize others into groups (Lalonde et al., 2015). Another reason for this focus on differences may be that it is very difficult to determine criteria for establishing universality. For example, Ara Norenzayan and Steven Heine (2005) differentiated between types of universals that depend on whether a phenomenon exists across cultures, is used to solve the same problems across cultures, and is equally accessible to individuals in those cultures. This activity

---

encourages you to consider similarities across cultures and their importance to our understanding of human behavior.

Directions: In his book on human universals, anthropologist Donald E. Brown (1991) presented a description of the *Universal People* (or UPs) as a means of explaining commonalities across cultures, societies, and language groups. For example, Brown suggested that the UPs have a language that allows them to think and speak about things that are not physically present, they have childhood fears, they distinguish right from wrong, they have specific standards of attractiveness and so on. In the space below, write a paragraph or two describing additional characteristics of the Universal People. What characteristics do all humans share? Some aspects you might address in your description of the UPs include language, emotions, self-concept, daily activities, social interaction, family and community structure, rituals, and view of outsiders.

Thinking Further:

1. Human universals nearly always aid survival in some way (Buss, 2001). They can be innate psychological tendencies, such as the ability to learn languages, or learned behaviors in response to human needs, such as counting systems (Norenzayan & Heine, 2005). Human universals may also reflect physical facts that are common across cultures, such as a preference for right handedness, (Brown, 2004). Choose one of the universals you identified in your description of the Universal People and discuss possible sources of that universal (an innate psychological tendency, learned behavior in response to human needs, a reflection of physical facts, or other sources).
2. What might be some of the costs of focusing on differences rather than similarities in research on culture and psychology? Please explain.

References:

Brown, D. E. (1991). *Human universals*. Temple University Press.
Brown, D. E. (2004). Human universals, human nature & human culture. *Daedalus, 133*(4), 47–54. https://doi.org/10.1162/0011526042365645
Buss, D. M. (2001). Human nature and culture: An evolutionary psychological perspective. *Journal of Personality, 69*(6), 955–978. https://doi.org/10.1111/1467-6494.696171

Lalonde, R. N., Cila, J., Lou, E., & Cribbie, R. A. (2015). Are we really that different from each other? The difficulties of focusing on similarities in cross-cultural research. *Peace and Conflict: Journal of Peace Psychology*, *21*(4), 525–534. https://doi.org/10.103 7/pac0000134

Norenzayan, A., & Heine, S. J. (2005). Psychological universals: What are they and how can we know? *Psychological Bulletin*, *131*(5), 763–784.

ACTIVITY 1.4
HANDOUT

CROSS-CULTURAL PSYCHOLOGY'S DEATH WISH

Walter Lonner (2018, p. 82) suggested that culture-oriented psychology has a "death wish" in that it strives to no longer exist as a separate field of psychology once cross-cultural perspectives become "a central and common-place component of psychological thinking, research, and application." This activity will allow you to investigate how close psychology has come to making this wish come true.

Directions: First, find a university-level textbook on a specific subtopic in psychology (e.g., research methods, biopsychology, states of consciousness, sensation and perception, lifespan development, motivation and emotion, learning, memory, cognition, gender and sexuality, health psychology, personality, social psychology, psychological disorders, counseling). You may also use a specific chapter of an introduction to psychology textbook (some complete textbooks are available online). Then answer the questions below.

1. State the author, title, and topic of the textbook or chapter you selected.
2. List and briefly describe the concepts or theories for which cultural perspectives have been included in the chapter or textbook.
3. Discuss at least one topic in the chapter or text where you believe a cultural perspective is necessary but has been omitted.

Thinking Further:

What changes over time do you think will facilitate the integration of cultural perspectives across areas of psychology?

Reference:

Lonner, W. J. (2018). The continuing growth of cross-cultural psychology: A first-person, annotated chronology. In K. D. Keith (Ed.), *Elements in psychology and culture* (pp. 1–92). Cambridge University Press.

ACTIVITY 1.5
HANDOUT

A SEARCH FOR INDIVIDUALISM AND COLLECTIVISM

The concepts of individualism and collectivism have received great attention in research on culture and psychology and continue to be debated and revised (e.g., Minkov et al., 2017; Taras et al., 2014; Wong et al., 2018). These terms stem from Hofstede's (1980) classic cross-cultural study of workplace values. According to Hofstede (2001, p. 225),

> Individualism stands for a society in which the ties between individuals are loose; everyone is expected to look after themselves and their immediate family only.

> Collectivism stands for a society in which people from birth onwards are integrated into strong cohesive in-groups, which throughout people's lifetime continue to protect them in exchange for unquestioning loyalty.

This activity encourages you to explore these concepts by seeking out real-life examples of individualism and collectivism.

Directions: Reread the definitions of individualism and collectivism above. Then identify one real-life example of individualism and one of collectivism (such as a behavior, an object, a song, or an advertising slogan). The ease with which you can find these examples will depend on whether you live in a more individualistic or collectivistic culture. However, you should be able to find some forms of collectivism within an individualistic culture and some forms of individualism within a collectivistic culture. Examples of individualism might include an advertisement for an electric blanket that has separate settings for the right and left sides or a brochure for a preschool curriculum in which activities depend on the individual child's skills and interests. Examples of collectivism might include information on a community bicycle-sharing program or a T-shirt imprinted with the insignia of your university. If possible, bring your examples – or photos of your examples – to class with this completed assignment.

1. Describe your example of individualism and explain why it illustrates individualism.
2. Describe your example of collectivism and explain why it illustrates collectivism.

Thinking Further:

1. Studies show that greater cross-cultural differences in individualism and collectivism are expressed in "cultural products," such as those you and your classmates collected, than in self-ratings of behaviors, beliefs, or feelings (Morling, 2016; Morling & Lamoreaux, 2008). Why might that be so?
2. Cultural values are not static but change over time. After analyzing 51 years of data from 78 countries, Henri Santos and colleagues (2017) reported that individualism is increasing and appears to accompany a country's socio-economic development. How might you explain this finding?
3. Hofstede cautioned against applying findings based on national culture dimensions like individualism and collectivism to individuals – an error that has been called the *ecological fallacy* and is not uncommon (Brewer & Venaik, 2014). Rather than measure individualism and collectivism on the individual level, researchers should instead measure the traits of idio-centrism and allocentrism respectively. As Hofstede (2001, p. 7) put it, "cultures are not king-size individuals." Why should we be concerned about researchers committing the ecological fallacy?

References:

Brewer, P., & Venaik, S. (2014). The ecological fallacy in national culture research. *Organization Studies, 35*(7), 1063–1086. https://doi.org/10. 1177/0170840613517602

Hofstede, G. (1980). *Culture's consequences: International differences in work-related values.* Sage.

Hofstede, G. (2001). *Culture's consequences: Comparing values, behaviors, and organizations across nations* (2nd ed.). Sage.

Minkov, M., Dutt, P., Schachner, M., Morales, O., Sanchez, C., Jandosova, J., Khassenbekov, Y., & Mudd, B. (2017). A revision of

Hofstede's individualism-collectivism dimension: A new national index from a 56-country study. *Cross Cultural & Strategic Management*, *24*(3), 386–404. https://doi.org/10.1108/CCSM-11-2016-0197

Morling, B. (2016). Cultural difference, inside and out. *Social and Personality Psychology Compass*, *10*(12), 693–706. https://doi.org/10.1111/spc3.12294

Morling, B., & Lamoreaux, M. (2008). Measuring culture outside the head: A meta-analysis of individualism-collectivism in cultural products. *Personality and Social Psychology Review*, *12*(3), 199–221. https://doi.org/10.1177/1088868308318260

Santos, H. C., Varnum, M. E. W., & Grossmann, I. (2017). Global increases in individualism. *Psychological Science*, *28*(9), 1228–1239. https://doi.org/10.1177/0956797617700622

Taras, V., Sarala, R., Muchinsky, P., et al. (2014). Opposite ends of the same stick? Multi-method test of the dimensionality of individualism and collectivism. *Journal of Cross-Cultural Psychology*, *45*(2), 213–245. https://doi.org/10.1177/0022022113509132

Wong, Y. J., Wang, S. Y., & Klann, E. M. (2018). The emperor with no clothes: A critique of collectivism and individualism. *Archives of Scientific Psychology*, *6*(1), 251. https://doi.org/10.1037/arc0000059

ACTIVITY 1.6
HANDOUT

CLEANLINESS BELIEFS

One of the complaints sojourners often have when they visit another culture is that cleanliness practices are not adequate. This activity will help you to explore your own cleanliness beliefs and put them in a cross-cultural perspective.

Directions: Respond to the items below to indicate your cleanliness beliefs.

1. People in my culture value cleanliness.

Strongly Disagree						Strongly Agree
1	2	3	4	5	6	7

Please explain:

2. One should wash one's body before entering a bathtub full of clean water.

Strongly Disagree						Strongly Agree
1	2	3	4	5	6	7

3. Blankets and rugs should be hung out daily to air.

Strongly Disagree						Strongly Agree
1	2	3	4	5	6	7

4. Shoes should be removed before entering a home.

Strongly Disagree						Strongly Agree
1	2	3	4	5	6	7

5. The left hand should not be used for eating or taking food from communal dishes.

Strongly Disagree						Strongly Agree
1	2	3	4	5	6	7

6. One should shower or bathe daily.

Strongly Disagree						Strongly Agree
1	2	3	4	5	6	7

7. Cleaning products should be used in the home to kill germs.

Strongly Disagree						Strongly Agree
1	2	3	4	5	6	7

8. One's hands should be washed upon returning home.

Strongly Disagree						Strongly Agree
1	2	3	4	5	6	7

9. One should use one washcloth and soap for the upper half of one's body and a different washcloth and soap for the lower half.

Strongly Disagree						Strongly Agree
1	2	3	4	5	6	7

10. After using the toilet, rinsing with water is more sanitary than using toilet paper.

Strongly Disagree						Strongly Agree
1	2	3	4	5	6	7

Thinking Further:

1. Look over your answers to the questions above. With which cleanliness practices did you AGREE most strongly? What cultural messages were you taught that support these practices?
2. With which practices did you DISAGREE most strongly? What cultural messages were you taught that conflict with these practices?
3. What other cleanliness practices not listed above are important to you?
4. Review your responses above. Are there any of your cleanliness beliefs that could be considered poor hygiene by someone from a culture other than your own?
5. Look back at your response to item 1. Is there anything you would like to add or change in your answer?

Sources:

Cleanliness belief items are based on the following sources:

Fernea, E., & Fernea, R. A. (1994). Cleanliness and culture. In W. J. Lonner & R. S. Malpass (Eds.), *Psychology and culture* (pp. 65–70). Allyn & Bacon.

Tseng, W.-S., & Streltzer, J. (2008). *Cultural competence in health care*. Springer.

Vivian, C., & Dundes, L. (2004). The crossroads of culture and health among the Roma. *Journal of Nursing Scholarship, 36*(1), 86–91. https://doi.org/10.1111/j.1547-5069.2004.04018.x

Waxler-Morrison, N., Anderson, J., & Richardson, E. (1990). *Cross-cultural caring: A handbook for health professionals in Western Canada*. University of British Columbia Press.

ACTIVITY 1.7
HANDOUT

ETHNIC GLOSS

Joseph Trimble (1990) coined the term "ethnic gloss" to refer to overgeneralized labels used to categorize ethnocultural groups. For example, Trimble and Bhadra (2013) noted that the single category "American Indian" is used to refer to over 500 individual tribal units, varying widely in terms of language and belief systems. If used to indicate ethnocultural identity without further specification, terms like "Asian Canadian," "Hispanic" or "Latinx," or "African American" may also be considered ethnic gloss. In psychological research, the use of broad ethnocultural labels such as these can result in inaccurate findings and may promote stereotypes.

The purpose of this activity is to increase awareness of ethnic gloss in cross-cultural research.

Directions: Find three psychology research articles that include an ethnocultural label in the title. Examine each article carefully paying particular attention to the studies' rationale, description of participants, results, and discussion. Then, answer the questions below.

Study 1:

1. Provide the complete reference for your article (see references throughout this book for examples of the format and content).
2. Did you observe the use of overgeneralized ethnocultural labels (ethnic gloss)? Please explain.

Study 2:

1. Provide the complete reference for your article (see references throughout this book for examples of the format and content).

---

2. Did you observe the use of overgeneralized ethnocultural labels (ethnic gloss)? Please explain.

Study 3:

1. Provide the complete reference for your article (see references throughout this book for examples of the format and content).
2. Did you observe the use of overgeneralized ethnocultural labels (ethnic gloss)? Please explain.

Thinking Further:

1. Does the concept of ethnic gloss apply to people of European ancestry? Why or why not?
2. It is clear that broad ethnocultural labels are problematic in psychological research. How might ethnic gloss be problematic in psychotherapy?
3. Are there any situations in which broad ethnocultural labels could be useful?

References:

Trimble, J. E. (1990). Ethnic specification, validation prospects, and the future of drug use research. *International Journal of the Addictions, 25*(supp 2), 149–170. https://doi.org/10.3109/10826089009071038

Trimble, J. E., & Bhadra, M. (2013). Ethnic gloss. In K. Keith (Ed.), *The Encyclopedia of Cross-Cultural Psychology*, Vol. 2 (pp. 500–504). Wiley-Blackwell.

ACTIVITY 1.8
HANDOUT

ETHNOCENTRISM, CULTURAL RELATIVISM,
AND UNIVERSAL HUMAN RIGHTS

When we encounter cultural practices or beliefs that differ from our own, there are several approaches we can take. An *ethnocentric* approach uses the standards of one's own culture to judge the practices of people from other cultures. In contrast, a *cultural relativist* approach involves evaluating an individual's behaviors based on their own cultural context. Most researchers of culture have adopted a philosophy of cultural relativism to some extent but view as unacceptable cultural practices

---

that violate *universal human rights*, such as the killing of women considered to have violated their family's honor (Woolf & Hulsizer, 2013). These concepts have important applications beyond the study of culture and psychology. For example, courts in many countries with multicultural populations are grappling with *cultural offense* cases in which an act viewed as appropriate among members of a specific subpopulation violates the laws of that country (Muzzica et al., 2015). This activity encourages you to explore the complexities of applying the concepts of ethnocentrism, cultural relativism, and universal rights.

Directions: For each of the incidents listed below, discuss your opinion and then indicate whether that opinion is driven by ethnocentrism, cultural relativism, or universal human rights.

1. The Supreme Court of Canada ruled that a 12-year-old Sikh boy should be allowed to wear his ceremonial sword – known as a kirpan – while he is at school. For devout Sikh men, wearing the kirpan is an essential part of the religious faith. The decision overturned one made by his school which banned him from carrying the small blunt metal dagger because they regarded it as a weapon.

   Do you believe the court made the correct decision? Is your response based on ethnocentrism, cultural relativism, or universal rights? Please explain.

2. Members of some Amish communities in the United States have contested local building codes requiring that homes have smoke alarms and carbon monoxide detectors. These requirements have been viewed as infringing on religious and cultural beliefs that discourage the use of technology. In 2015, the state of Wisconsin granted an exemption to these codes for members of the Amish community.

   Do you believe the state of Wisconsin made the correct decision? Is your response based on ethnocentrism, cultural relativism, or universal rights? Please explain.

3. In 2022, the Court of Justice of the European Union ruled that employers have the right to stop employees from wearing visible religious symbols, including Islamic clothing (such as the burka and niqab) and headscarves (such as hijab).

   Do you believe the European Court of Justice made the correct decision? Is your response based on ethnocentrism, cultural relativism, or universal rights? Please explain.

4. In 2005, King Abdulaziz University of Saudi Arabia paid Virginia Tech University $246,000 to design and operate summer courses for 60 of the King Abdulaziz faculty – courses that were held on the Virginia Tech campus. Following Saudi custom and the preferences of the King Abdulaziz University

professors, the 30 female Saudi professors and 30 male Saudi professors were taught in separate classes. Several Virginia Tech faculty members objected, stating that this action violated U.S. federal anti-discrimination laws.

Do you believe that Virginia Tech made the correct decision? Is your response based on ethnocentrism, cultural relativism, or universal rights? Please explain.

5. Although bullfighting is illegal in the United States, a bullfighting academy has been operating in Southern California since 1996. Students at this school do not train with real animals, yet the San Diego County Humane Society opposes the school, which it views as promoting animal cruelty. One of the founders of the academy, however, takes the position that bullfighting is an important cultural practice and should not be prohibited.

Do you believe this school should be allowed to operate? Is your response based on ethnocentrism, cultural relativism, or universal human (or animal) rights? Please explain.

Thinking Further:

Based on your answers to the questions above, write a brief statement explaining the conditions under which you believe it is justified to take an ethnocentric, cultural relativist, or universal rights perspective when considering the practices of cultures other than your own.

References:

Muzzica, R., Tamborra, T. L., & Amarelli, G. (2015). Emerging cultural conflicts in Italy: A challenge for criminal law. *International Journal of Criminology and Sociology*, *4*, 141–153. https://doi.org/10.6000/1929-4409.2015.04.15

Woolf, L. M., & Hulsizer, M. R. (2013). Human rights. In K. Keith (Ed.), *Encyclopedia of cross-cultural psychology* (pp. 668–671). Wiley-Blackwell.

ACTIVITY 1.9
HANDOUT
EXPLORING THE WORLD VILLAGE

This activity, based on the format of The World Village Project, is designed to help you gain a more accurate view of human characteristics worldwide.

Directions: Imagine a village of 100 people that represents planet Earth. Answer the questions below, assuming that all of the human ratios in the village are the same as those of the world.

Of the 100 inhabitants, indicate how many would fall into each of the following categories.

1. *Gender*[1]
_____ are male
_____ are female

2. *Age*
_____ are under age 15
_____ are over age 65

3. *Places of Origin*
_____ are Africans
_____ are Asians
_____ are Europeans
_____ are South Americans
_____ are North Americans
_____ are Oceanians (Australia, New Zealand, Papua New Guinea)

4. *Primary Language*
_____ speak Arabic
_____ speak Bengali
_____ speak English
_____ speak Hindi
_____ speak Japanese
_____ speak Mandarin
_____ speak Portuguese
_____ speak Punjabi
_____ speak Russian
_____ speak Spanish

5. *Religion*
_____ are atheists
_____ are Buddhists
_____ are Christians
_____ are Hindus
_____ are Muslims
_____ are non-religious
_____ are other religions

6. *Education*
_____ will be able to read and write
_____ complete high school
_____ hold a college degree

7. *Technology*
_____ have a cell phone
_____ have internet access
_____ have cars

8. *Health and Well-Being*
_____ have access to clean drinking water
_____ have access to basic sanitation
_____ are affected by mental health problems
_____ live with a disability

[1] No data is currently available on the number of individuals worldwide who identify as nonbinary.

_____ are food insecure
_____ live in urban areas
_____ live in substandard housing

_____ live in regions affected by climate change
_____ are refugees

9. *Wealth*
_____ live below the internationally defined poverty line
_____ control half of all wealth

ACTIVITY 1.10
HANDOUT

A GLOBAL VIEW OF PSYCHOLOGY

Much of what is published in psychology journals and textbooks takes a Western perspective and ignores the psychologies developed by scholars across the globe to address more local conditions. The purpose of this activity is twofold. First, it will acquaint you with some of the research interests of psychologists throughout the world. Second, it will encourage you to think about some of the forces that have shaped psychology in different regions, including the form labeled *Western psychology*.[2]

Directions: Read about the field of psychology in a country other than your own. There are several good sources for this kind of information, including professional associations (such as The Nigerian Psychological Association), publications of the International Psychology Division of the American Psychological Association, and of course, database or internet searches (e.g., "psychology in China" OR "history of psychology in Brazil"). You may need to use an online translator if you are not familiar with the language in which this information appears.

1. Provide the complete reference for your source (see references throughout this book for examples of format and content).
2. In a paragraph or two, describe below what you learned about the focus of psychology in the country you investigated.

---

[2] The term *Western psychology* can itself be viewed as ethnocentric in that it ignores the diverse cultures of the West and focuses only on those of European tradition. Some scholars have acknowledged this bias by using the term "Eurowestern" rather than "Western."

3. What social, cultural, political, historical, environmental, economic, and/or religious factors may have shaped the research focus of psychology in the country you selected?

Thinking Further:

Consider the theories, methods, and priorities of Western psychology. What do you conclude about the social, cultural, political, historical, environmental, economic, and/or religious factors that may have shaped its research focus? Please explain.

(Space for responses in these handouts has been reduced. Please see www.rou-tledge.com/9781032394336 for fillable versions of these handouts.)

–2–

Culture and Psychological Research

ACTIVITY 2.1
HANDOUT

FUNCTIONS OF CROSS-CULTURAL RESEARCH

As you have probably realized by now, cross-cultural research is not without its challenges. Efforts must be made to identify the appropriate cultures for testing a theory and to develop or select measures and procedures that will ensure cross-cultural comparisons are based on equivalent procedures and data. Why, then, would social scientists make the effort to conduct such research? Researchers choose to conduct cross-cultural studies for many different reasons. The purpose of this activity is to become familiar with the major functions of cross-cultural research.

Directions: Several functions of cross-cultural research have been identified and described (Berry et al., 2011; Brislin, 2000). Read the functions of cross-cultural research listed below. Then, for each of the research project descriptions that follow, indicate which of the functions is served by taking a cross-cultural approach. More than one function may be relevant to some of the project descriptions. Once you finish you can check your answers with your instructor.

Functions of Cross-Cultural Research:

1. Identifying culture-specific values, cognitive categories, or forms of behavior.
2. Unconfounding variables. Two variables that may be linked in one culture may be unrelated in another culture.
3. Expanding the range of variables.

DOI: 10.4324/9781003356820-15

4. Understanding the relationship between ecological and psychological variables.
5. Investigating possible human universals.
6. Testing the generality of psychological models or theories.
7. Studying the effect of cultural change.

Project Descriptions:

1. A Japanese expert on post-traumatic stress disorder constructed a model for predicting the likelihood that someone will develop psychological disturbances in response to extreme trauma. His original model was based on a study of survivors of the Fukushima earthquake and tsunami in Japan. He wondered if his model would also be a good predictor in other cultures, so he tested it on data from survivors of Hurricane Maria in Puerto Rico.

   What function was served by taking a cross-cultural approach? Please explain.
2. A community psychologist was interested in the effect of neighborhood stability on willingness to participate in community-based recycling programs. She was having some difficulty conducting her research because in her own country many neighborhoods had high residential mobility (people move homes frequently). By including several other countries in her study, she was able to explore "willingness to participate" within unstable, moderately stable, and highly stable neighborhoods.

   What function was served by taking a cross-cultural approach? Please explain.
3. A social psychologist was studying the impact of exposure to internet content on children's beliefs about the value of material goods. In her own country, only wealthy families have internet access, thus causing difficulty in separating the effects of internet content from the effects of growing up in a wealthy family. Instead, she decided to conduct her research in Canada where she could find children with different levels of exposure to internet content at both high- and low-income levels.

   What function was served by taking a cross-cultural approach? Please explain.
4. An experimental psychologist was interested in the effect of urban living on depth perception. He reasoned that city dwellers might be less sensitive than people in rural environments to depth cues that involve distance. He used stimuli to assess the perception of depth cues with

individuals living in cultures based in a variety of urban and rural environments.

What function was served by taking a cross-cultural approach? Please explain.

5. An interdisciplinary team of researchers was exploring the reasons why members of certain ethnic groups were underrepresented as clients of a community mediation center. They hypothesized that the techniques used to resolve disputes at the mediation center may be culturally inappropriate for some groups of people. Instead of encouraging members of those groups to use the mediation center, they decided to conduct a cross-cultural study to identify methods of resolving disputes that were indigenous to those ethnic groups.

What function was served by taking a cross-cultural approach? Please explain.

6. A clinical psychologist was interested in the impact of exposure to Western values on eating disorders. He decided to investigate changes over time in rates of anorexia and bulimia in areas with growing exposure to Western media.

What function was served by taking a cross-cultural approach? Please explain.

7. A student of psychology read that in her own country, boys outperformed girls in measures of mathematical achievement. She wondered if this might be due to biological sex differences and was found in all cultures or if it reflected differences in experience (such as educational or career opportunities). When she looked into the cross-cultural literature she discovered that in some countries researchers found gender differences in mathematical achievement scores and in others they did not.

What function was served by taking a cross-cultural approach? Please explain.

References:

Berry, J. W., Poortinga, Y. H., Breugelmans, S. M., Chasiotis, A., & Sam, D. L. (2011). *Cross-cultural psychology: Research and applications* (3rd ed.). Cambridge University Press.

Brislin, R. (2000). *Understanding culture's influence on behavior* (2nd ed.). Wadsworth.

ACTIVITY 2.2
HANDOUT

INSIDERS AND OUTSIDERS

Psychologists have long emphasized objectivity in research and have expressed concern about bias stemming from the researcher being too close to the groups they are studying. In contrast, anthropologists have traditionally taken an approach that involves participating in the circumstances they are describing or analyzing. What are the advantages of being a cultural outsider or a cultural insider? This activity is designed to clarify differences between the insider perspective and the outsider perspective in conducting cross-cultural research.

Directions: Find an organized group or club that is well-known on or off your campus. Identify two people to interview about this group: one who is a member (an insider) and one who has heard something about the group but is not a member (an outsider). Ask the same questions outlined below to both interviewees. Please assure your respondents that their identities will remain confidential. Do not include their names on these sheets.

Group: _____

Interview A: Insider (Member)

   1. How did you first learn about this group?
   2. What are the criteria for membership?
   3. How would you characterize the members of this group?
   4. What are the goals of this group?
   5. How effective is this group in achieving its goals? Please explain.
   6. What is the perception most nonmembers have of this group?

Interview B: Outsider (Nonmember)

   1. How did you first learn about this group?
   2. What are the criteria for membership?
   3. How would you characterize the members of this group?
   4. What are the goals of this group?
   5. How effective is this group in achieving its goals? Please explain.
   6. What is the perception most nonmembers have of this group?

First compare the responses from the two interviews, then answer the questions below.

1. Describe the major differences between the two accounts.
2. What are the advantages and disadvantages of using insiders as an information source?
3. What are the advantages and disadvantages of using outsiders as an information source?

Thinking Further:

What would you recommend for cross-cultural psychologists in terms of being an insider or outsider relative to the cultures they study?

ACTIVITY 2.3
HANDOUT

EMIC AND ETIC PERSPECTIVES

The purpose of this activity is to familiarize you with a key concept in studying culture and human behavior; the distinction between *emics* and *etics*. According to John Berry (1969, 1989), etic research takes an outsider's perspective and focuses on the search for human universals, whereas emic research takes an insider's perspective and addresses the way behaviors are expressed within a specific culture. Berry warned us about the danger of an *imposed etic* in which we assume that research concepts or methodologies developed in one culture have the same meaning across cultural groups. For example, people in all cultures make moral judgments, but a study that employs a measure of Kohlberg's stages of moral development across cultures is using an imposed etic. Instead, it may be possible to identify emic forms of moral behavior, such as *ahimsa*, an Indian principle of nonviolence based on respect for all life (Eckensberger & Zimba, 1997). Cross-cultural research should ideally lead to *derived etics*, based on common features across emic phenomena (Berry et al., 2011).

Directions: First add five etic categories to the list below. Then choose one of these etics, select a cultural group with which you are familiar, and then identify and describe an associated emic for that cultural group. For example, "social relationships" is an etic category, but the Chinese concept of *guanxi* addresses an emic aspect of social relationships, "the closeness of a relationship that is associated with a particular set of differentiated behavioral obligations based on social and ethical norms" (Mao et al., 2012, p. 1161). You may need to use published scholarly sources to find your emic.

Etics

a. childrearing practices   f. _____
b. gender roles   g. _____
c. leadership   h. _____
d. humor   i. _____
e. expression of emotion   j. _____

1. Identify the etic you selected.
2. Describe an associated emic.

References:

Berry, J. W. (1969). On cross-cultural comparability. *International Journal of Psychology, 4*, 119–128. https://doi.org/10.1080/00207596908247261

Berry, J. W. (1989). Imposed etics-emics-derived etics: The operationalization of a compelling idea. *International Journal of Psychology, 24*(6), 721–735. https://doi.org/10.1080/00207598908247841

Berry, J. W., Poortinga, Y. H., Breugelmans, S. M., Chasiotis, A., & Sam, D. L. (2011). *Cross-cultural psychology: Research and applications* (3rd ed.). Cambridge University Press.

Eckensberger, L. H., & Zimba, R. F. (1997). The development of moral judgment. In J. W. Berry, P. R. Dasen, & T. S. Saraswathi (Eds.), *Handbook of cross-cultural psychology*, Vol. 2: Basic processes and human development (2nd ed., pp. 299–338). Allyn & Bacon.

Mao, Y., Peng, K. Z., & Wong, C. (2012). Indigenous research on Asia: In search of the emic components of *guanxi. Asia Pacific Journal of Management, 29*(4), 1143–1168. https://psycnet.apa.org/doi/10.1007/s10490-012-9317-5

ACTIVITY 2.4
HANDOUT

CULTURAL DISTANCE

Cultural distance generally refers to "the degree to which cultural values in one country are different from those in another country" (Sousa & Bradley, 2006, p. 52).

The concept of cultural distance has been included in research on a wide range of cross-cultural topics, with the measurement used varying by topic. Some studies use a *country-level measure* of cultural distance in which each nation has been assigned a score based on an established index, such as the World Values Survey or the Hofstede Dimensions of Culture. For example, Yun Hyeong Choi and colleagues (2022) investigated the role of cultural distance between participating and host nations in the Summer Olympics as measured by country scores on the Hofstede Dimensions. The authors reported that cultural distance on the dimensions of Masculinity and Uncertainty Avoidance was negatively related to winning an Olympic medal. In contrast, many studies have used a subjective, *individual-level measure* of perceived cultural distance in which participants are asked to indicate how different or similar countries are on a set of criteria. For example, Kali Demes and Nicolas Geeraert (2014) developed an individual-level measure that details multiple components of perceived cultural distance (e.g., social norms, family life, language). Research on international student adjustment with individual-level measures has found a fairly consistent connection between greater perceived cultural distance and more severe adjustment difficulties (Malay et al., 2023). This activity will familiarize you with the concept of cultural distance in the context of intercultural adjustment.

Directions: Below you will find a number of dimensions on which cultures may differ. Numbering from 1 (most important) to 12 (least important), rank these areas of difference on their importance in creating a sense of cultural distance for you. For example, would a culture feel more distant to you if your primary language was not spoken there? Or if the foods you typically eat were not available?

_____ Languages spoken
_____ Directness of communication
_____ Pace of life
_____ Personal safety
_____ Environmental noise level
_____ Typical foods
_____ Gender equality
_____ Racial/ethnic diversity
_____ Religious beliefs
_____ Etiquette and manners
_____ Individualism/collectivism
_____ Personal space

What do you conclude about cultural distance from ranking these areas of cultural difference?

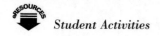

Thinking Further:

Michael Muthukrishna and colleagues (2020) developed a country-level measure of cultural distance with the goal of broadening the range of countries sampled in cross-cultural research and reducing the overrepresentation of U.S. Americans. How could a measure of cultural distance help to achieve this aim?

References:

Choi, Y. H., Wei, Q., Zhang, L., & Choi, S.-J. (2022). The impact of cultural distance on performance at the Summer Olympic Games. *SAGE Open, 12*(1). https://doi.org/10.1177/21582440221085265

Demes, K. A., & Geeraert, N. (2014). Measures matter: Scales for adaptation, cultural distance, and acculturation orientation revisited. *Journal of Cross-Cultural Psychology, 45*(1), 91–109. https://doi.org/10.1177/0022022113487590

Malay, E. D., Otten, S., & Coelen, R. J. (2023). Predicting adjustment of international students: The role of cultural intelligence and perceived cultural distance. *Research in Comparative and International Education.* https://doi.org/10.1177/17454999231159469

Muthukrishna, M., Bell, A. V., Henrich, J., Curtin, C. M., Gedranovich, A., McInerney, J., & Thue, B. (2020). Beyond Western, educated, industrial, rich, and democratic (WEIRD) psychology: Measuring and mapping scales of cultural and psychological distance. *Psychological Science, 31*(6), 678–701. https://doi.org/10.1177/0956797620916782

Sousa, C. M., & Bradley, F. (2006). Cultural distance and psychic distance: Two peas in a pod? *Journal of International Marketing, 14*(1), 49–70. https://journals.sagepub.com/doi/abs/10.1509/jimk.14.1.49

ACTIVITY 2.5
HANDOUT

WRITING TRANSLATABLE ITEMS

There is much controversy among those who study culture and psychology over the wisdom of translating materials developed in one culture for use in assessing the behaviors of individuals in another culture. However, most

---

would agree that if translation is to be used, there are practices that increase its accuracy. The purpose of this activity is to explore the process of preparing test materials for translation.

Directions: Using scholarly sources (such as those available on PsycINFO), locate a scale or test that is designed to measure some psychological phenomenon. Another good source to help you identify tests in your area of interest is the *Mental Measurements Yearbook* (https://buros.org/mental-measurements-yearbook) which contains descriptions, reviews, and references for hundreds of tests, many of which can be accessed online or through a library database. Once you have located a scale, choose five items of interest to you and write them below. Next, modify the wording of the items based on the rules on the following page, which were adapted from Richard Brislin, Walter Lonner, and Robert Thorndike's (1973) guidelines for writing translatable items.

1. State the author, source, and name of the scale.
2. List five of the original scale items.
   a.
   b.
   c.
   d.
   e.

Guidelines for writing translatable items:

   i. Use short, simple sentences.
  ii. Use active rather than passive words.
 iii. Repeat nouns instead of using pronouns.
 iv. Avoid metaphors and colloquialisms.
  v. Avoid the subjunctive tense (such as verb forms with *could* or *would*).
 vi. Avoid adverbs and prepositions telling where or when (such as *frequent, beyond, upper*).
 vii. Avoid possessive forms.
viii. Use specific rather than general terms (such as *cow, chicken,* or *pig* rather than *livestock*).
 ix. Avoid words indicating vagueness regarding some event or thing (such as *probably* or *frequently*).
  x. Avoid sentences with two different verbs if the verbs indicate two different actions.

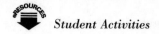

3. List the five modified items.
   a.
   b.
   c.
   d.
   e.

Sources:

Guidelines for writing translatable items adapted from Brislin, R., Lonner, W., & Thorndike, R. (1973). *Cross-cultural research methods.* Copyright © 1973 by John Wiley & Sons, Inc. Adapted with permission.

ACTIVITY 2.6
HANDOUT

BACK-TRANSLATION

One of the many concerns in conducting cross-cultural research is the accuracy of translated materials. This activity will provide you with an opportunity to try out a widely used technique for improving the quality of translated materials called *back-translation* (Brislin, 1980, 2000).

Directions: For this activity, you will need to enlist the help of two bilingual individuals who are skilled in the same two languages. The materials to be translated are the five test items you developed in Activity 2.5 or any other five psychological test items. The first bilingual individual is to translate the test items from the original language to a second (or target) language. You are then to hand the translated version to a second bilingual individual who is to translate them back into their original language. The two bilingual assistants are to work separately on this task. By comparing the original and back-translated versions of the test items, you can identify concepts or word forms that cannot be easily translated accurately.

1. State the author, source, name of the scale, and original language.
2. What is the target language for your translation?
3. List your five items from Activity 2.5 or other source.
   a.
   b.
   c.

---

d.

    e.

4. List the items as translated into the target language.

    a.

    b.

    c.

    d.

    e.

5. List the five items as back-translated into the original language.

    a.

    b.

    c.

    d.

    e.

6. List below any words or phrases that did not translate accurately or were difficult to translate. What might problems in translation tell you about cultural differences?

7. Based on the results of the back-translation, are there any modifications you think would be helpful to make to the *original* version to allow for a translation into equivalent versions? Please explain.

Thinking Further:

Perspectives on translation have changed since back-translation was first introduced, with a greater focus on the context around the material to be translated. Sonia Colina and colleagues (2017) suggested that the back-translation method focuses too much on the text to be translated and recommended that translations also consider characteristics of the audience (e.g., age, socioeconomic status), the communication method (e.g., read by the participant, spoken by an interviewer) and the purpose (e.g., to gather opinions, make a diagnosis). How might these factors play a role in the translation you conducted?

References:

Brislin, R. (1980). Translation and content analysis of oral and written materials. In H. Triandis and J. Berry (Eds.), *Handbook of cross-cultural psychology*, Vol. 2: Methodology (pp. 389–444). Allyn & Bacon.

Brislin, R. W. (2000). Back-translation. In A. E. Kazdin (Ed.), *Encyclopedia of psychology*, Vol. 1 (pp. 359–360). American Psychological Association.

Colina, S., Marrone, N., Ingram, M., & Sánchez, D. (2017). Translation quality assessment in health research: A functionalist alternative to back-translation. *Evaluation & the Health Professions*, *40*(3), 267–293. https://doi.org/10.1177/0163278716648191

ACTIVITY 2.7
HANDOUT

PAGTATANONG-TANONG: AN INDIGENOUS RESEARCH METHOD

This activity evaluates the cross-cultural applicability of the research methods typically used in "Western psychology" and explores an indigenous research method from the Philippines called *pagtatanong-tanong*.

Directions: Read the scenario and answer the questions that follow.

Scenario: Suppose that you have been trained at your university to uphold the following principles of research:

- The researcher must remain objective. It is important not to become too emotionally attached, or disclose personal information, to research participants.
- Procedures should be standardized. The questions asked of participants and the conditions under which they are asked should be as uniform as possible.
- Participants should not be subject to the influence of others during the testing or interview process (unless it is a condition of the experiment). Thus, participants should be tested or interviewed on an individual basis.

Now imagine that you are preparing to conduct a series of interviews in a rural community in the Philippines. Through reading and speaking with experts and members of this community you learn the following about the culture in which you are planning to conduct your research.

- People are unaccustomed to being asked a series of questions in sequence and responding in a regimented manner.
- People are uncomfortable discussing personal opinions or behaviors with a stranger with whom there will be no future relationship.

- People may be uncomfortable alone with a stranger, particularly if the stranger is of a different gender or social status.
- People are more comfortable speaking in a conversational manner in which each person discloses information and contributes to managing the process and content of the conversation.

1. Describe how you might modify your research methods in order to conduct your interviews more effectively. Which research principles would you be willing to reconsider, and which principles would you maintain?
2. Rogelia Pe-Pua (1989, 2006) described a social science research method indigenous to the Philippines called *pagtatanong-tanong*. In recent years, this technique has been used to investigate the concept of giftedness (Camitan & Bragas, 2020), caregiver coping mechanisms (Naldo et al., 2021), and envy of the success of others (Billote et al., 2021).

According to Pe-Pua, *Pagtatanong-tanong* has some of the following characteristics:

a. The researcher uses a tentative outline of questions that are revised based on input from the participants.
b. The researcher and the participants share equally in determining the content and structure of the interview.
c. A relationship is established between the researcher and the participants such that the participants feel comfortable asking the researcher questions and expect that they may have contact with the researcher in the future.
d. The researcher starts the interview with a group of participants rather than individuals. Interruptions in the interview process are not seen as distractions, but as an opportunity to check on the reliability of the information obtained.

What do you expect about the validity of the information you would collect in a rural community in the Philippines using the *pagtatanong-tanong* method?

Thinking Further:

If you are not from the rural Philippines yourself, do you think that *pagtatanong-tanong* would yield useful information in your culture? Please explain.

References:

Billote, W. J. S., De Sagon, G. A., Escoto, M. F., Pableo, A., Ponce, R., Ponce, T. E., Quibal, J., Quiloan, A., Comaya, M. A., & Ponce, J. M. (2021). Talangkang Pag-Iisip: An exposé of its positivity in the lens of students in a selected university in Baguio City. *JPAIR Multidisciplinary Research*, *43*(1), 36–56. https://doi.org/10.7719/jpair.v43i1.715

Camitan, D. S., & Bragas, B. M. (2020). Caught between two worlds: Conception of giftedness in the Dumagat-Remontados culture of Paglitao. *International Journal of Psychology and Educational Studies*. https://doi.org/10.6084/m9.figshare.12177405.v2

Naldo, G. Jr, Gacosta, M. K. N., Arevalo, K., & Orcales, L. (2021). Caregivers need help too: The lived experiences and coping mechanisms of the caregivers of the dengue patients in Palawan, Philippines. *Asian Journal of Resilience*, *3*(1), 17–25. https://asianjournalofresilience.com/index.php/ajr/article/view/25/12

Pe-Pua, R. (1989). Pagtatanong-tanong: A cross-cultural research method. *International Journal of Intercultural Relations*, *13*, 147–163. https://psycnet.apa.org/doi/10.1016/0147-1767(89)90003-5

Pe-Pua, R. (2006). From decolonizing psychology to the development of a cross-indigenous perspective in methodology: The Philippine experience. In U. Kim, K.-S. Yang, & K.-K. Hwang (Eds.), *Indigenous and cultural psychology: Understanding people in context* (pp. 109–137). Springer.

ACTIVITY 2.8
HANDOUT

ETHICS IN CROSS-CULTURAL RESEARCH

You are probably familiar with many of the ethical concerns faced by psychologists, such as obtaining informed consent from potential research participants, protecting them from harm and discomfort, and fully debriefing participants once the research has been completed. This activity encourages you to think about the additional ethical issues cross-cultural psychologists must address.

Directions: Read the following scenario and identify any ethical dilemmas. Next, propose an alternative research design that will remedy each ethical concern.

Scenario: A study conducted in the United States by Brinke et al. (2015) found that people were less successful in deceiving others when telling lies in a sparse environment (an empty office) than when telling lies in an enriched environment (a decorated and furnished office). The authors reasoned that a sparse environment creates feelings of discomfort and powerlessness, which results in the leakage of cues to deception. A Swiss researcher wonders if these findings would hold true in a natural environment as well. He decides to test this idea by replicating the study in two regions of Mexico, where he will be spending his vacation, one a desert environment (sparse) and the other a tropical environment (enriched). He reasons that since both are in the same country, this would eliminate any cultural differences between the two regions, which could be confounded with the differences in (sparse/enriched) environment. Early in the research process he befriends a local high school teacher and soon involves him in the project. The teacher takes primary responsibility for identifying potential research participants, translating data, and acting as a liaison with local authorities. The teacher also spends a considerable amount of time discussing possible interpretations of the data with the researcher. Participants are asked to sign an informed consent form prior to the start of the study and are given the researcher's email address in case any questions or concerns arise. The study, which is documented with both written and video records, identifies individuals in each location who are able to deceive others effectively. The research participants are paid the same amount of money per hour that the researcher has paid participants in Switzerland, though this is a far larger amount as compared with average salaries in Mexico than in Switzerland. Once the study is completed, the researcher returns to Switzerland to present his findings at a national conference, using the video materials as illustration. A few months later, he is the sole author of a journal article reporting the results of this study.

1. Discuss each of the ethical concerns illustrated by the above scenario.
2. What additional concerns might you have about the logic behind this research design?
3. Propose an alternative research design to remedy the ethical and design limitations of this study.

Reference:

ten Brinke, L., Khambatta, P., & Carney, D. R. (2015). Physically scarce (vs. enriched) environments decrease the ability to tell lies successfully. *Journal of Experimental Psychology: General, 144*(5), 982–992. https://doi.org/10.1037/xge0000103

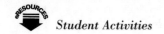

ACTIVITY 2.9
HANDOUT

TOWARD A MORE INCLUSIVE PSYCHOLOGY

If psychology as a discipline is to become more inclusive, those who consume and design psychological research will need to become more aware of various forms of bias. The purpose of this activity is to familiarize you with some of the forms of bias that frequently occur in designing studies in psychology.

Directions: Read the research project descriptions below and identify the form(s) of bias in each.

1. In a study of attachment behavior and academic achievement, children and their mothers are observed and interviewed at great length to determine the nature and degree of the bond between them.
2. A researcher is interested in investigating how gender roles may influence attraction in online dating. She has women rate profiles of men, and men rate profiles of women, who vary in attractiveness and conformity to traditional gender roles.
3. A researcher is interested in studying social interaction between people with and without disabilities. He simulates disability by having a nondisabled student confederate sit in a wheelchair in the coffee shop of the student center and then observes the interaction between the confederate and the (nondisabled) students who enter the room.
4. A study of adolescent risk-taking behavior in the U.S. compares data from Black, Latinx, and Asian American teens to data from White teens.
5. A study of friendship patterns in adults compares results across four different age groups. The groups consist of 18- to 29-year-olds, 30- to 45-year-olds, 46- to 59-year-olds, and individuals 60 years and over.

ACTIVITY 2.10
HANDOUT

DESIGNING CROSS-CULTURAL RESEARCH

Designing research that compares cultures on some psychological phenomenon involves several steps beyond what is required for research within a single culture. It rarely makes sense to conduct the study in exactly the same way using exactly the same materials in more than one culture. Although the way the

---

research is conducted in each culture should not be the *same*, it must be *equivalent*. This activity will acquaint you with some of the forms of equivalence that must be considered in conducting cross-cultural research.

Directions: For this activity, you will need to locate a journal article that reports a psychological study conducted within a single culture. Try to choose a relatively straightforward study in which the independent and dependent variables, the hypothesis, and the methods used are clearly understandable to you. Determine in which (different) culture you would replicate the study. In practice, the choice of cultures in which to conduct research should be based on aspects of the cultures that are relevant to the theories or concepts you are testing. For this activity, however, it is more important that you choose a culture that is somewhat familiar to you. Next, answer the questions below regarding various issues of cross-cultural equivalence.

1. Provide the complete reference for the journal article you have chosen (see the references in this book for examples of the format and content).
2. Briefly describe the study that you will prepare to replicate. Include the independent and dependent variables, the hypothesis, and the methods used.
3. Describe the culture in which the above study would be replicated.

Equivalence:

For each of the following forms of equivalence, determine whether the procedures used in the original study would be culturally appropriate if used in the second culture. If the procedure is not appropriate, suggest how you might modify the procedure in order to produce an outcome that is equivalent in both cultures.

1. *Construct Equivalence.* Does the primary phenomenon being investigated have the same meaning in both cultures? For example, the concept of *parenting behavior* may not have construct equivalence if comparing a culture in which parents are the primary caregivers with a culture in which the extended family or siblings play a major role in childrearing.
2. *Sampling Equivalence.* Does the method of recruiting research participants yield individuals who are similar on dimensions other than culture? For example, many studies are conducted with college students as participants. However, college students in a culture where a large proportion of the population attends college may differ in important ways (e.g., income, gender) from students in a culture where only the most privileged attend college.

3. *Item or Task Equivalence.* Do the questionnaire or interview items or experimental tasks that participants perform have the same meaning in both cultures? For example, it would be invalid for a cross-cultural study of music memory to use songs that are familiar to participants in one of the cultures and not in the other.

4. *Equivalence of the Test Situation.* Is the test situation likely to be perceived and valued similarly in both cultures? For example, in some cultures people are very familiar with strangers approaching them to ask somewhat personal questions as part of a study. In other cultures, this is a circumstance that would elicit suspicion and concern.

Thinking Further:

Those listed above are just a few of the forms of equivalence that need to be considered when making cross-cultural comparisons. Please make suggestions below for other aspects of research design and implementation that should have equivalent meaning to participants when conducting valid cross-cultural studies.

–3–

Culture and Basic Processes

ACTIVITY 3.1
HANDOUT

MAGICAL THINKING

Sometimes members of more traditional cultures are described as using forms of magical thinking that defy rules of logic and reason. Paul Rozin and Carol Nemeroff (2002) suggested that such thinking is not limited to traditional cultures but exists in some aspects of daily life in highly industrialized cultures as well. Their research on college students in the United States demonstrated the two forms of magical thinking below, described over a century ago by Sir James Frazer (1890/1959).

The law of contagion states that when two things (or beings) are in contact with each other, the properties of one can permanently transfer to the other. For example, Frazer described an ancient Chinese practice in which burial clothes were sewn by young women with the reasoning that their longevity would somehow pass into the clothes and ensure that the clothes themselves would live long (that is, not be used for many years).

The law of similarity holds that an image of an object or person takes on the characteristics of the actual object or person. For example, Frazer noted that in many cultures it was believed that by damaging footprints it is possible to injure the person who made them.

The purpose of this activity is to explore the use of magical thinking among college students and consider the meaning of such thinking for understanding the link between culture and cognition.

Directions: Identify two college students to act as participants in this activity. Then, using the interview forms below, ask each participant the two questions

DOI: 10.4324/9781003356820-16   *269*

about magical thinking (based on research by Rozin et al., 1986). Please interview the two participants separately and do not tell them that you are studying magical thinking. The first item addresses the law of contagion and the second item addresses the law of similarity.

Participant A

1. Would you rather wear a laundered shirt that had been previously worn by someone you like, someone you dislike, or someone you don't know? Please explain.
2. Would it be more difficult for you to throw darts at a dartboard depicting a picture of someone you like or someone you don't like? Please explain.

Participant B

1. Would you rather wear a laundered shirt that had been previously worn by someone you like, someone you dislike, or someone you don't know? Please explain.
2. Would it be more difficult for you to throw darts at a dartboard depicting a picture of someone you like or someone you don't like? Please explain.

To what extent did your participants manifest magical thinking? (On item 1, choosing the shirt worn by the liked person, and on item 2, having more difficulty throwing darts at the liked person, may indicate magical thinking.) Please explain.

Thinking Further:

1. Can you think of any alternative explanations for the "magical thinking" in the two questions asked of the participants?
2. Have you engaged in any other forms of magical thinking? Please explain.
3. To what extent does magical thinking interfere with rational thinking in everyday life in your culture?

Source:

Based on Rozin, P., Millman, L., & Nemeroff, C. (1986). Operation of the laws of sympathetic magic in disgust and other domains. Journal of Personality and Social Psychology, *50*(4), 703–712. https://doi.org/10.1037/0022-3514.50.4.703

References:

Frazer, J. G. (1959). *The new golden bough: A study in magic and religion*. MacMillan (Edited by T. H. Gaster, 1922; Original work published 1890).

Rozin, P., Millman, L., & Nemeroff, C. (1986). Operation of the laws of sympathetic magic in disgust and other domains. *Journal of Personality and Social Psychology*, *50*(4), 703–712. https://doi.org/10.1037/0022-3514.50.4.703

Rozin, P., & Nemeroff, C. (2002). Sympathetic magical thinking: The contagion and similarity "heuristics." In T. Gilovich, D. Griffin, & D. Kahneman (Eds.), *Heuristics and biases: The psychology of intuitive judgment* (pp. 201–215). Cambridge University Press.

ACTIVITY 3.2
HANDOUT

IMPLICIT THEORIES OF INTELLIGENCE

Patricia Ruzgis and Elena Grigorenko (1994) distinguished between cross-cultural research focusing on explicit and implicit theories of intelligence. They explained that studies of explicit theories have attempted to determine how cultural environments impact the development of different patterns of intellectual abilities. The data used to test explicit theories usually consists of scores on various tests of cognitive abilities. Explicit theories are constructed by scholars who are specialists in investigating cognitive abilities. Implicit theories (sometimes called "lay theories"), on the other hand, are the ideas that everyday people have about what constitutes intelligence. Data gathered to study implicit theories may include beliefs about the characteristics of an intelligent person or definitions of intelligence that are generated by research participants. Robert Sternberg and Elena Grigorenko (2004) investigated implicit theories of intelligence to better understand cultural differences in conceptions of intelligence. In this activity, you can explore your own implicit theory of intelligence and compare it to data on implicit theories of intelligence across cultures. We will also examine the concept of *giftedness* as a way to gain further insight into beliefs about intelligence.

Directions: Please respond to each of the questions below in the space provided.

1. Describe what the term *intelligent* means to you.
2. Describe what the term *gifted* means to you.
3. Read the list of items below and put an "X" in the blank next to any characteristic you associate with *an intelligent person.*
   _____ a. reasons logically
   _____ b. is verbally fluent
   _____ c. is sociable
   _____ d. can take another's point of view
   _____ e. works efficiently
   _____ f. identifies connections among ideas
   _____ g. speaks clearly and articulately
   _____ h. is humorous
   _____ i. is modest
   _____ j. plans ahead
   _____ k. makes clear decisions
   _____ l. is knowledgeable about a particular field of study
   _____ m. gets along well with others
   _____ n. admits mistakes in good grace
   _____ o. sees all aspects of a problem
4. For each of the items you selected above, add a point to the appropriate subscale below and calculate your scores for each of the five subscales (your scores should range from 0 to 3).
   _____ Practical Problem Solving: items a., f., and o.
   _____ Verbal Ability: items b., g., and l.
   _____ Positive Social Competence: items c., h., and m.
   _____ Receptive Social Competence: items d., i., and n.
   _____ Task Efficiency: items e., j., and k.
5. Hiroshi Azuma and Keiko Kashiwagi (1987) distinguished between positive social competence and receptive social competence. Look at the items that compose each of these subscales. How would you describe the difference between these two forms of social competence?
6. Look at your scores on the Positive Social Competence and Receptive Social Competence subscales. To what extent were these concepts part of your image of an intelligent person?
7. Ruzgis and Grigorenko observed that implicit theories of intelligence in more individualistic societies tend to include forms of Positive Social Competence whereas implicit theories of intelligence in more collectivist societies tend to include forms of Receptive Social

Competence. Why might Positive Social Competence be associated with individualism and Receptive Social Competence be associated with collectivism?

8. Reread your description of intelligence in question 1. Are there any characteristics in your description that would not be categorized under any of the five subscales? Please explain.

9. Carol Dweck has studied the implications of our implicit theories of intelligence for motivation to learn. She distinguished between a *fixed mindset*, the belief that intelligence is a static trait that cannot be meaningfully changed, and a *growth mindset*, the belief that intelligence is a quality that can be developed through effort and the willingness to try different strategies to achieve one's goal (Dweck, 2012). Her research suggests that under certain conditions a growth mindset is associated with greater well-being and academic success (Yeager & Dweck, 2020). These mindsets can vary with culture. For example, Jin Li and colleagues (2014) reported that Taiwanese mothers emphasize the "learning virtues" of diligence and perseverance (consistent with a growth mindset) more than do European American mothers. Does your implicit theory include the idea that intelligence is fixed, or do you believe that it can be changed?

10. Cross-cultural researchers have observed much variability in cultural conceptions of giftedness including some cultures in which there is no term for giftedness (Sternberg, 2007). For example, studies with the Keres Pueblo peoples in New Mexico (Romero, 1994) and with members of the Shona and Ndebele cultures of Zimbabwe (Ngara, 2006) indicated that the concept of giftedness had a more collectivist orientation in that it required that one's unique talents or abilities contributed to the well-being of the community.

    Reread your description of giftedness in question 2. To what extent does your description reflect individualist values? Collectivist values?

Thinking Further:

Sternberg (2020, p. 679) used the term *successful intelligence* to refer to "(1) the ability to formulate, strive for, and, to the extent possible, achieve one's goals in life, given one's sociocultural context, (2) by capitalizing on strengths and correcting or compensating for weaknesses (3) in order to adapt to, shape, and select environments (4) through a combination of analytical, creative, and practical abilities." Based on this definition, what are some everyday behaviors that would demonstrate successful intelligence in your culture?

Sources:

The Positive Social Competence, Receptive Social Competence, and Task Efficiency items were derived from Azuma, H. & Kashiwagi, K. (1987). Descriptors for an intelligent person: A Japanese study. *Japanese Psychological Research*, *29*, 17–26. Copyright © 1987 by Japanese Psychological Association. Adapted with permission.

The Practical Problem Solving and Verbal Ability items were derived from Sternberg, R. J., Conway, B. E., Ketron, J. L., & Bernstein, M. (1981). People's conceptions of intelligence. *Journal of Personality and Social Psychology*, *41*, 37–55. Copyright © 1981 by American Psychological Association. Adapted with permission.

References:

Azuma, H., & Kashiwagi, K. (1987). Descriptors for an intelligent person: A Japanese study. *Japanese Psychological Research*, *29*, 17–26. https://doi.org/10.4992/psycholres1954.29.17

Dweck, C. S. (2012). *Mindset: How you can fulfill your potential.* Constable & Robinson Limited.

Li, J., Fung, H., Bakeman, R., Rae, K., & Wei, W. (2014). How European, American and Taiwanese mothers talk to their children about learning. *Child Development*, *85*(3), 1206–1221. https://doi.org/10.1111/cdev.12172

Ngara, C. (2006). Indigenous conceptions of giftedness in Zimbabwe: A comparison of Shona and Ndebele cultures' conceptions of giftedness. *International Education*, *36*(1), 46–62.

Romero, M. E. (1994). Identifying giftedness among Keresan Pueblo Indians: The Keres Study. *Journal of American Indian Education*, *34*, 35–58. www.jstor.org/stable/24398400

Ruzgis, P., & Grigorenko, E. L. (1994). Cultural meaning systems, intelligence, and personality. In R. J. Sternberg & P. Ruzgis (Eds.), *Personality and intelligence* (pp. 248–270). Cambridge University Press.

Sternberg, R. J. (2007). Cultural concepts of giftedness. *Roeper Review*, *29*(3), 160–165. http://dx.doi.org/10.1080/02783190709554404

Sternberg, R. J. (2020). The augmented theory of successful intelligence. In R. Sternberg (Ed.), *The Cambridge handbook of intelligence* (pp. 679–708). Cambridge University Press.

Sternberg, R. J., & Grigorenko, E. L. (2004). Why cultural psychology is necessary and not just nice: The example of the study of intelligence. In R. J. Sternberg, & E. L. Grigorenko (Eds.), *Culture and competence: Contexts of life success* (pp. 207–223). American Psychological Society.

Yeager, D. S., & Dweck, C. S. (2020). What can be learned from growth mindset controversies? *American Psychologist, 75*(9), 1269–1284. https://doi.org/10.1037/amp0000794

ACTIVITY 3.3
HANDOUT

RACE AND IQ: INTERROGATING THE ASSUMPTIONS

Through the 1980s, it was common for psychology textbooks to mention diversity on one topic only – race and IQ. Since that time, studies attempting to find racial differences in intelligence have continued to surface from time to time, most recently due to the explosion of genetic research (Winston, 2020). Many scholars have criticized the logic that forms the foundation for these studies (e.g., Colman, 2016; Held, 2020; Nisbett, 2009). In fact, Robert Sternberg, Elena Grigorenko, and Kenneth Kidd (2005) state that race and IQ studies are based on folk beliefs rather than science. This activity explores the faulty logic of research on race and IQ.

Directions: Evaluate and discuss the logic behind one of the assumptions below. Locate and cite at least two scholarly sources (books or journal articles) to support your position.

- IQ test scores indicate fundamental intellectual ability.
- It is scientifically valid to examine "racial differences."
- Group differences in IQ reflect genetic differences.
- IQ is immutable (cannot be changed).
- High IQ leads to (causes) socioeconomic success.

Sources: In the space below, provide the full references for your articles (see the references in this book for examples of the format and content).

Evaluation/discussion of assumption: Indicate the assumption you are evaluating and discuss your findings below.

References:

Colman, A. M. (2016). Race differences in IQ: Hans Eysenck's contribution to the debate in the light of subsequent research. *Personality and Individual Differences, 103*, 182–189. https://doi.org/10.1016/j.paid.2016.04.050

Held, B. S. (2020). Epistemic violence in psychological science: Can knowledge of, from, and for the (othered) people solve the problem? *Theory & Psychology, 30*(3), 349–370. https://doi.org/10.1177/0959354319883943

Nisbett, R. E. (2009). *Intelligence and how to get it: Why schools and cultures count.* W. W. Norton & Company.

Sternberg, R. J., Grigorenko, E. L., & Kidd, K. K. (2005). Intelligence, race, and genetics. *American Psychologist, 60*, 46–59. https://doi.org/10.1037/0003-066X.60.1.46

Winston, A. S. (2020). Why mainstream research will not end scientific racism in psychology. *Theory & Psychology, 30*(3), 425–430. https://doi.org/10.1177/0959354320925176

ACTIVITY 3.4
HANDOUT

MEASURING CREATIVITY ACROSS CULTURES

Cross-cultural psychologists and cultural psychologists have traditionally had different views about testing psychological processes across cultures. *Cross-cultural psychologists* have tended to believe that once adjustments are made to a cognitive abilities test it can be used effectively in a culture other than the one for which it was originally developed. In fact, a significant portion of cross-cultural psychology focuses on how to modify tests (such as through translation or the use of culturally familiar materials and tasks) in order to make them cross-culturally appropriate. In studies of creativity, cross-cultural psychologists have generally focused on comparing creativity levels across cultures and identifying predictors of cultural differences. For example, most cross-cultural studies of creativity have compared samples on divergent thinking tasks (Guo et al., 2021), such as producing as many solutions as possible for an everyday problem or as many different uses as one can for a specific object.

Cultural psychologists, on the other hand, have tended to believe that psychological tests are themselves a product of culture. Patricia Greenfield (1997) explained that *symbolic culture* – that is, shared assumptions, knowledge, and communication – is embedded in any ability test. She argued that if the individuals tested do not share the symbolic culture of the test or tester, the result will be cultural misunderstandings that threaten the validity of the test. Greenfield recommended an alternative to taking tests from one culture and using it in another. She suggested that one should first identify characteristics and abilities that are valued within a particular culture and then develop culturally appropriate ways to measure them. This strategy might be called an *emic*, or culture-specific, approach. This activity asks that you consider how one might go about using the cultural psychologists' approach to studying creativity.

Directions: Imagine that you are investigating the concept of creativity in a culture where formal testing has never taken place. Describe how you would go about determining which behaviors or individuals are considered creative in this culture. (Be careful not to impose your own definition of creativity).

Thinking Further:

According to Vlad Petre Glăveanu (2019), in addition to determining *how* to measure creativity across cultures, we also need to consider *why* we would measure creativity across cultures. What are your thoughts about the benefits, if any, of doing so? Please explain.

References:

Glăveanu, V. P. (2019). Measuring creativity across cultures: Epistemological and methodological considerations. *Psychology of Aesthetics, Creativity, and the Arts, 13*(2), 227–232. https://doi.org/10.1037/aca0000216
Greenfield, P. M. (1997). You can't take it with you: Why ability assessments don't cross cultures. *American Psychologist, 52*, 1115–1124. https://doi.org/10.1037/0003-066X.52.10.1115
Guo, Y., Lin, S., Guo, J., Lu, Z., & Shangguan, C. (2021). Cross-cultural measurement invariance of divergent thinking measures. *Thinking Skills and Creativity, 41*(1). https://doi.org/10.1016/j.tsc.2021.100852

ACTIVITY 3.5
HANDOUT

CULTURAL NEUROSCIENCE

Cultural neuroscience is a relatively new approach to studying culture and human behavior which became possible due to the mapping of the human genome and advances in brain imaging. Lynda Lin and Eva Telzer (2018, p. 399) defined cultural neuroscience as an "interdisciplinary field that combines theories and methods from cultural and social psychology, anthropology, and social and cognitive neuroscience to investigate the interactions between culture, psychological processes, brain, and genes at different timescales." A wide range of topics has been explored using this approach, including language, music, mathematics, prejudice and stereo-typing, visual perception, and social cognition. This activity will acquaint you with the growing field of cultural neuroscience. Here are three examples of studies with a cultural neuroscience approach illustrating a focus on the brain, genes, and hormones respectively:

- A series of studies identified a common response to infants' cries in the brains of new mothers from several different countries. Marc Bornstein and colleagues (2017) found enhanced activity in areas of the brain linked to the intention to move, speak, and caregive (the supplementary motor area, Broca's area and the superior temporal regions associated with processing speech and complex sounds, and the midbrain and striatal regions associated with caregiving). This corresponds to their observa-tions of mothers across cultures responding to their infant's cries by picking up, holding, and talking to the infant. The authors suggested that these fMRI findings indicate the presence of a universal neurobiological basis for new mothers' responses to infants' cries.
- To better understand how gene-environment interaction shapes person-ality, Snežana Smederevac and colleagues (2020) investigated whether the genetic and environmental factors contributing to the Five Factor Model personality traits differed among monozygotic and dizygotic twins from Croatian, German, and Serbian cultures (twin studies are often used to assess the heritability of personality traits). Overall, the authors reported that the gene and environment correlation patterns were very similar across the three cultural groups, indicating a very limited role of culture in shaping personality traits.
- In an article titled "Feeling bad is not always unhealthy," Jiyoung Park and colleagues (2020) reported on the role of culture (U.S. American

---

and Japanese) in shaping the relationship between negative affect and biological stress responses (cortisol level). The participants tracked negative emotions over a one-month period while researchers assessed several biological health indices. The study found that for the U.S. participants, negative affect was associated with a greater cortical stress response, which is linked to a variety of health risks. For the Japanese participants there was no significant link between negative affect and cortisol response. The authors suggested that culture shapes how one interprets negative events, and that a more independent self-construal may result in a greater sense of responsibility for negative outcomes and thus more stress.

Directions: Identify a scholarly journal article describing a study that takes a cultural neuroscience approach to investigating emotions, cognition, personality, or social behavior. Then answer the questions below.

1. In the space below, provide the full reference for your article (see the references in this book for examples of the format and content).
2. Summarize the primary research question investigated in the study you selected.
3. Describe the neural, genetic, or hormonal mechanism investigated.
4. State the neuroscience measures used (such as functional magnetic resonance imaging [fMRI], functional near-infrared spectroscopy [fNIRS], genetic analysis, cortisol levels).
5. Discuss the primary conclusions of this study – what did the results indicate about the interaction between culture and neural mechanisms?

Thinking Further:

What insights were gained by taking a neuroscience approach to this topic that would not have been known otherwise?

References:

Bornstein, M. H., Putnick, D. L., Rigo, P., et al. (2017). Neurobiology of culturally common maternal responses to infant cry. *PNAS Proceedings of the National Academy of Sciences of the United States of America, 114*(45), E9465–E9473. https://doi.org/10.1073/pnas.1712022114

Lin, L. C., & Telzer, E. H. (2018). An introduction to cultural neuroscience. In J. M Causadias, E. H. Telzer, & N. A. Gonzales (Eds), *The handbook of culture and biology* (pp. 399–420). Wiley.

Park, J., Kitayama, S., Miyamoto, Y., & Coe, C. L. (2020). Feeling bad is not always unhealthy: Culture moderates the link between negative affect and diurnal cortisol profiles. *Emotion, 20*(5), 721–733. https://doi.org/10.1037/emo0000605

Smederevac, S., Mitrović, D., Sadiković, S., Riemann, R., Bratko, D., Prinz, M., & Budimlija, Z. (2020). Hereditary and environmental factors of the Five-Factor Model traits: A cross-cultural study. *Personality and Individual Differences, 162*, Article 109995. https://doi.org/10.1016/j.paid.2020.109995

ACTIVITY 3.6
HANDOUT

CULTURE AND MEMORY STRATEGIES

Although people in all cultures have the same *structural features of memory* (such as the sensory register, short-term, long-term, and working memory) and engage in the same *types of memory* (such as episodic memory – for events, semantic memory – for information, and procedural memory – for performing actions), there is much variability in *memory processes* depending on the cultural context. These processes include how memories are represented, what information is encoded, the memory's intended function, and how recalled material is reconstructed and expressed (Wang, 2021). This activity demonstrates the impact of the context on memory processes.

Directions: Complete each of the memory tasks below and then answer the questions that follow.

1. Quickly read through the list of words below then cover the list with a sheet of paper and in the space below, write down all the words that you remember.
   - hammer
   - envelope
   - pen
   - dish
   - wrench

- screwdriver
- spoon
- eraser
- fork
- pliers
- paper

Recalled words:

2. Describe the strategy you used to memorize the list of words.
3. In the space below, list the planets of the solar system.
4. Describe the strategy you used to recall the planets.
5. In the space below, draw a map of your campus or neighborhood.
6. Describe the strategy you used to remember the layout of your campus or neighborhood.
7. Based on this activity, what do you conclude about the impact of the context on memory processes?

Thinking Further:

Consider how each of the following research findings might be explained.

1. Michael Ross and Qi Wang (2010) reported that as compared with people from East Asian cultures, those from European and North American cultures are better able to visualize and recall autobiographical memories, such as childhood events. Why might this occur?
2. A series of studies (e.g., Masuda & Nisbett, 2001; Masuda et al., 2008) found that when presented with a scene, U.S. American participants tended to focus on objects in the foreground whereas Japanese participants attended equally to both the foreground objects and the background context. In fact, when participants from the U.S. and Japan were exposed to either a U.S. or Japanese street scene, both the Japanese and American participants who viewed the Japanese scenes attended more to contextual information than did those who viewed the American scenes (Miyamoto et al., 2006). Why might this occur?
3. Research on culture and memory has generally found that individuals who do not attend school perform poorly compared to schooled individuals on tasks involving memorizing lists of unrelated items, but that the two groups do equally well memorizing the items if they are placed in a diorama of a familiar setting (Cole, 2005). Why might this occur?

---

4. Research on culture and memory has generally found that individuals from cultures with a strong oral tradition may be quite skilled in memorizing large amounts of information relevant to daily life (Wang & Ross, 2007), such as family histories, star positions for navigating by sea, or agricultural facts. Why might this occur?

5. Studies have connected smartphone use with decreased ability to attend to and remember information (Wilmer et al., 2017). In fact, news stories have reported individuals who lose their phones and are unable to contact their spouse, close friends, or family because they don't know their phone numbers! Why might this occur?

6. Based on these research findings, what do you conclude about the influence of culture on memory?

References:

Cole, M. (2005). Cross-cultural and historical perspectives on the developmental consequences of education. *Human Development, 48*, 195–216. https://doi.org/10.1159/000086855

Masuda, T., Gonzalez, R., Kwan, L., & Nisbett, R. E. (2008). Culture and aesthetic preference: Comparing the attention to context of East Asians and Americans. *Personality and Social Psychology Bulletin, 34*(9), 1260–1275. https://doi.org/10.1177/0146167208320555

Masuda, T., & Nisbett, R. E. (2001). Attending holistically vs. analytically: Comparing the context sensitivity of Japanese and Americans. *Journal of Personality and Social Psychology, 81*, 922–934. https://doi.org/10.1037/0022-3514.81.5.922

Miyamoto, Y., Nisbett, R. E., & Masuda, T. (2006). Culture and the physical environment: Holistic versus analytic perceptual affordances. *Psychological Science, 17*(2), 113–119. https://doi.org/10.1111/j.1467-9280.2006.01673.x

Ross, M., & Wang, Q. (2010). Why we remember and what we remember: Culture and autobiographical memory. *Perspectives on Psychological Science, 5*(4), 401–409. https://doi.org/10.1177/1745691610375555

Wang, Q. (2021). The cultural foundation of human memory. *Annual Review of Psychology, 72*, 151–179. https://doi.org/10.1146/annurev-psych-070920-023638

Wang, Q., & Ross, M. (2007). Culture and memory. In S. Kitayama, & D. Cohen (Eds.), *Handbook of cultural psychology* (pp. 645–667). Guilford Press.

Wilmer, H. H., Sherman, L. E., & Chein, J. M. (2017). Smartphones and cognition: A review of research exploring the links between mobile technology habits and cognitive functioning. *Frontiers in Psychology*, *25*(8). https://doi.org/10.3389/fpsyg.2017.00605

ACTIVITY 3.7
HANDOUT

CULTURE AND AESTHETIC PREFERENCE

A fascinating way to explore culture and perception is to examine aesthetic responses. Aesthetic responses refer to perceiving something (such as artwork, music, poetry, or architecture) as pleasant, beautiful, attractive, or rewarding as opposed to unpleasant, ugly, unattractive, or unrewarding (Russell et al., 1997). By observing styles of art, music, architecture, and the like across cultures, we would quickly conclude that cultures vary markedly in what is deemed aesthetically pleasing. But are there any universal aspects of aesthetics that might be uncovered through cross-cultural research?

Building on the work of Daniel Berlyne (1960), several studies have found a curvilinear relationship between complexity and aesthetic preference (that is, preference was greatest for moderate levels of complexity), although individual and cultural differences also influence the direction of this relationship. For example, Nichola Street and colleagues (2016) tested preference for fractal images at different levels of complexity among a large number of participants from locations in Europe, North America, Central Asia, and Africa. They reported that although age, gender, and culture played a significant role in aesthetic preferences, the responses as a whole supported a preference for a moderate level of complexity. This activity explores the hypothesis that aesthetic preference is related to the complexity of the stimulus.

Directions: On the following pages you will find three drawings – one is relatively simple, another moderately complex, and another highly complex. Identify ten individuals to participate in this activity. Meet with each participant individually. Print out each drawing and place all three in front of your participant at once. Then ask the participant to rate the three items to indicate which they like most and like least (you might vary the order in which you place the drawings for different participants). Record the responses on the datasheet below by putting a "1" in the blank to indicate "most liked," a "3" to indicate "least liked," and a "2" to indicate the second-ranked stimulus. Once you have collected ratings of the three stimuli from each of your ten participants, calculate the average rating for each level of complexity. Then answer the questions that follow.

Data Sheet

1. Did your data support a relationship between level of complexity and aesthetic preference? Please explain.
2. If you were to replicate this study with participants from markedly different cultures, what changes might you need to make in terms of the methods you used?
3. Alexandra Forsythe and colleagues (2008) demonstrated that familiarity influences the extent to which we perceive an object as complex, with unfamiliar images viewed as more complex. How might you build a familiarity variable into the study you conducted?

	Level of Complexity		
Participant	Low	Moderate	High
1			
2			
3			
4			
5			
6			
7			
8			
9			
10			
Total Score			
Average Score			

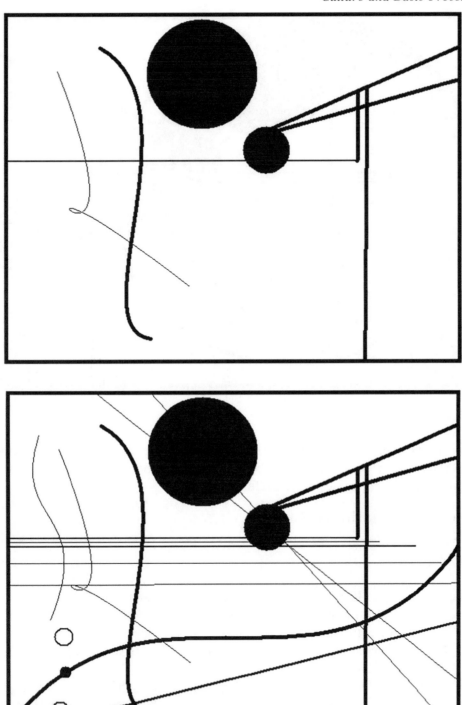

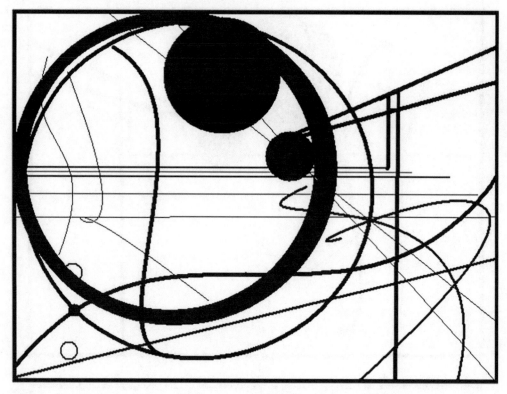

Thinking Further:

This activity has focused primarily on underlying *similarities* in aesthetic preferences across cultures. Describe below one factor that might help explain cultural *differences* in aesthetic preferences.

Drawings: Lauren Hisada (2006)

References:

Berlyne, D. E. (1960). *Conflict, arousal, and curiosity*. McGraw-Hill.

Forsythe, A., Mulhern, G., & Sawey, M. (2008). Confounds in pictorial sets: The role of complexity and familiarity in basic-level picture processing. *Behavior Research Methods*, *40*(1), 116–129. https://doi.org/10.3758/BRM.40.1.116

Russell, P. A., Deregowski, J. B., & Kinnear, P. R. (1997). Perception and aesthetics. In J. W. Berry, P. R. Dasen, & T. S. Saraswathi (Eds.), *Handbook of cross-cultural psychology*, Vol. 2: Basic processes and human development (2nd ed., pp. 107–142). Allyn & Bacon.

Street, N., Forsythe, A. M., Reilly, R., Taylor, R., & Helmy, M. S. (2016). A complex story: Universal preference vs. individual differences shaping aesthetic response to fractals patterns. *Frontiers in Human Neuroscience, 10*, Article 213. https://doi.org/10.3389/fnhum.2016.00213

ACTIVITY 3.8
HANDOUT

INTERPLANETARY PERCEPTION

This activity explores an experiment in interplanetary perception as a means to better understand the role of culture in shaping the way we perceive stimuli. On March 3, 1972, *Pioneer 10* was the first spacecraft to leave our solar system. It included a unique attempt to communicate with extraterrestrial life. Its message took the form of a 6- by 9-inch gold anodized plaque that had been designed by astronomer Carl Sagan. It was hoped that the message might be intercepted by intelligent inhabitants of another star system who would be able to "read" its contents. The spacecraft's signal was last detected on January 23, 2003. As William Gudykunst and Young Yun Kim (2003) observed, the *Pioneer 10* plaque illustrates the nonverbal strategy typically taken when communication involves individuals who do not share a common language. Nonverbal communication across cultures is used by many types of sojourners. This activity encourages you to think about the impact of culture on perception and the challenges of communicating nonverbally across cultures.

The components of the plaque (depicted below) are as follows:

1. The brackets indicate the height of the woman in comparison to the spacecraft. The man's arm is raised in a gesture of goodwill.
2. The two joined circles represent a reverse in the direction of the spin of the electron in a hydrogen atom.
3. The number 8 in binary form appears to the right of the woman, indicating that the woman is 168 cm or 5'5" tall.
4. The radial pattern indicates the location of our solar system in the galaxy.
5. The shorter solid bars indicate directions to various pulsars from our sun and the periods of the pulsars in binary form, allowing the recipient to estimate the date *Pioneer* was launched.
6. Our solar system appears at the bottom with the *Pioneer* originating from the Earth.

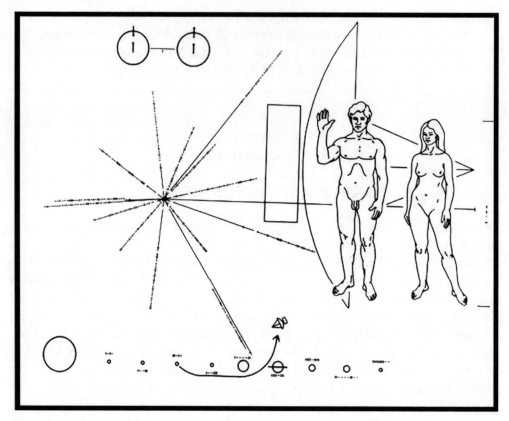

Directions: Examine the illustration of the *Pioneer 10* plaque above and read the description of its components. Then, in the space provided, draw on your knowledge of culture and perception to evaluate the likelihood that the plaque could effectively communicate with extraterrestrials. Below you will find two hints to start off your thinking on this matter.

Hint #1: Ramesh C. Mishra (1987) observed that the interpretation of pictorial symbols is in part dependent upon exposure to the objects these symbols represent. For example, Ewa Callahan (2005) discussed the failure of computer icons to be universally understood across cultures. Callahan described misunderstandings as a result of the mailbox and trashcan icons on computer interfaces given that in many countries people have mail delivered to their door or pick it up at a post office and that trashcans may have a very different appearance throughout the world.

Hint #2: A significant number of cross-cultural studies have examined the perception of three-dimensional objects depicted in two dimensions (as in a photograph or drawing). These studies have indicated that the ability to

---

perceive depth in such pictures varies greatly with exposure, educational background, and the nature of the task (Zuilkowski et al., 2016).

Discuss below the likelihood that the plaque could effectively communicate with extraterrestrials:

References:

Callahan, E. (2005). Interface design and culture. *Annual Review of Information Science and Technology, 39*(1), 255–310. http://dx.doi.org/10.1002/aris.1440390114

Gudykunst, W. B., & Kim, Y. Y. (2003). *Communicating with strangers: An approach to intercultural communication* (4th ed.). McGraw-Hill.

Mishra, R. C. (1987). A re-examination of sociocultural differences in the perception of pictorial symbols. *Indian Journal of Current Psychological Research, 2*, 65–73.

Zuilkowski, S. S., McCoy, D. C., Serpell, R., Matafwali, B., & Fink, G. (2016). Dimensionality and the development of cognitive assessments for children in sub-Saharan Africa. *Journal of Cross-Cultural Psychology, 47*(3), 341–354. https://doi.org/10.1177/0022022115624155

ACTIVITY 3.9
HANDOUT

SOUND SYMBOLISM

Clearly there are large differences between languages, but is there something universal about the way sounds are perceived across languages as well? This activity will familiarize you with the phenomenon of sound symbolism (once more commonly referred to as phonetic symbolism). This term refers to the idea that speech sounds may themselves carry some universal meaning, regardless of the language in which they are found. Edward Sapir's (1929) article on phonetic symbolism was one of the earliest cross-cultural research reports to be published in a psychological journal. Examples of recent research on this topic include a study demonstrating that higher frequency speech sounds in fictitious brand names increase the perception that a food product is healthy (Motoki et al., 2021) and studies on the impact of sound symbolism on the ease of learning (Lockwood et al., 2016) and remembering (Sonier et al., 2020) new words.

Directions: For each of the word pairs, place the letter after the word with the corresponding English meaning. For example, for the first word pair in Mandarin, if you believe *mei* means beautiful and *chŏu* means ugly, place a (b) next to *mei* and a (u) next to *chŏu*. If you believe *chŏu* means beautiful and *mei* means ugly, place a (b) next to *chŏu* and a (u) next to *mei*. Of course, if you are familiar with any of the three languages then you should not complete the word pairs for those languages.

English	Mandarin	Czech	Hindi
1. beautiful (b)	mei	ošklivé	badsurat
ugly (u)	chŏu	krásné	khubsurat
2. blunt (b)	kuài	tupy	tez
sharp (s)	dùn	spicaty	gothil
3. bright (b)	liang	tmavy	chamakdar
dark (d)	an	svetly	andhera
4. fast (f)	man	rychly	tez
slow (s)	kuài		sust
5. hard (h)	ying	mekky	sakht
soft (s)	ruăn		narm
6. light (l)	zhòng	tezky	wazani
soft (s)	qīng	lehky	halka
7. warm (w)	nuan	teply	thanda
cool (c)	liang	chladny	garam
8. wide (w)	zhăi	siroky	chaura
narrow (n)	kuān	uzky	sankara

Scoring: Check your responses against the answers provided by your instructor. Circle all correct word pairs. The higher the number of correct choices, the stronger the evidence for sound symbolism (remember that by chance you would correctly identify 12 of the 24 word pairs).

Number of correct responses: ___/24

Thinking Further:

What might be the source of similar sound-meaning associations across languages? How might they have developed?

Source:

Adapted from Brown, R. N., Black, A. H., & Horowitz, A. E. (1955). Phonetic symbolism in natural languages. *Journal of Abnormal and Social Psychology, 50*(3), 388–393.

References:

Lockwood, G., Dingemanse, M., & Hagoort, P. (2016). Sound-symbolism boosts novel word learning. *Journal of Experimental Psychology: Learning, Memory, and Cognition, 42*(8), 1274–1281.

Motoki, K., Park, J., Pathak, A., & Spence, C. (2021). Constructing healthy food names: On the sound symbolism of healthy food. *Food Quality and Preference, 90*, 13. https://doi.org/10.1016/j.foodqual.2020.104157

Sapir, E. (1929). A study in phonetic symbolism. *Journal of Experimental Psychology, 12*, 225–239.

Sonier, R., Poirier, M., Guitard, D., & Saint-Aubin, J. (2020). A round bouba is easier to remember than a curved kiki: Sound-symbolism can support associative memory. *Psychonomic Bulletin & Review, 27*(4), 776–782. https://doi.org/10.3758/s13423-020-01733-8

ACTIVITY 3.10
HANDOUT

LANGUAGE AND THOUGHT

One of the earliest topics of cross-cultural research was the relationship between language and thought. Benjamin Whorf (1956) proposed that the structure of the language one speaks influences how one views the world. This concept has been called *linguistic relativity*. A stronger version of this "Whorfian hypothesis" (also called the "Sapir-Whorf hypothesis" due to assistance Whorf received from linguist Edward Sapir) is that the language we speak *determines* the kinds of thoughts and perceptions we are capable of having. This idea is known as *linguistic determinism*. Many decades of linguistic, psychological, and anthropological research have provided conditional support for linguistic relativity in certain contexts (such as some spatial and numerical tasks). There has been far less evidence for the existence of linguistic determinism (Gleitman & Papafragou, 2013).

For example, you may be familiar with the Chihuahua dog breed, but did you know that there are "deer head" and "apple head" varieties? After learning these terms, do you think you would more easily recognize or remember the two types of Chihuahua (linguistic relativity)? Do you think you would be unable to differentiate between types if you did not know these terms (linguistic determinism)? This activity explores the concepts of linguistic relativity and linguistic determinism and asks you to consider the validity of the Whorfian hypothesis.

Directions: This activity requires that you collect three terms used by a subculture of interest to you. For example, Jerry Dunn (1997) investigated the specialized terms used by 75 subcultural groups, including mountain bike riders, disc jockeys, tabloid reporters, frisbee players, funeral directors, surfers, FBI agents, and science fiction fans. You can find such terms by interviewing group members, exploring their websites, or reading the literature of a particular subculture. Once you have collected the three terms, respond to the questions below. The terms should refer *to concepts that are new to you.* It is important that you do not use new words for familiar concepts.

1. Describe the subculture that you investigated.
2. List the three subcultural terms and their definitions.
   a.
   b.
   c.
3. How might having these new terms *influence* your thoughts or perceptions (linguistic relativity)? For example, might it be easier now to recognize or to remember the concepts represented by these terms?
4. Do you think you would be unable to think about these concepts if you didn't know these terms (linguistic determinism)? Please explain.
5. What do you conclude about linguistic relativity and linguistic determinism?

Thinking Further:

1. Several studies indicate that when given personality tests in two different languages bilingual people often produce two different personality profiles (e.g., Veltkamp et al., 2013). Based on your knowledge of linguistic relativity, why do you think this might occur?
2. John Lucy (2016) suggested that future research might investigate the effect of increasingly standardized language (due to higher literacy rates and greater access to formal education) on thought. Based on your knowledge of linguistic relativity, what do you predict about the effect of language standardization on the diversity of cultural worldviews?

References

Dunn, J. (1997). *Idiom savant: Slang as it is slung*. Henry Holt.

Gleitman, L., & Papafragou, A. (2013). Relations between language and thought. In D. Reisberg (Ed.), *The Oxford handbook of cognitive psychology* (pp. 504–523). Oxford University Press.

Lucy, J. A. (2016). Recent advances in the study of linguistic relativity in historical context: A critical assessment. *Language Learning, 66*(3), 487–515. https://doi.org/10.1111/lang.12195

Veltkamp, G. M., Recio, G., Jacobs, A. M., & Conrad, M. (2013). Is personality modulated by language? *International Journal of Bilingualism, 17*(4), 496–504. https://doi.org/10.1177/1367006912438894

Whorf, B. L. (1956). The relation of habitual thought and behavior to language. In J. B. Carroll (Ed.), *Language, thought, and reality: Selected writings of Benjamin Lee Whorf* (pp. 134–159). MIT Press.

–4–

Culture and Developmental Processes

ACTIVITY 4.1
HANDOUT

PARENTAL ETHNOTHEORIES

Anthropologist Sara Harkness and psychologist Charles Super (1996, 2021) have written extensively on cultural belief systems about parenting and child development, which they have termed *parental ethnotheories.* Jacqueline Goodnow (1996) pointed out that there are several reasons why it is useful to study parents' cultural beliefs. These beliefs (1) provide insight into the cognition and development of adults, (2) help us understand parenting behavior, (3) are one aspect of the context in which children develop, and (4) when studied across generations, can provide clues about cultural transmission and change. Parental ethnotheories have also been central to a number of interventions aimed at improving children's well-being (Harkness & Super, 2021). This activity will allow you to explore a variety of parental ethnotheories and examine the cultural basis for your own beliefs about childrearing.

Directions: Circle the number to indicate your view on each of the parental ethnotheories below.

1. Everyone in the household has responsibility for keeping an eye on a crawling child or toddler.

Strongly Disagree								Strongly Agree
1	2	3	4	5	6	7	8	9

    DOI: 10.4324/9781003356820-17

2. Praising a child for accomplishing a task leads to disobedience and selfishness.

Strongly Disagree								Strongly Agree
1	2	3	4	5	6	7	8	9

3. It is cruel and neglectful to put a baby alone in a room to sleep.

Strongly Disagree								Strongly Agree
1	2	3	4	5	6	7	8	9

4. Massage is a critical aspect of routine care for infants.

Strongly Disagree								Strongly Agree
1	2	3	4	5	6	7	8	9

5. Parents need to train their children in specific skills to prepare them for starting school.

Strongly Disagree								Strongly Agree
1	2	3	4	5	6	7	8	9

6. Babies should be encouraged to "sleep through the night" as soon as possible.

Strongly Disagree								Strongly Agree
1	2	3	4	5	6	7	8	9

7. Lactating women should freely nurse each other's children.

Strongly Disagree								Strongly Agree
1	2	3	4	5	6	7	8	9

8. Parents should respond immediately when their infant begins to cry.

Strongly Disagree								Strongly Agree
1	2	3	4	5	6	7	8	9

9. The role of parents is to protect and nurture their children, rather than stimulate their intellect.

Strongly Disagree								Strongly Agree
1	2	3	4	5	6	7	8	9

10. Children are happiest and most well-behaved when parents keep to a set daily routine.

Strongly Disagree								Strongly Agree
1	2	3	4	5	6	7	8	9

11. By age six or seven, children are capable of caring for younger siblings.

Strongly Disagree								Strongly Agree
1	2	3	4	5	6	7	8	9

12. Parents having difficulty with childrearing should consult medical or psychological experts or books written by such experts.

Strongly Disagree								Strongly Agree
1	2	3	4	5	6	7	8	9

Thinking Further:

1. With which parental ethnotheories did you most strongly agree? Why?
2. With which parental ethnotheories did you most strongly disagree? Why?
3. Meredith Small (1998) employed an *eco-cultural* perspective (Berry, 1976) in her approach to understanding childrearing. She described the many

ways in which parenting beliefs and practices evolved in response to environmental as well as sociocultural demands. For example, she cited the case of the Ache people of Paraguay who carry their children, rather than allowing them to crawl or walk – first in slings, then in baskets, and then piggyback – until they are about five years old. This practice makes sense considering the hazards for a small child crawling or walking in the forest environment of the Ache. How have the parental ethnotheories of your culture evolved in response to the physical or sociocultural environment? Please give an example below.

References:

Berry, J. W. (1976). *Human ecology and cognitive style: Comparative studies in cultural and psychological adaptation.* Sage/Halsted.

Goodnow, J. J. (1996). From household practices to parents' ideas about work and interpersonal relationships. In S. Harkness & C. M. Super (Eds.), *Parents' cultural belief systems: Their origins, expressions, and consequences* (pp. 313–344). Guilford.

Harkness, S., & Super, C. M. (1996). *Parents' cultural belief systems: Their origins, expressions, and consequences.* Guilford.

Harkness, S., & Super, C. M. (2021). Why understanding culture is essential for supporting children and families, *Applied Developmental Science*, 25(1), 14–25. https://doi.org/10.1080/10888691.2020.1789354

Small, M. F. (1998). *Our babies, ourselves: How biology and culture shape the way we parent.* Anchor Books.

ACTIVITY 4.2
HANDOUT

DEVELOPMENTAL NICHE

Sara Harkness and Charles Super created the developmental niche framework to better explain the role of culture in shaping human development. They asked, "How is it that growing up in a particular cultural setting – whether it be Boston, Rio de Janeiro, or the Serengeti plains of Tanzania – leads to the establishment of ways of thinking and acting so integral to one's identity that they will survive even radical changes of environment in later years?" (Super & Harkness, 1994, p. 95). The developmental niche is formed by three components (described below) that interact with each other and the larger environment. Although first introduced in the 1980s, this model continues to be the basis for empirical studies conducted throughout the world. The purpose of this activity is to familiarize you with the concept of developmental niche and its role in the study of culture and human development.

Directions: For each of the three components of the developmental niche detailed below, describe your own experiences, and then answer the questions that follow.

1. The physical and social setting (the child's living space, family composition, physical objects).
2. Customs and practices of child-rearing: (e.g., sleeping and feeding routines, childcare arrangements, interpersonal interaction styles, teaching approaches).
3. Caretaker psychology (psychological attributes of parents/caregivers and ethnotheories about the development and needs of children).

Thinking Further:

1. The components of the developmental niche not only shape the child, but the child has an influence on those components. Consider your individual traits and characteristics. How might you have influenced the components of your developmental niche?
2. One's developmental niche is also influenced by the larger ecological, economic, and sociopolitical context. How have these factors influenced your own developmental niche?
3. Researchers of culture and human behavior assume that although each child's developmental niche is unique, those of children within a specific community will share common features. What aspects of your developmental niche might you have shared with others in your community?
4. Researchers have used a variety of methods to study the developmental niche. More visible aspects might be observed, whereas other aspects could only be studied through the self-reports of parents and family members through interviews, questionnaires, or diaries. What type of research methods might be most successful in obtaining information about your own developmental niche?
5. According to Harkness and Super (2021), the components of the developmental niche work together as a system to provide children with a consistent message about the expectations of their culture. For example, Mieko Hobara (2003) studied the prevalence of transitional objects, such

as stuffed animals or blankets, in young children in Japan and the United States. She found that, as compared with the children in the United States, children in Japan were less likely to have an attachment to a transitional object (setting) and were more likely to co-sleep with parents (customs and practices). Hobara explained that in the United States, parents are more likely to believe that infants need to be socialized to become independent, whereas some level of dependence or inter-dependence between parents and children is viewed as natural in Japan (caretaker psychology).

Consider the three components of your developmental niche. What messages did they convey to you about the expectations of your culture?

References:

Harkness, S., & Super, C. M. (2021). Why understanding culture is essential for supporting children and families. *Applied Developmental Science, 25*(1), 14–25. https://doi.org/10.1080/10888691.2020.1789354

Hobara, M. (2003). Prevalence of transitional objects in young children in Tokyo and New York. *Infant Mental Health Journal, 24*, 174–191. http://dx.doi.org/10.1002/imhj.10046

Super, C. M., & Harkness, S. (1994). The developmental niche. In W. Lonner & R. Malpass (Eds.), *Psychology and culture* (pp. 95–99). Allyn & Bacon.

ACTIVITY 4.3
HANDOUT

ETHNIC-RACIAL SOCIALIZATION

Across the globe, children's ethnic/racial group membership has a significant effect on how they experience the world. As Martin Ruck and colleagues (2021, p. 944) explained, "dynamics related to race and ethnicity shape the developmental pathways of youth and have widespread implications for their physical, social, emotional, and academic well-being." Central to these outcomes is ethnic-racial socialization (ERS), the process by which young people learn about the values and traditions of their ethnic/racial group and learn to prepare for ethnicity- and race-related threats to their well-being (Hughes et al., 2006). Thus, researchers and practitioners have endeavored to better understand ERS. For example, researchers reported that the types of messages Chinese American adolescents received from parents about the wave of anti-Asian racism during the Covid-19 pandemic predicted racial discrimination-related stress and coping (Cheah et al., 2021; Ren et al., 2022). This activity will explore the content and agents of your own childhood ERS.

Directions: First think about the messages you received about your own race and ethnicity throughout your childhood. Then, in the box that indicates the appropriate message source and content, briefly describe the messages you received. There will likely be several empty boxes. Finally, based on your statements in the chart below, answer the questions that follow.

	SOURCES OF ETHNIC-RACIAL SOCIALIZATION				
MESSAGE CONTENT	*Parents/ Family*	*Peers*	*School*	*Community*	*Media*
Values, traditions, history of ethnic/racial group(s)					
Support for positive ethnic/racial identity					
Preparation for prejudice and discrimination					
Equality across ethnic/racial groups					
Anti-racist activism					
Other:					
Other:					

Thinking Further:

1. What kind of messages did you receive through explicit, direct statements? What kind of messages were communicated more indirectly (such as through stories, nonverbal behavior, or observation)? Please explain.
2. Did the ERS messages you received address your intersectional identities (that is, how your race/ethnicity interacts with other identities, such as gender identity, social class, sexual orientation, religion, or disability)? Please explain.

3. Did you observe any changes in the agents or messages of your ERS from early childhood through adolescence? Please explain.
4. Is there anything that was absent from your ERS that you wish had been included?
5. What do you conclude about the ERS you experienced?

References:

Cheah, C. S. L., Zong, X., Cho, H. S., Ren, H., Wang, S., Xue, X., & Wang, C. (2021). Chinese American adolescents' experiences of COVID-19 racial discrimination: Risk and protective factors for internalizing difficulties. *Cultural Diversity and Ethnic Minority Psychology*, 27(4), 559–568. https://doi.org/10.1037/cdp0000498

Hughes, D., Rodriguez, J., Smith, E. P., Johnson, D. J., Stevenson, H. C., & Spicer, P. (2006). Parents' ethnic–racial socialization practices: A review of research and directions for future study. *Developmental Psychology*, 42(5), 747–770. https://doi.org/10.1037/0012-1649.42.5.747

Ren, H., Cheah, C. S. L., Zong, X., Wang, S., Cho, H. S., Wang, C., & Xue, X. (2022). Age-varying associations between Chinese American parents' racial–ethnic socialization and children's difficulties during the COVID-19 pandemic. *Asian American Journal of Psychology*, 13(4), 351–363. https://doi.org/10.1037/aap0000278

Ruck, M. D., Hughes, D. L., & Niwa, E. Y. (2021). Through the looking glass: Ethnic racial socialization among children and adolescents. *Journal of Social Issues*, 77(4), 943–963. https://doi.org/10.1111/josi.12495

ACTIVITY 4.4
HANDOUT

FORMAL AND INFORMAL LEARNING

The United Nations Educational, Scientific and Cultural Organization (UNESCO; 2023) advocates for recognizing and valuing knowledge gained outside of a formal school environment through *informal learning*, which occurs in the course of daily life activities related to work, family, or leisure (they also recognize *nonformal learning*, such as apprenticeships). For example, weaving or small-scale farming skills might be more frequently learned informally whereas mathematical skills and historical dates may be more frequently learned through formal schooling. According to UNESCO, recognizing and certifying skills learned outside of a formal school environment can lead to social and economic benefits for individuals who have not had access to an educational system or cannot provide evidence of formal education due to migration from their home country. The purpose of this activity is to explore the value of informal education and some of the ways it differs from formal schooling.

Directions: List five skills that you learned through formal education and five skills that you learned through informal means. Then answer the questions that follow to compare these two forms of learning.

Formal Education:

1.
2.
3.
4.
5.

Informal Education:

1.
2.
3.
4.
5.

1. For each of the following statements, indicate by marking the appropriate blank with an "X" whether it better describes formal or informal education.

	Formal	Informal
a. Learning occurs in a specified setting and time period.	_____	_____
b. Learning occurs through observation.	_____	_____
c. Emotions are kept separate from the subject matter.	_____	_____
d. The teacher has a personal connection with the subject matter.	_____	_____
e. Teachers of a specific subject are basically interchangeable.	_____	_____
f. Cooperation more than competition characterizes the interaction among learners.	_____	_____

g. The subject matter is closely tied to life experiences.   _____   _____

h. The learning process is fairly structured and predictable.   _____   _____

2. What are your thoughts about the value of the skills and knowledge you learned through informal education as compared with those you learned through formal education?

Thinking Further:

1. What difficulties might arise for someone from a culture that depends heavily on informal education if they were to enter a formal schooling situation?
2. What characteristics of informal learning might be helpful to integrate into a formal educational setting?
3. Robert Serpell and Giyoo Hatano (1997) described how reading skills can be acquired outside of a school setting. What other skills that are typically taught in school might also be learned through informal means?

References:

Serpell, R., & Hatano, G. (1997). Education, schooling, and literacy. In J. W. Berry, P. R. Dasen, & S. Saraswathi (Eds.), *Handbook of cross-cultural psychology*, Vol. 2: Basic processes and human development (2nd ed., pp. 339–376). Allyn & Bacon.

UNESCO Institute for Lifelong Learning. (2023). International trends of lifelong learning in higher education: Research report. UNESCO. https://unesdoc.unesco.org/ark:/48223/pf0000385339

ACTIVITY 4.5
HANDOUT

HOME CULTURE AND SCHOOL CULTURE FIT

Cigdem Kagitcibasi (1990, 1997) stressed the importance of a fit between home culture and school environment for the academic success and well-being of children. According to Carrie Rothstein-Fisch and Elise Trumbull (2008), it is critical to

---

structure classrooms and curricula such that they avoid putting the students' home culture in conflict with their school culture. They further suggested that:

> teachers who are knowledgeable about the culture of school and culture of their students can serve as "cultural brokers," helping their students and students' families negotiate new cultural terrain and become biculturally proficient ... They can also share their cultural knowledge about families with other school personnel and help to influence the development of policies that are more culturally congruent ... (p. xvii)

Here are some examples of interventions aimed at creating a better fit between students' home culture and school culture:

- Based at the University of Alaska, Fairbanks, the Alaska Native Knowledge Network (ANKN, 2023) has developed an extensive curriculum aimed at adapting indigenous and Western knowledge systems to classrooms with a primarily Alaska Native student population. These resources include a focus on, for example, genealogy and oral history, the role of elders in children's education, and the importance of traditional ecological knowledge in contemporary society.
- The Center for Research on Education, Diversity, and Excellence Hawai'i Project (CREDE, n.d.) at the University of Hawai'i, Manoa, provides training and resources for teachers of native Hawaiian and other culturally and linguistically diverse students. Their "place-based" approach uses the local community and environment as a starting point to teach subjects across the curriculum, with themes such as gardening, the ocean, and Native Hawaiian plants.
- Carrie Rothstein-Fisch and Elise Trumbull (2008) collaborated with colleagues Patricia Greenfield and Blanca Quiroz to create The Bridging Cultures Project. This project was a five-year action research study of elementary classrooms in the U.S. with a high percentage of immigrant children from home cultures that emphasize collectivist values. These authors implemented a strategy for modifying individualist classroom structures to better fit a more collectivistic home culture, which they believe characterizes much of the world's population, including many of the Latinx immigrant students in U.S. classrooms. For example, they emphasized group-oriented, interdependent activities, which they have found to support academic and behavioral success.

This activity will encourage you to identify cultural values in the classroom and to consider your own experience with the compatibility of home and school cultures.

Directions: After obtaining any necessary permission, observe a preschool or elementary school class in your community. Make careful notes on what you observe about the students' behavior, the teachers' behavior, and the classroom setting. Finally, write an analysis of the cultural values implicitly or explicitly expressed in the class session. For example, Rothstein-Fisch and Trumbull (2008) noted the individualist values that underlie the practice of asking students to take a vote to resolve a disagreement about choosing a class activity. They suggested that for students with a more collectivistic social orientation, this practice could actually make the conflict worse.

Classroom Description and Analysis:

Thinking Further:

1. Select one of the behaviors you detailed in your classroom observation notes and discuss how it might be altered to be more culturally inclusive. Be sure to avoid the use of cultural stereotypes.
2. Consider the challenges of creating a home-culture and school-culture fit with a diverse student body. For example, Manuela Lavelli, Paula Döge, and Mara Bighin (2016) described a multicultural Italian preschool setting in which the families of Romanian, Moroccan, Nigerian, and Sri Lankan immigrant children had educational goals that differed significantly from each other and from those of the teachers. These authors suggested that this could be addressed both by greater cultural sensitivity in the curriculum as well as programs to create dialogue between teachers and immigrant parents. What strategies can you suggest to enhance home-culture and school-culture fit in a multicultural classroom?
3. Dina Birman and Nellie Tran (2015) described perhaps the most extreme form of home-school culture incompatibility, in which students with no experience in formal schooling are placed in a traditional education system. How might you attempt to create a harmonious home-culture–school-culture fit in that circumstance?
4. Think about the fit between your own home-culture and the school environment where your education took place. To what extent were they compatible? What changes could have been made to your classroom to make it more compatible with your home-culture?

References:

ANKN. (2023). *Alaska Native Knowledge Network.* www.ankn.uaf.edu/

Birman, D., & Tran, N. (2015). *The academic engagement of newly arriving Somali Bantu students in a U.S. elementary school.* Migration Policy Institute.

Center for Research on Education, Diversity, and Excellence Hawai'i Project. (n.d.). CREDE. http://manoa.hawaii.edu/coe/crede/

Kagitcibasi, C. (1990). Family and home-based intervention. In R. Brislin (Ed.), *Applied cross-cultural psychology* (pp. 121–141). Sage.

Kagitcibasi, C. (1997). Individualism and collectivism. In J. Berry, M. Segall, & C. Kagitcibasi (Eds.), *Handbook of cross-cultural psychology*, Vol. 3: Behavior and applications (2nd ed., pp. 1–49). Allyn & Bacon.

Lavelli, M., Döge, P., & Bighin, M. (2016). Socialization goals of immigrant mothers from diverse cultures and of their children's preschool teachers in Italy. *Journal of Cross-Cultural Psychology*, *47*(2), 197–214.

Rothstein-Fisch, C., & Trumbull, E. (2008). *Managing diverse classrooms: How to build on students' cultural strengths.* Association for Supervision and Curriculum Development.

ACTIVITY 4.6
HANDOUT

A CULTURALLY APPROPRIATE PIAGETIAN TASK

Early cross-cultural studies of cognitive abilities often found deficiencies in the mental abilities of individuals from less industrialized societies. Later studies of this type demonstrated, however, that these individuals' *performance* on cognitive tasks did not likely indicate their level of *competence*. One of the reasons for this was that the earlier studies tended to use materials that were not familiar to the participants. In a classic study demonstrating the importance of the familiarity of task materials (Irwin et al., 1974), nonliterate Liberian adults and U.S. college students were asked to perform two sorting tasks. One task involved sorting geometric figures differing in color, shape, and number. The second task involved sorting bowls of rice that differed in quantity, type of rice, and cleanness of the grains. The Americans performed better than the Liberians on the geometric figures task, whereas the Liberians performed better than the

Americans on the rice sorting task. Each group performed best on the task that utilized familiar materials.

A large number of cross-cultural studies of cognitive development have focused on Piagetian tasks. Jean Piaget's theory of cognitive development specifies a distinct structure of thought that differs at each of the four stages of development. Cross-cultural research generally supports the sequence of stages described by Piaget, although the age at which different stages are attained varies across cultures (Dasen, 2022). In addition, Piaget's fourth stage of development, formal operations, may be somewhat dependent on exposure to formal schooling (Keller, 2011). Children performing tasks with familiar materials were also more likely than those using unfamiliar materials to demonstrate mastery of the stages assessed (Price-Williams, 1981). The purpose of this activity is to think about how one might develop a culturally appropriate Piagetian task.

Directions: Use online materials or an introductory or developmental psychology textbook to review the concept of Piagetian conservation. Then devise a task to test conservation of quantity, mass, or number. This task should be appropriate for children in a specific culture or region with which you are familiar. Use materials for this task that are commonly found in the culture or region you selected. For example, Geoffrey Saxe and Thomas Moylan (1982) developed a Piagetian conservation task appropriate for the Oksapmin people of Papua New Guinea. The task involved the measurement of string bags, a commonly used object in Oksapmin culture, and required that people understand that the length of bags remains constant regardless of whether it is measured along the arm of a child or the arm of an adult.

In the spaces provided below, indicate the culture or region and conservation task you have selected and then describe the task and materials used.

1. The task below is intended to measure conservation of _____
   for members of the _____ culture/region.
2. Description of the task and materials:

References:

Dasen, P. R. (2022). Culture and cognitive development. *Journal of Cross-Cultural Psychology*, *53*(7–8), 789–816. https://doi.org/10.1177/00220221221092409

Irwin, M. H., Schafer, G. N., & Feiden, C. P. (1974). Emic and unfamiliar category sorting of Mano farmers and U.S. undergraduates. *Journal of Cross-Cultural Psychology*, 5, 407–423.

Keller, H. (2011). Culture and cognition: Developmental perspectives. *Journal of Cognitive Education and Psychology*, 10(1), 3–8.

Price-Williams, D. (1981). Concrete and formal operations. In R. H. Munroe, R. L. Monroe, & B. D. Whiting (Eds.), *Handbook of cross-cultural human development* (pp. 403–422). Garland Press.

Saxe, G. B., & Moylan, T. (1982). The development of measurement operations among the Oksapmin of Papua New Guinea. *Child Development*, 53, 1242–1248.

ACTIVITY 4.7
HANDOUT

GROWING UP AS A LANGUAGE BROKER

The term "language broker" has been used to refer to the children of immigrant families "who interpret and translate between culturally and linguistically different people and mediate interactions in a variety of situations including those found at home and school" (Tse, 1996, p. 226). Since professional interpreters are typically unavailable in daily activities, these children, adolescents, and young adults may be called upon to translate for family members in such situations as doctor visits, teacher meetings, government business, housing-related matters, and employment interviews. Research indicates that while acting as a language broker may be stressful for children at times, they typically emerge from this responsibility with skills that their non-language brokering peers may not have (Weisskirch, 2017).

Directions: Consider the experience of language brokering and then answer the questions below.

1. What types of knowledge might be gained from language brokering (consider knowledge about the outside world as well as knowledge about one's family and oneself)?
2. What specific intrapersonal skills (relating to one's own emotions and cognition) might emerge as a result of language brokering?

---

3. What specific interpersonal skills (relating to interactions with others) might emerge as a result of language brokering?

4. What specific intercultural skills (relating to interactions across cultures) might emerge as a result of language brokering?

Thinking Further:

How might the child's or adolescent's stage of development interact with their experiences as a language broker? Please explain.

References:

Tse, L. (1996). Who decides? The effect of language brokering on home-school communication. *The Journal of Educational Issues of Language Minority Students, 16,* 225–234.

Weisskirch, R. S. (Ed.). (2017). *Language brokering in immigrant families: Theories and contexts.* Routledge.

ACTIVITY 4.8
HANDOUT

"EAST-WEST" DIFFERENCES IN AGEISM: MYTH OR REALITY?

Research on cross-cultural differences in aging attitudes has long focused on comparisons between Eastern (Asian) and Western (European and North American) cultures. Much of this research is based on the idea that Confucian values in Asian societies would result in more positive attitudes towards aging and greater respect for older adults than in the West. This activity focuses on examining the assumption of more positive age-related attitudes in Eastern than Western nations.

Directions: Identify three individuals to answer the questions below and carefully record their ages and responses.

Participant A: Age _____

Do you think there are differences between Eastern and Western cultures in attitudes toward aging and older people? Please explain.

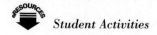

Participant B: Age _____

Do you think there are differences between Eastern and Western cultures in attitudes toward aging and older people? Please explain.

Participant C: Age _____

Do you think there are differences between Eastern and Western cultures in attitudes toward aging and older people? Please explain.

Did your participants express a belief in "East-West" differences? If so, to what did they attribute these differences?

Thinking Further:

Despite the widespread belief that older adults receive more respect in Asian cultures than in the West, research findings on such differences have been decidedly mixed. For example, Lindsay Ackerman and William Chopik (2021) measured implicit and explicit forms of age bias using data from over 900,000 individuals in 68 countries and found that participants living in collectivistic countries expressed less implicit and explicit age bias and greater feelings of warmth toward older adults compared with participants living in highly individualistic countries. In contrast, Michael North and Susan Fiske (2015) conducted a meta-analysis of 37 studies involving 23 countries that investigated cultural differences in age-related attitudes and found that older people in Western nations were viewed with greater respect than those in Eastern nations. In addition, Baozhen Luo and colleagues (2013) reported lower ageism among U.S. college students as compared to Chinese college students. What is more, Hui-Chuan Hsu and colleagues (2023) reported significant differences in age-related attitudes among Asian nations, with Japanese participants reporting more negative impressions about older adults than Taiwanese people, and Korean participants indicating that they were less willing to live with older adults than Taiwanese people. How might we make sense of these conflicting findings?

One strategy is *unpackaging culture* (Whiting, 1976) by identifying variables that may underlie the observed cultural differences. Some of the variables associated with cultural differences in attitudes about older people are listed below. Choose one of these variables and develop a hypothesis about why the variable you chose might predict more negative age-related attitudes:

- The proportion of older people in the country (Ayalon & Roy, 2022).
- Greater country-level socioeconomic development (Löckenhoff et al., 2009).
- The speed with which the country's population is aging (North & Fiske, 2015).

- "Marketized mentality" – focusing on a strong achievement orientation, excessive individualism, and the domination of others (Hövermann & Messner, 2023).
- Higher levels of country-level masculinity and long-term orientation (Ng & Lim-Soh, 2021). Hofstede's dimension of masculinity refers to "a preference in society for achievement, heroism, assertiveness, and material rewards for success" whereas long-term orientation indicates "thrift and efforts in modern education as a way to prepare for the future" (Hofstede Insights, 2023).
- More limited intergenerational interaction (Luo et al., 2013).

Your Hypothesis:

References:

Ackerman, L. S., & Chopik, W. J. (2021). Cross-cultural comparisons in implicit and explicit age bias. *Personality and Social Psychology Bulletin, 47*(6), 953–968. https://doi.org/10.1177/0146167220950070

Ayalon, L., & Roy, S. (2022). Combatting ageism in the Western Pacific region. *The Lancet Regional Health: Western Pacific.* https://doi.org/10.1016/j.lanwpc.2022.100593

Hofstede Insights. (2023). *Intercultural management.* www.hofstede-insights.com/intercultural-management

Hövermann, A., & Messner, S. F. (2023). Explaining when older persons are perceived as a burden: A cross-national analysis of ageism. *International Journal of Comparative Sociology, 64*(1), 3–21. https://doi.org/10.1177/00207152221102841

Hsu, H.-C., Chong, Y., & Osawa, E. (2023). Comparison of Asian countries and age groups in the attitudes toward active aging and impression of older adults. *Journal of Aging and Social Policy, 35*(4), 422–439. https://doi.org/10.1080/08959420.2022.2055418

Löckenhoff, C. E., De Fruyt, F., Terracciano, A., et al. (2009). Perceptions of aging across 26 cultures and their culture-level associates. *Psychology and Aging, 24*(4), 941–954. https://doi.org/10.1037/a0016901

Luo, B., Zhou, K., Jin, E. J., Newman, A., & Liang, J. (2013). Ageism among college students: A comparative study between U.S. and China. *Journal of Cross Cult Gerontology, 28*, 49–63. https://doi.org/10.1007/s10823-013-9186-5

Ng, R., & Lim-Soh, J. W. (2021). Ageism linked to culture, not demographics: Evidence from an 8-billion-word corpus across 20 countries. *The Journals of Gerontology: Series B*, *76*(9), 1791–1798. https://doi.org/10.1093/geronb/gbaa181

North, M. S., & Fiske, S. T. (2015). Modern attitudes toward older adults in the aging world: A cross-cultural meta-analysis. *Psychological Bulletin*, *141*(5), 993–1021. https://doi.org/10.1037/a0039469

Whiting, B. (1976). The problem of the packaged variable. In K. A. Riegel & J. A. Meacham (Eds.), *The developing individual in a changing world*, Vol. 1 (pp. 303–309). Mouton.

ACTIVITY 4.9
HANDOUT

ETHNOGRAPHIC STUDIES OF HUMAN DEVELOPMENT

Carol and Melvin Ember (2001) suggested that making cross-cultural comparisons is impossible without ethnography. Ethnography provides detailed, culture-specific information which allows us to identify patterns and possible universals. Ethnography involves recording observations of daily behavior, generally over an extended period of time. Ethnographic researchers typically take in-depth notes on their observations and may work closely with members of the community they are studying. At times ethnographic researchers may even take part in the activities they are investigating, a technique called *participant observation*.

In a research technique called the *holocultural* or *hologeistic* method, hypotheses about the relationship between variables across cultures are typically tested using collections of ethnographies. In this form of research, societies rather than individuals are used as the unit of analysis. One of the most widely used collections of ethnographies is the Human Relations Area Files (HRAF). The HRAF databases (*eHRAF World Cultures* and *eHRAF Collection of Archeology*) contain ethnographies from over 360 cultural, ethnic, religious, and national groups around the world and have been used in hundreds of studies. For example, using the HRAF, Carol Ember, Teferi Abate Adem, and Ian Skoggard (2013) identified a link between climate-related disasters, such as drought, and the likelihood of warfare. Another source of ethnographic studies is the Database of Places, Language, Culture, and Environment (D-Place), which contains cultural, linguistic, environmental, and geographic information for over 1400 human societies.

The following studies are examples of ethnographic research.

- Dina Birman and Nellie Tran (2017) spent two years conducting classroom observations and interviews to investigate how Somali Bantu refugee students adjusted to attending an elementary school in Chicago, U.S. They collected detailed accounts of the challenges faced by children and teachers. One outcome of this research was that they identified two different approaches that teachers took in dealing with cultural differences: an "assimilationist" approach, which emphasized a need for students to conform to U.S. culture and school rules, and a "multicultural" approach in which teachers showed respect for the students' expressions of their culture at school.
- David Lancy (2020) used ethnographic accounts to support the argument that young children experience a biologically based "helper stage" in which they express interest in helping older siblings and adults with everyday tasks. According to Lancy, this stage is facilitated by child-rearing practices in many cultural contexts, but is often extinguished by parenting behaviors in WEIRD societies.
- Tham Thithu Tran and Elizabeth Bifuh-Ambe (2021) used ethnographic methods to investigate ethnic identity among second-generation Vietnamese American adolescents who were members of a Buddhist youth program. Through interviews, focus groups, and observations, the authors identified sources and manifestations of ethnic pride (such as participating in Vietnamese traditions) and proposed that a strong ethnic identity facilitated by the Buddhist Youth program promoted family harmony and mitigated intergenerational and peer conflict.

The purpose of this activity is to become familiar with the method of ethnography, particularly as it informs our understanding of human development.

Directions: Using scholarly sources, locate a published ethnography addressing some aspect of human development. Such studies focus on understanding the context of experiences and adaptations throughout the lifespan. The research article you select should describe a study conducted in a culture other than your own. Many social science books and journals include ethnographies. However, some particularly good journal sources for ethnographic accounts include:

- *American Anthropologist*
- *American Ethnologist*
- *Culture & Psychology*
- *Journal of Aging Studies*
- *Journal of Black Studies*
- *Journal of Comparative Family Studies*

- *Current Anthropology Culture, Medicine, and Psychiatry*
- *Ethnic and Racial Studies*
- *Ethnography and Education*
- *American Journal of Sociology*
- *American Journal of Community Psychology*
- *Cross-Cultural Research*
- *Cultural Diversity and Ethnic Minority Psychology*
- *Ethos*
- *Field Methods*
- *Journal of Contemporary Ethnography*
- *Journal of Ethnography and Qualitative Research*
- *Social Anthropology*
- *Social Science & Medicine*

After carefully reading your ethnography, answer the questions below. Be sure to include a copy of your article with this assignment.

1. In the space below, provide the full reference for your article (see the references in this book for examples of the format and content).
2. In your own words, describe the purpose of this ethnographic study.
3. Describe the ethnographic methods that were involved in this study.
4. Summarize the findings of the study. In what way did this research contribute to our understanding of human development?
5. What do you think might be some strengths and weaknesses of the ethnographic approach?

References:

Birman, B. D., & Tran, N. (2017). When worlds collide: Academic adjustment of Somali Bantu students with limited formal education in a U.S. elementary school. *International Journal of Intercultural Relations, 60*, 132–144. https://doi.org/10.1016/j.ijintrel.2017.06.008

Ember, C. R., Adem, T. A., & Skoggard, I. (2013). Risk, uncertainty, and violence in eastern Africa: A cross-regional comparison. *Human Nature, 24*, 33–58. https://doi.org/10.1007/s12110-012-9157-5

Ember, C. R., & Ember, M. (2001). *Cross-cultural research methods.* Rowman & Littlefield.

Lancy, D. (2020). *Child helpers: A multidisciplinary perspective (Elements in Psychology and Culture).* Cambridge University Press.

Tran, T. T., & Bifuh-Ambe, E. (2021). Ethnic identity among second-generation Vietnamese American adolescents. *Journal of Ethnic and Cultural Studies, 8*(2), 167–186. https://doi.org/10.29333/ejecs/622

ACTIVITY 4.10
HANDOUT

TEXTBOOK REWRITE

As you learn more about culture and psychology you may find that you view your psychology lectures and reading materials from a new perspective. In fact, you may be tempted to fill in information about cultural variability or modify existing information to be more inclusive of diverse populations. This activity gives you an opportunity to do just that.

Directions:

1. Select a brief segment (1–2 paragraphs) of a developmental psychology textbook or the developmental chapter of an introductory psychology textbook.
2. Use scholarly articles or cross-cultural texts to locate material on cultural factors relevant to the aspect of development described in your text excerpt.
3. Rewrite the material so as to include the information about cultural influences. Be sure to make the appropriate citations for the material you include.
4. Include a copy of the original textbook passages with your rewrite.

The task of this activity involves not just adding information to the existing text passage, but significantly rewriting the material so as not to *marginalize* diverse perspectives. An example of this rewriting strategy is provided below.

Example:

One way to start this process is to identify the emic or culture-specific information in the original, which is often presented as if it is universal (in the example below, the three socialization patterns are culture-specific). Then identify the etic, or universal construct (in the example, the universal concept is childrearing style). Be sure that your rewrite is built around the etic and not the emic.

Original:

> Research based on Baumrind's (1971) model indicates that parents generally employ one of three socialization patterns: authoritarian, in which adults control children, permissive, in which there is little parental control, or authoritative socialization, in which parents set clear standards but also encourage independence.

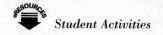

Cultural influences included but marginalized:

> Research based on Baumrind's (1971) model indicates that parents generally employ one of three socialization patterns: authoritarian, in which adults control children, permissive, in which there is little parental control, or authoritative socialization, in which parents set clear standards but also encourage independence. However, these patterns may not apply to all ethnocultural groups. Chao (1994), for example, found that Baumrind's model did not fit Chinese parenting styles.

Inclusive rewrite:

> Childrearing styles vary across ethnic and cultural groups. Baumrind (1971) identified three main socialization patterns in research on European American parents: authoritarian, permissive, or authoritative parenting. Chao (1994) found that the concept of *chiao shun*, which emphasizes training children to know what is expected of them, best characterizes the parenting style of Chinese Americans.

In the space below provide the complete reference for the textbook you have selected and your inclusive rewrite.

References:

Baumrind, D. (1971). Current patterns of parental authority. *Developmental Psychology Monographs, 4*(1), 1–103. https://doi.org/10.1037/h0030372

Chao, R. K. (1994). Beyond parental control and authoritarian parenting style: Understanding Chinese parenting through the cultural notion of training. *Child Development, 65,* 1111–1119. https://doi.org/10.2307/1131308

(Space for responses in these handouts has been reduced. Please see www.rou-tledge.com/9781032394336 for fillable versions of these handouts.)

–5–

Personality, Emotion, and the Self in Cultural Context

ACTIVITY 5.1
HANDOUT

THE INTERDEPENDENT AND INDEPENDENT SELVES

One of the most researched topics in cross-cultural psychology is Hazel Markus and Shinobu Kitayama's (1991) self-construal theory. They posited that our sociocultural context shapes how we perceive our self – as interdependent and thus defined in terms of our relationships and inseparable from the social context, or as independent, and focused on how our individual traits, abilities, goals, and preferences distinguish us from others. They suggested that an interdependent self-construal would be more common in a collectivist cultural context and an independent self-construal would be more common in an individualist cultural context. According to Markus and Kitayama, and the authors of many subsequent studies, the degree to which we hold an interdependent vs. independent self-construal affects how we process thoughts, how we experience and express emotions, and how and when we are motivated. Although there have been challenges to and modifications of the independent–interdependent framework, as well as scrutiny of the methods used in these studies, this topic continues to be one of considerable research interest. This activity will familiarize you with the concept of self-construal.

Directions: Read each of the items in the two columns below and place a check next to the item in each pair that best describes you.

DOI: 10.4324/9781003356820-18

1. ____ Success depends on help from others.   ____ Success depends on my abilities.

2. ____ I know more about others than I do about myself.   ____ I know more about myself than I do about others.

3. ____ Being excluded from my group would be very hard on me.   ____ Being dependent on others would be very hard on me.

4. ____ Silence is comfortable.   ____ Silence is embarrassing.

5. ____ It is important that my behavior is appropriate for the situation.   ____ It is important that my behavior and attitudes correspond.

6. ____ I sometimes feel ashamed.   ____ I sometimes feel guilty.

7. ____ Friendships are difficult to establish but are generally very intimate.   ____ Friendships are fairly easy to establish but often not very intimate.

8. ____ I generally socialize in groups.   ____ I generally socialize in pairs.

____ **Total number of checks**   ____ **Total number of checks**

1. The items in the column on the left indicate characteristics of the inter-dependent self, whereas items in the column on the right indicate character-istics of the independent self. According to the total number of checks for each column, is your self-construal more interdependent or independent? To what extent does your cultural background relate to this result?
2. It is possible that we each have both independent and interdependent self-construals. Harry Triandis (1994) suggested that individuals draw from different types of self-construal at any given moment depending on their cultural experiences and the situation. Describe below an instance in which you acted from an interdependent self-construal and one in which you acted from an independent self-construal.

Thinking Further:

Studies have shown that it is possible to *prime* people to think independently or interdependently regardless of their cultural background. For example, partici-pants may be asked to read one of two stories and count the number of pronouns (Brewer & Gardner, 1996). Those who read a story containing independent pronouns (e.g., *I, me, mine*) may act as if they have an independent self-construal and those who read a story containing interdependent pronouns (e.g., *we, us, our*) may act as if they have an interdependent self-construal. Several studies have found differences in self-construal as a result of priming (Cross et al., 2011). However, there is also some indication that priming may interact with sociocultural context. For example, Sandra Weltzien et al. (2019) used self-construal priming with children from India and the UK and then assessed their generosity in a resource allocation game. Children from both countries became more selfish following independence priming, but only the Indian children (particularly those living in traditional extended families) became more generous following the interdependence priming. What do the results of such priming studies tell us about how self-construal might develop?

References:

Brewer, M. B., & Gardner, W. L. (1996). Who is this "we"? Levels of collective identity and self representations. *Journal of Personality and Social Psychology, 71*, 83–93. http://dx.doi.org/10.1037/0022-3514.71.1.83

Cross, S. E., Hardin, E. E., & Gercek-Swing, B. (2011). The what, how, why, and where of self-construal. *Personality and Social Psychology Review, 15*(2), 142–179. https://doi.org/10.1177/1088868310373752

Markus, H., & Kitayama, S. (1991). Culture and self: Implications for cognition, emotion, and motivation. *Psychological Review, 98*, 224–253. http://dx.doi.org/10.1037/0033-295X.98.2.224

Triandis, H. C. (1994). *Culture and social psychology.* McGraw-Hill.

Weltzien, S., Marsh, L., Kanngiesser, P., Stuijfzand, B., & Hood, B. (2019). Considering self or others across two cultural contexts: How children's resource allocation is affected by self-construal manipulations. *Journal of Experimental Child Psychology, 184*, 139–157. https://doi.org/10.1016/j.jecp.2019.04.002

ACTIVITY 5.2
HANDOUT

MULTIPLE AND SHIFTING IDENTITIES

There are many aspects of our identity in addition to culture. These different identities contribute to the diversity within cultural groups. This activity is designed to encourage you to examine your multiple group identities. Henri

Tajfel's (1978) Social Identity Theory suggests that these group identities shape how we view ourselves and others. Marshall Singer (1998) used the term *identity group* in an intercultural communication context to refer to groups of people who perceive some aspect of the world similarly and who recognize and communicate about that similarity. According to Singer, the perceptions, values, attitudes, and beliefs that we learn from being a part of these groups, and the relative importance of our multiple identity groups, make each of us unique.

Directions: Think for a minute about your identity groups; that is, the group memberships that most clearly define who you are. These may include gender identity, nationality, religion, socioeconomic status, race/ethnicity, sexual orientation, age cohort, disability status, as well as such affiliations as political party, academic discipline, occupation, hobbies, and sports teams. Then answer the questions below in the space provided.

1. List your identity groups below:

    _____   _____

    _____   _____

    _____   _____

    _____   _____

    _____

Go back to your list of identity groups above and rank them by putting a (1) next to the group that you identify with most strongly, a (2) next to the group that is next most important to you, and so on.

2. Did you find the groups difficult to rank? Why or why not?
3. One reason that identity groups may be difficult to rank is that their importance may vary with the situation. Describe below a situation in which an identity group that you ranked as relatively unimportant could be much more important to you.
4. Dimensions of identity do not exist in isolation but interact with each other to influence our life experiences and behavior. Kimberlé Crenshaw (1989) introduced the term *intersectionality* to refer to the overlapping forms of social injustice associated with identity. For example, the effects of ageism differ for men and women; the effects of growing up poor differ by race/ethnicity. What would happen if one of your primary identity groups changed – for example, your gender identity, socioeconomic class, race/ethnicity, or sexual orientation? Would this affect your other identity groups? If so how?

References:

Crenshaw, K. (1989). Demarginalizing the intersection of race and sex: A Black feminist critique of antidiscrimination doctrine, feminist theory and antiracist politics. *University of Chicago Legal Forum, 1.* http://chicagounbound.uchicago.edu/uclf/vol1989/iss1/8

Singer, M. R. (1998). *Perception & identity in intercultural communication.* Intercultural Press.

Tajfel, H. (1978). The achievement of inter-group differentiation. In H. Tajfel (Ed.), *Differentiation between social groups* (pp. 77–100). Academic Press.

ACTIVITY 5.3
HANDOUT

MULTIRACIAL IDENTITY

The number of mixed-race individuals is increasing dramatically in several parts of the world. For example, the 2021 census in Britain showed a 40% increase since 2011 in the number of people identifying as being from "mixed/multiple ethnic groups" (Office for National Statistics, 2022), and the segment of the U.S. population that identified as "two or more races" increased by 276% between 2010 and 2020 (U.S. Census Bureau, 2020). At the same time, social science researchers have stepped up efforts to better understand multiracial identity development and the experiences of individuals with mixed racial/ethnic backgrounds.

As you might imagine, conducting research on multicultural identity is a complex endeavor. One reason is that multiracial individuals often identify with only one racial/ethnic group. In fact, a Pew Research Center survey (2015) found that only 39% of adults with mixed racial backgrounds identified as multiracial. In addition, the experiences of these individuals differ significantly depending on the specific racial/ethnic groups that make up their background. Despite these methodological challenges, researchers generally agree that the identity of mixed-race individuals can vary over time and across situations (Norman & Chen, 2020; Ream, 2023). Furthermore, siblings of the same mixed heritage may have very different racial/ethnic identities (Root, 1998). Research has identified a number of factors that may influence racial/ethnic identity among individuals with multiracial heritage. This activity will acquaint you with some of these factors.

Directions: Imagine that you are the child of a Black mother and an Asian father. In the space provided, describe how the different factors listed might affect the *strength* and *content* of your racial/ethnic identity.

1. Appearance – The degree to which your appearance is racially ambiguous or leads people to categorize you as a member of a specific race/ethnic group (Black or Asian).
2. Community – The degree to which you live in a racially mixed neighborhood and have friends from different ethnic/racial groups, or you live in a primarily segregated (Black or Asian) community.
3. Ethnic/racial socialization – the degree to which your parents and family members encourage or discourage discussion and knowledge of your ethnic and racial heritage.
4. Discrimination – the degree to which you and your family have experienced discrimination from people in your own ethnic groups (Black or Asian) or from people outside of your own ethnic groups (for example, from White people).
5. Your gender identity.

Thinking Further:

1. Discuss the relative importance of the factors listed above in terms of their contribution to ethnic/racial identity.
2. What other factors do you think might be relevant?
3. Maya Yampolsky, Catherine Amiot and Roxane de la Sablonnière (2016) found that individuals who are able to integrate their multiple cultural identities within their self-concept had greater well-being than those who focused on one predominant identity or those who compartmentalized and maintained separate identities depending on the situation. Based on the different factors listed above, what types of experiences might facilitate multicultural identity integration?

References:

Norman, J. B., & Chen, J. M. (2020). I am multiracial: Predictors of multiracial identification strength among mixed ancestry individuals. *Self and Identity*, *19*(5), 501–520. https://doi.org/10.1080/15298868.2019.1635522

Office for National Statistics. (2022). *Ethnic group, England and Wales: Census 2021*. www.ons.gov.uk/peoplepopulationandcommunity/

culturalidentity/ethnicity/bulletins/ethnicgroupenglandandwales/census2021#ethnic-groups-in-england-and-wales

Pew Research Center. (2015). *Multiracial in America: Proud, diverse and growing in numbers.* www.pewresearch.org/social-trends/2015/06/11/multiracial-in-america/

Ream, A. (2023). Three decades of multiracial identity research: A bibliometric review. *Identity.* https://doi.org/10.1080/15283488.2023.2223599

Root, M. P. P. (1998). Experiences and processes affecting racial identity development: Preliminary results from the biracial sibling project. *Cultural Diversity and Ethnic Minority Psychology, 4,* 237–247. https://doi.org/10.1037/1099-9809.4.3.237

U.S. Census Bureau. (2020). *Percentage of Population and Percent Change by Race: 2010 and 2020.* www2.census.gov/programs-surveys/decennial/2020/data/redistricting-supplementary-tables/redistricting-supplementary-table-02.xlsx

Yampolsky, M. A., Amiot, C. E., & de la Sablonnière, R. (2016). The multicultural identity integration scale (MULTIIS): Developing a comprehensive measure for configuring one's multiple cultural identities within the self. *Cultural Diversity and Ethnic Minority Psychology, 22*(2), 166–184. https://doi.org/10.1037/cdp0000043

ACTIVITY 5.4
HANDOUT

CULTURE AND SELF-CONSISTENCY

Across cultures studied, people recognize the existence of individual personality traits, and personality traits appear to be useful in predicting behavior. However there are cultural differences in perceived self-consistency, that is the extent to which people *believe* that their traits are stable and consistent. Numerous studies have found evidence that people in collectivistic cultures, especially some East Asian cultures, view their personality as less consistent as compared with people in individualist cultures. For example, Hyewon Choi and Shigehiro Oishi (2023) found that U.S. Americans were significantly more likely to agree with the statement "I act the same way no matter who I am with" than were Japanese participants. In addition, Velichko Fetvadjiev and colleagues (2018) found that more collectivist Black South Africans viewed their behavior as more variable than did more individualist White South Africans. Choi and Oishi explained that because one is expected to prioritize the needs of the group over personal goals in collectivist cultures, it is important to be able to draw on different traits and attributes depending on the social situation. In this activity, you will explore your own level of perceived self-consistency and consider how self-consistency may be related to other psychological phenomena.

Directions: Answer the questions below to assess your own level of self-consistency.

1. Do you believe that your personality traits have been consistent over time? Please explain.
2. Do you believe that your personality traits have been consistent across situations? Please explain.
3. Do you believe that your personality traits can reliably predict your behavior? Please explain.
4. To what extent do you think your culture's level of individualism/collectivism has influenced your own level of self-consistency?

Thinking Further:

1. Helen Boucher (2011) reported lower self-consistency among dialectical thinkers – individuals who are comfortable exploring and synthesizing contradictory ideas. How might you explain this finding?
2. Given that self-consistency beliefs have been found to vary across cultures, how might the psychological research topics relevant in cultures with low self-consistency differ from those relevant in cultures with high self-consistency?

References:

Boucher, H. C. (2011). The dialectical self-concept II: Cross-role and within-role consistency, well-being, self-certainty, and authenticity. *Journal of Cross-Cultural Psychology*, *42*(7), 1251–1271. https://doi.org/10.1177/0022022110383316

Choi, H., & Oishi, S. (2023). Cultural variations in perceived partner responsiveness: The role of self-consistency. *Journal of Cross-Cultural Psychology*, *54*(2), 303–318. https://doi.org/10.1177/00220221221132786

Fetvadjiev, V. H., Meiring, D., van de Vijver, F., Nel, J. A., Sekaja, L., & Laher, S. (2018). Personality and behavior prediction and consistency across cultures: A multimethod study of Blacks and Whites in South Africa. *Journal of Personality and Social Psychology*, *114*(3), 465–481. https://doi.org/10.1037/pspp0000129

ACTIVITY 5.5
HANDOUT

RELIGION AND UNDERSTANDING CULTURE

In 2003, Nalini Tarakeshwar, Jeffrey Stanton, and Kenneth Pargament pointed out that religion is a much-overlooked consideration in research on culture and psychology. In fact, their database search found that the percentage of articles dealing in some way with religion ranged from only 2% to just under 6% in cross-cultural journals. In the years since, the number of cross-cultural psychology publications addressing aspects of religion has increased markedly. For example, Jonathon McPhetres and colleagues (2021) conducted 11 studies to explore the universality of findings from the U.S. linking religiosity and anti-science attitudes. These authors found that whereas religiosity was correlated with both explicit and implicit negative attitudes toward science in the U.S., this pattern was not found consistently across the over 60 countries they studied.

Directions: For each of the aspects of culture listed below, give an example of how it may be related to one's religion. In order to do so, you may need to gather additional information about specific religions through scholarly sources of discussions with others.

1. Values
2. Child-rearing practices
3. Health-related behaviors
4. Prejudice and stereotyping
5. Gender roles
6. The concept of the self
7. Beliefs about interpersonal relationships
8. Beliefs about education and learning.

Thinking Further:

Despite the connections between religion and culture explored above, it is important to note that religious affiliation does not, itself, equate to culture.

For example, Michael Minkov and Anneli Kaasa (2022) analyzed 100 religious groups in 27 African countries and reported that nationality was a far better predictor of cultural ideologies than was religion. Why might this be the case?

References:

McPhetres, J., Jong, J., & Zuckerman, M. (2021). Religious Americans have less positive attitudes toward science, but this does not extend to other cultures. *Social Psychological and Personality Science*, *12*(4), 528–536. https://doi.org/10.1177/1948550620923239

Minkov, M., & Kaasa, A. (2022). Do religions account for important cultural differences? An analysis across 100 religious groups in 27 African countries. *Cross Cultural & Strategic Management*, *29*(4), 938–962. https://doi.org/10.1108/CCSM-09-2021-0163

Tarakeshwar, N., Stanton, J., & Pargament, K. I. (2003). Religion: An overlooked dimension in cross-cultural psychology. *Journal of Cross-Cultural Psychology*, *34*, 377–394. https://doi.org/10.1177/0022022103034004001

ACTIVITY 5.6
HANDOUT

PUTTING EMOTIONS INTO WORDS

Across cultures, there is much similarity in the emotions people report experiencing, the events that trigger those emotions, and the subjective and physiological responses that accompany those emotions (Matsumoto & Wilson, 2022). Cultures differ, however, in how emotions are expressed, both verbally and nonverbally. A growing area of research focuses on lexicalized emotion, or how emotions are put into words (Ogarkova, 2013). One way that verbal expressions of emotion differ across cultures is the frequency with which somatic referents are used. Somatic referents are terms that express emotional states by referring to specific parts of the body. For example, emotion words used by the Hmong of Laos often refer to the liver, such as *term tu siab*, literally "broken liver" or sadness (Postert et al., 2012). Many Persian emotion terms refer to the eye. For example, loving someone may be expressed as "having place on one's eye" (Sharifian, 2011). In this activity you will investigate the frequency of somatic referents for emotion in your own language.

Directions: Follow the steps below to investigate somatic referents of emotion in your language. First, list words that label six different emotions in the column on the left. Then look up each word in a thesaurus, and in the column on the right list any somatic referents that appear for that term. For example, if you listed the term "disgust" on the left, you might find the somatic referent "stomach-turning" and list it on the right.

Basic Emotion Terms   Somatic Referents

- _____   _____
- _____   _____
- _____   _____
- _____   _____
- _____   _____
- _____   _____

1. Considering the words that appeared in the thesaurus for each of your emotion terms, did you find somatic referents to be frequent? Rare? Please explain.
2. Is there anything you can conclude from this analysis about the degree to which speakers of the language you investigated view mind and body as connected or separate? Please explain.

Thinking Further:

1. Vivian Dzokoto and colleagues (2016), who identified a large number of somatic referents for emotions in two Ghanaian languages, suggested that somatic referents may be a way to express negative emotions in a manner that preserves social harmony. Why might this be the case?
2. How might cultural differences in the use of somatic referents to express emotions be relevant to counseling across cultures?

References:

Dzokoto, V., Senft, N., Kpobi, L., & Washington-Nortey, P. (2016). Their hands have lost their bones: Exploring cultural scripts in two West African affect lexica. *Journal of Psycholinguistic Research*, *45*(6), 1473–1497. https://doi.org/10.1007/s10936-016-9415-5

Matsumoto, D., & Wilson, M. (2022). A half-century assessment of the study of culture and emotion. *Journal of Cross-Cultural Psychology*, *53*(7–8), 917–934. https://doi.org/10.1177/00220221221084236

Ogarkova, A. (2013). Folk emotion concepts: Lexicalization of emotional experiences across languages and cultures. In J. J. R. Fontaine, K. R. Scherer, & C. Soriano (Eds.), *Components of emotional meaning: A sourcebook* (pp. 46–62). Oxford University Press.

Postert, C., Dannlowski, U., Müller, J. M., & Konrad, C. (2012). Beyond the blues: Towards a cross-cultural phenomenology of depressed mood. *Psychopathology*, *45*(3), 185–192. https://doi.org/10.1159/000330944

Sharifian, F. (2011). Conceptualizations of *cheshm* 'eye' in Persian. In Z. A. Maalej & N. Yu (Eds.), *Embodiment via body parts: Studies from various languages and cultures* (pp. 197–211). John Benjamins.

ACTIVITY 5.7
HANDOUT

CULTURAL DISPLAY RULES

Early studies by Paul Ekman and Wallace Friesen (Ekman, 1972) indicated that several emotions tend to be fairly universal in that they can be recognized across cultures. Yet, there are marked cultural differences in when and how emotions are expressed. This is due in large part to variability in *cultural display rules*. According to David Matsumoto and Hyi-Sung Hwang (2019), display rules are the guidelines one learns early in life about how to manage and modify the expression of emotions depending on the situation. For example, in one of the few studies of display rules conducted within Arab cultures, Sharon Flicker, Haneen Ayoub, and Melissa Guynn (2017) found that Palestinian students were more comfortable expressing powerless emotions (sadness and fear) to friends than parents. They suggested that this may be due to greater comfort with friends or an effort to protect their parents from observing their emotional distress. This activity is designed to familiarize you with the concept of cultural display rules and to help you to identify the display rules you follow.

Directions: Over the next day or two, keep a record of your emotions and their expression. When you experience an identifiable emotion, make an entry below indicating when you experienced the emotion; the type of emotion you

---

experienced (such as happiness, sadness, fear, anger, disgust, or surprise); the setting in which you experienced the emotion (Were you alone or with others? Were you in a public or private place?); and the manner in which the emotion was expressed (indicate the form – such as laughing, yelling, or frowning – and the intensity of the expression). Try to record ten instances of emotional expression then answer the questions that follow.

	Date/Time	*Emotion*	*Setting*	*Expression/Intensity*
1				
2				
3				
4				
5				
6				
7				
8				
9				
10				

1. Compare the instances of emotional expression that took place in private rather than public settings. What do you conclude about the display rules governing the public expression of emotion?
2. Compare the instances of emotional expression involving different types of emotions. Did you observe different rules governing the expression of positive (happiness, surprise) as opposed to negative (sadness, anger) emotions?
3. To what extent can you trace your display rules to your cultural background or gender socialization? Please explain.

Thinking Further:

1. Several studies support an association between collectivism and lower levels of emotional expressivity (e.g., Matsumoto et al., 2008). Why do you think this might be?
2. Adrienne Wood, Magdalena Rychlowska, and Paula Niedenthal (2016) identified an additional predictor of emotional expressivity, historical heterogeneity, which refers to the number of source countries that have made up a country's present-day population over the last 500 years. Why might historical heterogeneity be associated with more expressive display rules?
3. What cultural display rules govern the use of emojis? Moyu Liu (2023) investigated this question in Japan and found that emojis were more likely to be used: (1) with close friends or family, (2) in positive than in negative situations, (3) in private than in public contexts, and (4) in a manner that matches the intensity of the expression with the emotionality of the situation. If you live in Japan – or if you live elsewhere – do these rules describe your emoji use? Please explain and, if possible, provide an example.

References:

Ekman, P. (1972). Universal and cultural differences in facial expression of emotion. In J. R. Cole (Ed.), *Nebraska symposium on motivation, 1971* (pp. 207–283). University of Nebraska Press.

Flicker, S. M., Ayoub, H. J. S., & Guynn, M. J. (2017). Emotional display rules in Palestine: Ingroup/outgroup membership, status of interaction partner and gender. *International Journal of Psychology, 54*(1), 33–41. https://doi.org/10.1002/ijop.12429

Liu, M. (2023). Are you really smiling? Display rules for emojis and the relationship between emotion management and psychological well-being. *Frontiers in Psycholology, 14.* https://doi.org/10.3389/fpsyg.2023.1035742

Matsumoto, D., & Hwang, H.-S. (2019). Culture and emotion. In D. Matsumoto (Ed.), *Handbook of culture and psychology* (2nd ed., pp. 361–398). Oxford University Press.

Matsumoto, D., Yoo, S. H., Fontaine, J., et al. (2008). Mapping expressive differences around the world: The relationship between emotional display rules and individualism versus collectivism. *Journal*

of *Cross-Cultural Psychology*, *39*(1), 55–74. https://doi.org/10.1177/
   0022022107311854

Wood, A., Rychlowska, M., & Niedenthal, P. M. (2016). Heterogeneity
   of long-history migration predicts emotion recognition accuracy.
   Emotion, *16*(4), 413–420. https://doi.org/10.1037/emo0000137

ACTIVITY 5.8
HANDOUT

DEAR SIGMUND (OR CARL)

Nearly all of the early personality psychology theorists came from a similar Western tradition in terms of the cultural values and assumptions inherent in their theories. This activity encourages you to think about these classical theories from a cross-cultural perspective.

Directions: Select the personality theory of either Sigmund Freud or Carl Rogers. Below, make some notes about important concepts in the theory you chose. Then write a one-page letter to one of these theorists in the space provided. In your letter, identify aspects of the theory that are culture-bound and make recommendations for revision. For example, Freudian theory focuses on the role of the mother as primary caregiver, whereas in much of the world children are raised by multiple caregivers. Some suggestions are provided for concepts you might include in your consideration of each theory. It may also be helpful to refer to an introductory psychology or personality theories textbook for an overview of the theory you chose.

Freudian theory – some concepts for cultural consideration: psychosexual stages; superego development; psychoanalysis; the use of projective tests.

Rogerian theory – some concepts for cultural consideration: the self; unconditional positive regard; the fully functioning person; client-centered therapy.

Notes:

Dear_____,

ACTIVITY 5.9
HANDOUT

THE CULTURE AND PERSONALITY SCHOOL – OLD AND NEW

In the 1930s and 1940s, a major research focus of psychological anthro-pologists was the study of culture and personality. These studies were strongly influenced by Freudian research and often involved the use of psychoanalytic assessment tools (such as the Rorschach ink blots) to identify the basic personality type characterizing members of a specific culture. For example, in 1944, Cora DuBois published an analysis of the Alorese people based on her extensive fieldwork in a small mountain village in what was then the Dutch East Indies (now Indonesia). In this book she discussed the connection between childrearing practices and adult character. Her data included ethnographic descriptions as well as the results of several psycho-logical tests. She concluded that the structure of day-to-day activities led to the neglect of Alorese children and that this level of neglect resulted in such adult personality characteristics as emotional instability and distrust. DuBois's study typifies the culture and personality school. The purpose of this activity is to examine the assumptions underlying this significant area of research and to explore how, more than 80 years after the peak of the Culture and Personality School, some new research is using a different approach to once again ask whether cultural groups are characterized by specific personality profiles.

Directions: Read, and then evaluate, each of the five assumptions of the Culture and Personality School stated below (adapted from Bock, 1995).

1. *The continuity assumption* – Early childhood experiences (such as weaning and toilet training) are the primary determinants of adult personality. Similar childhood experiences are assumed to result in similar adult personality types.
   Do you agree or disagree? Please explain.
2. *The uniformity assumption* – Societies can be described in terms of a core personality type. Along with this assumption is the idea that since childrearing behaviors are shaped by culture, they are fairly similar across families within a culture.
   Do you agree or disagree? Please explain.
3. *The causal assumption* – Basic personality structure is an entity that is not only observable but can cause, or be caused by, cultural institutions. For example, if a society is characterized as having a core personality

---

trait of aggression, that trait can be described as causing a practice such as intergroup warfare. (Yet consider that the evidence for the core trait of aggression may come from observing such practices as intergroup warfare.)

Do you agree or disagree? Please explain.

4. *The projective assumption* – By using projective tests (such as Rorschach ink blots) it is possible to determine basic personality characteristics and unconscious conflicts. Further, it is assumed that projective tests can be effectively used to understand the psychological makeup of an individual who is a member of a markedly different culture from the one in which the test was developed and standardized.

Do you agree or disagree? Please explain.

5. *The objectivity assumption* – Cultural outsiders are able to accurately describe psychological characteristics and culturally patterned behaviors without imposing their own values or interpretations.

Do you agree or disagree? Please explain.

Thinking Further:

Rather than using projective tests, in recent decades national differences in personality have been studied by administering personality inventories to individuals in several countries and then comparing the aggregate scores for each country. For example, Jüri Allik and colleagues (2017) mapped NEO Personality Inventory scores (for Neuroticism, Extraversion, Openness to Experience, Agreeableness, and Conscientiousness) across 62 nations and identified clusters of nations with similar personality profiles. Country-level personality scores have been found to correlate with Hofstede's dimensions (Individualism/Collectivism, Power Distance, Masculinity/Femininity, and Uncertainty Avoidance; Hofstede & McCrae, 2004), economic indicators (Stolarski et al., 2013), political regime type (Barceló, 2017), environmental engagement (Milfont & Sibley, 2012), and the activities participants reported being engaged in at 7:00 pm the previous evening (Baranski et al., 2017)! However, these between-country differences tend to be small and have not been consistent across studies. Furthermore, results show that within-country differences in personality are significantly larger than between-country differences (Allik et al., 2017; Kajonius & Mac Giolla, 2017). Given the lack of evidence for large differences in personality across cultures, why do we have such strong stereotypes about people from specific countries?

Robert McCrae and colleagues (2013) investigated the association between national stereotypes and the personality test scores of individuals in 26 cultures. In line with the findings of previous studies of national stereotype accuracy,

---

they reported a great deal of agreement about the traits people associated with each country, but these perceptions were not accurate in that they did not correspond to the actual measures of those traits. Please answer the questions below to explore these findings.

1. Describe a stereotype that you have or are familiar with about a country other than your own.
2. What might be the source of this stereotype, considering the extent to which there tends to be agreement about these perceptions?
3. What purpose might national stereotypes serve? In other words, why are they maintained?
4. How might these national stereotypes be harmful?
5. What forces might cause these national stereotypes to change over time?

Source:

The five assumptions of the Culture and Personality School were adapted from Bock, P. K. (1995). *Rethinking psychological anthropology: Continuity and change in the study of human action.* Copyright © 1995 by Waveland Press. Adapted with permission.

References:

Allik, J., Church, A. T., Ortiz, F. A., Rossier, J., Hřebičkova, M., de Fruyt, F., Realo, A., & McCrae, R. R. (2017). Mean profiles of the NEO Personality Inventory. *Journal of Cross-Cultural Psychology, 48*(3), 402–420. https://doi.org/10.1177/0022022117692100

Baranski, E. N., Gardiner, G., Guillaume, E., et al. (2017). Comparisons of daily behavior across 21 countries. *Social Psychological and Personality Science, 8*(3), 252–266. https://doi.org/10.1177/1948550616676879

Barceló, J. (2017). National personality traits and regime type: A cross-national study of 47 countries. *Journal of Cross-Cultural Psychology, 48*(2), 195–216. https://doi.org/10.1177/0022022116678324

DuBois, C. (1944). *The people of Alor.* Harper & Row.

Hofstede, G., & McCrae, R. R. (2004). Personality and culture revisited: Linking traits and dimensions of culture. *Cross-Cultural Research, 38,* 52–88. https://doi.org/10.1177/1069397103259443

Kajonius, P., & Mac Giolla, E. (2017). Personality traits across countries: Support for similarities rather than differences. *PLoS ONE, 12*(6). https://doi.org/10.1371/journal.pone.0179646

McCrae, R. R., Chan, W., Jussim, L., et al. (2013). The inaccuracy of national character stereotypes. *Journal of Research in Personality*, *47*(6), 831–842. https://doi.org/10.1016/j.jrp.2013.08.006

Milfont, T. L., & Sibley, C. G. (2012). The big five personality traits and environmental engagement: Associations at the individual and societal level. *Journal of Environmental Psychology*, *32*(2), 187–195. https://doi.org/10.1016/j.jenvp.2011.12.006

Stolarski, M., Zajenkowski, M., & Meisenberg, G. (2013). National intelligence and personality: Their relationships and impact on national economic success. *Intelligence*, *41*(2), 94–101. https://doi.org/10.1016/j.intell.2012.11.003

ACTIVITY 5.10
HANDOUT

ETIC AND EMIC APPROACHES TO PERSONALITY

A major goal of research in personality psychology is identifying etic, or universal, dimensions of personality. Studies conducted by different researchers in various cultures, using a variety of measures, have found support for the existence of five basic personality traits (e.g., Allik et al., 2017; McCrae & Costa, 2006). These dimensions form the *Five Factor Model* (FFM). However, the measures used to assess personality in these studies were developed primarily by researchers with a Western orientation to psychology and then translated and administered in other cultures. This creates the danger of an *imposed etic* in which we assume that research concepts or methodologies developed in one culture have the same meaning across cultural groups. The majority of research on culture and personality has taken this imposed etic approach (Thalmayer et al., 2022). In contrast, an emic, or culture-specific, approach to personality assessment has sought to identify indigenous dimensions of personality. For example, a series of studies by Marcia Katigbak, Timothy Church, and colleagues (e.g., Katigbak et al., 2002) identified culture-specific dimensions of personality in the Philippines that added to the predictive power of the FFM. These include *Pagkamadaldal* (Social Curiosity), *Pagkamapagsapalaran* (Risk-Taking), and religiosity. Fanny Cheung, Fons van de Vijver, and Frederick Leong (2011) advocated for a combined emic-etic approach in which, in addition to testing the universality of FFM traits across cultures, indigenously derived traits are tested for universality. These authors suggested that indigenous research could lead to the discovery of aspects of personality that have been overlooked by Western researchers due to "cultural blind spots." For example, both the indigenously derived Cross-cultural (Chinese) Personality Assessment Inventory (CPAI; Cheung et al., 2013) and the South African Personality Inventory (SAPI; Fetvadjiev et al., 2015) may have identified universal dimensions of personality beyond those included in the FFM, including Interpersonal Relatedness. This activity will explore a combined emic-etic approach to better understanding this strategy for investigating personality across cultures.

Directions: There are three steps to this activity. First, in the column on the left side of the page, list ten traits or personality characteristics that describe you or someone you know. Second, read the descriptions of the FFM traits listed below and indicate in the column on the right the FFM trait category under which each of the traits on the left would fall. If the trait on the left does not fit clearly into any of the FFM categories, then leave the corresponding FFM space blank. Finally, read about three indigenous personality traits and determine whether these fit under the FFM classifications.

Trait	FFM Category?
1. _____	_____
2. _____	_____
3. _____	_____
4. _____	_____
5. _____	_____
6. _____	_____
7. _____	_____
8. _____	_____
9. _____	_____
10. _____	_____

The FFM (adapted from McCrae & Costa, 1987):

- *Openness* – Refers to the degree to which one is imaginative vs. down-to-earth, prefers variety vs. routine, and is independent vs. conforming.
- *Conscientiousness* – Refers to the degree to which one is organized vs. disorganized, careful vs. careless, and self-disciplined vs. weak willed.
- *Extraversion* – Refers to the degree to which one is sociable vs. introverted, fun loving vs. sober, and affectionate vs. reserved.

- *Agreeableness* – Refers to the degree to which one is softhearted vs. ruthless, trusting vs. suspicious, and helpful vs. uncooperative.
- *Neuroticism* – Refers to the degree to which one is worried vs. calm, insecure vs. secure, and self-pitying vs. self-satisfied.

1. Listed below are three traits considered to be indigenous aspects of personality. Read the descriptions of these traits and determine which FFM category, if any, could be used to classify the trait.

Trait and Definition	**FFM Category?**
• *Philotimo* (see Triandis & Vassiliou, 1972) involves being polite, generous, respectful, and meeting one's obligations. [Greek]	_____
• *Abnegation* (see Avendaño-Sandoval et al., 1997 cited in Fetvadjiev et al., 2015). The tendency to sacrifice oneself for others [Mexican]	_____
• *Amae* (see Doi, 1973) refers to a combination of childlike dependence on and obligation to another person. Rooted in the mother-child relationship, *amae* is also seen as characterizing the relationship between people of higher and lower status. [Japanese]	_____

2. Based on your findings, what do you conclude about the universality of the FFM?

Thinking Further:

Discuss how the combined etic-emic approach could be used to investigate an area of psychology other than personality.

Source:

The FFM descriptions were adapted from McCrae, R. R. & Costa, P. T. (1987). Validation of the five factor model of personality across instruments and observers. *Journal of Personality and Social Psychology*, *52*, 81–90. https://doi.org/10.1037/0022-3514.52.1.81

References:

Allik, J., Church, A. T., Ortiz, F. A., et al. (2017). Mean profiles of the NEO personality inventory. *Journal of Cross-Cultural Psychology*, *48*(3), 402–420. https://doi.org/10.1177/0022022117692100

Cheung, F. M., Cheung, S. F., & Fan, W. (2013). From Chinese to cross-cultural personality inventory: A combined emic–etic approach to the study of personality in culture. In M. Gelfand, C. Y. Chiu, & Y. Y. Hong (Eds.), *Advances in culture and psychology*, Vol. 3 (pp. 117–180). Oxford University Press.

Cheung, F. M., van de Vijver, F. J. R., & Leong, F. T. L. (2011). Toward a new approach to the study of personality in culture. *American Psychologist*, *66*(7), 593–603. https://doi.org/10.1037/a0022389

Doi, T. (1973). *The anatomy of dependence*. Harper Row.

Fetvadjiev, V. H., Meiring, D., van de Vijver, F. J. R., Nel, J. A., & Hill, C. (2015). The South African Personality Inventory (SAPI): A culture-informed instrument for the country's main ethnocultural groups. *Psychological Assessment*, *27*(3), 827–837. https://doi.org/10.1037/pas0000078

Katigbak, M. S., Church, A. T., Guanzon-Lapeña, M. A., Carlota, A. J., & del Pilar, G. H. (2002). Are indigenous personality dimensions culture-specific? Philippine inventories and the five-factor model. *Journal of Personality and Social Psychology*, *82*, 89–101. https://doi.org/10.1037/0022-3514.82.1.89

McCrae, R. R., & Costa, P. T., Jr. (2006). Cross-cultural perspectives on adult personality trait development. In D. K. Mroczek & T. D. Little (Eds.), *Handbook of personality development* (pp. 129–145). Lawrence Erlbaum Associates Publishers.

Thalmayer, A. G., Saucier, G., & Rotzinger, J. S. (2022). Absolutism, relativism, and universalism in personality traits across cultures: The case of the Big Five. *Journal of Cross-Cultural Psychology*, *53*(7–8), 935–956. https://doi.org/10.1177/00220221221111813

Triandis, H. C., & Vassiliou, V. (1972). Comparative analysis of subjective culture. In H. C. Triandis (Ed.), *The analysis of subjective culture* (pp. 299–338). Wiley.

–6–

Health, Stress, and Coping Across Cultures

ACTIVITY 6.1
HANDOUT

WHAT IS ABNORMAL?

Before exploring issues of culture and well-being, it is useful to consider what we mean when we talk about behavior that is normal or abnormal. This activity focuses on these concepts.

Directions: Please respond to each of the questions below.

1. Describe a behavior that, within your culture, is/was considered abnormal at one point in history, but normal at another point in history.
2. Describe a behavior that, within your culture, is considered abnormal in one setting, but is considered normal in another setting.
3. Describe a behavior that is considered normal in your culture, but abnormal in some other culture(s).
4. Describe a behavior that is considered abnormal in your culture, but normal in some other culture(s).
5. Describe a behavior that is considered abnormal in all societies.
6. Develop a set of criteria that can be used to determine if a behavior is abnormal.
7. Would the criteria you developed likely apply across cultures? Please explain.

DOI: 10.4324/9781003356820-19

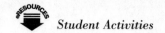

ACTIVITY 6.2
HANDOUT

CULTURE AND HEALTH: THE NI HON SAN STUDY

Several studies of culture and health have taken advantage of what one might consider a natural experiment; that is, changes in health as a specific ethnic group migrates to another culture. By comparing the health measures of members of an ethnic group who do not migrate with those who do, we can begin to separate genetic from behavioral influences on health. An example of this type of research is the landmark Ni Hon San study described below. The purpose of this activity is to encourage you to think about how culturally embedded behaviors may influence health. In addition, this activity will familiarize you with a form of research that provides significant insights into issues of culture and health.

Directions: Read the description of the Ni Hon San study below (based on Benfante, 1992) and then answer the questions that follow.

The Ni Hon San Study:

The Ni Hon San study began in 1964 as part of the Honolulu Heart Study and ran for over three decades. This research compared health data from three groups of men: Japanese men living in Hiroshima and Nagasaki, Japan; descendants of Japanese migrants to Hawaii; and descendants of Japanese migrants to San Francisco, California. One of the most striking findings of this study is that the rate of cardiovascular disease (heart disease) was lowest in the Japan group, highest in the California group, and intermediate in the Hawaii group.

1. What conclusions can you draw from the findings of the Ni Hon San study about the role of genetics and behavior in the development of cardiovascular disease?
2. What assumptions can you make about the distinction between individuals of Japanese ancestry living in Hawaii as opposed to California?
3. List some behavioral factors (things people do in daily life) that may have led to the findings of the Ni Hon San study.
4. List some environmental factors (aspects of the setting in which people live) that may have affected the findings of the Ni Hon San study.
5. The participants of the Ni Hon San study were all men. Would you have any concerns about extrapolating from this study to draw conclusions about the health practices of women? For example, is there reason to believe that gender might interact with acculturation processes? Please explain.

Thinking Further:

Another example of long-term health research is the Adventist Health Studies, which have investigated health behaviors and risks among tens of thousands of Seventh-Day Adventists over more than six decades (e.g., Fraser et al., 2020). The participants in these studies are from several ethnic groups but share the same set of dietary and lifestyle practices associated with the Adventist religion. How does this research design compare with that of the NI Hon San study? [Hint: Think about which variables are held constant and which vary.]

References:

Benfante, R. (1992). Studies of cardiovascular disease and cause-specific mortality trends in Japanese-American men living in Hawaii and risk factor comparisons with other Japanese populations in the Pacific region: A review. *Human Biology, 64*, 791–805. www.jstor.org/stable/41464340

Fraser, G. E., Cosgrove, C. M., Mashchak, A. D., Orlich, M. J., & Altekruse, S. F. (2020). Lower rates of cancer and all-cause mortality in an Adventist cohort compared with a US Census population. *Cancer, 126*(5), 1102–1111. https://doi.org/10.1002/cncr.32571

ACTIVITY 6.3
HANDOUT

THE GLOBAL OBESITY EPIDEMIC

According to the World Health Organization (WHO; 2021), the global rate of obesity has nearly tripled since 1975 and most of the world's population lives in countries where obesity is a greater threat to health than being underweight. In almost half of the Organization for Economic Co-operation and Development (OECD) countries, 50% or more of the population is overweight or obese, including one in six children (OECD, 2017). Although high-income countries continue to have the highest prevalence, the rate at which obesity among children and adolescents is increasing is much faster in low and middle-income countries (WHO, 2021). These changes have resulted in devastating physical and mental health, economic, and societal consequences. This activity will help you to understand the sociocultural influences shaping the global obesity epidemic.

Directions: Investigate the rise of obesity in a country other than your own. Report your findings below on the statistics, causes, consequences, prevention efforts, and additional cultural factors involved. Sources of information on this topic include the websites of the World Health Organization (WHO; www.who.int) and the Organization for Economic Co-operation and Development (OECD; www.oecd.org) as well as academic journal and news articles.

1. Country:
2. Statistics (e.g., percentage of adults and children who are obese; rate of increase):
3. Causes (e.g., poverty; food deserts; increased exposure to fast food; decrease in physical activity due to changes in technology or lack of neighborhood safety):
4. Consequences (e.g., high rates of diabetes, increased health care costs, greater employee absenteeism):
5. Prevention efforts (e.g., nutritional labeling of food products; increased access to healthier foods; counseling and support sessions):
6. Additional cultural factors involved (e.g., norms against exercise for women in some cultures; an association of heavier weight with wealth in some lower-income nations):

References:

Organization for Economic Co-operation and Development. (2017). *Obesity update [Fact sheet].* www.oecd.org/health/obesity-update.htm
World Health Organization. (2021). *Obesity and overweight [Fact sheet].* www.who.int/news-room/fact-sheets/detail/obesity-and-overweight

ACTIVITY 6.4
HANDOUT

CULTURE AND MENTAL HEALTH QUIZ

In recent decades, there has been a rapid increase in research on issues of culture and mental health. This activity will enable you to test your knowledge of a variety of key findings from this literature.

Directions: Decide whether each of the statements below is true or false. Then check your answers with your instructor.

1. Depression and schizophrenia appear to be universal in that these mental illnesses have been found across cultures studied.   TRUE / FALSE

2. The likelihood of recovering from schizophrenia is greater for patients in non-industrialized nations than for those in industrialized societies.   TRUE / FALSE

3. Across cultures, there is no consistent gender difference in rates of autism.   TRUE / FALSE

4. A syndrome widely recognized in Japan is a form of work-related stress that translates as "death by overwork."   TRUE / FALSE

5. Anorexia nervosa, a syndrome marked by self-starvation and a distorted body image, is specific to the relatively affluent cultures of North America and Europe.   TRUE / FALSE

6. Across cultures studied, most therapists surveyed agree that successful treatment for alcohol abuse requires complete abstinence from drinking.   TRUE / FALSE

7. Clients are less likely to drop out of therapy if they are paired with a therapist of their own race/ethnicity.   TRUE / FALSE

8. Attention Deficit Hyperactivity Disorder (ADHD) does not exist in some cultures.   TRUE / FALSE

9. When seeking help, people of Chinese cultural background tend to emphasize somatic (or physical), rather than psychological, symptoms of mental illness.   TRUE / FALSE

10. In addition to affecting the well-being of those targeted, racism also affects the well-being of those holding racist beliefs.   TRUE / FALSE

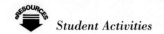

ACTIVITY 6.5
HANDOUT

SUBJECTIVE WELL-BEING ACROSS CULTURES

In recent decades, thousands of studies across the globe have investigated subjective well-being and over 40 countries have implemented a mechanism for assessing the subjective well-being of their citizens. Subjective well-being (SWB) has been defined as "a person's cognitive and affective evaluations of his or her life" (Diener et al., 2005, p. 63). Thus, SWB involves the way people think about their own life satisfaction (the cognitive component) and their general mood and emotions (the affective component). Some measures of SWB have simply asked people to rate their overall level of happiness on a numerical scale, whereas others have involved self-report questionnaires, sampling people's real-time experiences, asking people to reconstruct their prior day, measuring brain activity, and analyzing the use of positive and negative emotion words in social media (Myers & Diener, 2018, p. 218). SWB comparisons have been made both on an individual level and on a national level. The purpose of this activity is to learn about SWB while assessing common beliefs about its determinants.

Directions: Administer the following questionnaire to three individuals to learn about their beliefs about SWB, then respond to the questions that follow.

Participant A:

1. Throughout the world, what age group experiences the most rapid decline in subjective well-being? Please explain your answer.
2. Are people happier in rich countries or poor countries? Please explain your answer.
3. Is self-esteem related to happiness? Please explain your answer.

Participant B:

1. Throughout the world, what age group experiences the most rapid decline in subjective well-being? Please explain your answer.
2. Are people happier in rich countries or poor countries? Please explain your answer.
3. Is self-esteem related to happiness? Please explain your answer.

Participant C:

1. Throughout the world, what age group experiences the most rapid decline in subjective well-being? Please explain your answer.
2. Are people happier in rich countries or poor countries? Please explain your answer.
3. Is self-esteem related to happiness? Please explain your answer.

After reading the research findings below, indicate which of your respondents' answers were accurate and which were inaccurate. Discuss the possible source of any inaccurate beliefs.

- Recent research using Gallup World Poll data for 145 countries (Handa et al., 2023) shows a rapid decline in SWB for adolescents and young adults in much of the world. This decline was not found in most nations of South Asia, the Middle East, and North Africa where SWB tended to start out significantly lower. In addition to socioeconomic factors, SWB was associated with education, health, and civic engagement. In wealthier nations, SWB increases again in older adulthood, whereas in poorer nations SWB is stable or continues to decline with age (Lansford, 2018).
- People are generally less happy in poor countries than in wealthier ones, particularly in nations with greater income inequality (Wirajing et al., 2023). The higher levels of SWB in wealthier nations may be due not only to lower poverty rates, greater educational opportunities, and better health, but also to less ethnopolitical conflict (Myers & Diener, 2018).
- Self-esteem tends to be more strongly associated with SWB in Western cultures than in East Asian cultures (Suh & Choi, 2018). One explanation for this is that high self-esteem is more useful in individualistic Western societies where there is greater relational mobility (people more frequently form new relationships and leave old ones) than in more collectivist East Asian societies (Yuki et al., 2013). The idea here is that higher self-esteem would allow one to be socially successful in a context that involves dealing with more interpersonal rejection and risk-taking.

What is your assessment of the participants' responses?

Thinking Further:

1. Review the methods used to measure SWB that are described at the beginning of this activity. To what extent do you think cross-cultural differences in assessed SWB are a result of the methods used rather than actual differences in

---

SWB? [Consider, for example, whether culture or language might affect the cognitive and affective components of SWB or how participants from different countries perceive the terms researchers use to refer to SWB.]

2. Monitoring levels of SWB is important since people with higher SWB "tend to be healthier and longer-lived, thanks to a stronger immune system, better cardiovascular health, and healthier behaviors (exercising, wearing seat belts, even using sunscreen); have better relationships, have more friends, more often get and stay married, and rate their marriages as better; are more prosocial and are engaged organizational citizens; and succeed more at work" (Myers & Diener, 2018, p. 224).

Fortunately, it is possible to increase SWB on both an individual and societal level. SWB has been shown to increase over time with better social support, safety, human rights, environmental quality and green spaces, and income security and employment (Diener et al., 2015). In the space below, describe a specific intervention that could be implemented to increase SWB in your community.

References:

Diener, E., Lucas, R. E., & Oishi, S. (2005). Subjective well-being: The science of happiness and life satisfaction. In C. R. Snyder & S. J. Lopez (Eds.), *Handbook of positive psychology* (2nd ed., pp. 63–73). Oxford University Press.

Diener, E., Oishi, S., & Lucas, R. E. (2015). National accounts of subjective well-being. *American Psychologist, 70*(3), 234–242. https://doi.org/10.1037/a0038899

Handa, S., Pereira, A., & Holmqvist, G. (2023). The rapid decline of happiness: Exploring life satisfaction among young people across the world. *Applied Research in Quality Life, 18*, 1549–1579. https://doi.org/10.1007/s11482-023-10153-4

Lansford, J. E. (2018). Predictors of subjective well-being across cultures. In E. Diener, S. Oishi, & L. Tay (Eds.), *Handbook of well-being* (pp. 344–357). DEF Publishers.

Myers, D. G., & Diener, E. (2018). The scientific pursuit of happiness. *Perspectives on Psychological Science, 13*(2), 218–225. https://doi.org/10.1177/1745691618765171

Suh, E. M., & Choi, S. (2018). Predictors of subjective well-being across cultures. In E. Diener, S. Oishi, & L. Tay (Eds.), *Handbook of well-being* (pp. 768–779). DEF Publishers.

Wirajing, M. A. K., Nchofoung, T. N. & Nanfosso, R. T. (2023). Revisiting the inequality-well-being nexus: The case of developing countries. *Global Social Welfare*. https://doi.org/10.1007/s40609-023-00278-7

Yuki, M., Sato, K., Takemura, K., & Oishi, S. (2013). Social ecology moderates the association between self-esteem and happiness. *Journal of Experimental Social Psychology*, *49*(4), 741–746. https://doi.org/10.1016/j.jesp.2013.02.006

ACTIVITY 6.6
HANDOUT

CLIMATE CHANGE AND MENTAL HEALTH

A relatively new and concerning area of cross-cultural research deals with the current and potential psychological effects of climate change. Helen Louise Berry, Kathryn Bowen, and Tord Kjellstrom (2010) outlined the direct and indirect pathways through which climate change may affect mental health. Direct effects involve the psychological trauma associated with exposure to more frequent and intense climate-related disasters, such as drought, floods, hurricanes, and fires. Indirect effects stem from threats to physical health, such as increased vulnerability to disease and disruption to food supply, as well as from economic and social threats to one's community, such as loss of property, income, and social support. The purpose of this activity is to add to our understanding of the connection between climate change and mental health across cultures.

Directions: For this activity you are asked to search a psychology database (such as PsycINFO) to locate a journal article reporting research in a country other than your own on climate change and mental health and then to identify variables that could help us to understand this relationship. For example, here are three variables to consider. Each links climate change with mental health:

- Perceived harm to self and perceived harm to country – Both of these variables predicted climate anxiety in participants from China, India, Japan, and the United States, with climate anxiety higher in the Chinese and Indian samples than among the Japanese and U.S. American participants (Tam et al., 2023).
- Cultural norms for expression of distress – Studies in Maharashtra, India found that droughts and crop failures have led to large numbers of suicides among farmers in that region (Singh et al., 2023).

- Gender-based violence –Nahid Rezwana and Rachel Pain (2022) documented how violence toward women and girls increases as a result of disasters such as those related to climate change. The incidence of domestic abuse, child marriage, and sex trafficking increases along with the economic hardships and social disruption that accompany such disasters.

1. In the space below, provide the full reference for your article (see the references in this book for examples of the format and content).
2. Describe a variable addressed in your article that should be considered in research on climate change and mental health across cultures. Be sure to detail the evidence for the importance of that variable.

References:

Berry, H. L., Bowen, K., & Kjellstrom, T. (2010). Climate change and mental health: A causal pathways framework. *International Journal of Public Health*, *55*, 123–132. https://doi.org/10.1007/s00038-009-0112-0

Rezwana, N., & Pain, R. (2022). *Gender-based violence and layered disasters: Place, culture and survival.* Routledge.

Singh, R., Bindal, S., Gupta, A. K., & Kumari, M. (2023). Drought frequency assessment and implications of climate change for Maharashtra, India. In B. Phartiyal, R. Mohan, S. Chakraborty, V. Dutta, & A. Kumar Gupta (Eds.), *Climate change and environmental impacts: Past, present and future perspective* (pp. 369–381). Springer International.

Tam, K.-P., Chan, H.-W., & Clayton, S. (2023). Climate change anxiety in China, India, Japan, and the United States. *Journal of Environmental Psychology*, *87*. https://doi.org/10.1016/j.jenvp.2023.101991

ACTIVITY 6.7
HANDOUT

CULTURAL CONCEPTS OF DISTRESS

It has long been clear that culture shapes the way people experience, explain, label, and treat mental disorders. According to Junko Tanaka-Matsumi (2019), researchers have taken two major approaches to understanding cultural differences in mental disorders. One approach, the *universalist* view, holds that there exist similarities in disorders across cultures, but the expression of

---

these disorders differs from culture to culture. A second perspective, the *cultural relativist* approach, suggests that some disorders are unique to specific cultures and may only be understood within the context of those cultures.

Many clusters of symptoms that appear throughout the world do not clearly map onto Western categories of mental disorders such as those described in the *Diagnostic and Statistical Manual of Mental Disorders* (DSM) published by the American Psychiatric Association. These clusters of symptoms were once referred to as *culture-specific disorders* or *culture-bound syndromes*. However, this designation was problematic because it implied that these disorders are atypical and exotic whereas the disorders experienced in Western industrialized nations are universal and uninfluenced by culture. The DSM (DSM-5; APA, 2013) now reflects the current view among mental health researchers that mental disorders involve both etic (universal) and emic (culture-specific) components. In addition, it no longer uses terms like *culture-specific disorders* or *culture-bound syndromes* and instead provides information on three aspects of cultural concepts of distress: cultural syndromes, cultural idioms of distress, and cultural explanations. We will explore each of these below.

Directions: Choose a cultural concept of distress to investigate using scholarly sources (one appendix of the DSM-5 also includes detailed descriptions of cultural concepts of distress). Several cultural concepts of distress are listed below, though you may discover others in your search. Before you start, read through the questions that follow and be prepared to address these with the information you gather.

- Ataque de nervios
- Dhat syndrome
- Khyâl cap
- Kufingisisa
- Maladi moun
- Nervios
- Shenjing shuairuo
- Susto

1. State the cultural concept of distress you selected as well as the location(s) in which it occurs:
2. Describe the cultural syndrome – the clusters of symptoms that tend to occur in a specific cultural group, community, or context.
3. Describe the cultural idiom of distress – the way people express or communicate their emotional suffering.
4. Describe the cultural explanation for this mental illness – the way that the cause or origin of the disorder is explained within the specific culture.

---

5. All mental disorders can best be understood as having both etic (universal) and emic (culture-specific) aspects. For example, Lisa Marie Beardsley (1994) mapped the etic and emic symptoms of *taijin-kyofusho*, a type of social phobia found in Japan. In this disorder, patients, primarily males, become fearful that they will offend others by such acts as staring, blushing, or emitting odors.

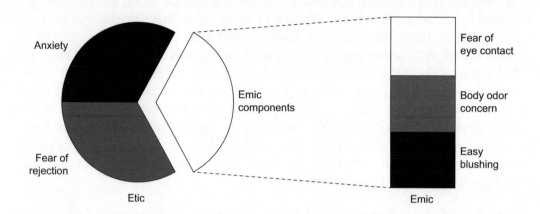

In the space provided below, diagram the emic and the etic components of the cultural concept of distress that you investigated.

Thinking Further:

Juris Draguns (1973) observed that the expression of mental disorders within a specified culture tends to be an *exaggeration of the normal*. In the case of *taijin-kyofusho*, the symptoms expressed indicate an exaggeration of the Japanese value of sensitivity toward others (Tanaka-Matsumi & Draguns, 1997). Consider the cultural context of the disorder you investigated. Can this disorder be viewed as an exaggeration of the normal? Please explain.

Source:

Figure reprinted from Beardsley, L. M. (1994). Medical diagnosis and treatment across cultures. In W. J. Lonner & R. S. Malpass (Eds.), *Psychology and culture* (pp. 279–284). Copyright © 1994 by Allyn & Bacon. Reprinted with permission.

References:

American Psychiatric Association. (2013). *Diagnostic and statistical manual of mental disorders* (5th ed.). American Psychiatric Publishing.

Beardsley, L. M. (1994). Medical diagnosis and treatment across cultures. In W. J. Lonner, & R. S. Malpass (Eds.), *Psychology and culture* (pp. 279–284). Allyn & Bacon.

Draguns, J. (1973). Comparison of psychopathology across cultures: Issues, findings, directions. *Journal of Cross-Cultural Psychology, 4,* 9–47. https://doi.org/10.1177/002202217300400104

Tanaka-Matsumi, J. (2019). Abnormal psychology and culture. In D. Matsumoto (Ed.), *Handbook of culture and psychology* (2nd ed., pp. 431–467). Oxford University Press.

Tanaka-Matsumi, J., & Draguns, J. (1997). Culture and psychopathology. In J. W. Berry, M. H. Segall, & C. Kagitcibasi (Eds.), *Handbook of cross-cultural psychology*, Vol. 3 (2nd ed., pp. 449–491). Allyn & Bacon.

ACTIVITY 6.8
HANDOUT

SELF-HELP AND CULTURAL IDEALS

According to Daniel Nehring and Dylan Kerrigan (2019), a multi-billion dollar self-help industry has taken hold in countries across the globe. Self-help books, podcasts, videos, websites, and apps provide advice on actions individuals can take to solve personal problems and have a more fulfilling life. They also provide clues about cultural ideals and concerns. For example, Scott McLean (2022) analyzed five best-selling self-help books in Mexico and identified connections between self-help themes and the increasing precarious-ness of social relations in Mexico (for example, a rising divorce rate and more informal work arrangements). This activity explores cultural perspectives on well-being by examining popular self-help books.

Directions: For this activity, you will need to visit your local bookstore or public library and investigate the self-help section, sometimes labeled "Psychology" or "Self-Improvement." (You could also complete this activity using an online bookstore if you are able to look inside and at the back cover of the books.) Spend some time looking at a good sampling of self-help books and then answer the questions below.

1. Based on the self-help books you examined, list five authors/titles of books addressing the well-being of women. Explain how you decided that women are the intended audience.
2. Based on the self-help books you examined, list five authors/titles of books addressing the well-being of men. Explain how you decided that men are the intended audience.
3. Was it easier to find self-help books targeting women or men? Please explain.
4. List the authors/titles of any self-help books that support individualist goals (such as independence, assertiveness, or individual achievement).
5. List the authors/titles of any self-help books that support collectivist goals (such as family harmony, fulfilling obligations to others, or working as a team).
6. Was it easier to find self-help books targeting individualist or collectivist goals? Please explain.
7. You may find that self-help books tend to address the well-being of some groups and ignore others. List some topics that you would add to make self-help books more inclusive of diverse readers and issues.
8. Based on your examination of self-help books, what characteristics or abilities are promoted as necessary for achieving well-being? Do these requirements for well-being differ by gender? Please explain.

Thinking Further:

Consider for a moment the concept of self-help book. What cultural values underlie this phenomenon? For example, culture may shape our ideas about the best sources of advice or about the ability of individuals to change the direction of their lives.

References:

McLean, S. (2022). The cultural logic of precariousness and the marginalization of the sociological imagination: Signs from Mexican self-help books. *Canadian Review of Sociology/Revue Canadienne de Sociologie, 59*, 115–134. http://dx.doi.org/10.1111/cars.12371

Nehring, D., & Kerrigan, D. (2019). *Therapeutic worlds: Popular psychology and the sociocultural organisation of intimate life.* Routledge.

ACTIVITY 6.9
HANDOUT

CLIENT'S AND COUNSELOR'S THOUGHTS

In the decades since the first publications on race, culture, and counseling in the mid-1970s, multicultural competence and social justice training have become central to counselor education and certification. Pamela Hays (2001) suggested that it is important for counselors to examine their own biases and inexperience regarding cultural and social groups. Her *ADDRESSING* model focuses on the interacting cultural influences of **A**ge, **D**evelopmental and acquired **D**isability, **R**ace, **E**thnicity, **S**ocial status, **S**exual orientation, **I**ndigenous heritage, **N**ational origin, and **G**ender. Some approaches to training practitioners of multicultural counseling, such as Paul Pedersen's (1994, 2000) Triad Training Model, use role plays in which participants other than those enacting the client and counselor make the cultural issues explicit. There are multiple versions of the Triad Training Model, but according to Tomoko Yoshida (2020), this approach generally makes four assumptions: (1) during a counseling session there will be many thoughts that the client doesn't verbalize or "hidden messages," (2) these thoughts are influenced by social identity group memberships, (3) the more differences between client and counselor, the greater the potential for misinterpretations, and (4) to be effective, the counselor must address the hidden messages. This activity, based on the Triad Training Model, encourages you to consider some of the complexities of multicultural counseling and the preparation of counselor trainees for intercultural interaction.

Directions: For this activity, you are asked to write two versions of a scenario that illustrates cultural differences between a client and counselor. The first version should consist of a dialogue between a client and a counselor in which there is some cultural misunderstanding or misperception that is NOT verbalized. In the second version, make the cultural issues explicit by including the thoughts of the client and of the counselor (see the example below). Be sure that you use this activity as an opportunity to dispel – rather than create – stereotypes. It is also important to remember that there is a great deal of variability within any social group, and the cultural differences illustrated in this activity should be thought of as illustrating dimensions on which cultural or identity groups may differ, but not a guide for determining the behavior or attitudes of particular individuals. Because age is considered a "critical component of multicultural diversity" (APA, 2009; updated 2018, p. 7) and some studies indicate that age-related bias affects the diagnosis and treatment

of older clients (e.g., Danzinger & Welfel, 2000; Fullen, 2018), the example below addresses age as a factor in a client–counselor interaction.

Example:

The following is a counseling session involving a 32-year-old male psychotherapist, Dr. Allen, and a 70-year-old female client, Mrs. Green.

Counselor: Come right in, Mrs. Green, I hope I haven't kept you waiting long.
Client: That's quite all right, I brought something to do in the waiting room.
Counselor: Well, fine. Now tell me why you've come to see me today.
Client: Well, I've been having some trouble with my mind.
Counselor: What do you mean, Mrs. Green?
Client: I guess it might be called "writer's block," but it's been going on for some time now and I'm rather concerned about it.
Counselor: Now when did you first realize you were having trouble with your memory?
Client: Uh … um … it's not my memory exactly … um it's more like my ability to generate creative new ideas in my writing. You see, after I retired from teaching I took up writing novels and uh …
Counselor: Mrs. Green, maybe you need some other activities. There's a crafts class right here at the clinic on Thursdays.
Client: Well, maybe I'll check into it.
Counselor: In the meantime, let's make an appointment for the same time next week.
Client: That should be fine, Dr. Allen. See you then.

The second version of the scenario includes the thoughts of the client and counselor:

The following is a counseling session involving a 32-year-old male psychotherapist, Dr. Allen, and a 70-year-old female client, Mrs. Green.

Counselor: Come right in, Mrs. Green, I hope I haven't kept you waiting long.
[*Counselor's Thoughts*: She looks like a nice grandmotherly type.]
Client: That's quite all right, I brought something to do in the waiting room.
[*Counselor's Thoughts*: Oh, that bag must be full of knitting or needlepoint.]
[*Client's Thoughts*: Good thing I brought my laptop to work on. I had no idea I'd have to wait for such a long time.]

Counselor:	Well, fine. Now tell me why you've come to see me today.
[Counselor's Thoughts:	I guess this isn't going to be one of my most exciting mornings.]
Client:	Well, I've been having some trouble with my mind.
Counselor:	What do you mean, Mrs. Green?
[Counselor's Thoughts:	Could be early signs of Alzheimer's.]
Client:	I guess it might be called "writer's block," but it's been going on for some time now and I'm rather concerned about it.
Counselor:	Now when did you first realize you were having trouble with your memory?
[Counselor's Thoughts:	Talk about memory problems … I can't seem to recall what I learned in graduate school about the diagnostic criteria for dementia.]
Client:	Uh … um … it's not my memory exactly … um it's more like my ability to generate creative new ideas in my writing.
[Client's Thoughts:	I get it! He thinks I'm senile!]
Client:	You see, after I retired from teaching I took up writing novels and uh …
[Client's Thoughts:	He's looking at me like I'm crazy. This is so unnerving.]
[Counselor's Thoughts:	Hmm … she forgot the end of her sentence. Not a good sign in terms of cognitive functioning.]
Counselor:	Mrs. Green, maybe you need some other activities … there's a crafts class right here at the clinic on Thursdays.
[Counselor's Thoughts:	She just needs to stay busy.]
Client:	Well, maybe I'll check into it.
[Client's Thoughts:	He doesn't understand my situation at all. I guess it was a big mistake to go to a counselor.]
Counselor:	In the meantime, let's make an appointment for the same time next week.
[Counselor's Thoughts:	I guess I should get her back to make a more thorough diagnosis of her memory deficits.]
Client:	That should be fine, Dr. Allen. See you then.
[Client's Thoughts:	I'll call and cancel the appointment as soon as I get home.]

Write your dialogue (**without** client or counselor thoughts) in the space below:

Write your dialogue (**with** client and counselor thoughts) in the space below:

References:

American Psychological Association. (2009; updated 2018). *Multicultural competency in geropsychology: A report of the APA Committee on Aging and its Working Group on Multicultural Competency in Geropsychology*. APA.

Danzinger, P. R., & Welfel, E. R. (2000). Age, gender and health bias in counselors: An empirical analysis. *Journal of Mental Health Counseling, 22*(2), 135–149.

Fullen, M. C. (2018). Ageism and the counseling profession: Causes, consequences, and methods for counteraction. *The Professional Counselor, 8*(2), 104–116. https://doi.org/10.15241/mcf.8.2.104

Hays, P. A. (2001). *Addressing cultural complexities in practice: A framework for clinicians and counselors*. American Psychological Association.

Pedersen, P. (1994). Simulating the client's internal dialogue as a counselor training technique. *Simulation and Gaming, 25*, 40–50.

Pedersen, P. (2000). *A handbook for developing multicultural awareness* (3rd ed.). American Association for Counseling and Development.

Yoshida, T. (2020). The Triad Training Model in counseling: Cultural diversity, and intercultural training. In D. Landis & D. P. S. Bhawuk (Eds.), *The Cambridge handbook of intercultural training* (4th ed., pp. 377–406). Cambridge University Press.

ACTIVITY 6.10
HANDOUT

CULTURE AND PSYCHOTHERAPY

This exercise will explore the ways in which your conception of therapy may be culture-bound and will help you to better understand one *indigenous* form of psychotherapy.

Directions: Use the space provided to respond to the questions below.

1. You are probably familiar with the use of psychotherapy to treat emotional or psychological difficulties. You may have read about therapy, seen therapists in the media, may know someone who has been to a therapist, or

may have been to a therapist yourself. Based on your perceptions, please define the term "therapy" below.

2. List some of the major features of therapy.

In the 1920s, a Japanese psychiatrist named Shoma Morita developed a therapy to treat neuroses that is based in part on Buddhist principles. Morita therapy is now practiced throughout the world (Sugg et al., 2020), often in a modified form designed for outpatients (Dijkstra & Nagatsu, 2022). Morita focuses on rest and isolation. In fact, David Reynolds (1976) observed a sign in one Morita clinic that read "People who converse will not get well." The traditional form of Morita therapy generally lasts from 4 to 8 weeks and consists of the following stages (as outlined by Prince, 1980, p. 299):

a. Total bed rest and isolation for 4 to 10 days; the patient is totally inactive and not permitted to converse, read, write, or listen to the radio.

b. For the next 7 to 14 days, the patient is out of bed and allowed to do light work in the garden; the patient begins to write a diary for the doctor, but other human contact is forbidden.

c. For a further week or two the patient is instructed to do heavier work, continue the diary, and attend lectures from the doctor on self-control, the evils of egocentricity, and so forth.

d. Finally, the patient gradually returns to full social life and his former occupation; the patient continues contact with the doctor and attends group sessions with other patients on an out-patient basis.

3. How do you think you would feel as a patient of Morita therapy?

4. Contrast Western psychotherapy and Morita therapy. How are they different?

5. Compare Western psychotherapy and Morita therapy. How are they the same?

6. Revise your definition of therapy to include both Morita therapy and Western psychotherapy. (*Hint*: focus on the *function* rather than the *process* of therapy.)

References:

Dijkstra, J. M., & Nagatsu, T. (2022). Cognitive behavioral therapy (CBT), acceptance and commitment therapy (ACT), and Morita therapy (MT); comparison of three established psychotherapies and possible common neural mechanisms of psychotherapies. *Journal of*

Neural Transmission, 129(5–6), 805–828. https://doi.org/10.1007/s00702-021-02450-9

Prince, R. (1980). Variations in psychotherapeutic procedures. In H. C. Triandis & J. Draguns (Eds.), *Handbook of cross-cultural psychology,* Vol. 6: Psychopathology (pp. 291–349). Allyn & Bacon.

Reynolds, D. K. (1976). *Morita therapy.* University of California Press.

Sugg, H. V. R., Richards, D. A., & Frost, J. (2020). What is Morita therapy? The nature, origins, and cross-cultural application of a unique Japanese psychotherapy. *Journal of Contemporary Psychotherapy, 50,* 313–322. https://doi.org/10.1007/s10879-020-09464-6

(Space for responses in these handouts has been reduced. Please see www. routledge.com/9781032394336 for fillable versions of these handouts.)

Culture and Social Behavior

ACTIVITY 7.1
HANDOUT

VIOLATING CULTURAL NORMS

Social norms are (often unspoken) rules or expectations about how people within a given group should behave. Social psychologists have found that people generally choose to conform to the social norms of the groups to which they belong. This activity explores the importance of the content and strength of social norms in defining a culture.

Directions: The statements below instruct you to list social norms, choose one of these norms to violate, and then answer a series of questions based on your experience.

1. Examples of social norms relevant to some cultures include:

   - Forming a line when a group of people are waiting.
   - Applauding when a performance is completed.
   - Saying "excuse me" if you bump into strangers in a crowded place.

   In the space provided, list five social norms that you have observed.

2. Choose one of the norms you listed above to violate. *Please be sure that your behavior is not illegal and does not put you or others in any danger.* Your norm violation need not be anything very dramatic. Sometimes we can learn more from subtle than drastic norm violations.

DOI: 10.4324/9781003356820-20

In the space below, describe your violation of a social norm, including (a) the setting, (b) the nature of the norm violation, (c) how you felt during the norm violation, and (d) how others responded to your behavior.

3. Discuss the cultural value that underlies the norm you chose to violate.
4. Why do you think we typically react negatively toward those who violate our social norms?
5. How did you learn the social norms of your own culture?
6. How would you go about learning the social norms of an unfamiliar culture?

Thinking Further:

Perrti Pelto (1968) distinguished between loose cultures, which have weaker social norms and greater tolerance for deviance, and tight cultures, which have strong norms and severe punishments for their violation. Michele Gelfand, Jesse Harrington, and Joshua Jackson (2017) explained the evolution of looseness-tightness in terms of threat. They suggested that in societies with a history of social and ecological threats (e.g., lack of resources, natural disasters, disease, warfare), strong norms evolved to facilitate coordinated action. Several Asian nations were among the tightest of those measured and several Eastern European nations were among the loosest (Gelfand et al., 2011).

How might someone from a loose culture experience life in a tight culture? How do you think someone from a tight culture would experience life in a loose culture?

References:

Gelfand, M. J., Harrington, J. R., & Jackson, J. C. (2017). The strength of social norms across human groups. *Perspectives on Psychological Science, 12*(5), 800–809. https://doi.org/10.1177/1745691617708631

Gelfand, M. J., Raver, J. L., Nishii, L., et al. (2011). Differences between tight and loose cultures: A 33-nation study. *Science, 332*, 1100–1104. https://doi.org/10.1126/science.1197754

Pelto, P. J. (1968). The differences between "tight" and "loose" societies. *Society, 5*(5), 37–40. https://doi.org/10.1007/BF03180447

ACTIVITY 7.2
HANDOUT

SHOPPING FOR CULTURAL VALUES

Sometimes it is easier to identify the cultural values of groups that are more foreign to us than to identify cultural values that permeate our day-to-day environment. Cultural values have been studied in a wide variety of settings including hospitals, schools, businesses, sports events, coffee shops, and children's birthday parties. This activity is designed to give you some perspective on the cultural values in your community through a trip to your neighborhood grocery store.

Directions: Select a grocery store in your community. Plan to spend 30 minutes to an hour making your observations. Take careful notes about the shoppers, the products available for purchase, and the layout of the store so that you can answer the questions below.

Name of store _____
Type of store _____
Time of day _____

1. What type of food or products were most plentiful in the store? What type of food or products were scarce?
2. What claims were used to promote food items? Did these claims emphasize taste, nutritional value, cost, ease of preparation?
3. What were the most expensive items in the store? When a wide range of prices exists for the same type of product, what distinguished the lower from the higher cost versions?
4. What type of behavior did you observe on the part of the shoppers? In what circumstances did shoppers interact with each other?
5. How were meats and poultry packaged? Were they labeled and displayed in a way that distances these products from their original animal form? Please explain.
6. What did you observe about the sizes in which different types of products were available? What did these sizes imply about the social settings in which the products will be used? For example, did you see more individual servings or family-size packaging?
7. How were foods from various ethnic groups distributed throughout the store? Were some ethnic foods presented as normative (integrated throughout the store) whereas others were placed in a separate section or presented as unusual or exotic?

---

8. What other observations did you make that informed you about cultural values?

9. Based on your answers to the questions above, what cultural values were evident in the supermarket setting?

Thinking Further:

Shalom Schwartz and colleagues have conducted extensive cross-cultural research on values. These studies support the existence of seven societal-level values and ten individual-level values across cultures. Although cultures may differ in terms of the degree to which specific values are endorsed, there appears to be a consistent structure to these values. Descriptions of the ten basic values pursued by individuals are listed below (Schwartz, 2011, p. 465).

- *Power:* Social status and prestige, control and dominance over people and resources.
- *Achievement:* Personal success through demonstrating competence according to social standards.
- *Hedonism:* Pleasure and sensuous gratification for oneself.
- *Stimulation:* Excitement, novelty, and challenge in life.
- *Self-Direction:* Independent thought, and action – choosing, creating, exploring.
- *Universalism:* Understanding, appreciation, tolerance, and protection for the welfare of all people and for nature.
- *Benevolence:* Preservation and enhancement of the welfare of people with whom one is in frequent personal contact.
- *Tradition:* Respect, commitment, and acceptance of the customs and ideas that traditional culture or religion provide the self.
- *Conformity:* Restraint of actions, inclinations, and impulses likely to upset or harm others and violate social expectations or norms.
- *Security:* Safety, harmony, and stability of society, of relationships, and of self.

Which of these values were most evident in the products and behaviors you observed in the grocery store? Please provide examples of how these values were expressed.

Reference:

Schwartz, S. H. (2011). Values: Individual and cultural. In F. J. R. van de Vijver, A. Chasiotis, & S. M. Breugelmans (Eds.), *Fundamental questions in cross-cultural psychology* (pp. 463–493). Cambridge University Press.

ACTIVITY 7.3
HANDOUT

CULTURE AND MORAL REASONING

Psychological research on moral reasoning has been dominated by theories developed by Western scholars studying the behavior of Western participants. Cross-cultural psychologists have raised questions about the universality of these theories and the methods used to test their validity. This activity focuses on one of those methods – the "trolley problem."

Directions: One way that researchers have studied moral reasoning is with the trolley problem (Foot, 1967). There are many versions of this problem, but two of the most widely used versions are below. Please respond to these two trolley problem scenarios and then answer the questions that follow.

1. In one version of the trolley problem, there is a runaway train car speeding down a hill, about to crash into – and kill – five people on the track. However, at the last minute you see that you could flip a switch and send the train onto another track. Unfortunately, there is a man on the other track who will be hit (and killed) by the train if you do so.

   Would you flip the switch to move the train onto the other track (saving the group of five but killing the one man)? Yes _____ No _____

2. A second version of the trolley problem is similar, but in this case you are standing on a bridge when you see the runaway train car about to hit five people. There is also a large man on the bridge, who you don't know. If you push him off the bridge he will land on the track and stop the train car from hitting the five people, although he would be killed. (Your own body is not large enough to stop the train car.)

   Would you push the man onto the track to stop the train car (saving the group of five but killing the one man)? Yes _____ No _____

3. Do you feel more comfortable about the first or the second scenario above? Please explain.

4. Across cultures, people almost always feel more comfortable with the first scenario than with the second scenario. For example, Awad et al. (2020) found this to be the case in a study of 70,000 participants from 42 countries. How can we explain this seemingly universal (or etic) phenomenon?

5. There are also some cultural differences in the percentage of people from different countries who answer "yes" to a version of the trolley problem. For example, Piotr Sorokowski and colleagues (2020) compared Canadians and Yali people from the remote Yalimo Valley of Papua, Indonesia on a

moral reasoning task. Because the trolley concept would be unfamiliar to the Yali, they used a more ecologically relevant "falling tree dilemma." In this scenario, a tree is about to fall on and kill five people. You have the opportunity to push the tree in a different direction, but doing so would kill one other person. In this study, 37% of Yali said they would push the tree as compared with 68% of Canadians. Sorokowski et al. suggested that the difference in willingness to kill one person while saving five may be due to religious beliefs (e.g., humans do not have the right to determine when someone will die) or perhaps due to the cultural consequences for causing someone's death (e.g., the likelihood that relatives of the deceased individual would seek retribution). Can you think of any other culture-specific (or emic) reasons why cultures may differ in the percentage of individuals willing to take action in versions of the trolley dilemma?

Thinking Further:

Research conducted in Western societies generally finds that moral identity (the degree to which being a moral person is important to one's self-concept) predicts moral behavior. However, studies conducted in several Asian societies has found that moral identity is not closely linked to moral behavior (Jia & Krettenauer, 2017). Why might this be so?

References:

Awad, E., Dsouza, S., Shariff, A., Rahwan, L., & Bonneto, J.-F. (2020). Universals and variations in moral decisions made in 42 countries by 70,000 participants. *PNAS Proceedings of the National Academy of Sciences of the United States of America, 117*(5), 2332–2337. https://doi.org/10.1073/pnas.1911517117

Foot, P. (1967). The problem of abortion and the doctrine of the double effect. *Oxford Review, 5,* 5–15.

Jia, F., & Krettenauer, T. (2017). Recognizing moral identity as a cultural construct. *Frontiers in Psychology, 8,* 412. https://doi.org/10.3389/fpsyg.2017.00412

Sorokowski, P., Marczak, M., Misiak, M., & Bialek, M. (2020). Trolley dilemma in Papua: Yali horticulturalists refuse to pull the lever. *Psychonomic Bulletin & Review, 27,* 398–403. https://doi.org/10.3758/s13423-019-01700-y

ACTIVITY 7.4
HANDOUT

BARE BRANCHES

For the first time in human history, there is a significant sex-ratio imbalance in China and India (Denyer & Gowen, 2018). Among those under 25, there are 116 males per 100 females in China and 110 males per 100 females in India (United Nations, 2023). The young men in these countries are sometimes described as "bare branches," since they are unlikely to find a marriage partner and expand the family tree. This situation is a result of cultural preferences for boys coupled with the one-child policy in China (from 1979–2016) and sex-selection abortion and female infanticide and neglect in both countries. Although the sex ratio has become more balanced in the past few years, scholars warn that this imbalance will likely have significant effects for the next 20 or 30 years – effects that extend beyond marriage rates to the state of regional and global economies as well. This activity explores the implications of this situation through a consideration of gender roles across cultures.

Directions: Think about the roles, behaviors, and traits generally associated with men and women throughout the world. Then discuss the changes that might occur in a hypothetical society as a result of a disproportional number of men. Consider that, across cultures, gender stereotypes change along with changes in the behaviors of women and men (Miller et al., 2015). Some potential matters to consider are listed below:

- Age markers or milestones
- Care of elderly parents
- Crime rates
- Economic conditions
- Education
- Gender discrimination
- Gender roles
- Government policies
- Health and health care
- Home ownership
- Immigration and emigration
- Income inequality/social class
- Leisure activities
- Marriage and divorce rates and attitudes
- Mass media
- Mental illness
- Military service
- Occupations
- Personality traits
- Religion
- Sexual behavior
- Social class
- Status of women

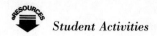

Your description of a society where men outnumber women:

References:

Denyer, S., & Gowen, A. (2018). Too many men: China and India battle with the consequences of gender imbalance. *The Washington Post*, April 24.

Miller, D. I., Eagly, A. H., & Linn, M. C. (2015). Women's representation in science predicts national gender-science stereotypes: Evidence from 66 nations. *Journal of Educational Psychology*, *107*(3), 631–644. https://doi.org/10.1037/edu0000005

United Nations Department of Economic and Social Affairs. (2023). *India overtakes China as the world's most populous country*. www.un.org/development/desa/dpad/wp-content/uploads/sites/45/PB153.pdf

---

ACTIVITY 7.5
HANDOUT

AGGRESSION ACROSS CULTURES: A QUIZ

This activity explores some of the factors that may help us to understand cross-cultural variation in aggressive behavior.

Directions: Decide whether each of the statements below is true or false. Then check your answers with your instructor.

1. Cross-cultural research indicates that about half of all conflicts between humans result in some form of aggressive behavior.   TRUE/FALSE

2. Across cultures, males are more physically aggressive than females   TRUE/FALSE

3. A link between exposure to violent media and aggressive behavior seems to apply less to Latinx samples than to other ethnic groups.   TRUE/FALSE

4. An increase in the population of undocumented immigrants is generally associated with an increase in the rate of violent crime.   TRUE/FALSE

5. The likelihood of warfare increases with the complexity of a society.   TRUE/FALSE

6. Driver aggression ("road rage") varies very little across cultures.   TRUE/FALSE

---

7. In addition to a far greater frequency of mass shootings in the United States as compared with most of the world's nations, in the U.S., a far greater proportion of shootings occur in the workplace as compared with other nations.   TRUE/FALSE

8. Across cultures studied, parental rejection is a strong predictor of children's violence.   TRUE/FALSE

9. People from the northern United States are more likely than people from the southern United States to react to insults with violence.   TRUE/FALSE

10. Video games have been used to decrease gender-based violence.   TRUE/FALSE

ACTIVITY 7.6
HANDOUT

CONFLICT COMMUNICATION STYLE

Much research has demonstrated cultural variability in conflict handling style. This activity will provide you with an indication of how you communicate in conflict situations.

Directions: Using the scale at the top of each page, circle the number that best describes how you feel about each of the following statements. Once you have completed the scale, calculate and plot your scores, and then answer the questions that follow.

Strongly Disagree	Disagree	Disagree Somewhat	Neutral	Agree Somewhat	Agree	Strongly Agree
1	2	3	4	5	6	7

1. When something I have purchased is found to be defective, I keep it anyway.   1 2 3 4 5 6 7

2. Showing your feelings in a dispute is a sign of weakness.   1 2 3 4 5 6 7

3. I would be embarrassed if neighbors heard me argue with a family member.   1 2 3 4 5 6 7

4. I rarely state my point of view unless I am asked.   1 2 3 4 5 6 7

5. I am drawn to conflict situations.   1 2 3 4 5 6 7

6. If I were upset with a friend I would discuss it with someone else rather than the friend who upset me.   1 2 3 4 5 6 7

7. An argument can be resolved more easily when people express their emotions.   1 2 3 4 5 6 7

Strongly Disagree	Disagree	Disagree Somewhat	Neutral	Agree Somewhat	Agree	Strongly Agree
1	2	3	4	5	6	7

8. I would feel uncomfortable arguing with one friend in the presence of other friends. 1 2 3 4 5 6 7

9. In a dispute, I try not to let the other person know what I am thinking. 1 2 3 4 5 6 7

10. I like when other people challenge my opinions. 1 2 3 4 5 6 7

11. After a dispute with a neighbor, I would feel uncomfortable seeing them again even if the conflict had been resolved. 1 2 3 4 5 6 7

12. If I become angry it is because I have lost control. 1 2 3 4 5 6 7

13. I don't mind being involved in an argument in a public place. 1 2 3 4 5 6 7

14. In a dispute, I want to know all about the other person's thoughts and beliefs. 1 2 3 4 5 6 7

15. I enjoy challenging the opinions of others. 1 2 3 4 5 6 7

16. When I have a conflict with someone I try to resolve it by being extra nice to them. 1 2 3 4 5 6 7

17. It shows strength to express emotions openly. 1 2 3 4 5 6 7

18. I feel uncomfortable seeing others argue in public. 1 2 3 4 5 6 7

19. There are not many people with whom I feel comfortable expressing disagreement. 1 2 3 4 5 6 7

20. I don't mind when others start arguments with me. 1 2 3 4 5 6 7

21. I feel more comfortable having an argument over the phone than in person. 1 2 3 4 5 6 7

22. Getting emotional only makes conflicts worse. 1 2 3 4 5 6 7

23. I am just as comfortable having an argument in a public place as in a private place. 1 2 3 4 5 6 7

24. In a dispute, I am glad when the other person asks me about my thoughts or opinions. 1 2 3 4 5 6 7

25. I feel upset after an argument. 1 2 3 4 5 6 7

26. I expect a family member to know what is on my mind without my telling them. 1 2 3 4 5 6 7

27. It makes me uncomfortable when other people express their emotions. 1 2 3 4 5 6 7

Strongly Disagree	Disagree	Disagree Somewhat	Neutral	Agree Somewhat	Agree	Strongly Agree
1	2	3	4	5	6	7

28. I am annoyed when someone refuses to discuss a disagreement with me because there are others around.   1 2 3 4 5 6 7

29. In a conflict situation I feel comfortable expressing my thoughts no matter who the others involved are.   1 2 3 4 5 6 7

30. I hate arguments.   1 2 3 4 5 6 7

31. I prefer to express points of disagreement with others by writing them notes rather than speaking with them directly.   1 2 3 4 5 6 7

32. It is a waste of time to involve emotions in a dispute.   1 2 3 4 5 6 7

33. I argue in public.   1 2 3 4 5 6 7

34. When involved in a dispute I often become silent.   1 2 3 4 5 6 7

35. I wait to see if a dispute will resolve itself before taking action.   1 2 3 4 5 6 7

36. If a coworker were interfering with my performance on the job I would rather speak to them directly than to tell the boss.   1 2 3 4 5 6 7

37. For me, expressing emotions is an important part of settling disputes.   1 2 3 4 5 6 7

38. I feel uncomfortable when others argue in my presence.   1 2 3 4 5 6 7

39. In a dispute there are many things about myself that I won't discuss.   1 2 3 4 5 6 7

40. Conflicts make relationships interesting.   1 2 3 4 5 6 7

41. If a friend owed me money, I would hint about it before asking directly to be paid.   1 2 3 4 5 6 7

42. In a dispute, I express my emotions openly.   1 2 3 4 5 6 7

43. When I am having a dispute with someone, I don't pay attention to whether others are around.   1 2 3 4 5 6 7

44. In an argument I try to reveal as little as possible about my point of view.   1 2 3 4 5 6 7

45. Arguments don't bother me.   1 2 3 4 5 6 7

46. I prefer to solve disputes through face-to-face discussion.   1 2 3 4 5 6 7

47. I avoid people who express their emotions easily.   1 2 3 4 5 6 7

48. I wouldn't mind if a friend told others about an argument that we had.   1 2 3 4 5 6 7

49. During a dispute I state my opinions openly.   1 2 3 4 5 6 7

50. Arguments can be fun.   1 2 3 4 5 6 7

Scoring:

This Conflict Communication Scale is composed of five subscales. To calculate your subscale scores, first copy your scores from each of the items into the columns on the next page, then reverse the scoring of the items marked with an asterisk (*) so that 1 = 7, 2 = 6, 3 = 5, 4 = 4, 5 = 3, 6 = 2, and 7 = 1. Finally, sum each item in the column to calculate the subscale score.

Confrontation		Emotional Expression		Public/Private Behavior		Self-Disclosure		Conflict Approach/Avoidance	
1*		2*		3*		4*		5	
6*		7		8*		9*		10	
11*		12*		13		14		15	
16*		17		18*		19*		20	
21*		22*		23		24		25*	
26*		27*		28		29		30*	
31*		32*		33		34*		35*	
36		37		38*		39*		40	
41*		42		43		44*		45	
46		47*		48		49		50	
Total		Total		Total		Total		Total	

Edward T. Hall (1976) distinguished between low- and high-context cultures. In low-context cultures, most of what is communicated is done explicitly. People in low-context cultures are more likely to directly state or indicate what they would like to say. In high-context cultures, a greater level of shared knowledge and experience allows the message to be communicated more indirectly.

Although now considered an overgeneralization, Hall described the United States (most likely referring to the dominant culture of the United States), Germany, and Scandinavia as representative of low-context cultures and placed China, Japan, and Korea near the high-context end of the continuum. Latin American, Greek, and Arab cultures have also been categorized as high-context. You may have observed that low-context cultures tend to be more individualistic, whereas high-context cultures are more collectivistic.

According to Stella Ting-Toomey (2015) high- and low-context cultures are expected to vary on several dimensions of conflict handling, with more confrontational behavior in low-context cultures. For example, suppose you have asked a favor of a coworker and he is unable to assist you. If this had occurred in a low-context culture, the coworker would likely tell you directly that unfortunately, he is unable to help. If this same event occurred in a high-context culture, however, the coworker might convey the same meaning by giving a vague reply stating that he will do his best to help.

In terms of the Conflict Communication Scale, we would expect low-context cultures to be characterized by greater levels of confrontation, public disputing behavior, self-disclosure, emotional expression, and conflict approach. Average scores for each of the subscales for U.S. undergraduates are as follows: Confrontation, 48; Public/Private, 31; Emotional Expression, 49; Conflict Approach/Avoidance, 35; and Self-Disclosure, 47. Scores below the mean indicate more indirect or high-context communication. Scores above the mean indicate more direct or low-context communication.

To what extent do your Conflict Communication Scale scores reflect low-context or high-context communication?

Thinking Further:

Differences in conflict communication styles are a common cause of intercultural (and interpersonal) misunderstandings. What strategies would you recommend for resolving conflicts between individuals with opposing styles?

Source:

Questionnaire items adapted from Goldstein, S. B. (1999). Construction and validation of a conflict communication scale. *Journal of Applied Social Psychology*, *29*, 1803–1832. https://doi.org/10.1111/j.1559-1816.1999.tb00153.x. Copyright © 1999 by Wiley-Blackwell. Adapted with permission.

References:

Hall, E. T. (1976). *Beyond culture*. Doubleday.
Ting-Toomey, S. (2015). Facework/Facework negotiation theory. In J. Bennett (Ed.), *Sage Encyclopedia of Intercultural Competence*, Vol. 1 (pp. 325–330). Sage.

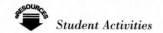

ACTIVITY 7.7
HANDOUT

WORK-RELATED VALUES

The basis of much cross-cultural research in – and outside of – the workplace is Geert Hofstede's (1980, 2001) cultural dimensions. Hofstede studied the values of IBM employees in over 70 countries. Based on this data he derived four dimensions of cultural variability: *individualism-collectivism*, *power distance*, *uncertainty avoidance*, and *masculinity-femininity*. Hofstede used the average scores of workers in each country to rank countries on the four dimensions. Several years later, the Chinese Culture Connection (1987), a group of researchers led by Michael Harris Bond, identified the value Confucian Work Dynamism. Hofstede added this dimension to his model, which he labeled *long- vs. short-term orientation* (Hofstede, 2001). Finally, a sixth dimension, *indulgence-restraint*, was added based on Michael Minkov's analysis of World Values Survey data (Hofstede et al., 2010). It is useful to be familiar with these dimensions because they are so widely used in cross-cultural research. However, it is important to note that our understanding of Hofstede's original dimensions is evolving and that recent studies have called these dimensions into question, particularly *uncertainty avoidance* and *masculinity-femininity* (Minkov & Kaasa, 2021). The purpose of this activity is to better understand these six dimensions by applying them to a workplace with which you are familiar.

Directions: First write a brief description of a work setting with which you are familiar. Then read the descriptions of the six dimensions below and in the questions that follow apply these dimensions to your work setting.

   Workplace Description (include type of business or occupation, approximate number of employees, and structure in terms of managers and subordinates):

Work-Related Values:

As compared to Individualistic cultures, cultures high in Collectivism tend to be characterized by:

- A focus on the goals of the group rather than individual goals
- Achievement attributed to the efforts of the group rather than the individual

---

- Avoidance of confrontation
- The perception that direct requests are an ineffective form of communication
- Working in groups

Cultures high in Power Distance tend to be characterized by:

- Clear distinctions between superiors and subordinates
- The acceptance of an unequal power distribution
- Dependence of subordinates on superiors
- Conformity

Cultures high in Uncertainty Avoidance tend to be characterized by:

- Lower tolerance for ambiguity
- Greater need for consensus
- Greater need for formal rules
- Avoidance of conflict
- Resistance to change

As compared to Feminine cultures, cultures high in Masculinity are characterized by:

- A high value on things as opposed to people
- A focus on power and competition as opposed to nurturance
- The perception that work is central to one's life
- An emphasis on distinct gender roles

As compared to cultures with Short-Term Orientation, those with Long-Term Orientation tend to be characterized by:

- Patience and perseverance
- Thrift
- Organizations modeled after the structure of the family
- Having a sense of shame

As compared to those high in Indulgence, cultures high in Restraint tend to be characterized by:

- A focus on controlling impulses
- A value on maintaining order

- Low importance of leisure
- Little sense of personal control in life
- Pessimism

1. Is this workplace more individualistic or collectivistic? Please explain.
2. Does this workplace have high, moderate, or low power distance? Please explain.
3. Does this workplace have high, moderate, or low uncertainty avoidance? Please explain.
4. Is this workplace more feminine or masculine? Please explain.
5. Does this workplace have more of a long-term or short-term orientation? Please explain.
6. Does this workplace have more indulgence or restraint? Please explain.

Thinking Further:

Are the values manifested in this workplace conducive to a diverse workforce? Please explain.

References:

Chinese Culture Connection. (1987). Chinese values and the search for culture-free dimensions of culture. *Journal of Cross-Cultural Psychology*, *18*, 143–164. https://doi.org/10.1177/0022002187018002002

Hofstede, G. (1980). *Culture's consequences: International differences in work-related values*. Sage.

Hofstede, G. (2001). *Culture's consequences: Comparing values, behaviors, and organizations across nations* (2nd ed.). Sage.

Hofstede, G., Hofstede, G. J., & Minkov, M. (2010). *Cultures and organizations: Software of the mind* (3rd ed.). McGraw-Hill.

Minkov, M., & Kaasa, A. (2021). A test of the Revised Minkov-Hofstede Model of Culture: Mirror images of subjective and objective culture across nations and the 50 US States. *Cross-Cultural Research*, *55*(2–3), 230–281. https://doi.org/10.1177/10693971211014468

ACTIVITY 7.8
HANDOUT

CULTURAL INFLUENCES ON LEADERSHIP

A major interest of those who study organizational behavior is how to select and train effective leaders. Leadership becomes an even greater concern when it involves international businesses or domestic organizations that have a diverse workforce. This activity explores universality and cultural variability in the concept of leadership.

Directions: Spend a few minutes thinking about your image of a leader. Then complete the five sentences below to describe characteristics of a good leader and answer the questions that follow.

- A good leader _____.
- A good leader _____.
- A good leader _____.
- A good leader _____.
- A good leader _____.

1. Do you think that the characteristics you described above are universal across cultures or are culture-specific? Please explain.
2. Project GLOBE is an extensive multi-stage study of leadership behavior across cultures for which questionnaire, interview, and observational data were collected in 62 countries in 2004 (House et al., 2004), 24 countries in 2014 (House et al., 2014) and 124 countries in the most recent wave of data collection which began in 2020. One goal of Project GLOBE researchers is to identify universal attributes of effective leaders and to determine how leadership varies across cultures. These researchers found that across cultures, leaders with charismatic behavior (they are encouraging, positive, motivational, and confidence builders) and team-oriented behavior (they build consensus and focus on collaborative problem-solving) have the most impact on the company's performance.

   Discuss how these findings compare with the characteristics of good leaders you listed above.
3. What basic human needs might be reflected in the universal preference for leaders with charisma and team-oriented behavior?

Thinking Further:

1. Project GLOBE also identified several cultural differences in leadership style. For example, the Southern Asia Cluster (India, Indonesia, Philippines, Malaysia, Thailand, and Iran) is characterized by leadership that has a family-like structure (Gupta et al., 2002). Jai B. P. Sinha (1995), for example, described the Indian manager as a nurturant task leader who acts toward the employees as a parent would toward a child. Treating each subordinate fairly, then, does not mean treating them all the same, but making sure that the needs of each are met to the extent possible. As these needs differ, so will the treatment. According to Sinha, leadership in the businesses of India involves more participation in the projects of subordinates rather than merely giving instructions as to which tasks are to be undertaken. Furthermore, there is little of the distinction between work and personal life that one finds in much of the Western world (Ly, 2020). The manager is expected to provide advice and at times intervene if an employee is experiencing problems unrelated to work. For example, a manager in India may suggest a marriage partner for an employee or provide guidance in family disputes.

   Would a person having the five characteristics you listed at the beginning of this activity make an effective leader in the Indian context Sinha describes? If not, what other characteristics would be important?

2. R. C. Sekhar (2008) noted that leadership in India varies a great deal from region to region. What factors do you think might influence such regional differences within countries?

3. Based on Project GLOBE data, Amanda Bullough and Mary Sully de Luque (2015) investigated the environments that are conducive for women to participate in as business and political leaders. Their results indicated that in settings where a charismatic leadership style is valued (emphasizing encouraging and motivating others), women are more likely to participate in both political and business leadership roles. However, women are less likely to participate in leadership roles, particularly in political positions, when a self-protective leadership style is valued (emphasizing competition and status).

   What might this mean for the participation of women in business and political leadership in your country?

4. Recent studies (e.g., Azevedo & Jugdev, 2022; Rosenauer et al., 2016) point to cultural intelligence as an important characteristic of competent leaders. Cultural intelligence is "a person's adaptation to new cultural settings and capability to deal effectively with other people with whom

the person does not share a common cultural background and understanding" (Earley & Ang, 2003, p. 34). Describe below any additional characteristics of a good leader that would facilitate their cultural intelligence.

References:

Azevedo, A., & Jugdev, K. (2022). Applying cultural intelligence to develop adaptive leadership. *Organization Development Journal*, *40*(4), 56–70.

Bullough, A., & de Luque, M. S. (2015). Women's participation in entrepreneurial and political leadership: The importance of culturally endorsed implicit leadership theories. *Leadership*, *11*(1), 36–56. https://doi.org/10.1177/17427150135044

Earley, P. C., & Ang, S. (2003). *Cultural intelligence: Individual interactions across cultures*. Stanford University Press.

Gupta, V., Hanges, P. J., & Dorman, P. (2002). Cultural clusters: Methodology and findings. *Journal of World Business*, *37*, 11–15. https://econpapers.repec.org/RePEc:eee:worbus:v:37:y:2002:i:1:p:11-15

House, R. J., Dorfman, P. W., Mansour, J., Hanges, P. J., & de Luque, M. S. (2014). *Strategic leadership across cultures: GLOBE Study of CEO leadership behavior and effectiveness in 24 countries*. Sage.

House, R. J., Hanges, P. J., Javidan, M., Dorfman, P. W., & Gupta, V. (2004). *Culture, leadership, and organizations: The GLOBE study of 62 societies*. Sage.

Ly, N.-B. (2020). Cultural influences on leadership: Western-dominated leadership and non-Western conceptualizations of leadership. *Sociology and Anthropology*, *8*(1), 1–12. https://doi.org/10.13189/SA.2020.080101

Rosenauer, D., Homan, A. C., Horstmeier, C. A. L., & Voelpel, S. C. (2016). Managing nationality diversity: The interactive effect of leaders' cultural intelligence and task interdependence. *British Journal of Management*, *27*(3), 628–645. https://doi.org/10.1111/1467-8551.12131

Sekhar, R. C. (2008). Trends in ethics and styles of leadership in India. *Business Ethics: A European Review*, *10*, 360–363. https://doi.org/10.1111/1467-8608.00252

Sinha, J. B. P. (1995). *The cultural context of leadership and power*. Sage.

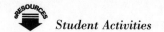

ACTIVITY 7.9
HANDOUT

CHOOSING A LIFE PARTNER

Starting in the late 1980s, David Buss (Buss et al., 1990) and other evolutionary psychologists conducted a number of cross-cultural studies to identify the characteristics women and men prefer in a long-term partner. This activity will familiarize you with some of the major findings of this research and allow you to compare your own partner preferences with these research findings.

Directions: Complete the items below using the five-point scale to indicate the importance you place on each characteristic in choosing a life partner, then answer the questions that follow.

	Very Unimportant				Very Important
	1	2	3	4	5

1. Kind and understanding	1 2 3 4 5
2. Family has good reputation	1 2 3 4 5
3. Similar religious beliefs	1 2 3 4 5
4. Exciting personality	1 2 3 4 5
5. Creative and artistic	1 2 3 4 5
6. Good housekeeper	1 2 3 4 5
7. Intelligent	1 2 3 4 5
8. Good earning capacity	1 2 3 4 5
9. Wants children	1 2 3 4 5
10. Easygoing	1 2 3 4 5
11. College graduate	1 2 3 4 5
12. Someone my family approves of	1 2 3 4 5
13. Physically attractive	1 2 3 4 5
14. Healthy	1 2 3 4 5
15. Someone I love	1 2 3 4 5

1. Circle the characteristics you rated as most important (4 or 5). What might be the reason why you selected these particular items?

2. Kathryn Walter and an international group of 75 colleagues (2020) replicated earlier studies by investigating sex differences in mate preferences across 45 countries. Their findings were representative of previous studies in that although both men and women preferred partners who are kind, healthy, and intelligent, men were more likely to value physical attractiveness in women and women were more likely to value a high earning potential in men. A recent 24-country study of 1.8 predominantly heterosexual online daters' *selections* (as opposed to just *preferences*) supported this latter finding in that earning potential increased attention received by men at nearly 2.5 times the rate that it increased attention to women (Jonason & Thomas, 2022). How do your responses compare with these findings?

3. Evolutionary psychologists suggest that heterosexual mate preferences are motivated by reproductive fitness. They have argued that when looking for a long-term partner, men will value physical attractiveness because it is a cue to their partner's fertility whereas women value economic security to provide for themselves and their children during the extended period of child care-giving after birth.

   An alternative explanation comes from biosocial role theory (Wood & Eagly, 2002), which suggests that sex differences in mate preference reflect a need to adopt traits and preferences that will be most helpful given the physical attributes of men and women as well as the gender roles that arise from a specific social and ecological context. According to this perspective, there should be fewer sex differences in mate preference in societies with more gender equality. This latter approach has had mixed support with some studies finding that the sex differences in mate preferences decrease with greater gender equality (e.g., Bech-Sørensen & Pollet, 2016) and others finding that level of gender equality is unrelated to mate preferences (Kennair et al., 2023).

   Walter et al. (2020) reported an interesting finding regarding long-term partners' age. In societies with greater gender inequality, women were more likely to have partners that were older than them and men were more likely to have partners that were younger than them. In other words, the sex difference in age of partner decreased as gender equality increased. Do you think this finding best fits an evolutionary perspective or a biosocial perspective? Please explain.

4. In one of the few studies applying the evolutionary model of mate preferences to same-sex relationships, Lisa Dillon and Daniel Saleh (2012) analyzed profiles of individuals seeking long-term or short-term same-sex partners on an online dating site. As in the studies of heterosexual men,

gay men seeking a long-term relationship were more likely to mention their financial security than any other combination of sex and relationship type. Why might this occur? [Remember that from the evolutionary perspective, the focus on financial assets in men is assumed to be associated with stability after a female partner gives birth.]

Thinking Further:

1. Studies show that love is viewed as an important basis for mate selection worldwide, although slightly more so in countries with greater wealth (Sprecher & Hatfield, 2017). Why might that be the case?
2. Although there appears to be a global trend away from formal arranged marriages (Dion & Dion, 2005), in many cultures throughout the world, families play a major part in mate selection, often identifying potential partners who will be a good fit with the family's needs and standards (Buunk et al., 2010). In fact, one study found that the majority of undergraduate students in eight countries wanted partners that aligned with their parents' preferences (Locke et al., 2020). What is the direct or indirect role of your family in your life partner selection? What advantages and disadvantages might there be to family input into this process?
3. You may be surprised to learn that media plays a significant role in perceptions of future mates across cultures (Chen & Austin, 2017). In what ways, if any, has the media influenced your preferences for a mate?

Source:

Items adapted from Shackelford, T. K., Schmitt, D. P., & Buss, D. M. (2005). Universal dimensions of human mate preferences. *Personality and Individual Differences*, *39*(2), 447–458. Copyright © 2005 by Elsevier. Adapted with permission.

References:

Bech-Sørensen, J., & Pollet, T. V. (2016). Sex differences in mate preferences: A replication study, 20 years later. *Evolutionary Psychological Science*, *2*, 71–176. https://doi.org/10.1007/s40806-016-0048-6
Buss, D. M., Abbott, M., Angleitner, A., et al. (1990). International preferences in selecting mates: A study of 37 cultures. *Journal of Cross-Cultural Psychology*, *21*, 5–47. http://dx.doi.org/10.1177/0022 022190211001

Buunk, A. P., Park, J. H., & Duncan, L. A. (2010). Cultural variation in parental influence on mate choice. *Cross-Cultural Research: The Journal of Comparative Social Science, 44*(1), 23–40. http://dx.doi.org/10.1177/1069397109337711

Chen, R., & Austin, J. P. (2017). The effect of external influences on mate selection necessity traits: Cross-cultural comparisons of Chinese and American men and women. *Marriage & Family Review, 53*(3), 246–261. http://dx.doi.org/10.1080/01494929.2016.1157562

Dillon, L. M., & Saleh, D. J. (2012). Sexual strategies theory: Evidence from homosexual personal advertisements. *Journal of Social, Evolutionary, and Cultural Psychology, 6*(2), 203–216. https://doi.org/10.1037/h0099214

Dion, K. L., & Dion, K. K. (2005). Culture and relationships: The downside of self-contained individualism. In R. M. Sorrentino, D. Cohen, J. M. Olson, & M. P. Zanna (Eds.), *Cultural and social behavior: The Ontario Symposium*, Vol. 10 (pp. 77–94). Erlbaum.

Jonason, P. K., & Thomas, A. G. (2022). Being more educated and earning more increases romantic interest: Data from 1.8 M online daters from 24 nations. *Human Nature, 33*(2), 115–131. https://doi.org/10.1007/s12110-022-09422-2

Kennair, L. E. O., Grøntvedt, T. V., Kessler, A. M., Gangestad, S. W., & Bendixen, M. (2023). Mating strategies in sexually egalitarian cultures. In D. M. Buss (Ed.), *The Oxford handbook of human mating* (pp. 262–285). Oxford University Press. https://doi.org/10.1093/oxfordhb/9780197536438.013.4

Locke, K. D., Mastor, K. A., MacDonald, G., et al. (2020). Young adults' partner preferences and parents' in-law preferences across generations, genders, and nations. *European Journal of Social Psychology, 50*(5), 903–920. https://doi.org/10.1002/ejsp.2662

Sprecher, S., & Hatfield, E. (2017). The importance of love as a basis of marriage: Revisiting Kephart (1967). *Journal of Family Issues, 38*, 312–335. https://doi.org/10.1177/0192513X15576197

Walter, K. V., Conroy-Beam, D., Buss, D. M., et al. (2020). Sex differences in mate preferences across 45 countries: A large-scale replication. *Psychological Science, 31*(4), 408–423. https://doi.org/10.1177/0956797620904154

Wood, W., & Eagly, A. H. (2002). A cross-cultural analysis of the behavior of women and men: Implications for the origins of sex differences. *Psychological Bulletin, 128*(5), 699–727. https://doi.org/10.1037/0033-2909.128.5.699

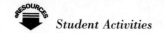

ACTIVITY 7.10
HANDOUT

INTERCULTURAL PARTNERSHIPS

The frequency of intercultural romantic partnerships is increasing rapidly in many parts of the world. Early writing on intercultural relationships focused on pathological motivation for entering into these unions, such as rebelling against one's own culture or even unconscious hatred of one's opposite-sex parent (and thus choosing a partner who does not physically resemble him or her!). We now know that most people enter intercultural relationships for the same reasons most people enter intracultural (same culture) relationships: warmth, love, affection, excitement, caring, intimacy, and solidarity (Jeter, 1982). In fact, people in enduring intercultural partnerships may even have or develop some special skills for dealing with cultural differences (Tili & Barker, 2015). This activity will allow you to explore some of the challenges and adaptations of people in intercultural relationships.

Directions: For this activity, you are to interview someone who is involved in an intercultural dating relationship, marriage, or committed partnership.

Select a respondent. It is up to you to determine what constitutes "intercultural" here. Researchers of intercultural relationships have focused primarily on individuals who differ in terms of race/ethnicity, religion, and nationality. For this activity, however, you may define intercultural more broadly.

Check for time constraints. Reserve at least 15 minutes for the interview.

Obtain informed consent. Explain the purpose of the interview (to explore the challenges of intercultural partnerships) and be sure that your respondent understands that their responses may be discussed in class or included in a written report.

Assure and maintain confidentiality. Be sure you tell your respondent that you will not in any way attach their name to the responses in reporting or discussing the responses to the interview. It is critical that you maintain this confidentiality in order to conduct the interview in an ethical manner.

Conduct the interview. Ask the interview questions in the order in which they appear in this activity. Be sure to take notes in the space provided or on a separate sheet.

Provide feedback to the respondent if appropriate. If you have some general conclusions about intercultural relationships based on discussing or analyzing the interview data with your class, you might convey these conclusions to your respondents.

Interview Questions:

1. In what way is your relationship with your partner an intercultural relationship? Please explain.
2. Please describe one or two cultural differences that have affected your relationship with your partner.
3. Please describe the most useful strategy you have used in dealing with cultural differences in your relationship.
4. Please describe the least useful strategy you have used in dealing with cultural differences in your relationship.
5. As a couple, do you spend more time with individuals from your own cultural background, from your partner's cultural background, both, or neither. Please explain how this has affected your relationship.
6. Have you learned any skills, as a result of being in an intercultural relationship, that would assist you in other types of intercultural situations?

Your Analysis:

1. The list below is adapted from Claude-Hélène Mayer's (2023) and Dugan Romano's (2001) work on common challenges for intercultural couples. Circle any of these challenges that seem to characterize the relationship of your interviewee.

a. values and rituals	g. friends	m. response to stress
b. food and drink	h. finances	n. conflict-handling style
c. politics	i. partner's family	o. response to illness
d. male-female roles	j. social class	p. sexual behavior
e. time	k. religion	q. communication or language
f. place of residence	l. raising children	r. future planning

Please explain how your interviewee has faced the challenges you indicated.

2. Romano (2001) described four types of relationships she identified in research on intercultural marriages, labeled Submission/Immersion, Obliteration, Compromise, and Consensus. After reading the explanations of each of these types, decide which best fits the circumstances of your interviewee.

- *Submission/Immersion*: One partner virtually abandons their own culture while immersing themself in the culture of the other partner.
- *Obliteration*: The couple forms a new third culture identity, maintaining none of the practices of their original cultures and thus eliminating all cultural differences.
- *Compromise*: Each partner gives up some (often important) aspects of their own culture to allow for the other's cultural practices or beliefs.
- *Consensus*: The couple makes an ongoing search for solutions in which neither partner sacrifices aspects of culture essential to their well-being. Partners allow each other to be different without viewing differences as threatening.

Which (if any) of the four types above best characterizes the relationship of your interviewee? Please explain.

3. Discuss what you have learned from this interview about effective and ineffective strategies for intercultural interaction.

Thinking Further:

1. Put an "X" in the blank to indicate which of the following relationships you would consider to be intercultural.

    _____ a. One partner is Swiss; the other is Chilean.
    _____ b. One partner is Buddhist; the other is Christian.
    _____ c. One partner is wealthy; the other is middle class.
    _____ d. One partner is Deaf; the other is hearing.
    _____ e. One partner is a first generation Korean immigrant; the other is a third generation Korean immigrant.
    _____ f. One partner comes from a rural area; the other partner comes from an urban area (of the same country).
    _____ g. One partner is male; the other is female.

2. Based on the items that you indicated above and on your interview data, write a definition of intercultural partnership.

References:

Jeter, K. (1982). Analytic essay: Intercultural and interracial marriage. *Marriage and Family Review*, 5, 105–111. https://doi.org/10.1300/J002 v05n01_10

Mayer, C. (2023). Challenges and coping of couples in intercultural romantic love relationships. *International Review of Psychiatry, 35*(1), 4–15. https://doi.org/10.1080/09540261.2023.2173000

Romano, D. (2001). *Intercultural marriage: Promises and pitfalls* (2nd ed.). Nicholas Brealey.

Tili, T. R., & Barker, G. G. (2015). Communication in intercultural marriages: Managing cultural differences and conflicts. *Southern Communication Journal, 80*(3), 189–210. https://doi.org/10.1080/1041 794X.2015.1023826

–8–

Intergroup Relations

ACTIVITY 8.1
HANDOUT

DISCRIMINATION INCIDENTS

Discrimination has been defined as "treating people differently from others based primarily on membership in a social group" (Kite et al., 2023, p. 18). A large number of psychological studies have focused on the characteristics of people who engage in discriminatory behavior and their cognitive processes. In recent decades, however, there has been increased attention to those experiencing discrimination as well as to causes of discrimination beyond the individual (e.g., Offermann et al., 2014). This activity is designed to encourage you to think about what constitutes discrimination, why it occurs, and the effects on the target of discrimination.

Directions: In the space provided below, please write an account of an incident of discrimination that you experienced, witnessed, or otherwise learned about. Then answer the questions on the following pages.
    Description of your incident:

1. Which of the following likely led to this incident of discrimination?

   • *Interpersonal* factors, such as an individual's attitudes or beliefs
   • *Institutional* factors, such as the policies or practices of an organization (e.g., a business, school, or government) that systematically favors some group(s) of people over others

DOI: 10.4324/9781003356820-21

- *Cultural* factors, such as widely held stereotypes or messages about values that are disseminated through popular culture and mass media Please explain.

2. Who is privileged by this form of discrimination?
3. What were (or might be) the short- and long-term effects of this incident on the target of the discrimination?
4. How could this form of discrimination be prevented?

References:

Kite, M. E., Whitley, B. E., & Wagner, L. S. (2023). *The psychology of prejudice and discrimination* (4th ed.). Routledge.

Offermann, L. R., Basford, T. E., Graebner, R., Jaffer, S., De Graaf, S. B., & Kaminsky, S. E. (2014). See no evil: Color blindness and perceptions of subtle racial discrimination in the workplace. *Cultural Diversity and Ethnic Minority Psychology, 20*(4), 499–507. https://doi.org/10.1037/a0037237

ACTIVITY 8.2
HANDOUT

EXPLORING PRIVILEGE

Although most of us readily acknowledge the discrimination that exists in our society, we often have difficulty recognizing the forms of unearned privilege that are the counterpart of discrimination. For example, imagine that a White woman and a Black woman walk into a clothing store at the same time. A salesperson starts monitoring the behavior of the Black customer. No one monitors the White customer. We can easily understand that the Black customer is the target of discrimination. What may be more difficult to understand is that the White customer is the recipient of an unearned privilege. This activity will help you explore this concept of privilege and understand how you as an individual may or may not be privileged.

Directions: For each of the categories below, read the example and write a second example of the form of privilege specified.

---

1. White skin privilege: [Example: I can be pretty sure that hiring decisions will be based on my skills and experience.]
2. Male privilege: [Example: I can travel on my own with little fear of being harassed.]
3. Heterosexual privilege: [Example: I can freely introduce my significant other to my family or coworkers.]
4. Able-bodied privilege: [Example: I can make plans without having to check whether transportation, parking, buildings, seating, or restrooms are accessible.]
5. Social class privilege: [Example: If I become ill, I can be confident that I will receive the medical treatment I need.]
6. What other forms of privilege exist? Identify one additional form of privilege and write a statement illustrating that form of privilege below.

Thinking Further:

1. Most people have not given much thought to the forms of privilege they experience. Why do you think we are relatively unaware of the privileges we receive?
2. Do you think that once we are aware of one form of privilege we are better able to understand other forms of privilege? Why or why not?
3. How can people become more aware of the ways in which they are privileged?

ACTIVITY 8.3
HANDOUT

INSTITUTIONAL DISCRIMINATION

The term *institutional racism* was first introduced by Stokely Carmichael and Charles V. Hamilton in their 1967 book, *Black Power*. They used this term to distinguish between the racist behavior of *individuals* and the policies and practices of *institutions* that perpetuate racism. Institutional discrimination is not limited to issues of race but includes the systematic perpetuation of other forms of inequality as well. This activity explores the concept of institutional discrimination; that is, policies or practices of organizations that *systematically* privilege members of some groups and discriminate against members of other groups.

Directions: For each of the policies below, determine whether it is a form of institutional discrimination. If you find it is, then answer the additional questions following each policy.

1. In many states in the U.S., people are required to show a government issued identification card in order to vote. Obtaining this card may require waiting in line at a department of motor vehicles or other government office, presenting proof of residency and a form of identification such as a birth certificate, and often paying a fee.
   a. This is institutional discrimination: Yes _____ No _____
   b. Against which groups, if any, might this policy discriminate?
   c. What is the purpose of this policy?
   d. If this purpose is a valid one, how else might it be achieved?
2. Children of alumni receive preference for admission into some colleges and universities.
   a. This is institutional discrimination: Yes _____ No _____
   b. Against which groups, if any, might this policy discriminate?
   c. What is the purpose of this policy?
   d. If this purpose is a valid one, how else might it be achieved?
3. As part of their marketing strategy, some retail companies seek people with a specific "look" to staff their stores.
   a. This is institutional discrimination: Yes _____ No _____
   b. Against which groups, if any, might this policy discriminate?
   c. What is the purpose of this policy?
   d. If this purpose is a valid one, how else might it be achieved?
4. In many states in the U.S., persons accused of a crime who cannot post bail remain in jail while awaiting trial.
   a. This is institutional discrimination: Yes _____ No _____
   b. Against which groups, if any, might this policy discriminate?
   c. What is the purpose of this policy?
   d. If this purpose is a valid one, how else might it be achieved?
5. Many corporations fill position openings "in-house" rather than advertise.
   a. This is institutional discrimination: Yes _____ No _____
   b. Against which groups, if any, might this policy discriminate?
   c. What is the purpose of this policy?
   d. If this purpose is a valid one, how else might it be achieved?
6. White actors are frequently chosen to play the part of People of Color.
   a. This is institutional discrimination: Yes _____ No _____
   b. Against which groups, if any, might this policy discriminate?
   c. What is the purpose of this policy?
   d. If this purpose is a valid one, how else might it be achieved?

Reference:

Carmichael, S., & Hamilton, C. V. (1967). *Black power: The politics of liberation in America*. Vintage Books.

ACTIVITY 8.4
HANDOUT

GEOGRAPHIC KNOWLEDGE AND INTERGROUP ATTITUDES

Several studies have found a link between geographical knowledge and attitudes about countries other than one's own. For example, a study conducted by Kyle Dropp for the *New York Times* found that U.S. Americans were more likely to support a diplomatic solution to conflicts with North Korea over military action if they could find North Korea on a map (only 36% could; Quealy, 2017). Fabio Lorenzi-Cioldi and colleagues (2011) had participants from Belgium, Ivory Coast, Italy, Kosovo, Portugal, and Switzerland draw the borders between their own and neighboring countries on boundary-free maps. They found that in general the tendency to underestimate the size of another country was associated with more negative attitudes toward that country.

Directions: For this activity, you will do your own informal test of the connection between geographic knowledge and intergroup attitudes. First, identify a current issue involving the relationship between your own and another country. Then write two questions to gauge attitudes about the issue and those involved. Finally, find an outline map – one that shows borders without labeling the countries (there are many available for classroom use online). Ask ten people to respond to your questions and to identify the country you have chosen on your outline map. Be sure to write down their responses and to use a clean copy of the outline map for each participant so that they won't be influenced by each other's responses. Examples below are based on the methods used in the studies conducted by Dropp and by Lorenzi-Cioldi and colleagues.

1. Briefly describe the issue and countries involved that you have chosen as your focus (for example, tensions between the U.S. and North Korea following a series of long-range missile tests by North Korea and an exchange of threats between the North Korean leader and a former U.S. President).

---

2. Below, list the questions you developed to assess intergroup attitudes (for example, "Do you think the U.S. should conduct airstrikes against North Korea?" and "Do you think most North Koreans are good people?").

3. Paste your outline map and instructions below (for example, "Make a mark on the map below to indicate the location of North Korea").

Did you find any relationship between the participants' ability to identify the country on a map and their answers to the two questions? (Note that this was an informal rather than scientific study, so we can't be certain that other factors did not influence the responses.) Please discuss your findings below.

Thinking Further:

1. How might we explain any relationship between attitudes about a country and the ability to locate it on a map?

2. In Dropp's study, those who could find North Korea on a map tended to be more educated, older (perhaps alive during the Korean War), know someone of Korean ancestry, or have traveled internationally. What factors might predict geographical knowledge in your survey?

3. Surveys conducted by the National Geographic Society show great variations in geographic literacy across countries, with students in the U.S. scoring particularly poorly (e.g., Council on Foreign Relations/ National Geographic Society, 2016, 2019). Other than differences in school curricula, such as requirements for geography coursework, what might contribute to these differences in geographic literacy?

4. What are some ideas for improving geographic literacy in young people today?

References:

Council on Foreign Relations/National Geographic Society. (2016). *What college-aged students know about the world: A survey on global literacy*. Author.

Council on Foreign Relations/National Geographic Society. (2019). *U.S. adults' knowledge about the world*. Author.

Lorenzi-Cioldi, F., Chatard, A., Marques, J. M., Selimbegovic, L., Konan, P., & Faniko, K. (2011). What do drawings reveal about people's attitudes towards countries and their citizens? *Social Psychology, 42*(3), 231–240. https://doi.org/10.1027/1864-9335/a000067

Quealy, K. (2017). If Americans can find North Korea on a map, they're more likely to prefer diplomacy. *New York Times*, July 5.

ACTIVITY 8.5
HANDOUT

INTERNALIZED OPPRESSION

One possible consequence of being the target of discrimination is *internalized oppression*. This occurs when people come to view and treat themselves and other members of their group in the same ways that they have been stereotyped or mistreated as targets. According to E. J. R. David and colleagues (2019), the field of psychology has neglected internalized oppression as an area of research. What we do know is that although internalized oppression does not always occur on a conscious level it can have serious physical and mental health consequences (Gale et al., 2020). For example, internalized racism is associated with glucose intolerance (a precursor to diabetes) among Afro-Caribbean women (Butler et al., 2002) and is a predictor of substance abuse among LGBTQIA+ individuals (Huynh et al., 2022). Understanding and addressing the societal sources of internalized oppression is therefore critical

---

for mental health professionals as well as for those involved in social justice education and advocacy (Gale et al., 2020). The aim of this activity is to explore the concept of internalized oppression.

Directions: Read the following list of behaviors and decide for each whether it indicates internalized oppression. Please explain your answer in the space provided.

1. Passing as a member of an ethnic/racial group other than one's own.
2. Using solutions or creams to lighten one's skin color.
3. Undergoing surgery to alter facial features associated with one's ethnic/racial group.
4. Telling jokes about one's own ethnic group, sexual identity, or disability status.
5. Undergoing "accent softening" training in which one works to attain an accent associated with a more upper-class manner of speaking.

Thinking Further:

It is important to recognize that internalized oppression occurs as a result of broader societal inequities. Choose one example of internalized oppression and discuss the possible social conditions contributing to that behavior.

References:

Butler, C., Tull, E. S., Chambers, E. C., & Taylor, J. (2002). Internalized racism, body fat distribution, and abnormal fasting glucose among African-Caribbean women in Dominica, West Indies. *Journal of the National Medical Association, 94,* 143–148.

David, E. J. R., Schroeder, T. M., & Fernandez, J. (2019). Internalized racism: A systematic review of the psychological literature on racism's most insidious consequence. *Journal of Social Issues, 75*(4), 1057–1086. https://doi.org/10.1111/josi.12350

Gale, M. M., Pieterse, A. L., Lee, D. L., Huynh, K., Powell, S., & Kirkinis, K. (2020). A meta-analysis of the relationship between internalized racial oppression and health-related outcomes. *The Counseling Psychologist, 48*(4), 498–525. https://doi.org/10.1177/0011000020904454

Huynh, K. D., Murgo, M. A. J., & Lee, D. L. (2022). Internalized heterosexism and substance use: A meta-analysis. *The Counseling Psychologist, 50*(5), 674–707. https://doi.org/10.1177/00110000221086910

ACTIVITY 8.6
HANDOUT

COGNITION AND STEREOTYPE FORMATION

Research in cognitive psychology indicates that stereotyping is in part a result of the way humans process information (see, for example, Hinton, 2016). The way we categorize, memorize, and explain events is generally adaptive, but under some circumstances can lead us to develop and maintain stereotypes. This activity will demonstrate some of the cognitive processes involved in stereotyping.

Directions: You will need to request the assistance of four volunteers for this activity. Each of the participants will listen to a slightly different description. Read the descriptions below to the participant indicated. The participant should then complete the appropriate questionnaire. You will note that the descriptions vary in terms of the age and gender of the stimulus person. Once you have collected responses from all four participants, answer the questions that follow.

Read to Participant A: We are asking for volunteers as part of a class project on the processes involved in forming mental imagery. Please listen to the following description and focus on the images that form in response. You will then be asked to complete a brief questionnaire.

Michelle is 27 years old. She is taking courses at her local community college and working part-time. A few years ago, she moved from a more urban area to an apartment complex in the suburbs. She lives alone, except for a pet. She is in good health and tries to get some exercise several times a week. She has made friends with one of her neighbors with whom she occasionally cooks a meal. She has several hobbies and enjoys the outdoors.

Read to Participant B: We are asking for volunteers as part of a class project on the processes involved in forming mental imagery. Please listen to the following description and focus on the images that form in response. You will then be asked to complete a brief questionnaire.

Michelle is 67 years old. She is taking courses at her local community college and working part-time. A few years ago, she moved from a more urban area to an apartment complex in the suburbs. She lives alone, except for a pet. She is in good health and tries to get some exercise several times a week. She has made friends with one of her neighbors with whom she occasionally cooks a meal. She has several hobbies and enjoys the outdoors.

Read to Participant C: We are asking for volunteers as part of a class project on the processes involved in forming mental imagery. Please listen to the following description and focus on the images that form in response. You will then be asked to complete a brief questionnaire.

Marcus is 27 years old. He is taking courses at his local community college and working part-time. A few years ago, he moved from a more urban area to an apartment complex in the suburbs. He lives alone, except for a pet. He is in good health and tries to get some exercise several times a week. He has made friends with one of his neighbors with whom he occasionally cooks a meal. He has several hobbies and enjoys the outdoors.

Read to Participant D: We are asking for volunteers as part of a class project on the processes involved in forming mental imagery. Please listen to the following description and focus on the images that form in response. You will then be asked to complete a brief questionnaire.

Marcus is 67 years old. He is taking courses at his local community college and working part-time. A few years ago, he moved from a more urban area to an apartment complex in the suburbs. He lives alone, except for a pet. He is in good health and tries to get some exercise several times a week. He has made friends with one of his neighbors with whom he occasionally cooks a meal. He has several hobbies and enjoys the outdoors.

Participant A:

Please think about the person who was just described to you for a moment. In the space below, write down everything you can remember about this person. When you have finished writing down what you remember, please answer the questions on the next page.

Based on your image of Michelle, please answer the following questions. If you do not have enough information to answer a particular question, **draw on your image** of Michelle to answer as best you can.

1. How old is Michelle?
2. What kind of courses was Michelle taking?
3. What kind of work did Michelle do?
4. Why did Michelle move to the suburbs?
5. What kind of pet did she have?
6. How is her health?
7. What kind of exercise does she do?
8. Why does she occasionally cook with her neighbor?

9. What do you think she cooks?
10. What are her hobbies?
11. What does she enjoy doing outdoors?
12. Do you think Michelle is someone you would enjoy meeting? Why or why not?

Participant B:

Please think about the person who was just described to you for a moment. In the space below, write down everything you can remember about this person. When you have finished writing down what you remember, please answer the questions on the next page.

Based on your image of Michelle, please answer the following questions. If you do not have enough information to answer a particular question, **draw on your image** of Michelle to answer as best you can.

1. How old is Michelle?
2. What kind of courses was Michelle taking?
3. What kind of work did Michelle do?
4. Why did Michelle move to the suburbs?
5. What kind of pet did she have?
6. How is her health?
7. What kind of exercise does she do?
8. Why does she occasionally cook with her neighbor?
9. What do you think she cooks?
10. What are her hobbies?
11. What does she enjoy doing outdoors?
12. Do you think Michelle is someone you would enjoy meeting? Why or why not?

Participant C:

Please think about the person who was just described to you for a moment. In the space below, write down everything you can remember about this person. When you have finished writing down what you remember, please answer the questions on the next page.

Based on your image of Marcus, please answer the following questions. If you do not have enough information to answer a particular question, **draw on your image** of Marcus to answer as best you can.

1. How old is Marcus?
2. What kind of courses was Marcus taking?
3. What kind of work did Marcus do?
4. Why did Marcus move to the suburbs?
5. What kind of pet did he have?
6. How is his health?
7. What kind of exercise does he do?
8. Why does he occasionally cook with his neighbor?
9. What do you think he cooks?
10. What are his hobbies?
11. What does he enjoy doing outdoors?
12. Do you think Marcus is someone you would enjoy meeting? Why or why not?

Participant D:

Please think about the person who was just described to you for a moment. In the space below, write down everything you can remember about this person. When you have finished writing down what you remember, please answer the questions on the next page.

Based on your image of Marcus, please answer the following questions. If you do not have enough information to answer a particular question, **draw on your image** of Marcus to answer as best you can.

1. How old is Marcus?
2. What kind of courses was Marcus taking?
3. What kind of work did Marcus do?
4. Why did Marcus move to the suburbs?
5. What kind of pet did he have?
6. How is his health?
7. What kind of exercise does he do?
8. Why does he occasionally cook with his neighbor?
9. What do you think he cooks?
10. What are his hobbies?
11. What does he enjoy doing outdoors?
12. Do you think Marcus is someone you would enjoy meeting? Why or why not?

Examine the responses of the four participants. In what ways did the shift in age or gender affect the images generated?

Thinking Further:

1. Studies of the role of cognition in the stereotyping process generally indicate the following:
   - We easily and readily place others into categories.
   - We tend to pay attention to and remember information consistent with our stereotypes.
   - We fill in gaps in memory with information that fits our stereotypes.
   - We tend to make judgments about causes of behavior that are stereotype-consistent.

      Discuss the extent to which the data you collected indicated any of these cognitive processes.
2. Discuss the possible sources of any stereotypes found in your data.
3. Discuss the implications of the existence of such stereotypes.

Reference:

Hinton, P. R. (2016). *The perception of people: Integrating cognition and culture*. Routledge.

ACTIVITY 8.7
HANDOUT

THE CONTENT OF STEREOTYPES

We know that stereotypes occur because of the human tendency to use categories to make sense of our world, but why is it that stereotypes of various groups differ from each other? For example, why is one group stereotyped as frail and helpless whereas another is stereotyped as violent and threatening? The stereotype content model developed by Susan Fiske and colleagues (2002) can help us understand why stereotypes vary and why they often include a combination of positive and negative attributes. These authors suggested that when we encounter someone from an outgroup, we ask ourselves two questions: (1) Does this person intend to harm me? (warmth) and (2) Is this person capable of harming me? (competence). These two dimensions, warmth and competence, determine the nature of specific stereotypes. For example, when the stereotype content model is applied to social class, people with high socioeconomic status are perceived as competent but cold, whereas people with low socioeconomic status are viewed as less competent but warmer (Durante et al., 2017). Differences in stereotype

---

content are important because they help to explain why a particular stereotype is associated with a specific type of treatment. This model can also guide strategies for reducing stereotyping. The purpose of this activity is to familiarize you with the stereotype content model and the implications of stereotype content for discriminatory treatment and stereotype reduction.

Directions: First identify a specific social group that you know to be stereotyped, then plot the stereotype content on the dimensions below. If you are unsure as to how that group is stereotyped, you might ask for others' opinions or find research on that social group.

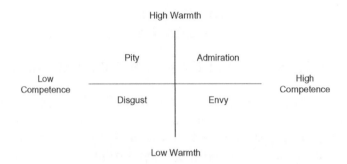

1. Based on the stereotype content model, what kind of treatment might you expect members of that group to experience?
2. Based on the stereotype content model, what might be some strategies for reducing this particular stereotype?

Thinking Further:

Susan Fiske (2017) observed that stereotype content (in terms of warmth and competence) is more consistent across cultures for sex, age, and social class than for race, ethnicity, and religion. Why might this occur?

References:

Durante, F., Tablante, C. B., & Fiske, S. T. (2017). Poor but warm, rich but cold (and competent): Social classes in the stereotype content model. *Journal of Social Issues, 73*(1), 138–157. https://doi.org/10.1111/josi.12208

Fiske, S. T. (2017). Prejudices in cultural contexts: Shared stereotypes (gender, age) versus variable stereotypes (race, ethnicity, religion). *Perspectives on Psychological Science*, *12*(5), 791–799. https://doi.org/10.1177/1745691617708204

Fiske, S. T., Cuddy, A. J. C., Glick, P., & Xu, J. (2002). A model of (often mixed) stereotype content: Competence and warmth respectively follow from perceived status and competition. *Journal of Personality and Social Psychology*, *82*(6), 878–902. https://doi.org/10.1037/0022-3514.82.6.878

ACTIVITY 8.8
HANDOUT

CULTURE AND THE STIGMA OF MENTAL ILLNESS

According to the World Health Organization (2022), approximately one in eight individuals worldwide lives with a mental illness. Despite the prevalence of mental illness, people dealing with these challenges often experience some form of stigmatization, such as labeling, separation, stereotyping, status loss, or other discriminatory actions (Hatzenbuehler et al., 2013). There are many harmful consequences to stigmatization, including increased psychiatric symptoms and a reduced likelihood of accessing mental health services (Oexle et al., 2018). The goal of this activity is to better understand this phenomenon by exploring cultural similarities and differences in mental health stigmatization.

In 1984, Edward E. Jones and colleagues proposed a general model of stigma that continues to be the basis of much domestic and cross-cultural research. This model details six dimensions related to the nature and severity of stigmatization, including:

- *Origin* – What is the source of the stigma and is it perceived to be under the individual's control?
- *Disruptiveness* – Does the condition impede social interaction or successful functioning in society?
- *Peril* – Is the condition viewed as potentially dangerous to others?
- *Stability* – Is the condition long-lasting rather than temporary?
- *Aesthetics* – Does the condition involve an unpleasant or devalued appearance?
- *Concealability* – Is the stigmatized identity visible to others?

In general, stigmatization is more severe when it is perceived as controllable, disruptive, perilous, stable, and not aesthetically appealing. The relationship between concealability and the severity of stigma is somewhat more complex. Reactions from others may be more severe for a discovered, concealable condition than for one that is readily visible. In addition, concealing a condition is often associated with greater anxiety and isolation for the stigmatized individual (Pachankis, 2007).

Directions: Using journal articles and other scholarly sources, read about mental illness stigma in a particular culture, country, or region, and then answer the questions below.

1. In the space below, provide the full reference for each of your sources (see the references in this book for examples of APA format).
2. Which of Jones et al.'s five dimensions of stigma above best address the form of mental illness stigma you investigated? Please explain.
3. What dimensions would you add to the Jones et al. model to describe the culture-specific form of mental illness stigma you investigated? Please explain.

References:

Hatzenbuehler, M. L., Phelan, J. C., & Link, B. G. (2013). Stigma as a fundamental cause of population health inequalities. *American Journal of Public Health*, *103*(5), 813–821. https://doi.org/10.2105/ajph.2012.301069

Jones, E. E., Farina, A., Hastorf, A. H., Markus, H. R., Miller, T., & Scott, R. (1984). *Social stigma: The psychology of marked relationships*. W. H. Freeman.

Oexle, N., Müller, M., Kawohl, W., Xu, Z., Viering, S., Wyss, C., Vetter, S., & Rüsch, N. (2018). Self-stigma as a barrier to recovery: A longitudinal study. *European Archives of Psychiatry and Clinical Neuroscience*, *268*(2), 209–212. https://doi.org/10.1007/s00406-017-0773-2

Pachankis, J. E. (2007). The psychological implications of concealing a stigma: A cognitive-affective-behavioral model. *Psychological Bulletin*, *133*(2), 328–345. https://doi.org/10.1037/0033-2909.133.2.328

World Health Organization. (2022). *World mental health report: Transforming mental health for all*. www.who.int/publications/i/item/9789240049338

ACTIVITY 8.9
HANDOUT

UNDERSTANDING ANTI-IMMIGRANT PREJUDICE

The number of refugees and other migrants across the globe has reached its highest level since World War II. The United Nations High Commission for Refugees (UNHCR, 2022) reported 108.4 million forcibly displaced people worldwide, 29.4 million of whom are refugees. Refugees are an internationally protected category of individuals fleeing armed conflict or persecution. Other people migrate to escape dangerous living circumstances, economic hardship, the aftermath of natural disasters, or the effects of climate change (World Bank, 2016). There are many challenges for displaced individuals seeking to resettle, including a lack of resources, particularly since the majority of displaced individuals are hosted in low- and middle-income nations. However, one of the biggest barriers is prejudice on the part of members of host nations. Anti-immigrant prejudice seems to be stronger among people who have greater exposure to mass media (White et al., 2012) and may also be influenced by language. For example, the term "illegal aliens" was found to evoke greater prejudice than "undocumented workers" (Pearson, 2010). This activity will help you to become familiar with the causes of anti-immigrant prejudice and possible strategies for prejudice reduction.

One model that has been useful in predicting anti-immigrant and anti-refugee attitudes in diverse nations and contexts is Walter and Cookie Stephan's (2000) Integrated Threat Model (e.g., Esses et al., 2017; Ramsay & Pang, 2017). According to this model, the likelihood of prejudice increases when these components are perceived to be present:

- *Realistic threats* to one's well-being, economic power, or political power
- *Symbolic threats* to one's values, beliefs, or worldview
- *Intergroup anxiety* about interacting with members of the outgroup
- Negative stereotypes

Directions: Citing specific news and social media sources, respond to the following questions to apply the Integrated Threat Model to anti-immigrant attitudes:

1. In your country, have immigrants been portrayed as a realistic threat? Give an example to support your answer.
2. In your country, have immigrants been portrayed as a symbolic threat? Give an example to support your answer.

---

3. Do you think nonimmigrant individuals in your country feel anxious about interacting with immigrants? Please explain.
4. In your country, have immigrants been portrayed using negative stereotypes? Give an example to support your answer.

Thinking Further:

Given what you have learned about predictors of anti-immigrant prejudice, describe one action that could be taken to reduce this form of bias.

References:

Esses, V. M., Hamilton, L. K., & Gaucher, D. (2017). The global refugee crisis: Empirical evidence and policy implications for improving public attitudes and facilitating refugee resettlement. *Social Issues and Policy Review, 11*(1), 78–123. https://doi.org/10.1111/sipr.12028

Pearson, M. R. (2010). How "undocumented workers" and "illegal aliens" affect prejudice toward Mexican immigrants. *Social Influence, 5*(2), 118–132. https://doi.org/10.1080/15534511003593679

Ramsay, J. E., & Pang, J. S. (2017). Anti-immigrant prejudice in rising East Asia: A stereotype content and integrated threat analysis. *Political Psychology, 38*(2), 227–244. https://doi.org/10.1111/pops.12312

Stephan, W. G., & Stephan, C. W. (2000). An integrated threat theory of prejudice. In S. Oskamp (Ed.), *The Claremont Symposium on Applied Social Psychology: Reducing prejudice and discrimination* (pp. 23–45). Lawrence Erlbaum.

UNHCR. (2022). *Global trends: Forced displacement in 2022.* www.unhcr.org/global-trends-report-2022

White, C., Duck, J. M., & Newcombe, P. A. (2012). The impact of media reliance on the role of perceived threat in predicting tolerance of Muslim cultural practice. *Journal of Applied Social Psychology, 42*(12), 3051–3082. https://doi.org/10.1111/j.1559-1816.2012.00973.x

World Bank. (2016). *Forcibly displaced: Toward a development approach supporting refugees, the internally displaced, and their hosts.* https://openknowledge.worldbank.org/entities/publication/a4bdb82b-01e7-5e8f-8b75-6dc1591d9da1

ACTIVITY 8.10
HANDOUT

THE CONTACT HYPOTHESIS

Many prejudice-reduction interventions are based on the idea that if people from different groups are brought together they will learn about each other, come to see their commonalities, and prejudice will diminish. Unfortunately, studies indicate that contact does not always result in decreased prejudice and under some conditions may actually worsen intergroup relations. Gordon Allport's (1954) *contact hypothesis* outlined the specific conditions required for prejudice reduction through intergroup contact. This activity will familiarize you with the contact conditions associated with an increase and decrease in prejudice (e.g., Pettigrew & Tropp, 2006).

Contact tends to *reduce* prejudice when:

- The contact is between groups that are roughly equal in social, economic, or task-related status.
- People in authority and/or the general social climate are in favor of and promote contact.
- The contact is intimate and informal enough to allow participants to get to know each other as individuals.
- Contact is pleasant or rewarding.
- Contact involves cooperation and interdependence.
- Superordinate goals are more important than individual goals.

Contact tends to *increase* prejudice when:

- Contact reinforces stereotypes.
- Contact produces competition between groups.
- Contact emphasizes boundaries between groups.
- Contact is unpleasant, involuntary, frustrating, or tense.
- Contact is between people of unequal status.

Interestingly, intergroup contact has been found to reduce prejudice even when it is virtual (online), vicarious (observing other ingroup and outgroup members interact), extended (learning that an ingroup member is friends with an outgroup member), or even imagined (visualizing oneself in intergroup interactions; Tropp et al., 2022). For example, Simina Oľhová and colleagues (2023) used passages from Harry Potter books to demonstrate positive intergroup contact and reduce anti-Roma prejudice in Slovak elementary schools.

Directions: Read the following scenario and answer the questions below based on the information provided about the contact hypothesis. This scenario illustrates the research finding that in everyday settings, there is often little intergroup contact *within* diverse populations (McKeown & Dixon, 2017).

Scenario:

Teachers in a high school in Northern Italy are dealing with a dilemma and have contacted you – an educational consultant – for advice. Two main groups make up the student body of this high school, native Italians and recent immigrants (from numerous countries, primarily in South Asia and North Africa). There is minimal interaction and sometimes outright hostility between the native Italians and immigrant groups. To make the situation more challenging, this is occurring at a time when there are some strong anti-immigrant attitudes in the surrounding community as well. Based on what you have learned about the contact hypothesis, describe the *specific actions* you would recommend to reduce prejudice in the situation described.

References:

Allport, G. W. (1954). *The nature of prejudice*. Perseus Books.

McKeown, S., & Dixon, J. (2017). The "contact hypothesis": Critical reflections and future directions. *Social and Personality Psychology Compass, 11*(1). https://doi.org/10.1111/spc3.12295

Oľhová, S., Lášticová, B., Kundrát, J., & Kanovský, M. (2023). Using fiction to improve intergroup attitudes: Testing indirect contact interventions in a school context. *Social Psychology of Education, 26*(1), 81–105. https://doi.org/10.1007/s11218-022-09708-4

Pettigrew, T. F., & Tropp, L. R. (2006). A meta-analytic test of intergroup contact theory. *Journal of Personality and Social Psychology, 90*, 751–783. https://doi.org/10.1037/0022-3514.90.5.751

Tropp, L. R., White, F., Rucinski, C. L., & Tredoux, C. (2022). Intergroup contact and prejudice reduction: Prospects and challenges in changing youth attitudes. *Review of General Psychology, 26*(3), 342–360. https://doi.org/10.1177/10892680211046517

(Space for responses in these handouts has been reduced. Please see www. routledge.com/9781032394336 for fillable versions of these handouts.)

–9–

Intercultural Interaction

ACTIVITY 9.1
HANDOUT

CULTURE MIXING

Although culture mixing has existed for centuries, it is a relatively new topic for cross-cultural researchers. Culture mixing refers to "the coexistence of representative symbols of different cultures in the same space at the same time" (Hao et al., 2016, p. 1257). There are many examples of culture mixing in food, such as the sushi burrito, ramen noodle burger, and poutine pizza. Researchers have created their own culturally mixed images, including the McDonald's Golden Arches superimposed on the Great Wall of China (Yang et al., 2016), a traditional Chinese paper-cutting in the shape of Mickey Mouse, and a Chinese porcelain plate with a picture of an American eagle in the middle (Cui et al., 2016). Several studies have focused on identifying factors that shape responses to culture mixing since this phenomenon is expected to increase in the coming years along with globalization and more frequent intercultural contact. The purpose of this activity is to explore the nature of and responses to culture mixing.

Directions: For this activity, you will first create an example of culture mixing and then gather reactions to your example from at least three people. Draw or describe your example of culture mixing in the space provided below or submit a photo of your example with this assignment.

 DOI: 10.4324/9781003356820-22

Example of Culture Mixing:

Participant A:

Use the rating scale below to indicate your feelings about this image:

Very Negative								Very Positive
1	2	3	4	5	6	7	8	9

Please explain:

Participant B:

Use the rating scale below to indicate your feelings about this image:

Very Negative								Very Positive
1	2	3	4	5	6	7	8	9

Please explain:

Participant C:

Use the rating scale below to indicate your feelings about this image:

Very Negative								Very Positive
1	2	3	4	5	6	7	8	9

Please explain:

1. What aspects of the image could influence reactions to culture mixing?
2. What aspects of the respondent's personality could influence reactions to culture mixing?

Thinking Further:

What might be the effect of repeated exposure to culture mixing?

References:

Cui, N., Xu, L., Wang, T., Qualls, W., & Hu, Y. (2016). How does framing strategy affect evaluation of culturally mixed products? The self–other asymmetry effect. *Journal of Cross-Cultural Psychology*, *47*(10), 1307–1320. https://doi.org/10.1177/0022022116670513

Hao, J., Li, D., Peng, L., Peng, S., & Torelli, C. J. (2016). Advancing our understanding of culture mixing. *Journal of Cross-Cultural Psychology*, *47*(10), 1257–1267. https://doi.org/10.1177/0022022116670514

Yang, D. Y.-J., Chen, X., Xu, J., Preston, J. L., & Chiu, C.-y. (2016). Cultural symbolism and spatial separation: Some ways to deactivate exclusionary responses to culture mixing. *Journal of Cross-Cultural Psychology*, *47*(10), 1286–1293. https://doi.org/10.1177/0022022116665169

ACTIVITY 9.2
HANDOUT

NONVERBAL COMMUNICATION

Is it possible to be in the same room as another person and not communicate? Even if we do not speak, we communicate through our facial expressions and gestures. Even if we do not move, we communicate through our posture, use of space, and appearance. Nonverbal behaviors serve several functions including complementing or accenting a verbal message, contradicting verbal cues, substituting for a verbal message, and regulating the flow of conversation (Ekman & Friesen, 1969). The ability to comprehend nonverbal communication is likely an important component of intercultural competence (Molinsky et al., 2005).

Some aspects of nonverbal behavior appear to be universal. For example, Caroline Keating and E. Gregory Keating (cited in Keating, 1994) found that in a variety of cultures tested, interpersonal distances (called *proxemics*) were closer between people who were acquainted than among strangers. In addition, the experience of crowding appears to be equally stressful across ethnocultural groups studied (Evans, 2000). On the other hand, there are also significant cultural differences in nonverbal behavior. Although it may be universal that acquaintances prefer smaller interpersonal distances than strangers and that people find over-crowding stressful, the preferred distance between people varies quite dramatically across cultures. According to Edward T. Hall (1966), members of low-contact cultures, such as Japan, tend to prefer significantly larger interpersonal distances than U.S. Americans and Canadians, who in turn prefer larger interpersonal distances than people in high-contact cultures such as many Arabs, Greeks, and Southern Italians. Individuals dealing with someone from a lower contact culture than themselves may feel rejected. Individuals dealing with someone from a higher contact culture than themselves may feel intruded upon.

Often when we think of nonverbal communication, we think of gestures that correspond to specific meanings (called *emblems*). Although the existence of emblems appears to be universal, as any traveler knows there are many cross-cultural differences in meaning. For example, the thumbs-up gesture indicates approval in some countries. But in several areas of West Africa and the Middle East it is equivalent to the use of the middle finger in many other parts of the world. Furthermore, the meaning of emblems changes over time and context. For example, at the time of this writing, the thumbs-up emoji is increasingly used to indicate sarcasm or hostility. The purpose of this activity is to better understand the function of nonverbal communication and the ways it differs from verbal communication.

Directions: In the space provided below, list all of the words or meanings that you know how to express nonverbally. Then answer the questions that follow.

1. Look back to your list of nonverbal expressions. In the space provided below, write/draw a dictionary entry for one of these expressions. It may be helpful to refer to an established dictionary for ideas about the format and content of your entry.
2. Think about the nonverbal expressions you listed above. How is nonverbal communication similar to verbal communication?
3. How is nonverbal communication different from verbal communication?
4. Do you think the potential for intercultural misunderstanding is greater in verbal or nonverbal communication? Please explain.

Thinking Further:

How could you go about learning how to communicate nonverbally in an unfamiliar culture?

References:

Ekman, P., & Friesen, W. (1969). The repertoire of nonverbal behavior: Categories, origins, usage, and coding. *Semiotica, 1,* 49–98. https://doi.org/10.1515/semi.1969.1.1.49

Evans, G. W. (2000). Cross-cultural differences in tolerance for crowding: Fact or fiction? *Journal of Personality and Social Psychology, 79*, 204–210. https://doi.org/10.1037/0022-3514.79.2.204

Hall, E. T. (1966). *The silent language*. Doubleday.

Keating, C. F. (1994). World without words: Messages from face and body. In W. J. Lonner, & R. S. Malpass (Eds.), *Psychology and culture* (pp. 175–182). Allyn & Bacon.

Molinsky, A. L., Krabberhoft, M. A., Ambady, N., & Choi, S. Y. (2005). Cracking the nonverbal code: Intercultural competence and gesture recognition across cultures. *Journal of Cross-Cultural Psychology, 36*, 380–395. https://dx.doi.org/10.1177/0022022104273658

ACTIVITY 9.3
HANDOUT

DISNEYLAND PARIS: AN INTERCULTURAL CONFLICT

Cases where individuals or organizations experience an intercultural misunderstanding are often used as teaching tools to increase intercultural competence. In this activity, you will analyze the case of Disneyland Paris and produce a training talk that identifies Disney's intercultural errors and discusses how they might have been avoided.

Directions: Read the brief description of the establishment of Disneyland Paris below. Next, identify areas of intercultural misunderstanding. Finally, in a page or two, write a script for a training talk that could have been given to Disney representatives to prevent the intercultural misunderstandings that occurred in the establishment of Disneyland Paris. You may need to do some research to identify the cultural differences underlying these misunderstandings.

The Disneyland Paris Case:

After a history of success opening theme parks in California, Florida, and Tokyo, the Walt Disney Company developed a plan to open a fourth location in Europe. Representatives from 200 locations bid to house the new park. However, Disney chose Marne-la-Vallée, France, 32 km (20 miles) east of Paris, due to its central location, with large populations living within a few hours' drive or flight. Reports indicate that early negotiations with the French government did not go smoothly and that there was opposition and protests

---

from French citizens who viewed the park as a threat to French culture. However, Disney pushed ahead with their plans. Their strategy was to implement many of the same policies and practices that had been successful in the U.S. and Japan. Euro-Disney (later renamed Disneyland Paris) opened in 1992 and by the end of the first year they were losing nearly one million U.S. dollars per day due to fewer visitors and shorter stays than expected.

Here are some of the *invalid assumptions* on which the Disney Company operated:

1. Visitors would spend four or five days in the park on vacation rather than a day or two.
2. Fewer visitors would come on Mondays and more would come on Fridays.
3. Visitors would view Disneyland as an acceptable activity for cold or rainy days.
4. Most visitors would arrive in cars.
5. Families would take children out of school to go to Disneyland.
6. Visitors would be enthusiastic about American culture.
7. Alcohol must be banned from the park to prevent behaviors associated with intoxication.
8. Dogs must not be allowed in restaurants.
9. Visitors would eat at various times, with many visitors snacking as they walked throughout the park.
10. The restrictions on the behavior of cast members (staff) that were implemented in the U.S. and Japan would also be appropriate in France. These included a dress code specifying acceptable clothing, hair length and dye colors, facial hair, make-up, and nail polish. Cast members were also prohibited from smoking, eating, or drinking in public and were expected to smile and be consistently polite when interacting with visitors.

List of Intercultural Misunderstandings:

Your Training Talk Script:

Sources:

Aupperle, K., & Karimalis, G. (2001). Using metaphors to facilitate cooperation and resolve conflict: Examining the case of Disneyland Paris. *Journal of Change Management, 2*(1), 23–32. https://doi.org/10.1080/714 042489

King, T. R. (1993). Euro Disney 3rd quarter loss to spur study of woes by U.S. concern. *Wall Street Journal*, July 9, A3.

Newell, L. A. (2013). Mickey goes to France: A case study of the Euro Disneyland negotiations. *Cardozo Journal of Conflict Resolution, 15*, 193–221.

Packman, H., & Casmir, F. L. (1999). Learning from the Euro Disney experience. *Gazette, 61*, 473–489. https://doi.org/10.1177/0016549299061 006002

Spencer, E. P. (1995). Educator insights: Euro Disney – What happened? What next? *Journal of International Marketing, 3*(3), 103–114. https://doi.org/ 10.1177/1069031X9500300308

ACTIVITY 9.4
HANDOUT

CLOCK TIME AND EVENT TIME

Robert Levine (1997), social psychologist and author of *A Geography of Time*, suggested that one of the most profound adjustments a sojourner must make is to cultural differences in the pace of life. These differences have also been noted by individuals who move between urban and rural settings, work environments, ethnic communities, and even academic disciplines. Research indicates that understanding cultural differences in time perception may be key to successful negotiations (MacDuff, 2006) and work outcomes (Nonis et al., 2005). The purpose of this activity is to provide you with a better under-standing of the role of temporal differences in cross-cultural adjustment.

Levine (1997, 2015) reported that a primary distinction in time perception is between *clock time* and *event time*. For cultures that follow clock time, the numbers on the clock signal when to begin and end activities. Cultures on event time, however, focus on the progression of the activity itself to determine when it begins or ends. Participants begin and end activities when it feels right to do so. Tamar Avnet and Anne-Laure Sellier (2011, p. 665) explained that "The main difference between these ways of scheduling tasks is that the decision to move to the next task is based on an internal cue in event-time versus an external cue in clock-time." From the perspective of someone on event time, for example, it would seem bizarre to end an exciting discussion or activity simply because you are "out of time." Cultures using clock time tend to be far more concerned with punctuality than those on event time. For example, you may have a 7:00 pm appointment to study for an exam with a friend. If you are on clock time, you might arrive at 7:00 pm, having decided in advance that you will stop studying at 9:00 pm since your friend has a meeting.

If a neighbor drops in with a video to show you they might be politely informed that you are studying and can't watch it right now. However, if you are on event time, another activity may delay your arrival for the appointment with your friend. In fact, if you arrived at exactly 7:00 pm your friend might not be there since you are not expected to arrive at the appointed time. On event time you would stop studying when you are finished even if this means that your friend is late for the meeting. If a neighbor drops in with a video on event time, you will likely invite them in for a while before you resume studying. In event time, time is much more flexible and less compartmentalized than in clock time.

Directions: First determine whether the culture in which you live is best characterized by clock time or event time. Then spend one day living as best you can according to the opposite time orientation. (Most participants in this activity will be accustomed to clock time and thus will spend a day using event time.) If possible, choose a day when you do not have any classes, work, or life-altering time commitments! Finally, respond to the questions that follow.

Description: In some detail, explain how you spent your day using a different time orientation and describe the emotions you experienced during this activity.

1. What priorities accompany the use of clock time? What priorities accompany the use of event time?
2. Sellier and Avnet (2019) found that even within a society, there are individual differences in *scheduling styles* – some individuals function better on clock time and others are more effective on event time. Which time orientation best suits you? Please explain.
3. Cultures on clock time tend to use time in a more monochronic manner. That is, activities are conducted sequentially; when one activity is completed another is begun. Cultures on event time tend to be more polychronic, conducting several tasks and social interactions simultaneously. For example, in monochromic societies, people line or queue up to be served at a store whereas in polychronic societies the shopkeeper might be helping three or four people at the same time. How might people with a monochronic orientation view polychromic behavior? How might people with a polychronic orientation view monochromic behavior?

Thinking Further:

Your experience with a different time orientation may have been made more challenging because others in your environment didn't make this change. How might it be for you to travel to a culture in which you and everyone else

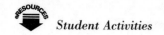

Student Activities

operated on a time orientation different from your current one? What strategies could you use to adjust to such a shift in time perception?

References:

Avnet, T., & Sellier, A. (2011). Clock time vs. event time: Temporal culture or self-regulation? *Journal of Experimental Social Psychology*, *47*(3), 665–667. https://doi.org/10.1016/j.jesp.2011.01.006

Levine, R. (1997). *A geography of time: The temporal misadventures of a social psychologist*. Basic Books.

Levine, R. (2015). Keeping time. In M. Stolarski et al. (Eds.), *Time perspective theory, review, research and application: Essays in honor of Philip G. Zimbardo* (pp. 189–197). Springer.

MacDuff, I. (2006). Your pace or mine? Culture, time, and negotiation. *Negotiation Journal*, *22*, 31–45. https://doi.org/10.1111/j.1571-9979.2006.00084.x

Nonis, S. A., Teng, J. K., & Ford, C. W. (2005). A cross-cultural investigation of time management practices and job outcomes. *International Journal of Intercultural Relations*, *29*, 409–428. https://doi.org/10.1016/j.ijintrel.2005.05.002

Sellier, A.-L., & Avnet, T. (2019). Scheduling styles. *Current Opinion in Psychology*, *26*, 76–79. https://doi.org/10.1016/j.copsyc.2018.06.003

**ACTIVITY 9.5
HANDOUT**

ACCULTURATION STRATEGIES

Much cross-cultural research has focused on acculturation. That is, the process by which people adjust to a culture other than their own. John Berry (1994, 2001) developed a model for understanding the strategies that people use in acculturation. This activity involves applying Berry's model to your own acculturation experience in order to better understand this process.

Directions: Think about an experience you have had acculturating, or adjusting, to another culture. You may have traveled outside of your country or to an unfamiliar region of your own country. Perhaps you have spent time with an ethnic group or social class different from your own. For people entering an unfamiliar academic culture, adjusting to college may even involve acculturation. In the space provided below, describe your acculturation experience (if you can't think of a time when you adjusted to an unfamiliar culture, you can ask someone you know about their acculturation experience and modify your responses accordingly). Then answer the questions based on Berry's model in order to analyze this experience.

Description of your acculturation experience:

1. Berry's (1994, 2001) model includes four types of acculturation strategies: Integration, Assimilation, Separation, and Marginalization. Read the descriptions of these strategies below and think about which best describes your own acculturation strategy.
   a. *Integration* – The individual maintains their own cultural identity while at the same time becoming a participant in the host culture.
   b. *Assimilation* – The individual gives up their own cultural identity and becomes absorbed into the host culture.
   c. *Separation* – The individual maintains their own cultural identity and rejects involvement with the host culture.
   d. *Marginalization* – The individual does not identify with or participate in either their own culture or the host culture.

Which of the four modes above best characterizes your acculturation strategy? Please explain.

2. Berry's (2001) model also includes four types of acculturation strategies adopted by the host culture: Multiculturalism, Melting Pot, Segregation, and Exclusion. Read the descriptions of these strategies below and think about which best describes the orientation of the society or group into which you acculturated.
   a. *Multiculturalism* – The society values and fosters diversity.
   b. *Melting Pot* – The society seeks assimilation.
   c. *Segregation* – The society forces separation.
   d. *Exclusion* – The society imposes marginalization.

Which of the four modes above best characterizes the orientation adopted by the host culture in your acculturation experience? Please explain.

3. Given the acculturation orientation of the host culture, do you believe that the acculturation strategy you adopted was effective? Please explain.

Thinking Further:

1. Jan Pieter van Oudenhoven and Veronica Benet-Martínez (2015) have further elaborated on Berry's integrative acculturation strategy, which they view as a form of biculturalism. These authors distinguished between those who have high *bicultural identity integration* (Benet-Martínez & Haritatos, 2005) and thus perceive the relationship between their heritage and host cultures as harmonious and overlapping, and those who are low on bicultural identity integration and perceive dissociation and tension between their two cultural identities. If you adopted an integrative acculturation strategy, do you think you had low, moderate, or high bicultural identity integration? Please explain.

2. Angela-Minh Tu D. Nguyen (2013) noted that acculturation is multi-dimensional in that it may differ depending on the domain, such as language use, social networks, daily living habits, cultural traditions, communication style, family socialization, and cultural knowledge. Did your acculturation strategy differ depending on these or other domains?

3. What other factors may have affected your acculturation strategy? Consider, for example, your personality, your resources, the degree to which your original cultural environment differed from that of the host culture (called *cultural distance*), and the degree to which the acculturation is voluntary or forced.

4. Paul G. Schmitz and Florian Schmitz (2022) reviewed 61 studies investigating correlates of acculturation strategy and found that, in general, the integration strategy was most beneficial. In other words, those who are engaged in both their heritage culture and the culture of the host society have better well-being than those who employ other acculturation strategies. Can you think of a situation, however, in which the separation strategy might be more preferred and beneficial?

References:

Benet-Martínez, V., & Haritatos, J. (2005). Bicultural identity integration (BII): Components and psychosocial antecedents. *Journal of Personality*, *73*, 1015–1050. https://doi.org/10.1111/10.1111/j.1467-6494.2005.00337.x

Berry, J. W. (1994). Acculturative stress. In W. J. Lonner & R. S. Malpass (Eds.), *Psychology and culture* (pp. 211–215). Allyn & Bacon.

Berry, J. W. (2001). A psychology of immigration. *Journal of Social Issues*, *57*, 615–631. https://doi.org/10.1111/10.1111/0022-4537.00231

Nguyen, A.-M. T. D. (2013). Acculturation. In K. Keith (Ed.), *Encyclopedia of cross-cultural psychology* (pp. 7–12). Wiley-Blackwell.

Schmitz, P. G., & Schmitz, F. (2022). Correlates of acculturation strategies: Personality, coping, and outcome. *Journal of Cross-Cultural Psychology*, *53*(7–8), 875–916. https://doi.org/10.1111/10.1177/00220221221109939

van Oudenhoven, J. P., & Benet-Martínez, V. (2015). In search of a cultural home: From acculturation to frame-switching and intercultural competencies. *International Journal of Intercultural Relations*, *46*, 47–54. https://doi.org/10.1111/10.1016/j.ijintrel.2015.03.022

ACTIVITY 9.6
HANDOUT

A SOJOURNER INTERVIEW

In this activity, you will conduct an interview with someone who has recently had or is currently having the experience of adjusting to an unfamiliar culture.

Directions: *Select an interviewee.* Find someone who has had or is having a significant cross-cultural experience. It should be someone who has spent at least several months in a culture different from their own. Typically, we think of crossing cultures as something that happens when one travels to another country. However, many other sojourns can result in life changing cross-cultural experiences. For example, when someone raised in a rural area spends time in a big city, when Students of Color attend a predominantly White institution, or when people travel to different regions of the same country, they may experience intercultural adjustment or even a sense of "culture shock."

Check for time constraints. Reserve at least 45 minutes to 1 hour for this interview. Oftentimes people are very excited about having someone to listen to their cross-cultural adventures and they may get a bit carried away with their storytelling!

Alter wording if necessary. The questions are worded for the situation in which the sojourn has been completed. If you interview someone who has a sojourn in progress, you may need to alter the wording of the interview questions somewhat.

Obtain informed consent. Explain the purpose of the interview and be sure that the interviewee understands that their responses may be discussed in class or included in a written report.

Assure and maintain confidentiality. Be sure you tell your interviewee that you will not in any way attach their name to the responses in reporting or discussing the responses to the interview. It is critical that you maintain this confidentiality in order to conduct the interview in an ethical manner.

Conduct the interview. Ask the interview questions in the order in which they appear in this exercise. Be sure to take notes in the spaces provided or on a separate sheet. Be aware of cultural differences in interview response style. Most psychology research texts suggest that the researcher will lose "objectivity" if they enter into a conversation with the interviewee in order to obtain the needed information. However, in many cultures it would seem inappropriate for the interviewer not to disclose information and opinions if they wish the interviewee to do so.

Provide feedback to the interviewee if appropriate. If you have some general conclusions about cross-cultural adjustment based on discussing or analyzing the interview data with your class you might convey these conclusions to your interviewee.

Interview Questions:

1. What is your home culture?
2. What is your host culture?
3. What preparation did you receive for your sojourn?
4. How much time did you spend in the host culture?
5. What did you expect the host culture to be like?
6. What was your role in the host culture (for example, international student, tourist, employee, missionary)?
7. How did members of the host culture react to you?
8. What does the term "culture shock" mean to you?
9. Do you think that you experienced culture shock? Why or why not?
10. Did you experience any negative psychological changes such as increased irritability, anxiety, suspiciousness, concern with cleanliness, or hostility toward the host culture?
11. Did you experience any positive psychological changes such as increased confidence, increased self-awareness, or greater openness to new experiences?
12. What was the hardest thing about being in the host culture?
13. What was the best thing about being in the host culture?
14. What was the funniest thing that happened during your sojourn?
15. Did you have social support from members of your home culture, members of the host culture, or members of another culture?
16. What new skills did you develop as a result of your sojourn?
17. What was most helpful in your adjustment to the host culture?

---

18. Can you think of anything that would have made your cross-cultural adjustment process easier?
19. Describe your re-entry into your home culture.
20. How would you compare the difficulty of the original adjustment to the host culture with the difficulty of the readjustment to your home culture?
21. How did others in your home culture respond to you upon your return?
22. What advice would you give to a friend who is about to leave for a cross-cultural sojourn?

Though we must be very cautious when drawing conclusions based on the responses of a single individual, summarize below what you have learned about the cross-cultural adjustment process.

Thinking Further:

Based on your interview, what recommendations do you have for designing a training session to prepare people for a cross-cultural experience? You can make your recommendations "culture-general" (skills or information that would be useful regardless of the host culture) or "culture-specific" (skills or information that fit a certain cultural context).

ACTIVITY 9.7
HANDOUT

INTERCULTURAL COMPETENCE: A SELF-ASSESSMENT

In recent decades, changes in communication, technology, transportation, immigration patterns, and policies of segregation have meant a dramatic increase in intercultural interaction. However, most of us are unprepared to interact competently with people from cultures that are unfamiliar to us. Darla Deardorff (2006, p. 249) defined intercultural competence as "the ability to communicate effectively and appropriately in intercultural situations based on one's intercultural knowledge, skills, and attitudes." Intercultural competence is particularly critical for individuals who provide essential services to others, such as teachers, medical professionals, and counselors.

A large volume of research has attempted to identify the characteristics of interculturally competent individuals. Some of these characteristics have been used to determine the type of person to *select* for intercultural or international programs or tasks. Others have been the focus of programs that *train* people to be more effective in intercultural interaction.

The components listed on the following pages were chosen because they reappear across studies of intercultural competence (e.g., Arasaratnam-Smith, 2017; Deardorff & Jones, 2012; Leung et al., 2014; Ramirez R., 2016; Rings & Allehyani, 2020; van der Zee & Van Oudenhoven, 2013). The purpose of this activity is to provide a means for you to evaluate your own intercultural competence and develop strategies for improving areas in which you indicate a lower level of competence.

Directions: Circle the number on each of the scales that follow to indicate your own level of intercultural competence. If you score 4 or below for any of the competence components, use the space provided to plan strategies for increasing your level of intercultural competence. Be creative in planning strategies for improvement. These could include such actions as reading on certain topics, gaining experience in a particular context, rewarding yourself for changing your behavior patterns, or practicing certain skills. Once you have described possible strategies for improvement, answer the Thinking Further question that follows.

Traits and Attitudes:

1. Respect for diverse cultures

1	2	3	4	5	6	7
Low						High

2. Openness to new experiences

1	2	3	4	5	6	7
Low						High

3. Tolerance for ambiguity

1	2	3	4	5	6	7
Low						High

4. Motivation for cultural learning

1	2	3	4	5	6	7
Low						High

5. Empathy

1	2	3	4	5	6	7
Low						High

Knowledge:

1. Cultural self-awareness

1	2	3	4	5	6	7
Low						High

2. Knowledge about language differences

1	2	3	4	5	6	7
Low						High

3. Knowledge about diverse cultures

Skills:

1. Ability to manage stress

1	2	3	4	5	6	7
Low						High

2. Ability to build relationships

1	2	3	4	5	6	7
Low						High

3. Ability to generate solutions and evaluate your own problem-solving strategies

1	2	3	4	5	6	7
Low						High

4. Communication and listening skills

1	2	3	4	5	6	7
Low						High

Student Activities

Strategies for Improvement:

Thinking Further:

Imagine that you are a manager tasked with choosing employees for an international assignment. On which of the components of intercultural competence could employees be trained? Which of the components could not be easily taught but would have to be used as selection criteria? Please explain.

References:

Arasaratnam-Smith, L. A. (2017). Intercultural competence: An overview. In D. Deardorff, & L. Arasaratnam-Smith (Eds.), *Intercultural competence in higher education* (pp. 7–18). Taylor & Francis.

Deardorff, D. K. (2006). Identification and assessment of intercultural competence as a student outcome of internationalization. *Journal of Studies in International Education, 10*(3), 241–266. https://doi.org/10.11 77/1028315306287002

Deardorff, D. K., & Jones, E. (2012). Intercultural competence: An emerging focus in international higher education. In D. K. Deardorff, H. de Wit, J. D. Heyl, & T. Adams (Eds.), *The Sage handbook of international higher education* (pp. 283–304). Sage.

Leung, K., Ang, S., & Tan, M. L. (2014). Intercultural competence. *Annual Review of Organizational Psychology and Organizational Behavior, 1,* 489–519.

Ramirez, E. (2016). Impact on intercultural competence when studying abroad and the moderating role of personality. *Journal of Teaching in International Business, 27*(2–3), 88–105. https://doi.org/10.1080/0897593 0.2016.1208784

Rings, G., & Allehyani, F. (2020). Personality traits as indicators of the development of intercultural communication competence. *International Journal of Curriculum and Instruction, 12*(1), 17–32.

van der Zee, K., & van Oudenhoven, J. P. (2013). Culture shock or challenge? The role of personality as a determinant of intercultural competence. *Journal of Cross-Cultural Psychology, 44*(6), 928–940. https://doi.org/10.1177/0022022113493138

ACTIVITY 9.8
HANDOUT

THE PSYCHOLOGY OF TOURISM

According to Colleen Ward, Stephen Bochner, and Adrian Furnham (2001), tourism is the most common form of international encounter. However, tourists may be the least likely of all sojourners to have meaningful intercultural interactions. In fact, often tourists have more contact with other tourists than with members of the host culture (Han et al., 2021). In this activity, you will observe tourist behavior in order to explore this unique form of cross-cultural encounter.

Directions: Taking detailed notes, spend an hour observing the behavior of people in a location that is popular among tourists. If there is no tourist destination near you, you can observe tourist behavior on one of the many live webcams located in tourist destinations around the world.

1. Briefly describe the tourist destination you selected.
2. Were you able to distinguish the tourists from the local people? How?
3. Describe the specific behaviors you observed on the part of the tourists.

Thinking Further:

1. In recent years there have been multiple news reports of tourists damaging ancient and sacred sites throughout the world, including such acts as riding scooters down Rome's Spanish Steps, knocking over and destroying a priceless 18th-century statue in Lisbon while taking a selfie, and carving initials into an ancient petroglyph in Big Bend National Park and into the walls of the Colosseum. What might explain this form of tourist behavior?
2. At times, tourism has been promoted as a mechanism for increasing intercultural understanding and promoting world peace (Ward et al., 2001). Under what circumstances might tourism work toward this goal?
3. Richard Slimbach (2010) introduced the concept of *mindful travel* to refer to the need for awareness of one's impact on the host community on several dimensions:
   • Economically – who benefits financially from the tourists' presence (e.g., local businesses or foreign hotel and restaurant chains)?
   • Culturally – How does exposure to tourist behaviors (e.g., language or clothing) and preferences (e.g., the items they seek to purchase) shape the host culture?

- Socially – How does the tourists' presence affect existing social structure and power dynamics (e.g., tensions between young and old, traditional and modern)?
- Ecologically – What is the effect of the act of traveling itself (e.g., CO_2 emissions, energy use) and the behavior of travelers (e.g., water, land use) on scarce resources in the host culture?
- Spiritually – How does tourism alter the host community's sources of meaning and wisdom (e.g., religious traditions)?

Describe a strategy that could be used to promote and reward at least one of these dimensions of mindful travel:

References:

Han, X., Praet, C., & Wang, L. (2021). Tourist-tourist interaction in the co-creation and co-destruction of tourism experiences among Chinese outbound tourists. *Tourism Planning and Development*, *18*(2), 189–209. https://doi.org/10.1080/21568316.2021.1873833

Slimbach, R. (2010). *Becoming world wise: A guide to global learning.* Stylus.

Ward, C., Bochner, S., & Furnham, A. (2001). *The psychology of culture shock* (2nd ed.). Taylor & Francis.

ACTIVITY 9.9
HANDOUT

CROSSING CULTURES WITH CRITICAL INCIDENTS

Critical incidents are often incorporated into training to prepare people for interacting effectively across cultures. According to Sarah Apedaile and Lenina Schill (2008, p. 7) "Critical incidents in intercultural communication training are brief descriptions of situations in which a misunderstanding, problem, or conflict arises as a result of the cultural differences of the interacting parties, or a problem of cross-cultural adaptation and communication." The goal of this form of training is to learn to make culturally congruent attributions. In other words, with enough exposure to critical incidents and the accompanying explanations, trainees learn to provide explanations similar to those that would be given by members of the cultures involved. This activity will familiarize you with the types of critical incidents that are used to prepare people for intercultural interaction.

Directions: Read the example of a critical incident below then develop your own critical incident and explanation. Critical incidents can take the form of a description, a first-person account, or a brief dialogue. They are designed to raise awareness about cultural differences in a variety of domains, including, but not limited to:

Conflict resolution	Space and time perception
Customs and traditions	Teacher–student interactions
Family relationships	Values
Formal and informal behavior	Verbal and nonverbal communication
Gender roles	Workplace expectations

Sample Critical Incident:

I think I'm adjusting well to studying in Austria, but one thing that I still can't get used to is how unfriendly people are. I mean, once you get to know people they are very nice, but I can't get over the coldness of the general public. In my hometown in the U.S., I'm used to greeting people passing by on the street with a smile, but if I give a smile here, people either ignore me, glare back, or look at me strangely. Maybe they treat me like that because they can tell that I'm a foreigner.

Explanation:

Smiling at strangers is not common in most parts of the world. In fact, in some countries, individuals who smile at strangers are perceived as odd, suspicious, or even unintelligent (Krys et al., 2016). The tendency to smile at strangers in the U.S. may stem from its immigrant history, in which smiling was a way to let others, who may not speak your language, know that you are friendly and mean them no harm.

Your Critical Incident:

Your Explanation:

References:

Apedaile, S., & Schill, L. (2008). *Critical incidents for intercultural communication: An interactive tool for developing awareness, knowledge, and skills.* NorQuest College.

Krys, K., Vauclair, C.-M., Capaldi, C. A., et al. (2016). Be careful where you smile: Culture shapes judgments of intelligence and honesty of smiling individuals. *Journal of Nonverbal Behavior, 40*(2), 101–116. https://doi.org/10.1007/10.1007/s10919-015-0226-4

ACTIVITY 9.10
HANDOUT

A DIVERSITY TRAINING INVESTIGATION

The use of diversity training programs in organizations has grown significantly over the past few decades in response to an increasingly global and diverse workforce, a greater emphasis on working in teams, and concern about meeting legal standards (Gebert et al., 2017). Such programs were developed to address sexism, racism, and other forms of discrimination while assisting members of the organization in viewing diversity as an asset (Paige & Martin, 1996). Diversity training programs vary greatly in terms of goals, content, and the method of training. Although many diversity training programs seem to be effective, others have not been able to achieve long-term changes in attitudes or behavior (Bezrukova et al., 2016). The most successful programs may be those that include modifications to the structure of the organization itself, such as in hiring, promotion, and leadership development (Kochan et al., 2003). This activity involves investigating the diversity training program of a single organization in order to learn more about this important form of intercultural training.

Directions: *Identify an organization* that has conducted some form of diversity training. The organization you select may be any type of business, government agency, or educational institution. In most organizations it may be best to contact the human resources office. In university settings, the office of student life or student affairs may also be involved in diversity training.

Make an appointment to speak with the person in charge of diversity training. It may be possible to conduct this interview over the phone, though it will likely take a minimum of 15 minutes.

Conduct the interview using the interview format included in this activity. Before conducting your interview, it will be helpful to read the "Thinking Further" questions below as well.

Answer the questions that follow to analyze the information that you gathered.

Name and description of the organization you selected:

Interview Questions:

1. Would you characterize your workforce as *diverse*? Please explain.
2. When did your organization start conducting diversity training?
3. What was the reason that diversity training was implemented?
4. Is the training conducted by someone from within or outside the organization?
5. Who participates in the training? Is participation voluntary or mandatory?
6. Please describe the content of the training program.
7. What do you hope will be accomplished by the diversity training?
8. Is there an evaluation or follow-up to this program?
9. Along with this training program, did your organization make any other changes to address diversity?

Thinking Further:

1. Were the goals of the program *cognitive* (focused on increasing knowledge and awareness), *affective* (focused on changing the way people feel about diversity and their own ability to perform well in diverse settings), or *behavioral* (focused on teaching specific skills and changing the way people act)? Do you think it would be easier to make cognitive, affective, or behavioral changes?
2. Was the content of the program *culture-specific* (addressing the experiences of particular groups, such as women, People of Color, or sexual minorities) or *culture-general* (addressing dimensions on which groups in general may differ, such as communication style or leadership behaviors)?
3. Was the training process more *didactic* (based on lectures or written materials) or *experiential* (based on discussion groups, role plays, or simulations)?
4. What criteria would you use to determine if a diversity training program has been effective?
5. In the space provided below, please give your overall assessment of the diversity training program you investigated. Do you think it will be effective? Why or why not?

References:

Bezrukova, K., Spell, C. S., Perry, J. L., & Jehn, K. A. (2016). A meta-analytical integration of over 40 years of research on diversity training evaluation. *Psychological Bulletin, 142*(11), 1227–1274. https://doi.org/10.1037/bul0000067

Gebert, D., Buengeler, C., & Heinitz, K. (2017). Tolerance: A neglected dimension in diversity training? *Academy of Management Learning & Education, 16*(3), 415–438. https://doi.org/10.5465/amle.2015.0252

Kochan, T., Bezrukova, K., Ely, R., Jackson, S., Joshi, A., Jehn, K., Leonard, J., Levine, D., & Thomas, D. (2003). The effects of diversity on business performance: Report of the diversity research network. *Human Resource Management, 42*, 3–21. https://doi.org/10.1002/hrm.10061

Paige, R. M., & Martin, J. N. (1996). Ethics in intercultural training. In D. Landis & R. S. Bhagat (Eds.), *Handbook of intercultural training* (2nd ed., pp. 35–60). Sage.